CRIME

IN ITS RELATIONS TO

SOCIAL PROGRESS

BY

ARTHUR CLEVELAND HALL, Ph.D.
Fellow in Sociology, Columbia, 1894-96.

"Oh, yet we trust that somehow good
Will be the final goal of ill."
Tennyson—IN MEMORIAM

New York
THE COLUMBIA UNIVERSITY PRESS
THE MACMILLAN COMPANY, AGENTS
LONDON: P. S. KING & SON
1902

STUDIES IN HISTORY, ECONOMICS AND PUBLIC LAW

EDITED BY THE FACULTY OF POLITICAL SCIENCE OF
COLUMBIA UNIVERSITY

VOLUME XV

THE AUTHOR'S PREFACE.

THE first few pages of this book seem very pessimistic, but in truth the author's view is a broadly optimistic one, growing more so with the progress of his work, which offers, to those who read, an answer to this strange enigma, by revealing the social good which rests within the growing mass of crime. The minds of many men to-day are filled with anxious fears and forebodings because of this increasing weight of evil, the fruit of our higher civilization; for they fail to trace within the gloom those strong forces working out social betterment by means of this very increase of crime which they so deplore.

Human good and human evil are many-sided—not fixed and unchanging, but largely relative—and compounded in ever-varying proportions the one with the other. Often, very often, evil is but good out of its proper time and place. Things must be looked at in their historic setting, if we would rightly value them. Only by a very wide, impersonal view—a long perspective—in which the individual and his immediate needs are merged in the continued welfare of the human race, can we see, "as through a glass, darkly," the vast outlines of eternal good, can we grow into that high-hearted and grandly reasonable hope that

> "There shall never be one lost good! What was, shall live as before;
> The evil is null, is naught, is silence implying sound;
> What was good, shall be good, with, for evil, so much good more;
> On the earth the broken arcs; in the heaven, a perfect round."
>
> (Browning.) *Abt Vogler.*

A student of these problems of crime for many years, the

author was in charge of the Bureau of Charities and Correction during the latter half of the Columbian Exposition, Chicago, 1893. The following spring he delivered a course of lectures on Criminology before graduate students of Johns Hopkins University, and in 1894–95 was Fellow in Sociology at Columbia University. Since July, 1895, the thoughts presented in this book have been slowly developing and growing clear before his mind, and the last three years have been devoted to a critical examination of the evidence—historical, legal and statistical—throwing light upon the subject.

Careful study of the valuable writings of the criminal anthropologists has strengthened the conviction that, in calling attention so forcibly to the physiological and psychological study of individual degeneration as the essential fact in criminology, we have been drawn away from the perception of another side of truth, perhaps equally important, namely: the evolutionary function and usefulness of crime and punishment. Crime is in large part a social product, increasing with the growth of knowledge, intelligence and social morality—increasing because of this growth. The persistent enlargement of the field of crime is a necessity for all truly progressive nations. Many acts formerly harmless, or socially beneficial, become harmful as civilization grows higher and more complex. An increase of crime, however, does not mean necessarily an increase of anti-social conduct. In fact, anti-social acts may have diminished while crime has grown larger in amount, or may have increased while crime has decreased. Society's conflict with its criminal members, due to the enforcement of new social prohibitions, is one of the chief means by which humanity, in every age, has risen from a lower to a higher plane of civilization, from almost uncontrolled license, selfishness and hate, into true liberty, love and mutual helpfulness.

The author desires to thank Professor Edwin R. A. Seligman and other professors of Columbia University who have aided him in the prosecution of his work; but especially is he indebted to Professor Franklin H. Giddings for criticism of his manuscript and proof sheets, and to Miss Katharine G. Spear for valuable assistance in proof reading, and for the making of the index.

A. C. H.

NEW YORK, *January*, 1902.

INTRODUCTION.

OUR theories of crime and our conception of the criminal have undergone profound modification since our notions of mankind were transformed by the researches of Mr. Darwin. Crime is still thought of by the uneducated as merely a black kind of wickedness, and by lawyers as merely a punishable act. But scientific students of mind and of society have learned that wicked and punishable acts are correlated with anthropological and physiological facts, and with social and historical conditions, that are deserving of investigation. The criminal is still thought of by a majority of law-abiding persons as an "evil-doer," who sins deliberately, because he "likes to"; who deserves the vengeance of man in this present world and the wrath of God in a world to come. But to the scientifically trained mind the criminal is a character who should be examined with painstaking care and by precise methods, to determine how far he is responsible. He may be an atavistic variant from normal mankind, and devoid of moral sense, a dangerous creature, to be restrained as a wild beast might be, but not to be punished by rational beings. He may be a weak or passionate person, not evil in disposition but liable to go wrong under stress of temptation or excitement. Or, finally, he may be nothing more nor less than a "professional"—a man who has gone into crime as a profitable business, exactly as he might have gone into politics or promoting. To those who have become familiar with these distinctions, it seems quite clear that professional criminals only are likely to be restrained by punishment, and that the "instinctive" and "occasional" criminals must be dealt with by other methods: equally clear that a sentimental charity towards professional criminals, who ought to be punished with such severity as would make their business unprofitable, must result in an increase of crime.

The methods of the anthropologists, however, are not the only ones that are suggested by an evolutionist philosophy, as applicable to the study of crime and the criminal. An undiscriminating notion of the criminal as in every instance a wicked man, or as in every instance a defective and irresponsible man, leading, as it must, to an undiscriminating policy of punishment or of mercy, is not the only cause affecting the amount of crime in the community. Granting the distinctions that have here been named, crime may increase or decrease in amount without any change in law or in policy. Changing social conditions determine the birth-rates of the atavistic and irresponsible; of the violent, the weak, the unscrupulous. Changing social conditions determine also the range of temptation and of opportunity. Crime and criminals, therefore, must be studied by the methods of the statistician, as well as by those of the anthropologist, if we are to obtain an adequate knowledge of the causes that control human well-being.

Even these methods, however, do not exhaust the possibilities of investigation offered by the phenomena of crime. Not every wicked act, not every injurious act, is a crime Certain acts (and negligences) society through its law-making authority formally prohibits, and through its executive authority solemnly punishes. These acts, which the state thus authoritatively brands, and no others, are crimes.

It is obvious therefore that crime may increase or diminish from age to age without any change whatever in the number of wrongful acts. Deeds which at one time are tolerated or even approved, at another time may be denounced and punished. Any change in the attitude of society toward human conduct must consequently make a corresponding change in the statistics of crime. It is well within the limits of possibility that a community might become, generation by generation, more moral, and produce increasing crops of the "peaceable fruits of righteousness," and yet show in its moral statistics a steady increase of crime, in excess of the increase of population.

This is a phase of the phenomena of crime which is unfamiliar to the general reader and to the average voter, and which, indeed, is understood only by those few persons among the well-informed who have devoted themselves to studies in comparative jurisprudence or in the history of legislation. It is this phase especially that Dr. Hall has investigated, and has set forth in the present volume with a thoroughness which, I think, has not characterized any preceding study of the relation of crime to civilization.

A moment's reflection will satisfy an intelligent reader that, by its very nature, civilization must now and then increase the sum total of crime. Civilization devises, extends and improves a moral order among men, and this order takes the form of legality. One after another the acts and negligences which civilized men regard as evil are branded, prohibited and punished as "crimes." Sometimes in a moment of mistaken zeal, acts that a sober second thought declares to be innocent in themselves, and harmless to mankind, are so stigmatized. Yet, on the whole, this process of converting immoralities into positive crimes is one of the most powerful means by which society in the long run eliminates the socially unfit, and gives an advantage in the struggle for existence to the thoughtful, the considerate, the far-seeing, the compassionate; so lifting its members to higher planes of character and of conduct. While it would be absurd to say that civilization is promoted by an increase of crime, if by "increase" we mean a multiplication of evil deeds, (the legal definition and the punishment of crime remaining the same) it is yet perfectly true to say that civilization in the long run is promoted by that "increase" of crime which is caused by *an extension of the category* of acts branded by society as criminal, the total number of evil deeds remaining unchanged.

I have some fear that Dr. Hall in these pages has not always been sufficiently careful to emphasize the distinction that I have just made. The attentive reader, however, will have no difficulty in discovering that Dr. Hall is not trying to demonstrate anything so absurd as a beneficial reaction of harmful deeds. And I am sure that those who examine the book as a study of results attributable to the long historical process of *extending the category*, "crime," over larger and larger areas within the field of socially injurious conduct, will find it a positive contribution to our present knowledge of this immensely important subject.

FRANKLIN H. GIDDINGS.

Columbia University.

TABLE OF CONTENTS

CHAPTER XII

Has Crime Increased During the Nineteenth Century?

CHAPTER XIII

Is Punishment Powerless against Crime?

CHAPTER XIV

The Trend of Crime in Modern Times. A Brightening Outlook.

CHAPTER I

THE EVOLUTIONARY FUNCTION AND USEFULNESS OF CRIME AND PUNISHMENT.

EACH human community, in every age, is busy moulding its individual members into conformity with its own type—into a closer resemblance to the social ideal. The American is different from the Englishman and both are unlike the German. The French type is markedly distinct and separate from both the Italian and the Spanish. A social education environs us from the cradle to the grave—a pressure to be this kind of man and not to be this other and antagonistic kind. If, for the most part, we are scarcely conscious of this moulding influence, it is because we are so used to it, and because we are ourselves scions of the national stock, inheriting these national traits and tendencies from our remote ancestors. Settle in a foreign land, and the pressure soon becomes disagreeably, perhaps painfully, apparent; and you must conform, in large measure, to these unwonted customs, rules and ways of doing things, if you would be happy and prosperous in the new environment.

In the furtherance of this social education, two great natural forces—strong, ever-present, social tendencies—are made use of, encouraged, trained, by the social group. One is the natural admiration and imitation of strong men, largely resembling their comrades, only somewhat better representatives of the developing social type; and the second is the instinctive abhorrence and persecution of individuals unlike their fellows—anti-social variations—dangerously hostile to the common weal. These two great socializing tendencies, or forces, work together in absolute harmony; and along the line of progress they induce, social pressure becomes more and more strongly developed, with increasing social evolution. This pressure is partly conscious and partly unconscious, in both directions: of praise or blame, of honor or persecution. The limits of the field of crime are largely coterminous with the extent of *conscious* persecution and punishment by the social group for wrongs against itself, and are continually being extended with the progress of civilization.

The creation of a new crime (that is, the branding by society of some form of conduct as criminal) always implies social punishment—a punishment enforced to raise the community to a higher plane of life, a nearer approach toward the social ideal. A new form of crime means either a step forward or a step backward for the nation choosing it. Wisely chosen, it is an active force driving man upward to a better, more truly social, stage of civilization; but the nation that persists in choosing its crimes wrongly is on the high road to degeneration and decay. Crime is to the body social much what pain is to the individual. Pain is the obverse of the shield of pleasure, and without the existence of pain there is no pleasure possible; without increasing pain there is no growth of higher pleasures. So, also, crime is the obverse of the shield of social good, and without increasing crime, there is probably no growth in social goodness—or, in other words, no development of the nation into the fullness of its strength, happiness and usefulness. It will cease to be a living force in the evolution of a higher, world civilization, and will become stationary, like the Chinese, or degenerate, like the American Indian.

Crime, therefore, is an inevitable social evil, the dark side of the shield of human progress. The most civilized and progressive states have the most crime. It is a social product, increasing with the growth of knowledge, intelligence and social morality — with all that is summed up in the words higher civilization.[1] The increase of crime largely takes the direction of acts in opposition to new social prohibitions. These prohibitions are neither accidental nor whimsical, but are inevitable consequences of the increasing complexity of life. In general, new crime follows lines of greatest resistance to the new life of society.

This book is an attempt to study some of the relations of crime to social progress; chiefly two great phases of the subject; namely: The evolutionary function and usefulness of crime and punishment; and, Crime as a social product, increasing with the increase of social prohibitions.

Nature's great task, throughout the ages, seems to have been the elevation of the individual, at the expense of his powers of reproduction—individuation versus procreation—resulting in the persistent rise in value of the individual life, as measured in terms of size, strength and activity of body and of brain. The forces preservative of race are two, writes Herbert Spencer, the power to maintain the individual—the power to generate the species. These vary inversely—as one decreases the other increases.[2] The evolution of larger, stronger, more highly developed forms of life is always accompanied by the same phenomenon, a decreasing birth rate. The minutest organisms multiply in their millions; the small compound types next above them in their thousands, while larger and more compound types

[1] There is scarcely a state in the American Union for which the census statistics do not show a large, and for the most part, progressive increase in the number of criminals (*i. e.* prisoners) in proportion to population, since 1850. The average numbers for these five census periods are: For Massachusetts, 1,899 prisoners per 1,000,000 population; for New York, 1,378; Maryland, 993; Missouri, 689; Arkansas, 651; Mississippi, 551; Utah (4 last census periods), 529; New Mexico (4 last census periods), 510.

[2] See *Principles of Biology*, II., 401.

multiply but in their hundreds or their tens, and the largest and most highly developed types only by twos or units.[1] Lowest organisms are marvelously prolific. The shallow seas of the Paleozoic age swarmed with minute life, which left its history written in the fossils of the hills, in the coral reefs of ocean, in chalk cliffs and silicious deposits everywhere, and in "the summits of great mountain ranges in Europe, Africa and India," formed of tiny shells of animals (known as numulites) which lived and died and helped to build our earth, during those early ages.[2] Undeveloped life is almost completely dependent upon its physical environment. The lower the organism the smaller its ability to contend with external dangers, and great fertility is absolutely necessary to preserve the species from destruction. Evolutionary forces act upon these lowly forms of life mainly *from the outside, upon whole groups*, rather than from within the group, upon its members singly.[3] The development produced by such means is enormously expensive. Nature seems to squander life, holding it of little worth.

"A thousand types are in the hills."

During the Mesozoic, or Reptilian age, natural selection was working along a low plain of individual self-interest; dominance was the reward of great size and enormous physical strength. But in united effort there is greater power than any gigantic brute can possess, and social life, with its mutual helpfulness against enemies and stimulation of mental

[1] See *Principles of Biology*, II., 426–7. [2] Mitchell, p. 47.

[3] A numerically large group of these microscopic organisms would occupy a very small space on the surface of our earth, and their environment would be practically the same for all individuals: that is, the forces acting upon them for good or evil would be in general the same throughout the entire group; and, being so very plastic under external influences, they would all develop in much the same way, until success or destruction came to the entire band. Another similar group, a little removed in space, might have a different set of forces acting upon it, have its individual units differently developed and perhaps succeed where the first group failed.

development, become the prime requisite for success in the struggle for existence; the great means to the attainment of a higher, more unselfish life.

After some mental activity has been aroused within the social group, there is, as it were, an effort of nature to promote upward growth by a less wasteful process, using the awakened individual intelligence, combined with the inherited social instinct, to induce evolution from within the group, by encouraging useful variation from the average—thus producing the leader—and punishing harmful variation, thus ultimately converting the mere malefactor into the criminal. Social pressure from within the group unites with the pressure from without to uplift and socialize the individual. One of the most important forms of this inner pressure is called among men criminal prosecution and punishment.

A social group is fundamentally a kindred group. Its members feel a resemblance among themselves and a sense of safety and of pleasure develops. There is general likeness with individual variation. The natural leaders are very like their fellows, being simply somewhat stronger exponents of the developing social type. Divergence from this type is disliked and antagonistic variation meets with conscious or unconscious persecution. And rightly so, for the social might stands as a shield before each and every member, protecting him from the destruction his weakness must call down, if left unaided. In so doing, society makes itself, as it were, responsible to nature for the acts of all its members. The individual whose persistent conduct weakens the social bond, or injures the effectiveness of the social group, must be made powerless to harm; for, since social life to a large extent prevents the immediate action of natural selection upon the individual, wise social selection must take its place, or destruction comes to all.

This is the explanation of crime and of the necessity for

its punishment. Individual variations, actively antagonistic to the prevalent social type, exist in all the higher social groups. Commonly they are social laggards, who have not kept pace with the average development toward the social ideal. The rebellious social laggard is the true criminal; other laggards belong to the pauper class. Even the higher animal societies collectively punish the most dangerous anti-social acts. Much the same conduct with a few additions is punished by the lowest human societies now known upon the earth; and, as social life attains to higher planes, more and more actions become socially harmful, are generally recognized as such, and added to the list of crimes—that is, the list of actions which society punishes as wrongs against itself, for the sake of the general welfare, for the preservation of the social life, for the elevation of the individual toward the ideal of the social type.

Thus the production of crime and criminals is one of the saving processes of nature, substituting a lesser for a greater evil, promoting upward progress at a smaller cost. For if nature had not induced this increasingly severe social selection and pressure within the group, toward the elevation of the individual and the improvement of the type, then that primitive and unreasoning form of pressure from physical forces without the group, which always persists, must have continued alone in operation, destroying countless individuals and groups, without, if we may so express it, the attempt to educate them into the true lines of their upward development.

Ancient human society was organized upon the basis of kindred—blood relationship—and not upon the possession of a common territory. Now, the individual is the unit, and is responsible to the state alone. Then, the kindred was the unit, and a wide system of group responsibility prevailed.[1]

[1] Hearn, p. 457; Maine, p. 126–7.

A man was responsible to his kindred, gens (or clan), his phratry, tribe and tribal confederacy, if this last existed. Each of these groups was likewise responsible for the man, for each and every member. It suffered for his misdeeds and could be rewarded for his good actions. The minor groups were originally independent—not yet included in any larger and more complex social body—and possessed, or, we may almost say, were possessed by, a wild and ferocious justice, reeking itself in fierce spasms of social vengeance, "half punishment, half outrage," upon some hated member of the band. Few acts, however, were punished by the social groups, as such, and few acts were therefore crimes. Injuries to individuals were left to private revenge, and there were other harmful acts—sins—supposed to be punished by the gods.

In gentile society, the household was the economic institution. Its chief function was the obtaining of a food supply. The Gens, or clan, was a mutual protective association, for help, defence and redress of grievances. Its function may be called judicial protective.[1] The Phratry, (φρατρια—brotherhood), was formed by a union of related gentes. It was the chief religious institution and had also social and judicial protective functions.[2] The Tribe or Tribal Confederacy, was primarily a military institution, standing for the unity and might of the gentile people.[3]

Each one of these social groups possessed judicial and penal authority, by right of ancestral, immemorial custom. Yet, in the most primitive legal codes which have come down to us, the evidence for such authority is very scanty. Why is this? Early Germanic codes of customary law embody but a part of the ancient penal customs of the race. Thus we find no mention of the father's right to punish for offences within the family. Such power was regulated, then as now, by

[1] Morgan, *Ancient Society*, pp. 76, 77. [2] *Ibid.*, p. 94. [3] *Ibid.*, p. 117.

social custom and existed none the less surely, though not chronicled in written laws.[1] Thus, also, crimes,[2] or authority to punish for such offences, are rarely mentioned; yet crimes existed, and the ability and will to punish were not lacking. These codes of the German barbarians afford us, nevertheless, by far the most clear and complete record we possess of ancient legal systems.[3] They deal almost entirely with offences which would now be classed as criminal, but which were not criminal then, in any true sense of that word.[4] They were injuries inflicted by man upon his fellow man, such as would now result in a civil suit for damages. These acts were not regarded nor punished by society, (or the State), as wrongs against itself, and in this consists the very essence of all crime. The laws, at first, simply afforded an opportunity for the injured party to accept compensation, rather than exact private vengeance (his undoubted right). The penalty was proportioned to the provocation, and not to the offence. Later, the laws hardened into a compulsory seeking and acceptance of composition offered for an offence, before private vengeance could be legally pursued. The man who refused to ask and accept an atonement for the injury received, and the offender who would not pay the customary price for his forgiveness, thus preserving the peace of the community, came to be regarded as untrue to the folk, and were solemnly declared outside of the law's protection—outlaws. Such men were true criminals; possibly the first dealt with, under the law, as distinguished from ancient social custom.[5]

[1] Offences against the father's authority have never been crimes in any age, no matter how great the paternal right of chastisement. They were sins rather.

[2] Brunner, ii, 603 et seq.

[3] Maine, p. 367.

[4] See article on Crime, *Encyclopædia Britannica*.

[5] R. R. Cherry, p. 14. For Iceland, see *The Story of Gisli, the Outlaw*; edited by Sir J. Dasent.

Thus we find in the earliest Germanic codes many penal laws, but not much *true criminal law*.[1] They were attempts, at first weak, but steadily gaining in firmness and hardening into law, to tame these wild men of the woods, by substituting an elaborate system of composition for the dearly loved right of blood revenge. But the lack of a developed criminal law is no evidence that crimes were not recognized and punished by early Germanic society. In fact, we have positive proof to the contrary, not only for the Germans, but for all other races of the great European–Aryan stock, and even for the lowest savage hordes known to man, such as the Australian Black-fellows and the African Bushman. Human society everywhere, writes Waitz, "has some common interest in opposition to the private interests of the individuals composing it."[2] Where the individual insists upon acting in opposition to social necessity, there we have the true criminal, and society must punish him or cease to exist.

How did primitive society punish the criminal? Just as private vengeance struck down the man who had harmed his fellow man, so social vengeance destroyed the malefactor who had injured the social body so seriously as to awaken in its members the passionate longing for revenge. There was no criminal law, because there was a separate action and procedure in the case of every criminal. Fundamentally instinctive, as are many acts of self-preservation, and for long largely unreasoning, like the lynch law of mobs, primitive society struck at its criminal members directly, through the folkmote, or assembly of all freemen. The people tried, condemned and punished, following the dictates of ancestral custom, with its roots deep in instinctive necessary action. Socially necessary action equals right action, because it is indispensable for social self-preservation and upward pro-

[1] Maine, p. 369–70.

[2] Waitz, *Anthropology*, p. 276.

gress. The people also slowly and almost unconsciously modified ancient custom to meet new needs.

No higher power—king, or priest, or noble—decreed what acts should be called criminal or compelled their punishment. Lowest savage tribes are intensely democratic and acknowledge no form of government, human or divine. Higher societies—Homeric Greeks, Romans of the days of Romulus, early Celts, Slavs and German barbarians of the first Christian century—elected their magistrates, chiefs and kings, who could also be deposed by the assembly of the freemen, and most important matters were always referred to its decision.[1] The people were sovereign, judge, and often executioner. They alone determined what constituted crime. They alone had power to condemn and punish criminals. Crime was and is a social product.

How then shall we define crime? Crime is any act or omission to act, punished by society as a wrong against itself. This is not merely the author's own definition of crime—possibly made to harmonize with his peculiar views—it is the condensed expression of opinions held in common by the whole school of historical jurisprudence, and generally accepted by modern writers on criminal law, as the reader may prove for himself by an examination of the following passages:

SIR HENRY SUMNER MAINE

"*Ancient Law.*"

In the primitive history of Criminal Law, "*the conception of crime*, as distinguished from that of *wrong or tort*, and from that of *sin*, involves the *idea of injury to the state or collective community*." "The commonwealth itself interposed directly and by isolated acts to avenge itself on the author of the evil which it had suffered." (p. 385.)

[1] Ihering, *Vorgeschichte der Indoeuropäer*, pp. 396–397.

"The earliest conception of a crimen or crime is an act involving such ***high issues*** that the state, instead of leaving its cognizance to the civil tribunal, or the religious court, directed a special law or privilegium against the perpetrator." "*The tribunal dispensing justice was the sovereign state itself.*" There was ***not*** "at this epoch any *Law of Crimes,* any Criminal Jurisprudence.[1] The procedure was identical with the forms of passing an ordinary statute." (p. 372–3.)

"Nothing can be simpler than the considerations which ultimately led ancient societies to the formation of a true criminal jurisprudence. *The State conceived itself to be wronged,* and the popular assembly struck straight at the offender with the same movement which accompanied its legislative action." (p. 381.)

Later, "when a regular criminal law with courts and officers had come into being, the old procedure remained practicable. *The people of Rome always retained the power of punishing by a special law offences against its majesty.*" So "the Athenian Bill of Pains and Penalties, or Εἰσαγγελία, survived the establishment of regular tribunals." (p. 373.) "The Heliæa of classical times was simply the *popular assembly* convened for *judicial purposes,* and the famous Dikasteries of Athens were only its subdivision or panels." "The history of Roman criminal jurisprudence *begins* with the old *judicia populi,* at which the kings are said to have presided. These were simply *solemn trials of great offenders* under legislative forms." (p. 382.) "When the *freemen of the Teutonic races assembled for legislation* they also claimed authority to punish *offences of peculiar blackness* or perpetrated by criminals of exalted station. Of this nature was the criminal jurisdiction of the Anglo-Saxon witenagemot." (p. 374.)

[1] **This is somewhat too sweeping a statement; as German students have proved.**

R. R. CHERRY

"*The Growth of Criminal Law in Ancient Communities.*"

"In *ancient law* the is *no such thing as a crime.*" "*Criminal law,* as distinct from *penal law,* involves some element of *public condemnation*—such as a sentence of outlawry." "The prototype of a modern criminal trial appears in the solemn proclamation at the tribe meeting, after full inquiry, of the sentence of outlawry." (p. 14.)

"*Criminal law originated, not in any command at all* (as the School of Analytical Jurisprudence seems to maintain), but in the *custom of retaliation,* at a time when there was no such thing as a sovereign body to issue a command, and no means of enforcing it, were it issued." (p. 16.)[1]

O. W. HOLMES, JR.

"*The Common Law.*"

"The germ of criminal law is found in the *desire for retaliation* against the offending thing itself . . . . *vengeance* was the original object." (p. 34.)

"The secret root from which the law draws all the juices of life . . . . *i. e.,* considerations of what is expedient for the community concerned; . . . . . generally the unconscious result of instinctive preferences and inarticulate convictions." (p. 35–6).

JOHN WILDER MAY

"*The Law of Crimes.*"

"Crime is a violation or neglect of duty of *so much public importance* that the law, either common or statute, takes no-

[1] John Austin, founder of the School of Analytical Jurisprudence, gives the following definition of law in his *Lectures on Jurisprudence* (Edition of 1869):

"Law is a rule laid down for the guidance of an intelligent being by an intelligent being having power over him." (p. 88). "Customary laws are positive laws fashioned by judicial legislation upon pre-existing customs." "These customs are merely rules set by opinions of the governed, and sanctioned or enforced morally" till they "are clothed with legal sanctions by the sovereign one or number." (p. 204.) Under these ancestral customs crime was punished by society long before law began.

tice of and punishes it." (p. 1.) "Not every act which is legally wrong is a crime. Private wrongs are redressed by suits *inter partes*. In a *criminal prosecution* the government itself is a party, and the government moves only when *the interest of the public is involved*. The basis of criminality is therefore the effect of the act complained of upon the public." (p. 4.)

"*Moral obliquity is not an essential element of crime*. What, therefore, is criminal in one jurisdiction may not be criminal in another, and what may be criminal at a particular period is often found not to have been criminal at a different period in the same jurisdiction." "The *general opinion of society*, finding expression through common law or through special statutes, *makes an act to be criminal or not* according to the view which it takes of the proper means of preserving order and promoting justice." "Adultery is a crime in some jurisdictions, while in others it is left within the domain of morals." "Embezzlement, which was, till within a comparatively recent period, a mere breach of trust, cognizable only by the civil courts, has been nearly, if not quite universally, brought by statute into the category of crimes as a modified larceny." "The sale of intoxicating liquors is or is not a crime, according to the different views of public policy entertained by different communities." (pp. 4 and 5.) "It is impossible to draw an exact line between offences that are criminal and those which are merely civil wrongs." The question to be settled is, "*Has the public security been endangered by the offence?*" (pp. 7 and 10.)[1]

[1] May classifies crimes as *treasons, felonies and misdemeanors*. Treason is a direct attack upon government and disturbs the foundations of society itself. It is "active disloyalty to the state." (This was probably the original form of crime.)

Beccaria (Marquis) *of Milan*:

"Observe, that by justice I understand nothing more than that bond which is necessary to keep the interest of individuals united, without which men would re-

"*American and English Encyclopædia of Law*," second edition, 1898; the latest and best work of the kind.

Article on Crime. "A Crime is more accurately characterized as a *wrong directly or indirectly affecting the public*, to the commission of which the state has annexed certain punishments and penalties, and which it prosecutes in *its own name* in what is called a criminal proceeding." (p. 248).

Crimes distinguished from civil injuries. In *State vs. Williams*, 7 Rob. (La.) 271, it is said: "The distinction of public wrongs from private, of crimes and misdemeanors from civil injuries, seems principally to consist in this; that private wrongs, or civil injuries, are an infringement or privation of the civil rights which belong to individuals, considered merely as individuals; public wrongs, or crimes and misdemeanors, are a breach and violation of the public rights and duties due to the whole community, considered as a community, in its social aggregate capacity." (4 Blackstone Com. 5.)

These extracts from the works of well-known writers on jurisprudence should suffice to give us clear ideas concerning the origin and nature of crime and criminal law. We see that among primitive peoples criminal law had scarcely yet come into existence. The penal laws first developed were laws of tort, or injuries of man to man; and laws of sin, or offenses against the gods. But the idea of crime as a serious injury to society itself, and the punishment of criminals by society, obedient to the passion for vengeance and the dictates of ancestral custom, are found everywhere among primitive Aryans and all other races of men. As

turn to the original state of barbarity. All punishments which exceed the necessity of preserving this bond, are in their nature unjust." See Beccaria, chapter II., *Of the Right to Punish*.

"Every punishment which does not arise from absolute necessity," says the great Montesquieu, "is tyrannical." (Same chapter.)

that great authority, Sir Henry Sumner Maine, writes in *Ancient Law* (p. 372):

"It is not to be supposed that a conception so simple and elementary as that of wrong done to the state was wanting in any primitive society. It means rather that the very distinctness with which this conception is realized is the true cause which at first prevents the growth of a criminal law." . . . . . "When the Roman community conceived itself wronged, the state avenged itself by a single act on the individual wrong-doer. . . . . "The trial of a criminal was a proceeding wholly extraordinary, wholly irregular, wholly independent of settled rules and fixed conditions."

Crime includes Misdemeanors. It is important that we should recognize this truth. There is no fixed line of moral heinousness beyond which all acts are crimes. That which is punished as a most serious offence in one age is often a simple misdemeanor in another, or perhaps no crime at all. On the other hand, harmless actions or petty misdemeanors of ancient days are now among our most troublesome and dangerous crimes. Is adultery a crime, misdemeanor, or civil injury? In New York it is legally a crime; in England, more of the nature of a tort, and in some countries it is simply a sin, unpunished by the law. Our ancestors very lightly regarded most forms of forgery and fraud, malicious injuries to property, painful wounds and attempts at murder. We deem them serious crimes. What shall we say of drunkenness, of the sale of intoxicants, of failure to have one's children educated? Most people see nothing immoral in such conduct, but a few states have made these actions criminal in recent years. The moral sense and intelligence of the community decide such questions, according to social needs, upon the plane of development attained.

The definition of Crime in the *American and English Encyclopædia of Law* (1898), is framed to include misdemeanors. On page 248 we read: "Although in common usage the word crime commonly denotes such offences as are of a deep and atrocious die, and similar faults and omissions of less consequence are comprised under the name of misdemeanors, yet "crime" and "misdemeanor" in legal language are synonymous terms and the word "crime" in a statute has frequently been held to include misdemeanors."[1] This is clearly recognized in the *Report on Forgery*, by the Select Committee on the Criminal Law of England, 1827. "Forgery is made *criminal* by the Common Law, and by various statutes. At Common Law it is a misdemeanor only; under the statutes it is frequently a felony. But, unless in raising the crime to a higher class," etc. (p. 1).

Sir James Fitz James Stephen writes: "A large number of misdemeanors were created by statute at different times, but especially in the 18th and 19th centuries, which differ in no essential respect from the common crimes distinguished as felonies. For instance, to obtain goods by false pretences, to misappropriate securities intrusted to the offender as agent, solicitor or banker, and to commit many other fraudulent or mischievous acts, are, *as far as moral guilt is concerned*, on a level with theft."[2]

It is very necessary that we should grasp clearly the distinction between tort, sin, crime, and acts of war. The field of crime has spread to such an extent as to cover many actions formerly classed under these other heads.

A tort is essentially a private injury as distinguished from a public wrong. It is a harm inflicted by a man upon his

[1] *Crime includes Misdemeanors.* England: Maine *vs.* Owen, 9 B. & C., 595; 17 E. C. L., 456. New York: Matter of Clark, 9 Wend. (N. Y.), 212. Penna.: Lehigh County *vs.*. Schock, 113 Pa. St., 373. Ill.: Van Meter *vs.* People, 60 Ill., 168. For many more such decisions see page 250, A. & E. Ency. of Law, 1898.

[2] *History of the Criminal Law of England*, i, 489. The criterion of a delete or tort is that, "the person who suffers it, and not the State, is conceived to be wronged." (Maine, p. 371.)

fellow man, not regarded as a wrong done the state, but giving rise to a civil suit for damages. In ancient times the injured man would have sought private vengeance, and a blood feud might have resulted. Later, it became customary to accept arbitration and pecuniary composition. Society gave to this arbitration a legal form and made the acceptance of the damages awarded compulsory, unless the plaintiff chose not to press his suit. Thus, for a tribesman to kill or steal from a man of another clan within his own tribe, was a tort demanding vengeance or compensation.

A sin is an offence against God, frequently punished as a crime by men. To kill one's blood brother was a fearful sin, punished by the community with the dread social doom of outlawry.

To kill or steal from a member of another tribe was an act of war, the weakening of a natural enemy and consequently praiseworthy. It was only very slowly and gradually that theft, murder, robbery and rape (within the social group) became crimes; regarded not merely as misfortunes or harms to an individual, but chiefly as wrongs to society itself, to be punished by society, utterly irrespective of the wishes of the persons chiefly concerned.[1]

Primitive man was, as Aristotle has well said, "the hardest of all animals to govern." The European Aryan was a sturdy individualist, passionate, rebellious at restraint, loving war and vengeance as his duty and his right—as that which makes a man. The blood feud had its use. It tended to consolidate the family group and to develop responsibility. It was a rough and terrible means of preserving peace; for even the boldest man would hesitate before bringing the vengeance of an entire kindred upon his house from genera-

[1] Maine, p. 370–371, and *Encyclopædia Britannica* (article on Crime): "In very primitive tribes, murder, robbery and rape are not crimes—not at least in the modern sense."

tion to generation. It was also a weighty reason for the developing of strength, courage and weapon skill. Every hand must guard its own head and every freeman his own home. Thus it made for social stability and warlike power.

The tribal state was but a weak institution, chiefly for military purposes. It punished a few acts as crimes because they had to be punished if the social group was to hold together, but at first it dared not interfere with individual vengeance, the right of private war.[1] Arbitration and composition for harm were very early offered as a substitute for blood revenge, but even when the state became strong enough to make arbitration compulsory, it yet preserved for long (in its trials) the semblance of a purely voluntary agreement.[2]

What primitive society needed most was strong, despotic law, to bind it firmly together, and give it strength and power to grow. Such law was most difficult to create and to enforce.[3] It formed first where most needed, strengthening the outer shell of association, hardening the tribe for war. Just as in the evolving sphere of earth the outside crust forms and hardens first, while the inside matter is yet hot and molten, so in primitive human society, the outside shell of legal custom hardened over the unruly passions of men unused to restraint, whose explosive natures were continually driving them into fierce words and bloody deeds.[4] In this stage of development, writes Steinmetz, there is as yet a kind of indifference to internal affairs, and only occasional punishment of differing characters (by death, expulsion or the like) takes place. The moral and disciplinary consideration of crime is entirely absent. There is as yet no proper compulsory state power.[5] Actions considered crimes were necessarily very few, while intense popular abhorrence and

[1] Hearn, pp. 430–1. [2] Maine, p. 374.
[3] See Bagehot's *Physics and Politics*, p. 21, and Hearn, p. 393.
[4] Hearn, pp. 430–432. [5] Steinmetz, chapter 5, book ii.

"almost physical loathing" of the criminal must have made him a very rare type of man.[1] Only the necessity for internal peace (for the blood feud was simply civil war socially sanctioned), strengthened the hands of society to substitute compulsory arbitration and composition for private vengeance, at a time when the development of wealth made compensation possible, and the increasing cultivation of the soil made internal peace more and more indispensable.[2] Composition became a favorable factor in the struggle for existence, and society, by gradually changing certain torts into crimes, intrenched itself, as it were, on a higher plane of human existence. The number of acts punished as crimes was increased. The number of criminals was greatly multiplied, but social welfare was conserved and individual security and freedom were enlarged.

No depth of moral heinousness is sufficient in itself to make an action criminal. Sin is never crime unless society makes it such. The mere fact that laws exist decreeing punishment for certain conduct, will not make that conduct criminal. In the statute books of England and the United States, there are many penal statutes (Blue Laws) never repealed, but unenforced for generations. The acts they were aimed to punish are certainly not crimes now, and they may never have been crimes. For it is not sufficient that society desire to punish, make laws to punish, or even try to punish. Unless it actually *succeeds* in punishing, often enough to make the average citizen believe offenders likely to be brought to justice, the act is not yet a true crime. On the other hand, social punishment need not fall upon a majority of offenders to make their conduct criminal. In the United States to-day, comparatively few men are executed, or imprisoned, for the many murders committed; but the average

[1] Maine, p. 120.

[2] Steinmetz, book i., pp. 427–8; also Hearn, p. 393.

citizen, not called upon to investigate such matters closely, does not realize this, and believes that "murder will out," and in general be punished. Laws need not exist and be enforced to make the actions they prohibit crimes. Lynch violence may do the work neglected by the courts of justice.

The essentials of crime are two.

First. The act must be one that society abhors and desires to punish as a wrong against its welfare.

Second. The act must be punished often enough to make the displeasure of society evident and its deterrent force plainly felt. Then, and not till then, does the action become a crime. But, if society is at all united in the intention to punish, it will generally succeed in inflicting some form of penalty, and this the more surely as social organization becomes stronger and more effective.

For it is ***the social standard of right action that determines what conduct shall be criminal.*** Society says: You must live up to a certain standard, at your peril. The test is essentially an objective one, and deals with manifest conduct, not the motive behind the act. A man thoroughly bad morally, need not fear punishment if he keep within the letter of the law. Again, it matters not how good a man's intentions may be, if he breaks the law he will be punished as a criminal; for society thinks he ought to have known better—unless, indeed, he prove idiotic or insane.[1] The standard is not fixed and unchanging, but is modified from age to age, according to the general level of knowledge, intelligence and social morality, and the actual needs of an advancing civilization.

Social evolution implies increasing complexity of life, a larger interdependence among men, and necessitates a nicer adjustment of mutual rights and duties, which must be enforced (largely through the criminal law), if society is to

[1] Holmes, pp. 110–113.

hold together and maintain a healthy growth. "Man, unlike the lower animals, has had to be his own domesticator."[1]

The criminal is the rebellious social laggard and must in some way be prevented from destroying, or seriously harming, the social life. There are many ways of accomplishing this end: by his death, imprisonment, education, reformation; but all are forms of punishment[2] for the man who refuses to live up to the standard of right action set by his fellow men, and the social welfare imperatively demands that such rebels be punished. With increasing civilization, more and more actions become socially bad, are perceived to be injurious by the common sense of the community, and are punished as crimes, thus increasing the number of criminals.

So long as social progress continues, so long as there is growth from a lower to a higher plane of brotherly love and mutual helpfulness, so long as the rebellious social laggard continues upon earth, for so long will crime continue to exist and possibly also to increase.[3] That it has increased till now this book will give the evidence, so far, at least, as the English-speaking people is concerned. But the nature of crime has changed and will continue to change, from more to less heinous offences, if we judge from the standpoint of present public opinion. Under the rule of law men have been slowly and painfully learning to curb their hasty passions. Crimes of force show a very great decrease during the last few centuries, and they are decreasing still.

[1] Bagehot, p. 51.

[2] See the hatred of Elmira and other Reformatory prisoners for education, the parole system and the indeterminate sentence.

[3] If in any age and nation a larger amount of crime is punished than in a later and higher stage of social development, it is probably because actions not rightly criminal are being punished in the former time, or because degeneration, which often brings non-punishment for even very dangerous offences, is setting in at the latter period.

If crime shall ever cease upon earth, it can be only when obedience to social commands has become an overmastering habit in the individual;[1] when society has grown so wise as to prohibit only the true crimes of its age; so strong and efficient that the mere dread of its displeasure is quite enough for the prevention of evil acts; when, in a word, the aim of Christianity, the brotherhood of man, is realized on earth. Then social morality can rise to higher and higher planes without increasing crime. Hitherto the social mind has had in every age "le défaut de ses qualités," and has punished or tried to punish as crimes, actions helpful or at least not harmful to the social welfare.[2]

It is an old truth that the greatest benefactors of the world have been also its greatest martyrs. New liberty, new life, have come to men often under a criminal ban. Are we wiser than our fathers? Do we no longer make these old mistakes? Thus much seems sure. The nation that persists in choosing its crimes wrongly is on the high road to social degeneration and destruction; and since the English-speaking people has continued to grow more strong, more united, more dominant upon the earth, we may believe that it has, upon the whole, through many errors, chosen its crimes rightly, and that it will continue to be, through coming years, the great teacher of Christianity and of civilization.[3]

[1] A condition practically fulfilled among lowest savage tribes, where obedience to a few fundamental ancient customs is thoroughly instinctive and unreasoning, because run into the very fibre of the race, by stern processes of natural selection, teaching elementary social necessities.

[2] The Statutes of Laborers in England, the subsequent attempts to make labor unions criminal, and the punishments of the Inquisition in Spain, will serve as examples; as will also the attempts, in our own day, to make trusts as such criminal, and not simply the abuses of trnsts.

[3] A crime and a form of crime express two closely related yet diverse ideas, between which we should distinguish clearly. A crime is an act, the act of a criminal, punished by society as a wrong against itself. A form of crime is a kind of conduct which society would punish in this manner, if the act were perpetrated, if

the criminal existed. Thus, treason is and has always been (as far back as we can trace) a most heinous form of crime among men. Throughout the centuries acts of treason have been very frequent, and severely punished as crimes; but among lowest savage hordes and the most highly civilized modern nations we find almost no instances of punishment for this offence. The traitor has practically disappeared from the English criminal statistics during the last half century, and abhorrence of the traitorous act is so intense among lowest savages that no one is found to commit this most heinous of crimes. A form of conduct may therefore be criminal without the actual infliction of social punishment, but such instances are very rare. Piracy is an example for modern times.

We may dream of a nation, in some future age, when even a new form of crime may not necessarily mean an increase of criminals. With us, the transgressor is so very natural and customary a result of the prohibition that we expect him as a matter of course, and are never pleasantly disappointed by his non-appearance. He is not, however, an absolutely inevitable social product, provided knowledge, intelligence and morality are high and strong enough, and the habit of obedience dominant enough in the social group.

CHAPTER II

SOCIAL PUNISHMENT AMONG ANIMALS.

DOES crime exist among animals? If so, it must be something very different from those destructive acts by which an animal secures his food, defends himself, strengthens his own band, or weakens that of his enemies; acts which have often mistakenly been called the crimes of animals. It must be conduct distinctly harmful to his own kind, his own social group; awakening against himself general dislike and vengeance. Many facts unite to prove that such noxious individuals are occasionally found among the more intelligent animal communities, that they frequently manifest signs of degeneration, like those common among human criminals, and that severe social punishment is often inflicted upon them.

In the different groups of monkeys, writes Brehm, when the struggle for command has resulted in the dominance of some sturdy male, any monkey refusing obedience is brought to reason by force, with cuffs and bitings.

The "cinocefali" are well organized for brigandage. They post sentinels to warn the devastating horde of the approach of man, and death is the penalty inflicted if one prove faithless or negligent in the discharge of this most necessary social duty.[1]

When the band is on the march toward the orchard destined for pillage, profound silence is compulsory. The ignorant youngster who begins to chatter is well thrashed.

[1] Brehm. *Les Mammifères* i, 81. Ferre, vol. iii, p. 291. Marchi, vol. xix, pp. 145–153. Lombroso, *L'Homme Criminel*, pp. 30, 31.

From the moment he is weaned, stealing is a part of the young monkey's education. Indeed, his very life depends upon his success in theft. According to Dr. Brehm, the mother monkey robs her own child. There is no chance for him while his elders are feeding peacefully; but they are sure to wrangle over some dainty morsel and then the young monkey seizes all he can and escapes. Woe to the unskillful thief who is caught in the act. He not only loses his booty, but is severely beaten by the older monkeys. Stealing has the entire approval of the monkey race. It is not thieving, but lack of skill in thieving, which the monkeys unite to punish,—a practice said to have been customary among the Spartans also.

Here is good evidence that social punishment is inflicted by monkey bands for *certain acts akin to treason*, that is, active disloyalty to the community; and for *lack of skill in thieving*. The actions punished are thoroughly destructive of the social welfare, by preventing, or endangering, the obtaining of the food supply. They are acts in direct opposition to the strong trend of the social life, which is, education and organization of the monkey band for stealthy marauding expeditions.

Perhaps the most intelligent of the anthropoid apes is a species of chimpanzee called the Soko, discovered and most carefully described by Livingstone. "They live in communities consisting of about a dozen individuals, and are strictly monogamous in their conjugal relations. If a Soko tries to seize the female of another, he is caught on the ground and all unite in boxing and biting the offender." Here is true social punishment for adulterous, or more probably, incestuous assault.

Elephants are very sociable by nature and lovers of peace, but they occasionally expel from the herd a "rogue" elephant, "always distinguished as unusually malicious." Once driven out from his own herd, the "rogue" is never admitted to another, although Saunderson found them occasionally in company with another solitary of their own species. Sir J. Tennant records, that even when driven into the keddah, a "rogue" was never allowed to enter the herd of captives with which he was enclosed. In isolation, the rogue is noted for malignant ferocity toward men as well as other elephants. His actions are often abnormal and he appears to be suffering from excitement which sometimes passes away. Good temper appears to be a fundamental condition of membership in elephant society. A malicious, unsociable fellow is punished with something like outlawry, "doubtless because of conduct obnoxious to the rest—probably aggressive."[1]

The ferocity of the "rogue" buffalo and "rogue" hippopotamus must probably be accounted for in the same way. Intolerable to their own kind and outlawed from society, they revenge themselves by the indulgence of their malicious nature and criminal instincts. Herds of wild cattle, in northern Scotland, have been known to punish offending individuals with death.[2] We may believe, therefore, that herds of elephants, hippopotami, buffaloes and wild cattle, punish with outlawry or death the few incurably malicious, anti-social individuals found among them.

Rodet, a distinguished French veterinary surgeon, states that in every troop of cavalry may be found a few horses thoroughly bad and rebellious against all discipline, letting no opportunity escape them of doing harm to man or their companions. Frequently it is found necessary to separate them from other horses in the stable, for they try to steal their companions' food. M. Rodet calls them "chevaux à nez busqué," because of their narrow and retreating foreheads; and Cornevin, who had noted these same facts, tells

[1] Spencer, *Justice*, p. 13.

[2] MacDonald, p. 20.

us that the Arabs will not admit into their studs the progeny of horses thus affected and showing this peculiar physiognomy.[1] This would seem to support the views of the criminal anthropologists, by showing, even among horses, the co-existence of criminal instincts with physical abnormities, and also the probably hereditary nature of such instincts and signs of degeneration.

Brehm states that wild goats are at times possessed with a species of frenzy, as if dangerously ill, and are then disposed to kill other animals and men. Another observer tells us that goats, after eating of coffee, become furious. The eating of poppy seeds makes certain cows dangerous. Bees made drunk on honey mixed with alcohol quickly lose their industrious habits and become robber bees. Excessive use of alcohol among men is a potent influence toward degeneration and crime, and it is known that a sect of Eastern assassins excite the homicidal furor by a mixture of hemp and opium.[2]

In rabbit communities there occur individuals instinctively disliked and persecuted by all the others. Similar facts have been noticed among domestic poultry and the mild, ringed pigeons; showing strong social antipathy and physical punishment of a few individuals, seemingly far divergent from the type.[3]

Adulterous conduct, contrary to nature, excites violent abhorrence among some of the most intelligent and sociable birds, and brings down the penalty of death upon offenders, if we may believe the numerous stories on record. For example: A pair of storks built their nest upon the chimney of a house near Berlin, and laid therein a single egg, for

[1] Rodet, *Notions Élémentaire de Vétérinaire.* Lombroso: *L'Homme Criminel,* p. 9.

[2] E. Ferre, vol. iii, p. 293. Lombroso: *L' Homme Criminel,* p. 22.

[3] Marchi, vol. xix, 145–153.

which the owner of the house substituted, by stealth, a goose egg. The advent of the gosling greatly excited the male stork, which finally flew away, leaving the female bird tenderly caring for her supposititious young one. Early on the fourth day the male reappeared, bringing with him nearly five hundred storks, "which held a mass meeting in an adjacent field," deliberating almost the entire forenoon. "Suddenly the meeting broke up, and all the storks pounced upon the unfortunate female and her baby gosling, killed them both, and after destroying the polluted nest, took wing and departed, and were never seen there again."

A community of ravens are reported to have destroyed a nest in which they found a young owl, killing both the birds —members of their band—whose house had thus been disgraced. Even the domestic cock has been known in several instances to kill hens which hatched out partridges or ducks.[1]

Karl Vogt, the celebrated German naturalist, observed an act which closely resembled murder among the storks. In a village near Salette two of these birds had for several years made their nest. One day, during the absence of the male, a younger stork began to court the female, which at first repulsed, then tolerated, and finally welcomed him. After many clandestine meetings the two birds flew, one morning, to the field where the husband was hunting frogs, and killed him.

There are many remarkable stories of birds meeting in large numbers, holding "courts of justice," and, after long "discussion," inflicting the death penalty upon the offenders; but these are probably human imaginings, based upon the fact recorded by Brehm, that certain migrating birds, assembled for their southern flight, kill individuals that will not or from weakness cannot accompany them. The phenomena

[1] Evans, pp. 231–4.

have been been observed among rooks, crows, ravens, storks, sparrows, and a few other birds.

Signor Muccioli, Secretary to the Roman Society for Pigeon Breeding, has made a careful scientific study of his dove-cotes, and published some important observations of degeneration and criminality among his birds. These carrier pigeons, he tells us, are in general sociable, loving their little ones and those of their own species, mild and peaceable by disposition, scrupulously neat, very jealous of their nest, and monogamous, with almost absolute faithfulness to the conjugal tie. But as among men, there exist lazy, weak degenerates among the pigeons, and experience has taught him that these are found usually among the birds discarded as good for nothing in the messenger service. They are the most lazy and the least intelligent of the dove-cote. He studies his pigeons one by one, and attributes the victories of his messengers largely to the care with which he eliminates degenerates from among them. He finds that these present a greater number of mental lesions and other defects, and prevent the perfecting of the species. "How great," he writes, "is the intelligence of the perfect pigeon, and how deficient that of the degenerate." The strong and bright birds lend themselves readily to his hands when he is seeking a messenger, eagerly volunteering for the expedition from which they are sure to return victorious. Those that hang back are frequently the ones that hurt or lose themselves if sent. Active anti-social conduct occurs, but is not common. Grown males have been known to commit violent incest upon their young male offspring, having none of the developed instruments of sex, and they occasionally ravish little young females; but "veritable incest is rather rare." A mother pigeon of the Liegest variety habitually killed her little ones by peckings on the head until the brains came out. "It seemed," writes our author, "a crime without the slightest social stimulus among pigeons, from whom I eliminated without difficulty these true born criminals." There are thieves among pigeons, which try to steal the straws collected by the others for their nests, and there are vicious birds, "ready to wound for a mere nothing." These offenders are in general lazy, unintelligent and bad messengers. Serious combats occur, the fighting being done by strokes of the beak upon the neck, but the struggle has never been observed to cause death.[1]

Keepers of parks, where wild animals are inclosed, have often observed the great differences among individuals of the same species; some remaining always savage and morose, while many of their fellows were becoming quite tame and friendly to man. Among domestic animals also—horses, dogs and cattle—there are always some untamably ferocious individuals, cruel and violent, seemingly from innate wickedness.

Sir John Lubbock's most careful experiments with ants seem to show individual differences between those of the same species, just as between men; but whether there are any free individuals punished by the ant community we do not know. The greatest harmony appears to reign, and as a rule, according to Huber, not even the slaves are subject to the slightest compulsion; yet insurrections of these slaves are mercilessly punished with death. Affection can hardly be the bond holding together these great communities, sometimes numbering 500,000 ants, for experiments have shown that hatred is much the stronger passion with them.

Many facts thus unite to prove that the higher, more intelligent animal communities do inflict severe social punishment for a few acts, dangerously antagonistic to the social welfare; such as: 1. *Active disloyalty to the community—i. e.*, rebellion against constituted authority, and faithlessness or negligence

[1] Muccioli, xiv, pp. 39–42.

in the performance of military duty: Monkeys. 2. ***Intolerably anti-social disposition***, manifested by repeated acts of malignant ferocity against those of their own kind: Elephants, hippopotami, buffaloes, wild cattle, and possibly rabbits, pigeons, and other social and intelligent birds. 3. *The revolt of slaves:* Ants. The first and second of these sets of noxious acts may be classed under the one term, *Treason;* and, if the malignant ferocity, mentioned under two, take the form of violent opposition to the acknowledged leader of the band, this also would be a treasonable offence.

There is one other form of conduct which seems to waken intense abhorrence, and bring severe punishment from some animal groups, namely: ***adulterous acts against nature;*** and in one instance, ***incest***, or adultery: Anthropoid apes (the Soko), storks, ravens and domestic poultry.

True instances of murder and theft are known among animals, but such conduct does not seem to be socially punished. In all the animal communities, actively anti-social individuals appear to be very few, and social punishment for such offenders consequently infrequent. As we descend lower in the scale of intelligence and sociability, the evidence of a true social penalty grows weak and soon disappears, although traces of malignantly anti-social conduct continue for some time longer.[1]

The scientific study of animal psychology and sociology is yet in its infancy, and the facts at our disposal are necessarily few, yet they seem to warrant fully the belief that the

[1] "Forse s'avvera anche qui nel mondo animale quell'áltra legge del mondo umano, cbe la criminalita cresce in rapporto diretto della genialità e dell' intelligenza." *Lombroso.*

The author did not discover the sentence just quoted from *Archivio di Psichiatria*, xiv, 450, until *Civilization Through Crime* was mostly written and completely thought out. He is glad of the support afforded by the words of so distinguished a thinker, but is not aware that Professor Lombroso has ever developed his idea.

conduct punished by animal communities is such as strikes directly at social unity and racial effectiveness; actions which, if left unrepressed, would soon destroy the social group. But this certainly does not prove the belief of animals in individual moral guilt, nor any *thought* that the acts punished are essentially bad for the social welfare.

Scientific investigators into animal psychology are generally agreed that to morality no brute can aspire; ideas of good and evil are beyond their comprehension. How, then, shall we explain the collective punishment by animals of conduct which *we* know to be thoroughly bad for the social group? The answer is not far to seek. Such punishment is due to what we may call *Social Reflex Action*—to instinctive antipathy, innate aversion, a feeling that certain individuals are radically unlike their fellows, and that they *must* be punished, followed by the infliction of social vengeance. The phenomenon is one of instinctive defensive reaction against the trangressor of old and necessary social customs. Such social reaction implies a common consciousness of injury done, but does not imply judicial punishment. *Animals do not know why they punish.* To this extent, therefore, crime, in the full human meaning of that word, does not exist among the brutes.

The actions of animals are for the most part automatic, obedient to impressions registered in the nervous system throughout countless generations of ancestors. These impressions, coming from the external world along the nerve channels, have reference to self preservation, and induce certain acts, warding off the harmful stimulus and supporting the beneficial one. Animals which react in a certain way are rewarded with life and dominance, while those reacting in other ways die out and disappear from the earth. Thus, by constant repetition, the helpful reaction becomes habitual, and is performed instinctively and often unconsciously and instantaneously. What would become of our eyes if a conscious message was required from the brain to make the eyelids shut before approaching danger? Lifting of the arms when falling is another instance of instinctive defensive reaction against anticipated harm. A man struck by another in the street instinctively returns the blow, and only a strong exertion of the will by one well used to self-control can prevent the customary reaction. Even the coward will strike back and then run away. The child passionately kicking a door which has jammed his finger is acting in a strictly natural manner.

But frequently, according to Professor James, the stimulus to action is but a sign of some distant circumstance of practical importance.[1] Then "the animal's acts are addressed to this circumstance, so as to avoid its perils, or secure its benefits," as the case may be. To an outside observer, all such acts might seem inspired by intelligence, for in them there seems to be a choice of proper means for the attainment of the end in view; but we know that some occur in entire unconsciousness on the part of the actor, while others are accompanied by consciousness—sometimes intense consciousness—but no volition. In this latter class would seem to fall the punishment of offenders by animal communities. For the habits of associating individuals grow more and more alike through natural selection and imitation, and become the social customs of the community. Strict obedience to custom is required from all on pain of death or banishment. Should the social group fail to enforce this obedience, it must itself perish, for through the ages, the record of those acts requisite for individual and social survival has been registered in the nerve centres, and disobedience is death. Indeed disobedience is often impossible, for through long ancestral habit many reactions have be-

[1] James, i, 12.

come unconscious and purely reflex. In other cases, the reactions are accompanied by consciousness, and appear to be less certain and but semi-reflex, as if the habit had not yet had time to become wholly fixed and despotic. Finally we reach habits which are entirely the result of individual education and are purely voluntary. To quote Prof. James: "Thus the animal's reflex and voluntary performances shade into each other gradually, being connected by acts which may often occur automatically, but may also be modified by conscious intelligence."[1]

Every animal has the instinct of self-defence, and will strike back when attacked. Every society has this same instinct, and will react in like manner against an injurer. Evidently to be without this instinct courts destruction. In union is strength: brute strength and the strength of intellect. Life in society is the chief means for the development of intelligence, and as such natural selection enforces it. The anti-social individual, growing up unlike his fell ws, becomes actively hurtful and more and more hateful to them, till instinctive antipathy brings social punishment upon him. The headlong rush of a mob of citizens, frenzied by some recent rape and murder, upon the supposed criminal, the fierce determination to hang him first and try him afterwards, the immediate execution, the grim feeling of satisfied vengeance; such lynch law is but too well known even among civilized men to-day. What is it but the instinctive social punishment of a crime so black that it has stirred the community to its very depths, awakening uncontrollable abhorrence and an imperative craving for vengeance, which the immediate death of the culprit alone can satisfy. Although calmed by many centuries of growing obedience to law, ancestral instincts at times reassert their sway over calmer, slow-voiced reason. The impulsive animal nature conquers

[1] James, i, 13.

for a time the intelligence of the rational man. Social punishment for crime is once more very close to social reflex action. And how easily this lynch law may again become customary is indicated by the action of an Ohio judge, who refused to surrender a supposed murderer to Kentucky authorities, on the ground that the great number of lynchings in that State rendered a legal trial improbable.

The lower we get in the scale of intelligence, the more despotic is the sway of reflex action over both individuals and social groups; that is, the stronger is the chain which compels them to follow, in unquestioning obedience, the dictates of ancestral habit or group custom. Therefore we should not expect to find aggressively anti-social, or, in other words, criminal members, in the lowest animal communities. We have no evidence that such exist.

As we rise to higher and higher types of mind, we find more and more acts which seem caused, sometimes by instinct, sometimes by conscious choice—semi-reflex acts we may call them. But the ultimate basis of reprisal for harmful acts lies in instinctive self-defence, reflex action, whether individual or social. Self preservation is the first law of nature, but it is *recognized as a law* only by men when they begin to deliberate upon their actions, after the purely reflex stage is ended. Then man develops the first law of punishment for wrong-doing—the law of revenge—an eye for an eye and a tooth for a tooth. But punishment for harmful acts had existed long before; had existed, so far as only the individual is concerned, since the beginning of life upon the earth—while social punishment for acts harmful to the social group is found, as we have seen, among the higher animals, as well as among men. Punishment for crime is born of vengeance—social vengeance—and has its warrant and justification in the necessity for self-defence. Punishment for crime is fundamentally instinctive, and is precedent to all ideas of morality, all thought of individuals or their actions as good or evil. Punishment for crime is primarily meted out for acts most harmful to the social existence, whether committed intentionally or through ignorance, it matters not. Indeed, primitive law is filled with punishments to be inflicted upon trees, stones and animals, as well as men. The thing that does the harm is accursed and must be punished. So we read in Exodus, xxi. 28: "If an ox gore a man or a woman that they die; then the ox shall be surely stoned, and his flesh shall not be eaten; but the owner of the ox shall be quit." In England, so late as the reign of Edward I., "If a man fell from a tree and was killed, the tree was 'deodand' (forfeited to the relatives of the deceased). If he drown in a well, the well was to be filled up."[1] Some will see in this but a late and strong evidence of the imputation of moral intelligence to trees and wells and their punishment as evil doers; but ancient penal law is full of evidence that it aimed directly at the satisfaction of vengeance, and that punishment was not proportioned to moral obliquity.

Far down into historic times, Roman and Germanic law punished the thief taken in the act much more severely than one who evaded capture until men's passions had had tfme to cool. Primitive punishment was proportioned to provocation. Among savage and semi-civilized men, as well as animals, individual or social vengeance fell upon the thing that did the harm, irrespective of intent. Thus the savage Kukis of southern Asia hack in pieces a tree from which a kinsman has fallen to his death. If a tiger kills one of their number, his relatives are disgraced until they have slain and eaten either this tiger or another one.

Punishment was originally individual or social reflex action, obedient to imperative demands of habit or custom,

[1] Holmes, p. 24.

imbedded deep in animal nature by the workings of natural law. Those who believe that punishment for crime is essentially a retribution for individual moral guilt, or that its true object is the reformation of the offender, may well study punishments among criminals and savage men. True social punishment existed before moral thought was possible, and it has generically nothing whatever to do with the motives of the individual. It has its roots deep in the necessity of self-defence, and is born of instinctive social vengeance. It deals with acts and not with motives, and its aim is the welfare of society, and not of the individual offender.

NOTE.—It is certainly wise when investigating problems in animal psychology, to accept the simplest theory that will thoroughly harmonize and explain the facts. Such, the author believes, is the theory of punishment by social reflex action. The mind of the brute is so unlike ours that we are working in an unknown medium, and can at best do little more than guess. It is rash, indeed, to impute to animals a moral intelligence with difficulty discernible among lowest savage men.

CHAPTER III

CRIME AMONG SAVAGES.

In every aggregation of living creatures may be found two great tendencies which we cannot explain—a tendency of offspring to be like their ancestors, and, on the other hand, a tendency to differ somewhat from their ancestors. These tendencies are mutually antagonistic and destructive, yet both are essentially necessary to the social welfare; for the one makes social life possible and the other makes possible social progress. How to foster both these tendencies toward the upbuilding of the social strength and effectiveness, is the great fundamental problem of every human society. The exclusive development of the principle of likeness will result in social stagnation, while the dominance of the principle of unlikeness will soon bring social disruption and death. In the ages before history, the great danger seems to have been from the latter tendency, and it was necessary to fuse every available social force into united opposition to the stiff-necked individualism of the human race. In historic times the difficulty has been reversed, and we have had to struggle manfully to prevent the crust of social custom from hardening so closely round us that individual and social growth be made impossible.

When human life was very young upon the earth, men were like children, utterly wayward and impulsive, passionate, revengeful, thoughtless, cruel from ignorance, easily frightened and intensely superstitious, yet recovering quickly from the immediate effects of all impressions, both good and bad; easily plastic in any direction, but as easily diverted into another channel. They were natural fighters—the males of these wild human hordes—fighting with strange men and fierce animals without the group; fighting also among themselves; recovering very quickly from terrible wounds (as do lowest savages to-day), full of savage vigor and ferocity, untamed as yet—creatures of boundless possibilities, because not yet set and hardened in their ways. Our primitive human progenitors differed from the lowest modern savage, at least, in this: their lives were not yet run into the mould of a curiously twisted and contorted custom; but it is probable that in very many respects the resemblance was a close one. Social customs they undoubtedly must have inherited from a yet lower stage of social existence; but we may believe that earliest man was not quite so slavishly obedient to these despotic rules of life, as are the brutes; even as the higher orders of the merely animal world are somewhat less inflexibly bound by them than are the lower orders. Certainly, all social custom was then, as it were, in the stalk, and very many centuries were required for the development of the delicate branching twigs and of the curving leaves and flowers. Aristotle and Plato and Xenophon—so unlike in most of their teachings—all unite in telling us of the exceeding great difficulty of inducing men to submit themselves continuously to any form of social discipline. These great thinkers lived when the nations had not yet "had time to forget" that man is the "hardest of all animals to govern."[1] In other words, the highest form of life tended far more strongly than lower forms toward individualism, toward divergence from its fellows, toward independence: that is, the thinking and acting for oneself.

But human betterment—intellectual and moral—positively demanded a social medium for its development. Moreover, mutual aid in war and peace was the prime requisite for

[1] Bagehot, p. 25.

survival, in the struggle for existence with other types of men and animals. For, among the rough hordes that roamed the untilled earth, which would secure the best hunting grounds, which would conquer their enemies, growing stronger and more dominant with time? Surely those that most speedily developed mutual aid among fellow members; that restrained by social pressure individual quarrels and strife within the group, especially in presence of the common enemy. As Walter Bagehot, in that wonderful little book *Physics and Politics*[1] puts it: "The slightest symptom of legal development, the least indication of a military bond, is then enough to turn the scale. The compact tribes win and the compact tribes are the tamest. Civilization begins, because the beginning of civilization is a military advantage."

Those hordes which first succeeded in taming themselves, in uniting their forces for war, by the development and collective enforcement of a few social customs, securing cohesion and military effectiveness—these were the conquering hordes which grew into barbaric empires. This process meant the social fostering of certain tendencies toward likeness and the social repression of certain tendencies toward unlikeness. Those who refused obedience to this social pressure, awakened general abhorrence and both merited and obtained collective punishment—in a word, became criminals.

At first it was unnecessary and surely impossible to curb savage liberty, or shall we call it license, in many directions. The actions punished as crimes were exceedingly few. Even the most necessary social discipline was endured with great difficulty, and any attempt to enlarge its sphere was sure to bring violent resistence and the probable destruction of the social bond.

Thus it was imperative to unite all available social forces for the safe-guarding of the veriest fundamentals, making

[1] Bagehot, p. 52.

social life of any kind possible; and especially for the securing of that prime requisite for survival, military strength and efficiency; hardening the outside shell of the tribe for war, by turning the spear points outward against the common foe.

Three strong instincts, found everywhere in the lowest human communities, were seized upon to do this work, linked together and sometimes united finally into one. Each is a true socializing force, developing centres of attraction, round which the hitherto almost homogeneous living mass begins to circle, resulting in a certain differentiation of function and co-ordination of efforts for the general welfare. These three instincts are manifest in practically every individual of the primitive social group. They are:

1. Instinctive admiration and deference for strongest fighters.

2. Intense reverence for ancient customs.

3. Boundless superstition and fear of the unknown and mysterious.

In no sense antagonistic and disruptive forces, they favor most strongly social unity and effectiveness. The first tendency calls into existence leaders in war and representatives of the social group. The second tendency raises up elders wise in the ancient customs of the race. The third tendency brings out witch doctors, medicine men, priests of heathendom; and around each set of leaders there is a natural grouping for, first war, second justice, third religion and medicine.

In direct antagonism to these three strong trends of the primitive social life arise the three great crimes of savage peoples:

1. Treason: The crime against the warlike strength and unity of the group.

2. Incest: The typical crime against ancient social

custom, and against that fundamental bond of kinship upon which all primitive society is based. For incest, if generally practised, would utterly confound and confuse the ties of relationship, greatly weaken the racial stock, both physically and mentally, and prevent the development of that respect and reverence for elders, so important in the uplifting and strengthening of savage communities.

3. Evil-Witchcraft: The superstitious fears of the people —giving great influence and rewards to socially helpful wizards—make the use of their supernatural powers against the community a crime of the deepest heinousness.

Among lowest savage hordes and tribes everywhere, in Australia and the Pacific Islands, in Greenland, in North and South America, in Asia and in Africa, these three forms of conduct are alike abhorred and severely punished by the social group, as wrongs against the whole community. Moreover, these are, in general, the only offences thus punished, or in other words, the only true crimes.[r]

Other bad actions, adultery, murder, theft, are regarded as simple harms to an individual, or family group, to be revenged by the individual or family, unless vengeance is bought off by composition, *i, e.*, payment of valuables.

The use of the ferocious blood feud in repressing savage passions, through fear of undying hatred and the sleepless quest for blood, has already been mentioned; as has also the slow development of arbitration—first voluntary, then compulsory—the use of outlawry and the change from tort to crime, striking evidence of which will be given in the study of Anglo-Saxon England.

Originally, there was no idea of individual moral guilt connected with the three great fundamental crimes: Treason, Incest, Witchcraft. Even to-day, the traitor may be a man

[r] See next chapter. The few notes for which the attention of the general reader is desired, are marked r.

thoroughly honorable and moral in every private relationship. Lowest savages—the Australian Blackfellows—abhor and punish incest with death, without the remotest idea that such conduct is sinful. Their ancient traditions show a clear perception that incest was very bad for the social welfare, and this is most interesting and important, as showing the essentially social reason for social punishment.

The Dieyerie Tribe dwell between Mount Freeling and Pirigundi Lake. Mr. Samuel Gason lived for over nine years among them, and his writings are believed to be most trustworthy. The Dieyerie believe in Mooramoora (a good spirit), who created the sun, while men were created by the moon at the bidding of Mooramoora. The tradition regarding original promiscuity and the reasons for change is as follows:

"After the creation . . . fathers, mothers, sisters, brothers, and others of the closest kin *intermarried promiscuously*, until the *evil effects of these alliances becoming manifest*, a council of the chiefs was assembled to consider in what way they might be averted; the result of their deliberation being a petition to the Mooramoora, in answer to which he ordered that the tribe should be divided into branches and distinguished one from the other by different names, after objects animate and inanimate, such as dogs, mice, emu, rain, iguana, and so forth, the *members of any such branch not to intermarry*, but with permission for one branch to mingle with another. Thus the son of a dog might not marry the daughter of a dog, but either might form an alliance with a mouse, an emu, a rat, or other family. This custom is still observed, and the first question asked of a stranger is 'What murdoo?'—namely, of what family are you?"[1]

We are informed that other low savage races hold this idea, *i. e.*, that incest breeds degenerates. Thus, among the

[1] Curr. ii, 48–9.

New Zealanders: "Any one outside brother and sister could marry, although marriage of first cousins was greatly disliked. They seem aware of the weakening effects of the inbreeding."[1]

"By the old custom of the Aht tribes (Indians of Vancouver Island), no marriage was permitted within the degree of second cousin. Intermarriage with other tribes is sought by the higher classes to strengthen the foreign connections of their own tribe, and, I think also, with some idea of preventing degeneracy of race."[2]

Incest is thus made highly criminal, and the word incestuous the most disgraceful and opprobrious epithet in the language, by a race (the Australians), among whom promiscuous intercourse before marriage is quite permissible, and adultery, with the consent or by command of the husband, thoroughly honorable and customary.[3] Indeed, among most savage peoples, the loose sexual intercourse with unmarried females that prevails, is strikingly in contrast with the utter social detestation and vengeance which destroys those who dare to commit incest.

Thus Kolbe, who studied the Hottentots of South Africa in the early 18th century, writes: "They have a tradition which condemns both the man and woman who marry, or commit fornication, within the proscribed degrees, to death under the club; and they say that this law has always existed among them. It is certain, that any one convicted of such an act is punished without pity, whatever be his rank in the nation."[4]

Also, Dobrizhoffer, missionary to the Abipones of South America early in the 19th century, states: "Long experience has convinced me, that the respect for consanguinity, by which they are deterred from marrying into their own

[1] Tregear. p. 102.
[2] Sproat. p. 99.
[3] See Spencer and Gillen.
[4] Kolbe, i, 268–9.

families, is implanted by nature in the minds of most of the people of Paraguay. In this opinion I was greatly confirmed by the Cacique Roy, leader of the savages in the woods of Mbaevira, who, when I happened to make mention of incestuous nuptials, broke out into these words—'you say right, Father! marriage with relatives is a most shameful thing. This have we learned from our ancestors.' Such are the feelings of these wood savages, though they think it neither irrational nor improper to marry many wives and reject them whenever they like." [1]

Nor was witchcraft regarded as in any way sinful, although this became in later ages the very essence of the offence. Originally it was not traffic with evil spirits which was punished as crime. Almost all savage peoples fear and honor the wizard, and make use of his services freely. Witchcraft in itself was neither sin nor crime. But the evil wizard, who used his occult powers against a member of his own community, thereby breeding widespread suspicion, hatred and fear within the social group, he *had* to be destroyed, if the tribe was to continue strong and united. Thus evil-witchcraft became a most heinous crime. Again, the reason is essentially a social one.

The tradition of the Dieyrie tribe, just given, affords strong evidence that some among the Australian Blackfellows believe in the existence of a good spirit interested in human welfare; but the same work from which this quotation is taken—a work recognized as the best and practically the only good general comparative study of Australian tribes [2]—arrives at the conclusion that the western tribes have no words at all to express God or good spirit, and it is very doubtful whether there was any such idea among the more intelligent tribes of the south and east until the coming of

[1] Dobrizhoffer, ii, 212–13.

[2] *Science of Man*, Sidney, Australia, May 22, 1899.

the whites. "That nothing of the nature of worship, prayer or sacrifice has been observed is certain." [1]

This same utter lack of the idea of a good God, and wise, all ruling Father of men, was found among the Indian tribes of North America at the coming of the French and English. "In no Indian language could the early missionaries find a word to express the idea of God. Manitou and Oki meant anything endowed with supernatural powers, from a snake-skin, or a greasy Indian conjurer, up to Manabozho and Jouskeha." [2] The Jesuits introduced the idea of "The Great Chief of Men," and the Indians accepted it readily, even tribes in no sense Christian.

"In the primitive Indian's conception of a God the *idea of moral good has no part.*" He does not dispense justice here or hereafter, but leaves man under the power of a host of subordinate spirits. "Nor is the good and evil of these inferior beings a *moral good and evil.* The good spirit is the spirit that gives good luck and ministers to the necessities and desires of mankind; the evil spirit is simply a malicious agent of disease, death and mischance." [3] "The primitive Indian believed in the immortality of the soul, but he did not always believe in a state of future reward and punishment. Nor, when such a belief existed, was the *good to be rewarded a moral good, or the evil to be punished a moral evil. Skillful hunters, brave warriors, men of influence and consideration,* went after death to the happy hunting-ground; while the *slothful, the cowardly and the weak* were doomed to eat serpents and ashes in dreary regions of mist and darkness." [4]

Yet, among all these people who possessed almost no idea of moral good and evil, crime existed and was punished, because essentially bad for the social welfare. Their good was a social good, and their evil a social evil. They possessed

[1] Curr, *The Australian Race.*

[2] Parkman, p. lxxix. [3] *Ibid.*, p. lxxviii. [4] *Ibid.*, p. lxxx.

an ethical standard, but it was a social standard of right action, not a religious standard of right motive.

We are told that the Bushmen of Africa have apparently not the least conception of a Supreme Being. They have been known to offer prayers to a caterpillar insect.[1] These Bushmen are probably the earliest remaining aborigines of South Africa, and "rank with the savages of Australia as the lowest existing type of mankind," yet they unite to punish evil witchcraft with death.

Intellectually very low in the scale of life, the Australians are morally even lower. Some writers have denied them any moral feelings,[2] while others, like Sir John Lubbock, agree with Curr, that they have no religion.[3] All their tribes believe in the existence of evil spirits, to whose malevolence and to the charms of sorcerers they attribute almost all their ills, including death; for they have no conception of death from natural causes. They believe also in the soul and in life beyond the grave, but all their thoughts on such subjects are very hazy and confused: indeed it is only with the greatest difficulty that they can grasp any abstract idea. Among the western Blackfellows there are no words for God or justice, and but few terms of endearment. Yet all their languages have words for theft, incest and cowardice, the last two being terms of greatest insult.[4]

Words for "good" and "bad" are invariably found in use among Australian tribes, and they are applied to actions beneficial or injurious to the social group. Thus Collins writes: "On our speaking of cannibalism to the natives of New South Wales, they expressed great horror and said it

[1] Lichtenstein, ii, 200.

[2] Wake, "*Evolution of Morality*," pp. 293-5.

[3] Lubbock, "*Prehistoric Times*," p. 436.

[4] There are often no words for murder, adultery or rape, and no words for love, virtue and mercy. See Dr. Maudsley.

was 'wee-ree' (bad). When we punished some of our people for ill-treating them, they expressed their approbation and said it was 'bood-yer-re' (good). Midnight murders they reprobated, and applauded acts of kindness and generosity."[1] Thieves, when detected, make no resistance, evidently considering their actions bad and deserving of punishment.[2] "Their notions of duty relate mostly to neighborly service and social interest." "They are not at all thieves and liars, but capable of many good deeds."[3]

They punish incest and evil-witchcraft with death, as awful crimes. Evidently they possess a social standard of right action, to which members of the tribe must conform. "With the customs of his tribe," writes Curr, "the Australian Aborigine must in a general way comply, and for exceptional infractions pay established penalties." Persistent disregard of tribal customs results in death or outlawry, which is sure to be speedily followed by death.[4] "As amongst all savage tribes, the Australian native is bound hand and foot by custom. What his fathers did before him he must do." "Any infringement of custom, within certain limitations, is visited with sure and often severe punishment."[5]

Yet, ultra conservative as the Blackfellows are, changes in custom have been introduced, however difficult. The traditions and festival customs of the tribes of Central Australia and of the natives dwelling near Perigundi Lake show this plainly. There has been some social growth, some upward progress, and this progress has been enforced and safeguarded by the production of a great new crime.

The Deyerie tradition states that promiscuity and incestuous cohabitation were at one time generally practiced. (As the Bible puts it: "All flesh had corrupted his way upon the

[1] Wake, i, 319. [2] Waitz, p. 297.
[3] *Encyclopædia Britannica*, article on Australian Blackfellows.
[4] Curr, i, 62. [5] Spencer and Gillen, pp. 11–12.

earth.") But at last incest was made highly criminal; and this must have been far back in the history of the human race, because of the intense abhorrence now occasioned by breaches of this ancient social custom. For the ***antiquity*** of ***a crime*** among low savages must be measured by the ***intensity of the detestation*** it awakens in the community, by the ***rareness of its occurrence*** and the ***sureness*** and ***severity*** of the ***penalty inflicted.*** Custom rules with a rod of iron among lowest men (as instinct among beasts), and obedience will be more instinctive, more unquestioning, the longer the binding yoke of custom has existed. It is more easy to find instances of the social punishment of evil-witchcraft than of social vengeance for incest, and yet this latter is perhaps even more widely abhorred and more generally forbidden by sacred, immemorial custom. Treason, or active hostility to the warlike strength and efficiency of the social group, is practically unknown among lowest races—we hear absolutely nothing about it, because it does not exist. Somewhat higher in the social scale we begin to meet with it, but the crime is still exceedingly infrequent. The punishment is always death, or outlawry, which is worse than death itself and speedily includes it. Thus we are told that the natives of Tonga exhibit intense loyalty.[1] The Aht Indians of Vancouver Island are "devotedly loyal" to their "own tribe."[2] Among the New Zealanders, outlawry is enforced for a very few offences, "black-treachery," etc., "so rare as to be scarcely worth noticing."[3] The betrayer of the secrets of the community is punished with death by the Aleuts of Alaska.[4] These peoples, though far removed from the lowest savages, have not yet developed royalty—they have no king to rule over them and take the lead in war.

When the king comes, the crime of treason is enlarged,

[1] Martin, ii, 142, 146.

[2] Sproat, p. 151.

[3] Tregear, p. 107.

[4] Petroff, p. 152.

to protect his person, ensure him honor, and enforce his authority, for the social welfare demands this. Instances of treason become increasingly frequent, as we find them among the negro kingdoms of Africa.

Accordingly, the author believes that treason—active disloyalty to the social group—striking directly at its warlike strength and effectiveness, is the great fundamental and first crime of the human race.

The evidence of social punishment among animals supports this theory. Nothing else is so absolutely indispensable to the savage horde as power to fight well and successfully. There must be absolute unity of all strength within the group to this end, for the struggle means always social victory or death. As Walter Bagehot well says: "In this early time, every intellectual gain, so to speak, that a nation possessed was invested and taken out in war, all else perished;"[1] and every superiority a tribe possessed, moral, mental, physical, was valued and estimated in terms of the military advantage found in it. This was true of the strong legal customs binding men together—true of monarchical despotism—true of religious faith. "Nation making is the occupation of men in these early ages, and it is war that makes nations."[2]

Steinmetz, in a paragraph of his valuable book upon "The First Development of Punishments," recognizes the possibility that treason against the community was the crime first punished, despite the fact that instances of such treason occur first among peoples by whom "public punishments" have been "already highly developed." "We may believe," he writes, "that sudden outbursts of wrath of the whole people against the traitor often occurred, although they do not appear in our sources of information. They would be, then, the first beginnings of these public punishments. That we

[1] *Physics and Politics*, p. 49.

[2] *Ibid.*, pp. 65–77.

do not find them in evidence, tends to show that the traitor in this stage of culture very seldom existed. The enemy would be too intensely and too generally hated. The crime gave too little inducement and means of reward. The traitor, who must leave his own folk, would surely be regarded as an enemy by other people . . . . The punishments inflicted would have been at once impulsive and seldom required."[1]

Lowest known human societies are groups of kindred and are very democratic. They have no king, no form of government, and no religion but vague dreams, fetish worship, and propitiation of the multitudinous powers of evil, to whom —even if they believe at all in good supernatural beings—they think the earth is entirely given over.

Social punishment, therefore, cannot be due to a religious command, for the malevolent spirits, hating man, certainly cannot be imagined as commanding punishment for actions which must be pleasing to the demons, because harmful to the tribes of men. Neither can they originate in the commands of rulers who do not exist among them. Thus, Curr, writing of the Australian aborigines in general, states that no fact is more surely established concerning them than this: they have no form of government; if by this word we mean "the habitual exercise of authority by one or a few individuals over a community or body of persons."[2]

The Blackfellows live in small local groups or petty tribes of from 25 to 500 individuals, whose members are closely related by blood and live in the "strictest alliance, offensive and defensive." Again, we find absolute loyalty to the social bond—treason unknown. There is no such thing as a chief among the central Australians; but fame in fighting, hunting, or knowledge of the ancient traditions and customs of his people raises some man to the position of "alatunja" in each community. "He has no definite power over

[1] Steinmetz, ii, 339-340. [2] Curr, i, 60.

the persons of the individuals who are members of his group," and all his authority is very vague. But "he calls together the elder men, who always consult concerning any important business, such as the holding of sacred ceremonies or the punishment of individuals who have broken tribal custom." His judgement upon any case need not be followed by the council.[1] These religious ceremonies ("engwura") are, as the natives say, to make "men very good:" "Ertwa murra oknizra," = "man, good, great, or very." They believe that the passing of this ordeal strengthens, "imparts courage and wisdom, makes the man more kindly natured and less apt to quarrel." Not until these ceremonies have been undergone is a man recognized as "a perfectly developed member of the tribe."[2] Goodness evidently consists in conduct socially beneficial, and every male is educated up to the requirements of the social standard of right action.

The Bushmen are sworn enemies to the pastoral life, and live by hunting and plunder. The temporary villages or kraals number about twenty-five huts, one hut to a family.[3] "Not the least approach to any tribal unity appears in their wandering groups." "They have no chiefs, bodily strength alone forming a distinction among them."[4]

Among the Gilbert Islanders, "in war and other matters, the heads of families formed the deliberative assembly or government for the time being." "They were constantly at war with each other."[5]

The Maoris of New Zealand are described as living in a republic with leading men and no proper form of government.[6] At the assemblies of the people for the administra-

[1] Spencer and Gillen, pp. 9, 10.
[2] *Ibid.*, p. 271.
[3] Barrow, i, 275.
[4] *Encyclopædia Britannica.* Article on the Bushmen.
[5] Turner, pp. 295, 305.
[6] Tregear, pp. 102–107.

tion of justice women as well as men expressed their opinions.[1]

Among the western tribes of Torres Straits, Australia, "there was no recognized government or state, nor any system of religion." Ancient customs were their laws.[2]

The Greenland Esquimaux are very low in the intellectual and moral scale. Their notions of supernatural beings are extremely hazy—they have no definite religion, and "absolutely no political organization among them."[3] The Greenlanders' "first social law is to help others. On this law and on the principle of common suffering and common enjoyment, all the small communities depend for their existence."[4] Their grand idea of virtue is "to have been dexterous and diligent at their work," to have performed great exploits, mastered many whales and seals to be distributed among the members of the group according to old and definite rules.[5] Only those who have performed such acts (good social actions, utterly irrespective of motive), will go to the Elysium where the feast is always preparing. They believe "wicked people and witches especially" will be banished to a place of torment.[6]

Among "the Indians," writes Schoolcraft, "the democratic principle is implanted a little too deep. The chief has no authority to act for the tribe, and dare not do it. If he does he will be severely beaten or killed at some future time. All business is done by the majority of the band assembling and consulting each other." The motion "that appears the best is adopted by general consent and the chief has to be governed according to the voice or opinion of the tribe."[7]

[1] Thomson, *New Zealand.*

[2] Haddon, p. 314.

[3] Nansen, ii, 340: Hall, ii, 316; Crantz.

[4] Nansen, ii, 304.

[5] See Crantz, and Nansen, ii, 302.

[6] Crantz. For impulsive social vengeance upon witches, see i, 194.

[7] Schoolcraft, ii, 182–3.

Among the Hill tribes of India each little village is practically an independent community. Every man is as good as his neighbor. There are meetings of the elders for arbitration, to prevent individual vengeance, and Punjayets, or councils of the whole tribe for judicial purposes, etc. Thus, the Nágás " have no kind of internal government," no priesthood apparently, and very few religious ceremonies. " Petty disputes and disagreements . . . are settled by a council of elders, the litigants voluntarily submitting to their arbitration. But, correctly speaking, there is not the shadow of a constituted authority in the Nágá community, and wonderful as it may seem, this want of government does not lead to any marked degree of anarchy and confusion."[1] They exhibit intense love for their native village. Terrible blood feuds exist among them, and " the Nágá's religion, the Nágá's principle and sense of honor is comprised in one word, and that word is revenge—deep, deadly revenge—and the prosecution of it to the extremest lengths for the most trifling offences."[2] Ancient custom is intensely strong among all these peoples.

MacGahan writes in *Campaigning on the Oxus*, (p. 350), " The state does not exist among the Turcomans. There is no body politic, no recognized authority, no supreme power, no higher tribunal than public opinion. Their head men, it is true, have a kind of nominal authority to settle disputes; but they have no power to enforce decisions. These the litigants can accept, or fight out their quarrel, just as they please. And yet they have such well-defined notions of right and wrong as between themselves, and public opinion is so strong in enforcing these notions, that there are *rarely dissensions or quarrels among them*." This shows the great power of social custom in repressing criminal instincts. Each member of a tribe, of course, obeys his tribal customs.

[1] Stewart, xxiv, 608. [2] *Ibid.*, xxiv, 609.

The origin of crime and social punishment, therefore, cannot be traced to the command of supernatural powers, nor to the dictates of any king or human ruler. Where, then, shall we seek it? The answer is surely manifest. The strong and sufficient cause for the social punishment of crime must be looked for in those ancient and time-honored customs, for which savages can give no reason, but which they follow instinctively, in blind reverence and unquestioning obedience; for they are the teachings of Mother Nature, drilled into countless generations of savage ancestors. They are lessons in social necessity, in social selection, where failure to learn, or refusal to obey, means the inevitable destruction of the social group—means social death. Crime is essentially a social product.

But are the imperative commands of immemorial custom everywhere so strong and binding upon low savage men? The evidence is overwhelming. Turn where you will, you find the same answer. The mere mass of testimony is so great, from America, Asia, Africa and Oceanica, that it would be folly to attempt to give, here, other than a few examples, some of them already referred to.

AUSTRALIA.—"As amongst all savage tribes, the Australian native is bound hand and foot by custom. What his fathers did before him he must do. Any infringement of custom, within certain limitations, is visited with sure and often severe punishment."[1]

In the *Islands of the Pacific Ocean*, law is scarcely ever separated at all from ancestral custom, which is very powerful.[2]

AMERICA.—Among the American Indians ancient social customs define and are most powerful for maintaining mutual rights and duties.

Aleuts.—"The Aleuts still maintain that a failure to ob-

[1] Spencer and Gillen, pp. 11–12. [2] See p. 77. *Papuan Islanders.*

serve the customs of their forefathers, and especially a wilful neglect of the same, is attended with all kinds of disasters and punishments."[1]

Dakotas.—Children of the Dakota are taught all the ancient customs of the race and obedience to them.[2]

Araucanians of South America.—Their "laws are nothing more than primordial usages, or tacit conventions, that have been established among them." The Araucanians elect their chiefs, who are regarded simply as "the first among equals." This people "cannot endure despotism," and "compel" the chiefs "to keep within the bounds prescribed by their customs."[3]

ASIA.—*Khonds.*—There is unfaltering devotion to the common cause and to the ancient customs of the race.[4]

Karens.—"The Karens ascribe all their laws to the elders of preceding generations and have no idea of any period when they did not exist." These traditional commands meet all the relations of man to man, moral and political, civil and religious.[5]

AFRICA.—*Gold Coast Negroes.*—"A semi-political and religious custom called Egbo is the most potent controlling influence in old Callebar and fulfils all the purposes of a natural code of laws."[6]

Hottentots.—The office of captain of each kraal (*i. e.*, village) is hereditary, "but he is not installed until he has solemnly engaged, in the presence of the people, not to alter or deviate from the ancient laws and customs of the kraal." The usual explanation or argument of this people is: "'Tis Hottentot custom and ever was so."[7]

[1] Petroff, p. 156.
[2] Schoolcraft.
[3] Thompson's Alcedo, i, 405.
[4] Campbell, p. 239; Macpherson's *Report*, p. 52.
[5] Mason, xxxvii. Pt. ii, 131 and 143.
[6] *Jour. Ethn. Soc.*, 1848, i, 247.
[7] Kolbe, i, 162.

Dahomans.—"Custom rules everybody and everything at the Court of Dahomy."[1]

Ashantes.—The king is represented as an absolutely despotic monarch, but he is under "obligation to observe the national customs which have been handed down to the people from remote antiquity, and a practical disregard of this obligation, in the attempt to change some of the customs of their forefathers, cost Osai Quamina his throne."[2]

The violation of a few fundamental and most socially necessary of these ancient customs, awakens in the savage breast everywhere, intense abhorrence and a passionate longing for vengeance, which brings immediate or speedy death, or outlawry, upon the hated individual.[3]

Oftentimes the horror occasioned by the crime is so overmastering and the social revenge so immediate, impulsive and irregular, that one is tempted to classify the punishment under the head of social reflex action, like the vengeance inflicted by animal communities; and surely those death penalties, meted out by savage races in moments of wild fury and excitement, do occasionally deserve the name of semi-reflex, and remind us forcibly of the probably instinctive and utterly unreasoning beginnings of punishment for crime, precedent to all ideas of morality, and of the fierce warrant and justification for such conduct, in the absolute necessity of social self-defence. But the evidence varies

[1] Forbes, ii, 176. [2] Beecham, p. 90, et seq.

[3] See p. 26. *Social Punishment Among Animals.* The few strong customs which induce social punishment for crime are certainly not the only customs binding savage men. Their whole lives are often enmeshed in a multitude of petty and burdensome regulations, which seem to us in many cases perfectly ridiculous, but which usually contain at bottom a discipline or lesson useful for their stage of social development. At any rate the savages themselves thoroughly believe in the usefulness of these minor rules of life; but the transgressor is punished, not by an outraged social group, but by the terrible fear of impending evil, physical or mental, the dread of sickness, malformation, torture, from unseen supernatural powers, angered by his act.

greatly. Sometimes the most frenzied and immediate social vengeance is found among savage races (like the negroes), fairly well advanced politically and socially, and even among highly civilized nations; while among the very lowest hordes (like certain tribes of the Australian Blackfellows), collective punishment is sometimes inflicted after long deliberation and in an orderly and regular manner. Among the fierce African Bushmen and the mild and peace-loving Greenland Esquimaux—both among the lowest human beings known to man—social vengeance is wreaked upon the hated malefactor in a thoroughly tumultuous and ferocious manner.

Esquimaux.—"Their procedure with witches is very short. If a rumor prevails that a certain old woman is a witch, because the poor old creature made pretences to charms and quackery, all the country will join to stone her, or she will be thrown into the sea, or hewn to pieces, according as their rage dictates to them." [1]

Bushmen.—Among the Bushmen there are "people who are considered as magicians and who are believed to have the power of commanding rain, wind and thunder, at their pleasure. If, unluckily, one of these magicians happens to have predicted falsely several times in succession, he is thrust out of the kraal, and very likely burned, or put to death in some other way." [2]

Tasmanians.—"They had few crimes against each other. Faults not immediately punished were usually overlooked. Injuries were soon forgotten." [3]

Fijians.—"Nearly all sudden deaths are ascribed to this cause" (*i. e.*, witchcraft). "Persons detected in the act of burying these deadly charms are *summarily* dealt with, or if found out afterwards, their houses are burnt and they themselves killed." [4]

[1] Crantz, i, 194.

[2] Lichtenstein, ii, 61.

[3] Bonwick, p. 10.

[4] Williams and Calvert, p. 195.

Iroquois and Hurons.—"Witches, with whom the Hurons and Iroquois were grievously infested, were objects of utter abomination to both, and any one might kill them at any time."[1]

Araucanians of South America.—"Justice is administered in a tumultuous and irregular manner, and without any of those preliminary formalities that are observed among civilized nations. The criminal who is convicted of a capital offence is immediately put to death." Such offences are "treachery, witchcraft, adultery, and the robbery of any valuable article." Other offences of less importance are punished by individual retaliation, which is much in use among them.[2]

Hill Tribes of India.—*Bheels.*—The Bheels "are loosely united among themselves and have a rude system of customary justice, which their chiefs rarely venture to break or change." For harms to an individual—such as "robbery, murder or theft"—reparation is demanded by "the chief, or family of the sufferer. If refused, immediate resort is had to acts of retaliation or reprisal, which provoke much further violence and loss of life on both sides. These proceedings are, however, only the effusions of sudden rage, and the elders of the tribes, when that is cooled, interfere, and in all quarrels and disputes, great or trifling, they have resort to Punjayets. These often consist of several hundred members, and proceed to settle the terms on which the murder, robbery or theft is to be compounded. Fines in cattle or money are high upon murders, but Bheel Punjayets never inflict death." Such judicial settlements of individual injuries of man to man, very closely resemble the procedure everywhere in use among the early Teutons and the Anglo-Saxons in England. So much for offences of tort—now for true crimes among the Bheels. "If the crime

[1] Parkman, p. lxiii.

[2] Thompson's Alcedo, i, 405.

committed be of so atrocious a nature as not to be compounded or forgiven, the culprit is pursued and destroyed by those whom this act has made his enemies; but he must be put to death in what they term an affray, that is, in warm blood; to take the life of each other coolly is ***revolting to their usages.***" [1]

Mishmis.—"Theft is punished by a fine inflicted by a meeting of all the gams (*i. e.*, head men). If the fine is not paid, or the offender refuses to pay, he is slain in a general attack, being cut up by the company assembled." Murder is punished in the same way, but the fine is heavier.[2]

AFRICA.—*Hottentots.*—Every Hottentot kraal "has a court for the administration of justice, composed of the captain and all the men of the kraal." It is held in an open field, the men squatting in a circle. Guilt or innocence is determined by a majority of voices. If the prisoner is convicted and adjudged worthy of death, sentence is immediately pronounced and immediately executed on the spot." The captain "as chief executioner, leaps with a kind of fury upon the criminal, striking him a terrific blow with his club. Then the rest of the assembly throw themselves also upon him, and although he is very soon dead, they do not cease to rain blows upon his head, stomach and side, until the head is all in pieces." [3]

Malagasy.—"Until a very recent date, persons detected in the act of stealing in the public markets, by cutting off the corner of the lamba in which money is usually tied up, were ***mobbed*** by the ***populace*** and ***killed without a trial.***" [4]

Savage tribes are of necessity organized primarily and principally for war; courage and success in battle form the cardinal virtue—the summum bonum.[5] Originally these

[1] Malcolm, i, 576.

[2] Griffith's *Journals*, p. 35, et seq.

[3] Kolbe, i, 165–172.

[4] Sibree, p. 305.

[5] The two ideas are generally merged into one in the savage mind. The successful warrior is the courageous man, and *vice versa.*

tribes are intensely democratic, but long-continued warfare—especially when the group attains to any considerable size and becomes a conquering nation—usually raises to increasingly despotic dominance, a head chief or king. The feeling of kindred and of common descent aids in this, for the king is soon regarded as the "father of his people," and he is always a king of men, not territory; king of the English, not king of England. He is himself the great warrior and war leader, like Saul or David—the "koennig: the man who can"—and he gathers around himself as his advisers the elders wise in ancient custom, and the medicine men or priests. Soon he begins to unite all their functions in himself. He is not only leader in war, but also judge in peace, sworn to observe and to enforce the sacred, ancient customs of the race. He becomes priest and prophet—finally he is worshipped as a god—supported in all this by the people, as the manifestation of the social unity, the preserver of the social life and effectiveness. He is the keystone of the arch, thus producing compactness and strength of organization, first for war and then for other purposes as well. Offences against him personally become regarded as wrongs against the whole community, and are punished as crimes, thus enlarging the sphere of treason, and introducing entirely new criminal offences. Naturally this process multiplies criminals; and yet it is thoroughly astounding to see how abject and unquestioning oftentimes, is the obedience of a truly brave and warlike people to a thoroughly bad sovereign, who kills their nearest and dearest to gratify a whim, so long as he does not seek to change or deviate from their time-honored customs.[1]

Their reverence and love are so deeply seated that it seems almost impossible to shake them. "The king can do no wrong;" without him they feel they cannot live. In this

[1] See The Dahomans and Ashantees, Dalzel, p. 69.

lies the great danger that people once so warlike, so independent, finding government of any kind very irksome and very hard to bear, may become too tame, with the manly fibre killed in them—as it was among the ancient Peruvians and Mexicans—under the yoke of a deified emperor and a cruel and implacable religion. They are full of humility, obeying every one, writes Zurita of the Mexicans;[1] and they are thoroughly indolent, for they have become accustomed to act only from fear of punishment. This is not the stuff out of which the enduringly progressive civilizations of the world are made. The caste system hardens around them, making helpful as well as harmful variation alike practically impossible. Upward growth ceases, and we have an arrested civilization, or an utterly unprogressive savage tribe, according to the time of the hardening of the outer crust of custom.

While the first successful and conquering groups were those that most easily tamed themselves, the final conquerors and leaders of the world's civilization were and are those who found this taming process so exceedingly difficult that for many centuries they lagged behind, and were despised as mere barbarians and savages, by the great nations of Egypt, Assyria, Babylonia and Persia. But the Greek, Roman and Teutonic peoples succeeded at last in securing national stability, while preserving and safe-guarding a strong tendency to variation—the spirit of individual liberty—which has always been so masterful in these races that it has compelled a place for itself, the safe-guarding of a fitting sphere for its development, as the price and condition of individual submission to the social needs.

Free discussion was the great means for the attainment of this good end.[2] Among the Teutons, it was those that most surely preserved their old love of liberty, their democratic customs of self-government, and slowly developed a

[1] Zurita, p. 186.

[2] Bagehot, pp. 158–162.

national polity of their own, that became the world's leaders and rulers. The tribes that wandered far from home and adopted to a large extent the laws and usages of the effete Roman civilization, came as conquerors and grew up into mighty kingdoms, that lasted for a day or for a hundred years—where are they now? While England, that struggled for a thousand years to unite its clashing races and little, liberty-loving kingdoms into a strong nation, a united people, before finally succeeding in the seventeenth century; America, which has at last merged local differences and jealousies, with greatest difficulty, under the Federal Government of the United States; and Germany, where the Teutonic peoples could not overcome their seemingly irresistible tendency to split up into little warring, independent states, until 1871—all three great peoples conquering themselves finally only under the pressure of a terrible war—these are the leaders of the world's civilization to-day; the conservatively progressive, world conquerors and educators and Christianizers, upon whom the hope of the future seems to rest.[1]

The great barbarian monarchies, as we now call those peoples which once scorned our savage ancestors, established a stable, but unprogressive equilibrium. The Eastern Races did not, and they do not to-day, understand what we mean by progress; this constant desire for change and upward growth. Change is what they most fear and hate. But Greece, Rome, and the Teutonic civilizations are progressive equilibriums, where the rights of the social whole are being constantly balanced with the rights of each individual member. This makes strong, intelligent and moral

[1] Shall we include Italy also, at last united in 1871 into a great kingdom, and at the present time rapidly developing, in her northern states, manufactures, industry and commerce, and it is hoped preparing for a great new birth—intellectual, artistic and moral? Then there is Russia also—the great unknown.

freemen, as well as good citizens, but it makes criminals also, or at least has made them, till now; and this great increase of criminality is a part of the price we are paying for growth to better things—for a larger, more abundant, more Christ-like life.

CHAPTER IV

SAVAGE RACES—IN AUSTRALIA, AMERICA, ASIA AND AFRICA

Lowest Savage Races.—What little social organization there is among lowest savages, is mainly for purposes of warfare, offensive and defensive. Their petty villages or tribes are almost continually at war with one another. Of course there are exceptions, such as the forest Veddahs of Ceylon; but the Veddahs have practically no social organization at all, and no punishment of criminals is found among them. These last facts are true also with regard to the miserable inhabitants of Tierra del Fuego. "Each family circle lives apart, and they combine only in small groups against some common enemy, but recognize not even a temporary leader." If social life does not exist, social punishment for crime is of course impossible.

Among almost all these low savage races, however, there is found the head man, or chief, possessed of a small and jealously limited authority, that varies with his character and warlike prowess. Elders, wise in ancient customs, are nearly everywhere in evidence, as are also witch-doctors, or medicine men, who are both feared and honored. Some of these tribes have no form of worship, no idea, apparently, of a good Spirit, interested in human welfare.

They are intensely devoted to their savage liberty, and to the absolutely sacred duty of personal blood revenge for injury to a man or his family. Every male is a fighter and can surely be relied on to defend the common cause. Among themselves they are, in general, peaceful, mutually helpful and even kindly—in reverential obedience to old ancestral customs. Incest and evil witchcraft awaken, everywhere, the most violent abhorrence and bring down speedy social vengeance upon the guilty, destroying them, oftentimes with their possessions; but such true criminals are very rare. Instances of treason are not found at all among the lowest groups. In those somewhat more highly developed, "black treachery" does, most infrequently, occur; or at least there is a known social penalty of death or outlawry for the offence. Infanticide of twins, weakly or deformed children, and the killing of the aged are very generally practised; not to propitiate any demon, but because the group cannot afford to be burdened with thoroughly useless members of the community. Aged people, themselves, are the last to wish these customs changed, and we can readily see how they aid social strength and effectiveness. "They know" that the mother could not possibly rear both twins, and if the two are boy and girl, such close connection of nearest relatives within the womb is abhorrent to them, as thoroughly incestuous.[1]

In the following tables R (revenge) stands for a tumultuous, impulsive and speedy vengeance; while P (punishment) represents a deferred, more calm and reasoned procedure; but it is very difficult, from scanty evidence, to draw such distinctions, and therefore the letter P is generally used. However, in all cases of treason, incest and evil-witchcraft, the evidence itself is given, and the reader can, if he chooses, draw his own conclusions.

SR = Social Revenge.
SP = Social Punishment.
S = Ancient social customs, strongly opposed to such conduct.
P = Punishment.
IR = Individual Revenge.
IP = Individual Punishment.
C = Composition: (Pecuniary compensation).

[1] Spencer and Gillen, p. 52. Danks, p. 292. Turner, pp. 284, 286, 304; 335–6.

D = Death.	M = Mutilation.
O = Outlawry.	W = Whipping.
H = Honorable.	N = No.

All harms of man to man are shown to be of rare occurrence within these savage groups. The evidence is both abundant and conclusive. If tort offences are so infrequent, instances of true crimes are far more rare and hard to obtain, but they can occasionally be found.[1] The location of the various races and tribes in the tables, follows, in general, the degree of social development attained; but the order, thus determined, does not pretend to any degree of scientific exactness, nor is it necessary that such should be secured.

[1] "The rude, rough man, left entirely in a state of nature, is not in himself evil and wicked, still less is he so from principle; but he follows blindly the impulse of his passions, which lead him to acts, that to us, in the high point of civilization we have attained, appear as crimes." Lichtenstein, ii, 51.

Crimes and Offences Punished by the Lowest Human Races

	Treason.	*Incest.*	*Witchcraft.*	*Adultery.*	*Theft.*	*Murder.*	*Infanticide and Killing of Weak and Aged.*	*Other Offences.*	*Very Few Offenders.*
Australians		S P D or O	S P D	I R D	I P D	I P D or wounding	H		yes
Bushmen		S	S R D or O	N P	N P				yes
Veddahs		P D				P C			yes
Tasmanians		S		I R W			H		yes
New Guineans			S R D	I R D or C	I P C			*arson* I P	yes
Gilbert Islanders		S P D	S P D	I R D	I P D	I R D	H		
Western Tribe of Torres Straits		S		I R D	I R	I R D	H	*sacrilege* P D	theft very rare
New Caledonians and people of New Hebrides		S P	S P D	I R D or possibly S P D	I R D		H		yes
Dyaks		S P D or (heavy fine, etc.)	S R D	I P D or W	P	I P C or D			yes
New Zealanders	S P O	S	S	I R D or C	I P C	I R D			
Sumatrans				I P C	I P C	I P C			yes
Fijians			S R D	I R D	P	I R D	H		
Tahitians or Society Islanders	S P D or O			I R D	I R D				
Hawaiians			S	banishment or I P D	I R D	P O			yes
Samoans	S P O	S		I R D or M	I R	I R D or C or S P O		*assault* I P	yes

TREASON.—*Tongans, S.*—The natives of Tonga are intensely loyal, respectful and obedient to their chiefs. The respect that is always paid to them "forms the stable basis of their government," and is regarded as "a superior sacred duty." It is "supposed the gods would punish" disrespect to chiefs "almost as severely as disrespect to themselves." Public assemblies are held to discuss important matters of state.[1]

New Zealanders, S P O.—Outlawry is enforced for a very few offences, "black treachery," etc., "so rare as to be scarcely worth noticing."[2] "The head, and frequently the whole person of a New Zealand chief, is strictly tapu," and peculiarly sacred.[3]

Tahitians, or Society Islanders, S P D, or O.—"They had no regular code of laws, nor any public courts of justice, and, excepting in offences against the king and chiefs, the leaders were seldom appealed to. The people in general avenged their own injuries. Destitute, however, as they were of even oral laws or institutes, there were many acts which by general consent were considered criminal and deserving punishment. These were summed up in the term orurehan: rebellion, or shaking the government, withholding supplies, or even speaking contemptuously of the king or his administration. So heinous was this offence that the criminal was not only liable to banishment, or to the forfeiture of his life, but a human sacrifice must be offered to atone for the guilt, and appease the displeasure of the gods against the people of the land in which it had been committed."[4]

Samoans, S P O.—"When the chiefs decided on war, every man and boy under their jurisdiction old enough to handle a club, had to take his place as a soldier, or risk the loss of his lands and property, and banishment from the place."[5]

[1] Martin, ii, 155, 159. [2] Tregear, p. 107. [3] Angas, i, 320, 330.
[4] Ellis, iii, 123. [5] Turner, p. 229.

INCEST.—*Australians, S P D.*—The Australian Blackfellows are in general kindly disposed to other members of the same tribe.[1] "In the matter of morality, their code differs radically from ours, but it cannot be denied that their conduct is governed by it, and that any known breaches are dealt with both surely and severely."[2] If a man breaks through the strict marriage laws, the elders and head men consult long together, and if he is adjudged guilty, they are known to have inflicted the death penalty, by means of a party organized for this purpose, called an "ininja.[3]" "A man in these tribes (Urabenen Tribe, etc.) may be put to death for wrongful intercourse . . . . . connection with a woman of the wrong group . . . . . because it is a serious offence against tribal laws, and its punishment has no relation to the individual." Sexual jealousy is very weak among them.[4]

Australians, S P D or O.—"Chastity," writes Curr, "is a virtue beyond the native conception," and the Blackfellows exhibit a deplorable lack of moral restraint; yet cohabitation with persons of near kin they regard with a horror which "they are unable to analyze or explain." [5]

If a man seizes a "gin" (*i. e.*, woman) within the proscribed degrees, he is punished with death or outlawed by the tribe, and can be killed by any one without fear of consequences.[6]

"Marriage within the class," writes the Rev. John Mathew, "is forbidden on pain of death. Even in cases of rape the class rules are respected." The profound submission of the blacks to "restrictions fettered upon them by tradition, and for which they can give no better reason than that such is the practice, points to a very powerful originating cause."[7]

[1] Spencer and Gillen, p. 32. [2] *Ibid.*, p. 46. [3] *Ibid.*, p. 15.
[4] *Ibid.*, pp. 100 and 110. See also 492 and 495.
[5] Curr, i, 43, 62. [6] Wyndham. [7] See also Grey, ii, 110 and 242.

Bushmen of Africa, S.—Brothers and sisters, parents and children may not marry.[1]

Veddahs, P D.—"There was an ancient custom among the Veddahs which has scarcely yet become extinct. It is that which sanctions the marriage of a man with his younger sister. To marry an elder sister or aunt would in their estimation be incestuous, a connection in every respect as revolting to them as it would be to us."

They have "the tradition of a man, whose name even has been preserved, and whose family still exists, who, they say, was eaten by worms for having exceeded the authorized limit, and formed connections with his elder sisters and aunts. By whom this punishment was inflicted they do not pretend to say; but the painful death they regard as the direct consequence of the incest."[2]

Tasmanians, S.—"All sanguineous connection would be illicit or incestuous."[3]

Gilbert Islanders, S P D.—"There was no king, but the heads of families met and ruled. The penalty for incest was strangulation, and the body thrown into the sea."[4]

Western Tribe of Torres Straits, S.—"Marriage was forbidden to cousins and also to the sister of a man's particular friend."[5]

Ths New Britain Group.—"No man may marry a woman of his own class. To do so would bring instant destruction upon the woman, and if not immediate death to the man, his life would never be secure. The nearest relative (male) of the woman would immediately seek her and kill her the moment he found her. I have been told by natives that both man and woman would be killed as early as possible." But as a matter of fact, a case of incest (connection within the totem) "never occurs in a thickly populated district."[6]

[1] Barrow, i, 276. [2] Bailey, ii, 295 and note. [3] Bonwick, p. 62.
[4] Turner, p. 295. [5] Haddon, p. 315. [6] Danks, p. 282–3.

Northern New Hebrides and Banks Island, S P.—"Irregular intercourse between members of the same division is a heinous offence; should such become known, the members of the other (totemic) division will destroy the property of the one in which the guilt is found, without resistance or complaint."[1]

New Caledonia, S P D.—"A law of private revenge allowed the murder of the thief and the adulterer. In a neighboring district the parties guilty of adultery" [or more probably incest] "were tried, dressed up, fed before the multitude and then publicly strangled. A man of the friends of the woman took one end of the cord and a man of the friends of the man took the other."[2]

Dyaks, S P D, etc.—When incest was committed by the Dyaks (Biadju) the whole town was defiled and the criminals were deemed deserving of death. Accordingly, they were separated in hampers and drowned.[3]

"Incest is held in abhorrence, and even the marriage of cousins is not allowed." The land Dyaks heavily fined a chief who had married his granddaughter and degraded him from the rank of chief.[4]

New Zealanders, S.—"Any one outside brother and sister could marry, although marriage of first cousins was greatly disliked. *They seem aware of the weakening effects of the "inbreeding.*" "There are cases in which (especially in legend) even these bonds were broken, but not as proper social practice." Widespread denunciation and stigma for offspring always resulted.[5]

Samoans, S.—Social customs were strongly opposed to incest.[6]

[1] Codrington, p. 307. [2] Turner, p. 343.
[3] Perelaer, p. 59. Quoted by Steinmetz, ii, 336.
[4] Low, pp. 300–301. See also Brooke, ii., 3.
[5] Tregear, p. 102. [6] Turner, p. 92.

EVIL-WITCHCRAFT.—*Australians, S P D.*—"Should a man of influence and well connected, that is, having numerous relatives, die suddenly, or after a long illness, the tribe believe that he has been killed by some charm. A secret council is held and some unhappy innocent is accused, condemned and dealt with by the Pinya"—an "armed band, entrusted with the office of executing offenders," by the council of old men and the chief (*i. e.*, native of superior influence: head man).[1]

Australians, S P D.—Among the aborigines of Moreton Bay . . . . when one is accused of having caused the death of another individual, through sorcery, he is by his own tribe delivered over to death.[2]

Australians, S P D.—"There are three bad men in our camp whom we *Iliaura* do not like, they must be killed." "Two are iturka" (incestuous: the most opprobrious word in their language), "the other is *very quarrelsome* and *strong in magic*." The elders accordingly condemned these men, enticed them to a certain camp-fire, and let members of another tribe kill them, they themselves standing quietly by. The two women who belonged to the iturka men were away. But the Iliaura men would certainly punish them severely and most probably kill them when captured.[3]

Bushmen of Africa, S K D or O.—Among the Bushmen there are "people who are considered as magicians, and who are believed to have the power of commanding rain, wind and thunder, at their pleasure. If, unluckily, one of these magicians happens to have predicted falsely several times in succession, he is thrust out of the kraal, and very likely burned, or put to death in some other way. One of the Bojesmans (*i. e.* Bushmen), who visited the general on

[1] Curr, ii., 53.

[2] Lang, pp. 342, 358. Quoted by Steinmetz, ii., 331.

[3] Spencer & Gillen, pp. 491–5.

this journey, related that such had been the case with his wife. Although at first a very great magician, latterly her prophecies had all proved false, and she was therefore put to death by the rest."[1]

Gilbert Islanders: "Nine, or Savage Island," S R D.—"Of old there were kings, but as they were high priests as well, and were supposed to cause the food to grow, the people got angry with them in times of scarcity and killed them; and as one after another was killed, the end of it was that there was no one wished to be king."[2]

New Guineans, S R D.—In the English part of New Guinea there dwells a whole stock of wizards. The other natives both abhor and fear them, and, when they dare, persecute and destroy them.[3]

"The Nufoers of New Guinea attribute witchcraft, with its results of disease and death, especially to women."[4]

New Caledonians, S P D.—"If a man among themselves was suspected of witchcraft, and supposed to have caused the death of several persons, he was formally condemned. A great festival was held"; the face and body of the convicted man was painted black, and he was dressed in flowers and shells. "He then came dashing forward . . . . jumped over the rocks into the sea and was seen no more."[5]

Dyaks, S R D.—"If a Dyak (Biadju) is thought to be an evil wizard, his life is not safe. For the public welfare and security it is thought necessary to put him to death, and his murder is deemed a praiseworthy act." Among the hill Dyaks a wizard is cruelly tortured to death.[6]

The New Zealanders, S.—New Zealanders "all dread cutting their nails, lest the parings should fall into the sorcerer's hands."[7]

[1] Lichtenstein, ii., 61.
[2] Turner, p. 305.
[3] Lindt, p. 113. Quoted bp Steinmetz, ii., 330.
[4] Crawley, p. 224.
[5] Turner, p. 342.
[6] Perelaer, p. 28. Quoted by Steinmetz, ii, 330.
[7] Thomson, i, 317.

"Some of the aged women among the New Zealanders are supposed to possess the power of witchcraft and sorcery."[1]

Fijians, S R D.—"Nearly all sudden deaths are ascribed to this cause," *i. e.*, witchcraft. "Persons detected in the act of burying these deadly charms are summarily dealt with; or, if found out afterwards, their houses are burnt, and they themselves killed. Professed practisers of witchcraft are dreaded by all classes, and by destroying mutual confidence, shake the security and comfort of society. Some of these wizards, but not all, are priests."[2]

Hawaiians, S.—They are a very superstitious people; think all death due to the power of evil spirits, poison, or the incantations of sorcerers, employed by some enemy; unless the deceased are known to have been killed by some act of violence.[3]

Javans, S P D.—According to the ancient code of Java, which is in force to this day (1820) in Bali, evil witchcraft is punished with death to the offender, and "if the matter be very clear,"—so runs the law—"let the punishment of death be extended to his parents, to his children, and to his grandchildren. Let no one escape; and let their property of every description be confiscated."[4]

OFFENCES OF ALL KINDS WITHIN THE GROUP VERY RARE

Australians.—"A more treacherous race I do not believe exists." A stranger "Blackfellow" is always treated as an enemy, and killed as soon as possible. Yet within the tribal group there is peace, kindliness and mutual aid. They love their children and are very tender toward them; yet murder about thirty per cent., including twins and all sickly and deformed infants, social custom demanding this. "They do not steal from one another to any great extent. I do not

[1] Angas, i, 317.
[2] Williams and Calvert, pp. 140, 195.
[3] Ellis, iv, 293.
[4] Crawford, i, 57.

remember," writes Lumholtz, "a single instance of weapons being stolen;" and these, with household instruments and ornaments are almost all the personal property they possess. Adultery is counted the most serious form of theft, and as such is punished—the offender having to fight with the man whose wife he has stolen. "Within the tribe lovers occasionally abscond, but they are soon overtaken, and the woman cruelly beaten." Lumholtz knew of but two instances where men eloping were permitted to retain as wives women already married in the tribe.[1]

Bushmen.—Adultery is not punished among the Bushmen—neither is theft; they are not addicted to it. A Bushman boasted before Livingstone of killing men, women and children of his own people, and thought such deeds manly and clever.[2] [Probably they were members of some other village or "kraal."]

Veddahs.—Serious offences are very rarely committed. Murder is almost unknown among them. There is great conjugal fidelity. They live generally in pairs, and assemble together only on extraordinary occasions.[3]

Tasmanians.—"They had few crimes against each other. Faults not immediately punished were usually overlooked. Injuries were soon forgotten."[4]

New Guineans.—"Theft is considered a very grave offence, and is of very rare occurrence. Adultery is unknown among them."[5]

The Western Tribe of Torres Straits.—"As there was no recognized government or state, nor any system of religion, all crimes were of a purely personal nature, and were individually revenged." Theft was prohibited and was very

[1] Lumholtz, pp. 126, 147. Curr, ii, 45. Spencer and Gillen.
[2] Livingstone, p. 159, and Lichtenstein, ii, 194–200.
[3] De Butts, p. 149.
[4] Bonwick, p. 10.
[5] Earl's *Papuans*, pp. 80–1.

rare. "Death was the penalty for infringing the rules connected with the initiation period, *i. e.*, for sacrilege;" but it does not appear by whom the punishment was inflicted.[1]

Papuan Islanders.—"These simple Arafuras, without hope of reward or fear of punishment after death, live in such peace and brotherly love with one another that they recognize the right of property in the fullest sense of the word; without there being any authority among them other than the decisions of their elders, according to the customs of their forefathers, which are held in the highest regard."[2]

New Caledonians.—A law of private revenge allowed the murder of the thief and the adulterer.

Dyaks. — "The Dyaks' minds are as healthy as their bodies; theft and brawling and adultery are unknown among them."[3]

"Adultery is a crime unknown and no Dyak ever recollected an instance of its occurrence."[4]

Sumatrans.—Theft among the Sumatrans is almost unknown. It is compounded for by double value. Adultery is of rare occurrence, and is punished by fine. There is no distinction between wilful murder and manslaughter. The compensation to the family is the same in both cases.[5]

Tahitians.—"Theft is practiced, but less frequently among themselves than toward their foreign visitors. Among themselves, if detected, the thief experienced no mercy, but was often murdered on the spot." Adultery is sometimes punished with death.[6]

In Otahitè "every man seems to be the sole judge of his own actions, and to know no punisment but death, and this perhaps is never inflicted but upon a public enemy.[7]

[1] *Jour. Anth. Inst.*, 1899, pp. 314, 316, 335.
[2] Earl's *Kolff's Voyages of the Dourga*, p. 161.
[3] Boyle, p. 235; also 91.
[4] Low, p. 300.
[5] Marsden, pp. 188, 207–10, 223.
[6] Ellis, iii, 125.
[7] Cook, p. 100.

Hawaiians.—"Murder is very rarely committed by the natives." Theft among themselves is severely punished by individual revenge.[1]

Samoans.—Theft, murder and adultery were punished by individual revenge, or, in the case of murder, by outlawry and forfeiture for those who fled. For adultery, the eyes were taken out, or nose and ears bitten off. The thief was killed. Both murder and adultery were very rare.[2]

NORTH AND SOUTH AMERICANS.

The Indian tribes of North and South America are groups of relatives, by birth or by adoption. Kinship has always been the fundamental bond holding them together. The main social requisites for survival were success in war and on the hunting field. These were the savage virtues of the race. The "brave," who took many scalps and killed many buffalo to share among his friends was a good man, and would become a chief. The traitor, the coward, the inefficient hunter, the evil-wizard, and the incestuous fellow—these were essentially bad Indians. Goodness consisted in the performance of good social actions, and not at all in the intention and moral nature of the man, and badness was the exact opposite of their idea of goodness. The standard was essentially a social one, determined by the social needs of the race.

When food was plenty, all ate and rejoiced; when there was famine, all suffered together. Each had his share of the joy and woe that came to the common life. The great council of the tribe met to discuss and decide those most weighty problems which affected the whole community, such as the making of war or peace, and the trial of most heinous criminals. In these councils even the women of some tribes

[1] Ellis, iv, 420. [2] Turner, pp. 178–9.

had a voice and a vote. Chiefs were elected and possessed but little authority, except when leading war parties. None but the great council could condemn a fellow-tribesman to death, and social outlawry was a dreaded penalty among them. True criminals were very rare. Violent in his love of liberty, every Indian revenged his own injuries, or called upon his family to help him, as ancient custom demanded; unless the clan or clans most interested induced arbitration and composition for the offence, thus warding off reprisals and the terrible blood feud. But among the Indians, we do not find anywhere that increasing social pressure for peace and domestic security had made composition compulsory. The man who refused to purchase forgiveness, or to relinquish his time-honored right of vengeance, was not yet a criminal. Few, indeed, were the offences socially punished, even among the most highly developed and progressive of Indian races—the Iroquois. Prominent among the crimes stand out the three great fundamental wrongs against the tribe — treason, incest and evil-witchcraft. Everywhere among North American races, including even the peace-loving Esquimaux, and their relatives, the Aleuts of Alaska, we find direct evidence of intense social abhorrence and the public infliction of the death penalty for these evil acts. We know less about the tribes of South America, but there also the evidence all tends in the same direction. A few other misdeeds are occasionally punished by a social group here and there; such as the breach of hunting and fishing regulations among the Omahas (S P O) and among the Aleuts; cowardice among the Chinooks (S P D); cannibalism (S P D) among the Ojibways and other northern Indians; and sacrilege among the Aleuts. The Omaha Indians are known to have inflicted the social punishment of outlawry upon a merely malicious and thoroughly quarrelsome fellow, who had committed, apparently, no overt act of wrong — thus reminding us strongly of similar procedure among animals.[1] The council of the Iroquois punished women convicted of adultery by a public whipping, and the evidence seems to indicate that among both the Araucanians and Caribs immediate social vengeance brought death upon the guilty pair; but it seems probable that these last were cases of incest rather than adultery. Among the Dakotas "there are some instances where a murderer has been put to death by authority of the Council." Probably these were instances of parricide, fratricide, or the murder of a noted chief.[2]

[1] An instance of such social punishment of a very quarrelsome individual occurred also in the Iliaura tribe of Australian Blackfellows.

[2] Schoolcraft, ii, 183.

CRIMES AND OTHER OFFENCES PUNISHED—NORTH AND SOUTH AMERICANS

	Treason.	*Incest.*	*Witch-craft.*	*Sacrilege.*	*Adultery.*	*Theft.*	*Murder.*	*Other Offences.*	*Infanticide and Killing of Aged and Weaklings.*	*Very Few Offenders.*
Esquimaux		S	S R D		I R		I R D		H	yes
Aleuts of Alaska	S P D	S P D		S P		P	P D			
Ahts of Vancouver	S	S	S P D		I R	I R or C	I P C or R		H	yes
Wyandots	S P D	S	S P D	P M or I P C	I R M	I P C or R	I P C or I R D			
Ojibways	S	S P D	S P D or I R D		I R M	Public disgrace	I R D	*cannibalism* S P D		yes
Dakotas	S P D	S				I R W	I R D or rarely S P D		H[1]	yes
Iroquois	S P D	S P	S P D		S P W	I P C	I R D or I P C			yes
South American Indians.										
Tupis		S			I R		I R D		H	yes
Abipones		S	S				I R D		H	yes
Guaranis		S								
Brazilians			S R D							
Guiana Indians					I R D		I R D		H	yes
Patagonians			S R D			(I R D or W or C)				
Araucanians	S R D	S	S R D		S R D?	S R D or I R D	I R D or C			
Caribs		S R D			S R D? or I R D		I R D	*wounding* I R	H	

[1] Contradicted by Keating, i, 404.

TREASON.—*Aleuts of Alaska, S P D.*—"The betrayer of the secrets of the community was punished with death."[1]

Aht Indians of Vancouver Island, S.—"Sincere in friendship" and "devotedly loyal to his own tribe."[2]

Wyandots, S P D.—"Treason consists in revealing the secrets of the medicine preparations, or giving other information or assistance to the enemies of the tribe, and is punished with death. The trial is before the council of the tribe."[3]

Ojibways, S.—"The fear of the nation's censure acted as a mighty bond, binding all in one honorable compact."[4]

Dakotas, S P D.—"The chief has no authority to act for the tribe and dare not do it. If he does, he will be severely beaten, or killed at some future time."[5]

Iroquois, S P D.—"If any person was guilty of treason, or by his character and conduct made himself obnoxious to the public, the council of chiefs and old men held a secret session on his case, condemned him to death and appointed some young man to kill him. . . . . . Acting by authority, he could not be held answerable" to the relatives of the slain. "The council, however, commonly obviated all difficulty (of punishing the traitor) in advance, by charging the culprit with witchcraft, thus alienating his best friends."[6]

Araucanians, S R D.—"The criminal who is convicted of a capital offence is immediately put to death. Such offences are treachery," etc.[7]

INCEST.—*Esquimaux, S.*—"Marriage between children of the same family, or even near relatives, is altogether inadmissible, and it is preferred that the contracting parties should belong to different settlements, which is, of course, a very sensible custom."[8]

"If a boy and girl, although in no way related, have been

[1] Petroff, p. 152. [2] Sproat, p. 151. [3] Powell, p. 67.
[4] Copway, p. 141. [5] Schoolcraft, ii, 182. [6] Parkman, p. lxiii.
[7] Thompson's Alcedo, i., 405. [8] Nansen, ii., 330.

brought up in the same family, they are looked upon as brother and sister, and are not allowed to marry."[1]

Aleuts of Alaska, S P D.—"Incest was considered the gravest crime, and was punished with great severity."[2]

The Aht Indians of Vancouver Island, S.—"By the old custom of the Aht tribes, no marriage was permitted within the degree of second cousin. Intermarriage with other tribes is sought by the higher classes to strengthen the foreign connections of their own tribe, and, I think also, with some idea of preventing degeneracy of race."[3]

Wyandots, S.—"Marriage between members of the same gens is forbidden."[4]

Ojibways, S P D.—The Ojibways formerly punished marriages among members of the same totem with death.[5]

Dakotas, S.—Dakota nations "will not allow marriage in the same totem."[6]

Iroquois, S.—"At no time in the history of the Iroquois could a man marry a woman of his own tribe, even in another nation. All the members of a tribe were within the prohibited degrees of consanguinity; and to this day, among the descendants of the Iroquois, this law is religiously observed."[7]

Potawatamis, S.—"An incestuous connection was at all times considered as highly criminal, but no punishment was attached to it." Several instances are given of the offence by chiefs. "But all these connections are held in utter abhorrence by the nation at large."[8]

South American Indians, Tupis, S.—The word "Atourassap" signifies "a friend who is loved like a brother. The tie was held as sacred as consanguinity, and one could not marry the daughter or sister of the other."[9]

[1] *Jour. Eth. Soc.* (1848), i., 148. See also Crantz, i., 147.
[2] Petroff, p. 155. [3] Sproat, p. 99. [4] Powell, p. 63. [5] Warren, p. 42.
[6] Burton, p. 132. [7] Morgan, p. 325. [8] Keating, p. 114.
[9] Southey, i., 240, and Waitz, iii., 422.

Abipones, *S*.—"The Abipones, instructed by nature and the example of their ancestors, abhor the very thought of marrying any one related to them by the most distant tie of relationship."[1]

Guaranis, *S*.—"Marriage with the most distant relatives they shun as highly criminal."[2]

Araucanians, *S*.—"In their marriages they scrupulously avoid the more immediate degrees of relationship."[3]

Caribs, *S R D*.—"When father and daughter were detected in incest, the punishment was the stake, where they were burnt alive, or torn in a thousand pieces."[4]

EVIL-WITCHCRAFT.—*The Greenland Esquimaux*, *S R D*. —"Their procedure with witches is very short. If a rumor prevails that a certain old woman is a witch, because the poor old creature made pretences to charms and quackery, all the country will join to stone her, or she will be thrown into the sea, or hewn to pieces, according as their rage dictates to them."[5]

Aht Indians of Vancouver Island, *S P D*.—"All the people live in constant apprehension of danger from the unseen world. An instrument called min-okey-ak was supposed to be thrown from an unseen hand and the person struck by it sickened and died. No one was allowed to live who knew how to make the min-okey-ak." The last person who possessed this knowledge among the "Ohyahts—the tribe from which I derived the information—was a young man of a family of eight men, and it was resolved at a meeting of the chiefs, that the whole family should be exterminated." Accordingly all the men were killed and all the women sold into slavery, and the house and property of the family destroyed. Since then, "no one

[1] Dobrizhoffer, ii., 212.
[2] Dobrizhoffer, i., 63.
[3] Smith.
[4] De Rochefort.
[5] Crantz, i., 194.

among the Ohyahts has known how to make the min-okey-ak."[1]

Wyandots, S P D.—"Witchcraft is punished by death, stabbing, tomahawking or burning. Charges of witchcraft are investigated by the grand council of the tribe."[2]

Ojibways, S P D or I R D.—"Formerly, when any notorious necromancer was suspected of having bewitched any one, he was often condemned by the councils of the different tribes to execution; but this was done always with great caution, lest the conjuror should get the advantage over them and thus bewitch the whole assembly." Sometimes "a relative of the person thought to be bewitched will go secretly and put the necromancer to death."[3]

Chinooks, S P D or I R D.—The chiefs believe themselves and their sons too important to die in a natural manner, and "whenever the event takes place, they attribute it to the malevolent influence of some other person, whom they fix upon . . . . frequently selecting those the most dear to themselves or the deceased. The person so selected is sacrificed without hesitation."[4]

Iroquois, S P D.—"Witches, with whom the Hurons and Iroquois were grievously infested, were objects of utter abomination to both, and anyone might kill them at any time."[5]

"Witchcraft was punishable with death." "Witnesses were called and examined, and if they established the charge to the satisfaction of the council, which they rarely failed to do, condemnation followed with a death sentence."[6]

Chippewayans, S.—The death of a chief was generally

[1] Sproat, p. 158, 175. All the chiefs of the tribe are chosen by the people and act as their representatives. *Ibid.*, p. 187.

[2] Powell, p. 67.

[3] Jones, p. 146.

[4] Kane, p. 177.

[5] Parkman, p. lxiii.

[6] Morgan, pp. 330, 333.

believed due to evil conjuration of "some of their own countrymen," or enemies of other tribes.

South American Indians—Abipones, S. — "The jugglers are commonly thought to be the authors of disease, as well as of death, and the sick Abipones imagine that they shall recover as soon as ever these persons are removed." [1]

Brazilians, S R D—"The misfortunes, sickness and death of the neighbors are often ascribed to his (the South Brazil paje's) sorceries, and he then atones for his practises with his life." [2]

Patagonians, S R D.—"The profession of wizards is very dangerous, notwithstanding the respect that is sometimes paid to them; for it often happens, when an Indian chief dies, that some of the wizards are killed; especially if they had any dispute with the deceased just before his death; the Indians, in this case, attributing the loss of their cacique, *i. e.*, chief, to the wizards and their demons." The same occurs in times of pestilence.[3]

Araucanians, S R D.—They are great believers in witchcraft, and "most unwilling to have their portraits taken, lest the one having possession of it may kill or injure the one represented. There is the same superstitious dread about revealing their names, lest the one knowing it acquire supernatural power against them." [4]

"Justice is administered in a tumultuous, irregular manner. The criminal who is convicted of a capital offence is immediately put to death. Such offences are witchcraft," *etc.* "Those accused of sorcery are first tortured by fire, and then stabbed with daggers." [5]

[1] Dobrizhoffer, ii, 223 and 226.

[2] Spix and Martius, ii, 244.

[3] Fitz Roy, ii, 163.

[4] Smith, p. 222.

[5] Thompson's Alcedo, i, 405.

OFFENCES OF ALL KINDS WITHIN THE GROUP VERY RARE.

Esquimaux.—They are a very peaceful folk, and quarrels among them are very rare. "Theft from members of his household or settlement is regarded as an abomination, and is very seldom practiced." "The pacific disposition of the Eskimo makes murder a very rare occurrence, and the slaying of a fellow creature is considered a great barbarity." When an Eskimo refrains from adultery with another man's wife, it is from desire not to fall out with the man, "rather than that he sees anything wrong in the act."[1]

"The Innuits among themselves are strictly honest."[2]

The Aht Indians of Vancouver Island.—This people is "very degraded and exceedingly revengeful," yet "the members of an Aht tribe live together in much social harmony. The men rarely quarrel except with their tongues, and a blow is seldom given." If struck in anger "it must be paid for next day with a present, unless the striker chooses to leave the dispute open," when an "implacable family feud" results.

"I have never witnessed a fight between sober natives, and quarreling is also rare among the children. Larceny of a fellow tribesman's property is rarely heard of, and the aggravation of taking it from the house or person is almost unknown."[3]

Comanches.—"There are not many private wrongs perpetrated among them, and family or personal feuds seldom arise. They live together in a degree of social harmony, which contrasts strikingly with the domestic incidents of some pseudo-civilized communities that vaunt of their enlightenment."[4]

Ojibways.—"Murder is seldom heard of among them."

[1] Nansen. ii, 329, 335–6.
[2] Hall, ii, 312.
[3] Sproat, pp. 51, 153, 159 and 186.
[4] Schoolcraft, i, 231.

"The old men all agree in saying that before the white man found and resided among them, there were fewer murders, thefts and less lying, more chastity in man and woman." [1]

Dakotas.—"Among the Dakotas I never knew an instance of blood being shed in any disputes or difficulties on the hunting grounds." Instances of theft are mostly among women and children. The men say it is too low a practice for them.[2]

Iroquois.—"Crimes and offences were so infrequent under their social system that the Iroquois can scarcely be said to have had a criminal code."[3]

"It was only in rare cases that crime among the Iroquois or Hurons was punished by public authority."[4]

Chippewayans.—Theft is "extremely rare among them."[5]

South American Indians..—Tupis.—"Boys rarely or never quarreled among themselves, although no other principles were inculcated than those of revenge and hatred. Savages are seldom quarrelsome when they are sober; and among the Tupis the feeling of good-will toward each other was so habitual that they seem not to have lost it even when they were drunk. De Lery lived among them a year, and witnessed only two quarrels. But if, on these occasions, any injury was inflicted, the law of retaliation was rigorously executed by the kinsmen of the sufferer.[6]

Abipones.—"Another admirable trait in the character of the savage Abipones is their conjugal fidelity. You never hear of this being shaken or even attempted." [7]

Guiana Indians.—Adultery of married women is very rare, probably because of the fearful punishment inflicted.[8]

The Indians of Guiana are not addicted to stealing.[9]

Araucanians.—This people, notwithstanding their propen-

[1] Schoolcraft, ii, 139.
[2] *Ibid.*, ii, 184-5.
[3] Morgan, p. 330.
[4] Parkman, p. lxi.
[5] Franklin, p. 156.
[6] Southey, i. 240.
[7] Dobrizhoffer, ii, 213.
[8] Humboldt, ii, 266.
[9] Brett, p. 348.

sity to violence, rarely employ arms in their private quarrels, but decide them with the fist or with a club.[1]

ASIATICS.

Among the "hill tribes of India," some, like the Gonds and Santals, have a numerous population of from one to three millions and live in comparative peacefulness, under a foreign domination, which has not attempted to change much their ancient customs and mode of life. The rest are "unmitigated savages," wild forest rangers, few in number, very loosely organized for war and pillage, with no recognized head or chief for any of their tribes, except, perhaps, the Bheels.[2] Dwelling in little migratory village groups of from twenty-five to a few hundred people, they are very democratic and often sociable among themselves; yet intensely devoted to a ferocious liberty, whose cardinal principal is revenge—deep, bloody revenge—for every personal injury, in accordance with their ancient customs.[3]

"A Karen always thinks himself right in taking the law into his own hands, for it is the custom of the country, which has the effect of law. He is never interfered with, unless he is guilty of some act contrary to Karen ideas of propriety, when the elders and the villagers interfere and exercise a check upon him."[4]

Beyond the limits of each Khond hamlet, or group of related villages, "all is discord and confusion; everywhere is seen an incipient or a dying feud," yet within the group "order and security prevail," and there is unfaltering devo-

[1] Thompson's Alcedo, i, 406.

[2] Forsyth's *Report*, v. 154.

[3] For Nagas: Stewart, *J. A. S. B.* xxiv, 609; For Karens: Mason, *J. A. S. B.* xxxvii, pt. ii, 145; For Mishmis: Rowlatt, *J. A. S. B.* xiv, 491.

[4] Mason, *J. A. S. B.*, xxxvii, pt. ii, 145.

tion to the common cause. Thus there is no room for treason.[1]

The elders have for centuries been striving to limit the instinctive passion for vengeance to the harmful acts of men of other villages or hostile tribes; and have been entirely successful in introducing the custom of composition for offences among fellow townsmen, which very rarely occur; and even in making the seeking and offering of the atonement compulsory, upon pain of social outlawry, for him who will not yield himself to this demand. The evil-doer who does not or will not make composition for his offence, becomes a criminal,--not because of the murder or theft he may have committed, for that is only an unfortunate harm to an individual or family, but because he will not do his best to restore peace to the community by preventing a bloody feud; because he will not submit to the social pressure for the general welfare.

Among all the hill tribes of India, and also among the savage hordes of northern and central Asia and the Bedouin Arabs of the desert, immemorial ancient customs take the place of laws, regulate the simple relations of man with man, and are religiously observed. Many of these customs teach the terrible duty of blood revenge, of unrelenting family feuds; but there are others which foster intense social abhorrence of a few actions; *i.e.*, treason or treachery to the community, incest between near relations, and evil-witchcraft—that is sorcery, practiced within the group, aiming at the destruction of a fellow tribesman and thus breeding mutual distrust and fear. Intense devotion to these ancestral customs makes the offender against them an exceedingly rare type of man—so rare that it is very difficult to find instances of his existence--but when such an one is discovered, the

[1] Macpherson's *Report*, pp. 42, 52, and Campbell, p. 239.

violent abhorrence awakened by his act brings down upon him a speedy and ferocious social punishment.

We must believe, therefore, that among these low and densely ignorant savage races, there are a few most heinous offences, punished by the collective might as wrongs against foundation principles of social life. Such are treason, incest and witchcraft. Refusal to preserve the folk peace by the seeking and giving of composition—in lieu of vengeance—has also more recently been made a crime in many tribes; after centuries of social pressure. All harms of man to man within the little group are rare, prevented primarily by fear of the blood feud; but far more rare are true crimes—wrongs to the whole community—and yet the criminal is occasionally found and punished among them.

CRIMES AND OFFENCES PUNISHED—ASIA.

	Treason.	*Incest.*	*Witchcraft.*	*Sacrilege.*	*Adultery.*	*Theft.*	*Murder.*	*Cowardice.*	*Infanticide or Killing of Aged and Weaklings.*	*Very Few Offenders.*
Todas		S							H	yes
Bheels	(S R D for most atrocious crimes.)					I R or C	I R or C			
Kukis	S R D	S			I R D or C	slavery				yes, almost none
Khonds		S P D	S P D		I R D for man	I R or C or S P O	I R D or C		H	yes
Karens			S P D or slavery		I P C	C or slavery	I R D			
Nágás		S P			I R D or C	I R D or C	I R D			yes
Mishmis	(S R D for refusal to pay fine imposed by society.)				I R D or C	I R or C	I P C or R			yes
Bodo & Dhimals.	(S P O for most serious crimes.)				I P W					yes, almost none
Gonds		S	S P O						H	yes
Santals	(S P O for most serious crimes.)				(C for minor offences.)					yes, almost none
					Central Asiatic Races.					
Kalmucks	S P D	S	S P		P C	I P C	I P C	S P D or slavery		yes
Kirghis				S P		I R	P			
					Northern Asiatic Races.					
Ostyaks		S								
Tschuktschi					I R D				H	
Kamtschadales ..		S			I R	I R or C or S P O	I R D		H	yes
(Arabs) Bedouin.	(S P O or D for most serious crimes.)					I R or C	I R D or C			

SOCIAL PUNISHMENT FOR THE MOST SERIOUS CRIMES.

Bheels, S R D.—The Bheels are unmitigated savages, living in small village groups, of from 25 to 50 people, organized for plunder, like the monkeys. There is absolute fidelity to their native chiefs, with no idea of the possibility of choice on their part. Therefore treason is unknown among them. The natural instinct of the Bheels leads them to individual or family revenge for murder, robbery and theft; but after their first wild rage has spent itself, resort is had to Punjayets, or councils, which "often consist of several hundred members." These councils make the best terms they can for the guilty party, by inducing the acceptance of a composition or atonement, in lieu of the infliction of vengeance. The offences dealt with are torts, or harms of man to man—not regarded as wrongs against the tribe. Ancient customs guide them. "Fines in cattle or money are high for murders, but Bheel Punjayets never inflict death." However, "if the crime committed be of so atrocious a nature as not to be compounded or forgiven, the culprit is pursued and destroyed by those whom this act has made his enemies; but he must be put to death in what they term an affray, that is, in warm blood; to take the life of each other coolly is revolting to their usages."[1] These last "atrocious" offences are probably true crimes.

Mishmis, S R D.—The Mishmis are semi-nomads, dwelling in little village groups. They are "a hospitable and even social race," indulging in a constant round of festivity. Every clan has a nominal head, or "gam," but his power is extremely limited. "Theft is punished by a fine inflicted by a meeting of all the gams; if the fine is not paid, or the offender refuses to pay, he is slain in a general attack, being cut up by the company assembled," "Murder is punished

[1] Malcolm, i, 576–7.

in the same way, but by a heavier fine. Adultery, against the consent of the husband, or at least elopement, is punished with death." [1]

The Mishmis seem to have reached the stage of compulsory composition for individual offences, which we shall find very prevalent among the Anglo-Saxons, after Alfred's time. Social pressure compels the injured man to seek and accept an atonement for the evil done him, unless he prefers to drop the whole matter. When judgment is given against the accused by the vote of the popular assembly, he must pay the fine, in compensation to the man or family he has harmed, or become a public criminal (an outlaw), and, when present, " he is slain in a general attack, being cut up by the company assembled." It is his refusal to pay the atonement and thus preserve the peace of the community, that makes him a criminal; not the murder or theft committed.

Santals, S P O. — The Santals number one and a half to two million people, and are only " half savages." Caste is unknown among them, and they are " sociable to a fault among themselves." The village elders meet to discuss public affairs and to punish the guilty. " So strong is the family feeling that expulsion from the clan is the only form of punishment known. Other clans will not receive the outcast." The idea of the destruction of the ties of kindred is " insupportable to the Santal." However, " for minor offences" reconciliation with his people is easily obtained by " twenty gallons of beer, and about ten shillings, to buy the materials of a feast for his clansmen. In more heinous cases, the difficulty of reconciliation is so great that the unfortunate man yields to his destiny, and, taking with him his bow and arrows, departs into the jungle, whence he never returns. A woman, once fallen, cannot regain her position." [2]

[1] Griffith's *Journals*, p. 35 *et seq.*

[2] Hunter, i, 202–3.

Among the Santals also, we find the practice of compulsory composition for minor offences, following on the public threat of banishment, or outlawry. It is doubtful whether the fine is paid to the family harmed, or to the entire community. For "heinous" crimes the dread doom of outlawry is socially enforced, and how terrible is the punishment may be judged from the quotation given.

Bodo and Dhimals, S P O.—These people are semi-nomadic forest-dwellers, in little village communities of from ten to forty households, owning a voluntary obedience to their chief, or Gra. Offenders against ancient "customs are admonished, fined or excommunicated, according to the degree of the offence," by the Gra, a few elders and the village priest.[1]

Here we have much the same judicial procedure as among the Santals—composition for minor offences and excommunication, which is more than the equivalent of outlawry, for serious crimes. Individual punishment is customary in cases of adultery, the delinquents being beaten by the injured husband.

TREASON—*Kukis, S R D.*—"The only crime punishable by death among the Kukis was high treason, or an attempt at violence on the person of the king, and treacherous commerce with an enemy of the clan. The victim in these cases was cut to pieces with dhaos, but, of course, no such extreme measures can be resorted to by them in the present day."[2]

Turkomans, S P D or C.—The Turkomans (Circassians), during their wars with the Russians in the beginning of this century, punished the traitor with death, the slavery of his whole family, or the confiscation of all the possessions of the guilty ones. The profits of this punishment were divided

[1] Hodgson, *Kocch, Bodo and Dhimals*, p. 159.

[2] Stewart, *J. A. S. B.*, xxiv, 627–8.

between the revealers of the plot and those who aided in inflicting the punishment. Sometimes the death penalties could be bought off for two hundred rubels.[1]

Kalmucks, S P D etc.—The written laws of the Kalmucks have penalties against: 1. Chiefs who stir up strife or neglect to quell disturbances; 2. Cowardice and incompetency in battle; 3. Neglecting to provide post-horses, etc., for government couriers. The most serious crimes are punished by death, mutilation or slavery.[2]

Bedouin Arabs, S P O or D.—The Bedouins are said to have attained the highest possible development of the pastoral life. Among them, the fiercest, strongest and most crafty rule. Then "there is the terrible blood feud, which even the most reckless fear for their posterity." The revealed law of the Koran is openly disregarded, as not meant for desert folk. But amid this ferocious development of individual liberty, exist the immemorial customs of the "Kazi el Arab," which "form a system stringent in the extreme," and are generally adhered to strictly.

"Grave offences of some kinds are punished with death." In capital proceedings the trial lasts many days—witnesses are sworn in, and appeal is granted from lower to higher courts, as is also a delay or respite after conviction. Beheading is the customary penalty. "A chief who has drawn the bond of allegiance too tight is deposed or abandoned. A man who has disgraced himself by a breach of their species of morality is shunned by his whole tribe, and is finally forced to leave it as an outcast." Here is true social punishment.[3]

INCEST.—*Hill Tribes of India, Todas, S.*—"There are degrees of kinship within whose limits the union of the sexes is held in actual abhorrence."[4]

[1] Bell, i, 237, and ii, 141, 161.
[2] Pallas, i, 193–218.
[3] Burton, *El Medinah*, ii, 86–7.
[4] Marshall, p. 220.

Kukis, S.—"The most strict rules exist, forbidding too close intermarriage in families; cousins cannot be so allied."[1]

Khonds, S P D.—" Intermarriage between persons of the same tribe, however large or scattered, is considered incestuous and punishable with death."[2]

Nágás, S P.—"The social rules and penalties by which individual life in a Nágá village is regulated, include prohibitions to marry within a man's own khel," *i. e.*, group of kindred or clan.[3]

Bodo and Dhimals, S.—" Neither Bodo nor Dhimal can marry beyond the limits of his own people, and if he does he is severely fined. Within those limits only two or three of the closest natural ties are deemed a bar to marriage."[4]

Gonds, S.—Subdivisions worshiping exactly the same gods cannot intermarry.[5]

Santals, S.—" No man is allowed to take a wife of his own clan."[6]

Central and Northern Asiatic Races.

Kalmucks, S.— " They have a strong objection to marrying within their own families or tribes, considering all the descendants of one father or head of a tribe as brothers and sisters, however distant their actual relationship may be. So universal is this custom, says the writer (Rev. W. Swan), that I never knew or heard of an instance of its being violated." [7]

Ostyaks, S.— "The Ostyaks deem it as a great sin and

[1] Stewart, *Jour. As. Soc., Bengal*, xxiv, 640.
[2] Spencer's *Descriptive Sociology*, Asia.
[3] Godden, *Jour. Anth. Inst.*, 1897, pp. 167, 173.
[4] Hodgson, p. 159.
[5] *Report Jubbulpore Expedition*, ii, 58. See Spencer's *Descriptive Sociology*, Asia, p. 9.
[6] Hunter, i, 202.
[7] Michie, p. 188.

shame to marry relatives, so that bride and bridegroom are always of different clans." [1]

Kamtschadales, S.—Marriage is prohibited only between father and daughter, mother and son. First cousins marry frequently, Divorce is easy to obtain. Yet "when a Kamtschadal resolves to marry, he looks about for a bride in some of the neighboring villages, seldom in his own." [2]

EVIL-WITCHCRAFT.—"The belief in witchcraft is common to almost all classes in India." [3]

Bheels and Khonds, S P D.—Serious disease or death "they invariably attribute to the evil influence of a Dhákan or witch." They consider it their duty to detect this Dhákan by various ceremonies, music, peacock's feathers, etc. "In some cases more cruel means are used." Burning or drowning are the penalties for those convicted.[4]

Karens, S P D or Slavery.—"It is considered a meritorious deed to put to death one guilty of poisoning:" *i. e.*, evil-witchcraft. "If such" imaginary poisons "are found on a man, he is sometimes, by the voice of the people, bound and spread out in the sun three days," his poisons destroyed, and he must "swear the most solemn oaths that he has no more and will never procure more; or he is sold into slavery." [5]

Gonds, S P O.—The belief in witchcraft is strong, and the modes of testing a witch various. They beat the suspected woman with castroil rods, and if she feel pain they believe they have found the witch; or they throw her, bound hand and foot, into deep water, when, if she swim, she is surely guilty. Men are sometimes considered wizards, but this is

[1] Bastian, iii, 299.
[2] Grieve, pp. 212–215. See Spencer's *Descriptive Soc.* Asia, p. 10.
[3] Malcolm, *Trans. Roy. As. Soc.*, i, 84 note.
[4] See above, and also Campbell, pp. 44–46.
[5] Mason, *J. A. S. B.*, xxxvii., 149.

comparatively rare.[1] A man convicted of killing a fellow Gond by sorcery is expelled from the district, and his property is destroyed.[2]

Central Asiatic Races — Kalmucks, S P. — The Kalmucks have a written law, or rule, with penalties, against the practice of sorcery.[3]

OFFENCES OF ALL KINDS WITHIN THE GROUP VERY RARE.

Todas.—Among the Todas there is great "respect for rights of meum and tuum." [4]

Kukis. — "Heinous crimes are very infrequent among these people. Theft is almost unknown." [5]

Khonds.—"While within each tribe order and security prevail, beyond all is discord and confusion; everywhere is seen an incipient or a dying feud." [6]

Nágás.—"Correctly speaking, there is not the shadow of a constituted authority in the Nágá community, and wonderful as it may seem, this want of government does not lead to any marked degree of anarchy and confusion." Differences rarely occur between two men of the same village. They are honest people. [7]

Mishmis.—"Laws and punishments seem scarcely to exist, and with the exception of murder and abduction, no other crimes against each other appear of common occurrence." [8]

Bodo and Dhimals.—"Crimes of a deeper dye are almost unknown, and breaches of the peace very rare." [9]

Gonds.—The Gonds are not naturally given to crime. Adultery very rarely occurs.[10]

[1] Spencer's *Descriptive Sociology*—Asia, p. 36.
[2] Dalton, p. 283.
[3] Pallas i, 193, etc.
[4] Harkness, p. 17.
[5] Stewart, *J. A. S. B.*, xxiv, 627.
[6] Macpherson's *Report*, p. 42.
[7] Stewart, *J. A. S. B.*, xxiv, 608 and 610.
[8] Rawlatt, *J. A. S. B.*, xiv, 491.
[9] Hodgson, *Kocch*, etc., pp. 158–9.
[10] Forsyth's *Highlands*, pp. 149, 155.

Santals.—" Among the pure Santals crime and criminal officers are almost unknown." [1]

Kalmucks.—I never knew or heard of an instance of incest, to which they have strong objections.[2]

Theft is infrequent among them.[3]

Kamtschadales.—" In spite of extreme poverty, they are an example of honesty." [4]

AFRICANS.

The population of Africa is much more numerous than that of any of the lands we have been studying, and the negro races have risen to a somewhat higher plain of social development.[5] Everywhere, among them, we find a strong trend toward the monarchical form of government, which has culminated, among the more intelligent and progressive peoples, in a tyrannical despotism, which is, in theory, absolute. In practice, however, the king is greatly limited by the ancient social customs of the race, which he has sworn to observe and to defend; and by the power of the tribal chiefs, who are collectively far too strong for him, although his vengeance often falls upon them individually. An attempt to cast aside these ancestral usages, which the people love and cling to, has been known to cost a most powerful ruler his throne—which must mean also his speedy death, at the hands of those he has made his enemies.

That despotic monarchy has greatly aided the general welfare, there can be no doubt; for it has united into a more or less compact and orderly nation, many little warring tribes of the same racial stock, thus bringing mutual aid and military effectiveness—their greatest social need. Most naturally, this development of royalty has occasioned an exten-

[1] Hunter, i, 217.
[2] Michie, p. 188.
[3] Pallas, i, 105.
[4] Krusenstern, ii, 254.
[5] Some of the Asiatic peoples mentioned are exceptions.

sion of the crime of treason—that wrong against warlike strength and unity—to protect the person and authority of the king, and make even the tokens of his government sacred and inviolable. The growing despot, supported by the people, as defender of themselves and of their ancient customs, becomes not only leader in war and judge in peace, but he and his whole family are surrounded by a ceremonial of religious reverence and dread, which must be observed most strictly, upon pain of death or other true social punishment. Thus he unites in his single person the three great attractions toward respect and obedience, found instinctive in every savage breast.[1] He becomes the embodiment of the great socializing forces of the race, and the welfare of his people becomes linked, indissolubly, for many centuries, with the power and welfare of their kings. But even the king is punished as a traitor to his people, if he seek to subvert their ancient rights and liberties, as imbedded in the teachings of immemorial custom. In fact, it becomes increasingly easy to find examples of treason and its punishment, simply because of the extension of the treason field, *to include conduct not yet made strongly abhorrent by the inherited social instinct or habits of the race.*

Not only along lines of treason is there an increase of crime and criminals. The widening of the social bond to include kindred tribes and conquered peoples of unrelated stock, weakens somewhat the instinctive trust between individuals within the group—that good fruit of many centuries of social pressure. Men and women of the tribe are much more frequently suspected of evil-witchcraft; and boundless superstition and fear make conviction easy and social punishment cruel. "All African peoples have the utmost dread of sorcery and thousands of persons fall victims every year to the belief in its use," writes Wake;[2] and Du Chaillu, that

[1] See p. 41.

[2] P. 343.

wide traveler in unexplored regions of the continent, writes: "Great numbers of people are compelled to drink poison to prove their innocence of sorcery," this "taking away more lives than any slave trade ever did."[1] The Negro races, to whom these quotations relate, number many millions of people, and it is probable that very frequently individual rather than social vengeance fell upon the supposed wizard, who may also have been a member of another and perhaps hostile group. Very few instances of punishment for incest are narrated. The strict military organization of Negro nations under despotic kings, is evidenced by the widespread social punishment of death for cowardice, of which we have instances among the Dahomans, Ashantes and Malagasy. Beside these primitive offences, there are other new forms of crime. Thus among the Congo people and the Kaffirs, the trial of poisoners is held before the king or chief and the penalty is death—often visited upon all the relatives of the guilty man—together with confiscation of their property.[2] Savages, however, frequently confound poisoning with evil witchcraft. Premeditated murder by a chief is punished by the Kaffirs with outlawry.[3] The man in whose house a destructive fire breaks out is punished in Dahomey with death, which is their usual penalty for all offences, even falling, when dancing before the king.[4] But after all, very few actions are punished as crimes. Murder, adultery and theft, with almost all other offences against the individual, continue to be regarded simply as torts, atoned for by composition, or revenged by the person or family harmed, if they wish to take the trouble, in obedience to ancient usage. The total amount of criminality must be comparatively small; but when crime is punished the penalties are frightfully severe, as is generally the case among all savage peoples.

[1] *A Journey to Ashango Land*, p. 435.
[2] Tuckey, pp. 87, 162–3.
[3] Barrow, i, 207.
[4] Burton, i, 289.

CRIMES AND OFFENCES PUNISHED—AFRICA.

	Treason.	*Incest.*	*Witchcraft.*	*Sacrilege.*	*Adultery.*	*Theft.*	*Murder.*	*Poisoning and Other Offences.*	*Infanticide and Killing of Aged and Sickly.*	*Offences of all Kinds Rare.*
East Africans ..			S P D or (slavery)		I R D or C	I R D or C	I R D or C			
Gold Coast Negroes.....			S P (slavery)	S P	I P slavery	I P C	I P C or D	S		
Congo People..	S P D or (slavery)				I R D	I P C		S P D		
Hottentots	S	S	S P		P D					
South Africans: Cape Colony to Natal.....		S P	S R D		P C	S P O or I R D	S P O or I R D	*Arson.* S P O or I R D		
Zulus and Other Kaffirs......	S P D		S P D		I P C or D	I P C	(S P O or I P D or C)	S P D	H	Murder not frequent
Dahomans	S P D				D	D or C	D	*Cowardice.* S P D		
Ashantes......	S P D				I P C or D	I P C or D	I P D or C	S P D		
Malagasy......	S P D	S	S P D	S P	I P C	S R D or I P C	I P C	S P D	H	
Abyssinians....	S P D	S P O		P D or (mutilation)		(Prison or flogging)	I R D			

TREASON.—*Zulus, S P D.*—Conveying information to the enemy, desertion from the tribe, contriving the death of the king or chief, or speaking evil against him, are punished among the Zulus by death and confiscation of goods.[1]

Congo People, S P D. — Lack of proper respect to the king or the king's wives is punished by death or slavery.[2]

Dahomans, S P D.—In Dahomey, treason and cowardice are punished with death.[3] The greatest respect to the king is compulsory.[4] After war, the king, as judge, holds an open court of justice. Any individual may comment on the conduct of any other man during the war, and "if the charge be substantiated, punishment follows. Great liberty of spirit is enjoyed, and distinctions of rank laid aside."[5]

The Dahomans "reverence" their king, "with a mixture of love and fear, little short of adoration." Even after horrible tyranny—when there was not an individual in the kingdom who had not lost some near and dear relative through the king's avarice or anger—their loyalty and attachment usually remained unshaken; for "whatever the king does they are persuaded is right." Yet, in the reign of Ahadee—a terrible tyrant—who had been chosen king by the Prime Ministers, over the head of his elder brother, Zingah; this brother, with other conspirators, plotted to seize the government; but they were discovered, seized, and all put to death. "The prince was sewed up in a hammock and drowned" in the sea—this being the punishment appointed by the law for offences of the royal family.[6] Later in the same reign, one of the Prime Ministers (the "Mayhou") rebelled, but was defeated and killed in battle, while all pris-

[1] Gardiner, pp. 94–5. Shooter, p. 156.

[2] Burton, *A Mission to Gelele*, i., 192, note. Pinkerton, xvi., 330.

[3] Forbes, i., 26.

[4] Dalzel, p. 133. Burton, *A Mission to Gelele*, i., 231, note.

[5] Forbes, ii., 86.

[6] Dalzel, pp. 67–70.

oners taken were put to death. Here is wholesale punishment for treason.

Ashantes, S P D.—The king is represented as an absolutely despotic monarch, but he is under "obligations to observe the national customs, which have been handed down to the people from remote antiquity; and a practical disregard of this obligation, in the attempt to change some of the customs of their forefathers, cost Osai Quamina his throne."[1] Individuals are subject to the most despotic authority and are frequently victims of the royal jealousy or displeasure. "To speak disrespectfully of the king is a treasonable offence" in Ashantee; so also, "To speak of the death of a former king, or to inquire concerning the successor to the reigning sovereign." Everybody must get out of the way when the king's wives go abroad.[2]

Malagasy, S P D.—Desertion from the army and cowardice in battle were punished with death.[3]

"Rataffe was seized, and a public court of military and civil judges declared him guilty of disloyalty. Within four hours a spear was thrust through his heart."[4]

Abyssinians, S P D.—The government is in the form of an absolute monarchy. Their legal system is based upon the ancient Code Justinian, but the king is "above all laws" and "often judges capital crimes himself." "It is death to strike, or lift the hand to strike, before the king." It is high treason to sit upon any seat of the king's.[5]

INCEST—*Hottentots, S.*—"The Hottentots allow not marriages between first and second cousins." They punish adultery with death.[6]

South African Tribes between Cape Colony and Natal, S P.—"A man and woman whose origin can be traced to a

[1] Beecham, p. 90, et seq. Reade, p. 43.
[2] Beecham, pp. 4, 95, 123.
[3] Drury, p. 151.
[4] Ellis, *Hist. of Madagascar*, ii, 368, 410.
[5] Bruce, iv., 462–4, iv., 16.
[6] Kolbe, i, 155 and 157.

common ancestor cannot marry; nor can they, without breach of the law, have sexual intercourse one with another. Fines invariably follow breaches of the marriage law." [1]

Abyssinians, S P O., etc.—"Incest is looked upon by the Abyssinians in its proper light. I remember only two or three instances of its occurrence; and in these the heinousness of the crime made such an impression on the feelings of the guilty persons that they confessed their sin publicly." Severe punishment with banishment into the mountains followed. The people "hooted" them out of the place, manifesting great "disgust." [2]

EVIL-WITCHCRAFT—*East Africans, S P D or slavery.*—The crime of "uchawe or black magic" is punished by burning to death, or sometimes by selling into slavery.[3]

Gold Coast Negroes, S *P.*—"The Bulloms have a saying among themselves that a Bullom man cannot die, unless his death be occasioned by poison or witchcraft." Those believed guilty of killing a member of the tribe by witchcraft are sold as slaves. "The accused person frequently acknowledges the charge, and submits to his sentence without repining." [4]

Hottentots, S P.—"They (the Korannas) are much addicted to a mischievous sort of witchcraft, by means of which they often grievously torment each other." [5] All sudden sickness, pain and death they ascribe commonly to witchcraft. Old women among them are thought to be especially given over to this abominable art.[6]

South African Tribes between Cape Colony amd Natal, S R D.—When any one falls ill, his friends go to the witch

[1] Macdonald, *Jour. Anth. Inst,* (1890), p. 270.
[2] Parkyns, ii, 220-21.
[3] Burton, *Lake Regions of Central Africa,* i, 113, 265.
[4] Winterbottom, i, 237-8, 260; ii, 10, note.
[5] Thompson, ii, 35.
[6] Kolbe, i, 219-20.

doctor to learn the cause of the disease. After a long while sitting in silence, he says oracularly, "You are being killed." "How, and by whom?" they ask. He replies that he cannot tell. They must return the following day, and meanwhile send a beast as his fee. The next day all the neighbors must attend the meeting. The witch doctor names to the chief the man who has bewitched "our brother;" all immediately separate themselves from the miscreant, and he is despatched that night. When the Rain Doctors fail to make rain fall after several attempts, "chiefs have been known to sacrifice every doctor belonging to the tribe in one huge holocaust."[1]

Zulus, S P D.—Poisoning and practises with an evil intent termed witchcraft are punished by death and confiscation.[2]

Malagasy, S P D.—Among the Malagasy "chicanery, lying, cheating and defrauding are mere trifles, compared with the enormous offences of trampling or dancing upon a grave (sacrilege), eating pork in certain districts where it is prohibited, running after an owl or wild cat, *or preparing enchantments*. In order that the land may be purged from the evils of witchcraft, it is imbued with the innocent blood of the unfortunately suspected victim—poisoned, speared, strangled, or dashed over the fatal precipice." Not to lie to foreigners on political matters is a crime.[3]

ANCIENT PERUVIANS, MEXICANS AND CENTRAL AMERICANS.

Following those strong tendencies toward absolute monarchy, as seen in Africa, to their natural conclusion, we find terrible despotisms, like the empires of the ancient Peruvians and Aztecs, as they existed at the time of the Spanish conquest in the 17th century. The emperor is not only

[1] Macdonald, *Jour. Anth. Inst.* (1890), pp. 294–5.
[2] Gardiner, pp. 94–5.
[3] Ellis, *History of Madagascar*, i, 144, 389, 394.

commander-in-chief of all the war forces of the nation, not only the fountain of law and of all justice, but he has become a god, directly descended from the high god of the nation. An organized priesthood support him with the dread sanctions of a most cruel and blood-thirsty religion. Military governors and judges support him, for they lose both power and life at his nod. All things strengthen the binding yoke of the custom of obedience upon the people, who become the slaves of their God and king, while the fighting quality —the manly fibre—is gradually crushed out of them. Ancient usages of the nation are for the most part maintained and enforced, for they make toward social stability and strengthen the power of the emperor. His far-reaching authority is developed and safeguarded, also, by the creation of many new prohibitions, unknown in savage communities, and supported by ferocious penalties for disobedience; such as death with all relatives to the fourth degree, death as sacrifice, death by burning, stoning or burial alive. "Laws were few and exceedingly severe," wrote Vega (ii, chap. 3), of the Peruvians, and the same was written by Zurita (p. 303), of the Mexicans; "under the ancient government the Indians had so few laws that they knew them all by heart." But what they had "related almost wholly to criminal matters,"[1] and offences were not only crimes but sins also. Social punishments were very effective in repressing crime, and criminals were comparatively few. Guzman calls the Peruvians the "innocents of this country" (p. 96). They are "obedient, industrious, patient and friendly" among themselves. The Mexicans never seem to preserve the remembrance of an injury. "They are full of humility, obeying every one and knowing but submission and labor."[2] They are thoroughly indolent, for they have become accustomed to act

[1] Prescott, *Conquest of Peru*, i, 44.

[2] Zurita, p. 186.

only from fear of punishment. The influence of the Aztec religion upon moral life seems to have been pernicious on the whole, but "the wish to have the good opinion of the tribe was productive of noble deeds." What we should call good actions were caused by social, not religious approval. Morality was apparently injured by religion, fostered by social pressure. Among the Peruvians there was "no money, little trade, and hardly anything that would be called fixed property,"[1] and thus the numerous business offences which furnish so large a part of our modern criminality could not have existed among them.

A glance at the following table will show very clearly how the coming of an absolute despotism increased the number of actions punished as crimes and thus multiplied criminals. At the same time, the intense social pressure, crushing out all tendency to individual variation, even at birth, kept criminals comparatively few; but prevented, likewise, all possibility of growth to a higher plane of social life, with greater intelligence and better morality—a growth which would inevitably have brought with it the necessity for nicer social adjustments between man and man—an increase in the number of acts deemed criminal and a growing mass of offenders against the state.

The nations of Central America, when conquered by the Spaniards, had not attained the high state of social and political development witnessed in the two great barbaric empires of the new world. Actions known to have been punished as crimes were very few in number, and in Yucatan and Guatemala, adultery, murder and theft were still mere harms against the individual, punished or excused at the option of the injured. In studying the tables it must always be remembered that S P and S R mean the action has become, or is becoming, a true criminal offence.

[1] Prescott, *Peru*, i, ch. 2.

CRIMES AND OFFENCES PUNISHED BY ANCIENT NATIONS OF CENTRAL AMERICA, PERU AND MEXICO.

	Treason.	*Incest.*	*Witch-craft.*	*Sacrilege.*	*Adultery.*	*Theft.*	*Murder.*	*Other Offences.*	
Yucatans	S P D				I R D at option of offended or S P D	I P C or slavery	I R D or I P C	*Arson.* I P D or P C *Rape.* P D	
Guatemalas ..	S P D		S P D	S P D or slavery	*Fornication.* I P C or poss. D	I P C or poss. S P D			
Chibchas	S P D	S P D			S P D or W or C	S P W or C or utter social infamy	S P D or C	The abominable sin S P D and a few other offences	Very few criminals
Peruvians ...	S P D	S P D		S P D	I R D	D less if act necessary to support life		*Arson.* Severe punishment or S P D *Unnatural Offences.* S P D	
Mexicans ...	S P D	S P D		S P D	S P D or I P M or D		S P D even for killing of slave.	*Unnatural Offences.* S P D	

Crimes Against the Emperor.

	Rebellion.	*Exporting Gold or Silver.*	*Killing Guano or Other Birds.*	*Unjust Judges.*	*Removing from one Province to Another.*
Peruvians ...	Destruction for inhabitants.	S P D. All reserved for use of Yncas.	S P D	S P D	

	Maltreating Ambassadors or Royal Couriers.	*Stealing Gold or Silver.*	*Giving Away a Prisoner of War, or Depriving Another of His Booty.*	*Disloyal Tax Collectors, etc.*	*Corrupt Prosecutors.*
Mexicans ...	S P D	S P D as sacrifice.	S P D	S P D	Slavery to Emperor or composition.

Mexicans ... Making use of the badges of the Emperor of Mexico, and those of the Lord Chief Justice of Mexico, was punished by death and confiscation of goods.

CRIMES AND OFFENCES AGAINST THE GENERAL SOCIAL WELFARE.

	Turning off Water from Neighbor's Land.	*Neglect to Irrigate Land at Proper Seasons.*	*Changing Boundaries.*	*Trespassing on Fields or Dwellings by Travelers.*	*Removing Landmarks.*
Peruvians . . .	Severe punishment.	Severe flogging.	Severe punishment.	Punishment.	Severe punishment.
	Fighting or Other Offences in Market Places.	*Altering Measures.*	*Changing Boundaries.*	*Selling Strayed Child as Slave.*	*Procuresses.*
Mexicans. . . .	S P D	S R D immediate.	S P D	S P slavery and forfeiture.	S P D
	Father, for not Rightly Training Child.	*Extravagance in Dress or Superfluity in Eating.*	*Killing any Game.*	*Disorderly People.*	
Peruvians . . .	Punished.	Prohibited.	S P D	Flogging.	
	Dressing Like One of the Opposite Sex.	*Lying or Defamation of Character.*	*Selling Possessions of Another Held in Farm.*	*Any Private Fighting.*	*Drunkenness.*
Mexicans. . . .	S P D hanged.	Mutilation.	Punished.	Rigorously punished.	S P D for youths; severe penalty for adults.
	Rape.	*Selling Stolen Goods.*			
Mexicans. . . .	P D	Punished.	A lord, taken prisoner in war, ***who returned home* was *condemned to death***, because not manly enough to die in battle.		

The Peruvians "never imposed a pecuniary fine, nor punished by confiscation of goods. Although the aggrieved person separated himself from the quarrel, justice was enforced by the ordinary judgment of officers, who inflicted the full punishment established by law for each offence." Here is true social punishment for crime. (Vega, Book II, Chap. 12.)

PROBABLE ORDER OF CHANGE FROM TORT TO CRIME OF THE THREE GREAT PRIMITIVE TORT OFFENCES.

It is our belief that adultery was the first of the three great primitive tort offences to be converted into a true crime—that is punished by society as a wrong against itself, irrespective of the wishes of the person injured. It was then regarded as the most heinous form of theft, and serious theft, in general, was probably made truly criminal before murder, which was for many centuries undistinguished from involuntary homicide, and which was always the harm most imperatively demanding individual revenge—blood for blood—in those early days. So Grey writes: "The most sacred duty of the Australian is to avenge the death of his nearest relation; until he has accomplished this he is mocked by the old women; his wives, if he be married, would soon leave him. If unmarried, no girl speaks to him; his own mother would constantly cry and lament as having given birth to so degenerate a son; his father would treat him with contempt."[1] Yet the murder of father, or brother, was undoubtedly an exception to this general rule; for then the murderer was himself the nearest of kin, the natural avenger of the deed of blood, and the horror created by the unnatural act brought with it the dread social doom of outlawry. Likewise, the murder of a beloved chieftain has sometimes been avenged by the entire savage community.

Reasons for this general order—1, adultery; 2, theft; 3, murder;—in the change from tort to crime may be readily found. There is very little private property among savage hordes, what few goods they possess being held for the most part in common; but the most highly valued and jealously guarded personal possession is the wife.[2] Later, when pastoral and agricultural life had increased property and made it

[1] Grey, ii, 240.

[2] See Australians.

a most important aid to social strength and effectiveness, all serious forms of theft were made criminal by the infliction of a true social punishment, and adultery, as the most intensely disliked form of theft, was probably changed first. The evidence, though scanty, from many different and widely scattered races, points in this direction.

Adultery punished as crime.—The Australians punish serious theft by death, or by expulsion from the social group, and they punish adultery as theft.[1] "If a young couple of Australians abscond, or if a man absconds with the wife of another, the whole tribe instantly goes in pursuit. In the former case death is the punishment of the female."[2] The word "expulsion" and the action by the whole tribe look like true social punishment in these cases, but all other authorities known to the author are agreed that adultery and theft among Australians are punished by individual revenge. For New Caledonians, see under Incest.[3]

Caribs.—By the Caribs the adulteress is done to death by the people in the public place.[4]

For *Araucanians*. See p. 59, "Crime Among Savages." Seems like *S R D for adultery. Theft, S R D or I R D. Murder, I R D or I P C.*

Iroquois.—"Adultery was punished by whipping." A council was held upon the question, and if the charge was sustained, they ordered the woman to be publicly whipped by persons appointed for the purpose.[5]

Murder and homicide within the group grievously weaken the community, but constant danger of life and limb fosters skill and preparedness for war—prime requisites for survival

[1] Stuart's *Australia*, ii, 117, 276.

[2] *Trans. Eth. Soc., N. S.*, iii, 249.

[3] Adultery usually *I R D*—one instance *S P D*. Theft, *I R D*.

[4] Gumilla, i, 207. Quoted by Steinmetz, ii, chap. 9. Adultery usually *I R D*; one instance, *S P D*; murder, *I R D*.

[5] Morgan, p. 331. Adultery, *S P W*. Theft, *I P C*. Murder, *I R D* or *I P C*.

among savage tribes. Man's business was to kill, and he must be well trained and always ready to fight the common enemy. Callous to suffering, cruel and impulsive by nature, trained to revenge as a religion, the power to fight well and kill was too highly prized and honored to permit punishment of homicide as crime by low savage communities. Not until passionate human nature had been somewhat curbed by social pressure in other directions, and until agricultural life had made killing within the group both more easy and more harmful, was even intentional homicide made crime.[1]

[1] See Anglo-Saxon England.

CHAPTER V

THE EUROPEAN—ARYANS.

THE researches of philologists in recent years have given us an outline picture of our primitive Aryan ancestors nearly 4000 years ago, when the forefathers of Greek and Roman, Teuton, Celt and Slav had not yet parted from the original mother stock, to begin their long and varied separate migrations. They were strangely low in the scale of civilization—these early progenitors of ours—when compared with the Chaldeans and Babylonians of their own era. Grouped in tribal communities around leading men or princes, the Aryans were a shepherd race, ignorant of agriculture, unacquainted with the art of metal working, living in tents or rude wooden houses, knowing nothing of town life, polygamous, and almost naked; with no words even to distinguish between law, custom and religious observance, for "âgas" meant an offence against both gods and men, and was equivalent in their language to the word "rna," fault or sin.

We know, however, that the right of individual vengeance was already recognized among them, and that the rod was a favorite instrument of punishment, not only for scourging, but also for the infliction of the terrible death penalty.[1] One word sufficed the primitive Aryans for the ideas guilty, thief, debt or loan, and it is highly probable that they placed the unfortunate debtor, whose relatives or friends would not redeem him, on a par with the detected thief. By both a man

[1] Ihering, p. 74–5. Suetonius (*Nero*, 49) specially mentions the "corpus virgis ad necem caedi" as "mos majorum," the custom of the ancients.

had been deprived of his property, and against both he had the same right of unlimited flogging. The amount of the debt or theft bore no relation to the penalty inflicted.[1] There were at least nine different methods of appeal to divine judgment—of which ordeals by fire, water and poison were the most severe—but we do not know to what offences these tests and punishments were applied. Have we then any evidence at all that crime was punished by the early Aryans? Was everything left to individual revenge, or were there some few actions so instinctively abhorrent to the community that they called for social condemnation and collective vengeance? Two facts indicate this latter conclusion. Outlawry was known among the Aryans, and this custom we have found associated with the beginnings of true public punishment, both among animals and low savage men.[2] Also, Ihering, the great German student of comparative jurisprudence, does not hesitate to state that this rude people "prohibited marriage between near relatives."[3] Thus, incest was probably a crime among our ancestors, 4000 years ago, just as we know it to be criminal among low savage tribes to-day.

The necessities of the long migratory period changed the sluggish, unprogressive, primitive Aryan into the energetic, war-like, progressive European. Hunger was the spur driving onward to new lands, into conflict with new foes. It was always the strongest and bravest who went forward from each temporary home. Natural selection and social selection were both joined in developing the masterful stock whence sprang the victorious, liberty-loving nations of western Europe. When history opens, the race is already

[1] See the Roman Twelve Tables, where the "in partes secare" took the place of scourging to death, "si plus minusve secuerint sine fraude esto."

[2] The rod and expulsion from the community of the Aryans are the two forms of punishment mentioned by Zimmer. See Ihering, p. 74–5.

[3] Ihering, p. 46–7.

widely scattered and national lines are beginning to form. From henceforth our study is of European progress in civilization. Do the records we possess of the early Aryan national groupings on the continent of Europe warrant a belief in the primal sovereignty of the people, and the direct social punishment of crime, in obedience, not to the command of any king or ruler, but to the dictates of time-honored ancestral custom? What conduct was prohibited by the community? What penalties were inflicted?

Crime is a Social Product.—"In the primitive law of almost all the races which have peopled western Europe," writes Sir Henry Sumner Maine, "there are vestiges of the archaic notion that the punishment of crime belongs to the general assembly of the freemen."[1]

The Aryan state, in its rudimentary form, writes Hearn, "dealt exclusively with its own affairs." It punished the person who betrayed its secrets to the enemy, or who, whether in the field or by less open aid, took part against his country. But it did not interfere in the private quarrels of its citizens. "Every man took care of his own property and his own household, and every hand guarded its own head." Injury brought individual revenge or reprisal, or might be followed by composition. "The state cared for none of these things."[2] Yet "when any new worship was introduced, or when any sorcerer or magician practiced his mysterious arts, the whole force of the community was directed to repress the common enemy, and the state did not hesitate to repel a danger that seemed to threaten as well itself as all its subjects."[3] "Our whole system of personal and political liberty rests upon the two principles—that individual freedom of action is the rule and that the interference of the state is the exception."[4]

[1] p. 383. [2] Hearn, p. 431. [3] *Ibid.*, p. 432. [4] *Ibid.*, p. 394.

Romans.—The Roman people certainly possessed a genius for law making. Their early kings, and especially Romulus, stand as the representatives of antiquity. The instructions and laws accredited to them—and very possibly promulgated by them—usually embody old social customs, handed down through many centuries. Their legal system begins with a code—the famous code of the XII. Tables—regarded with an almost superstitious reverence by the Roman people, and committed to memory by every Roman schoolboy. Compiled as early as 451 B. C., graven on brazen tablets in the heart of the city, many of these laws were not superseded till the enactment of the Code Justinian, 529–534 A. D., and their importance to the Roman nation can hardly be overestimated.[1] The fragments of the XII. Tables which have come down to us bear within themselves the evidence that these laws were really the condensed expression of very ancient legal customs of the race.[2] They "are little more than brief legal maxims or mementoes of settled legal principles, which must have owed all their life, and even their meaning, to a quantity of special notions widely diffused abroad, as well as to an infinity of detailed usages, of which no account whatever is contained in the words of the law itself."[3] This earliest of all codes bears ample witness to the sovereignty of the Roman people and to the customary punishment of criminals by the popular assembly. Thus, under Table IX. (de jure publico) we read:

Fr. 2. "De capite civis, nisi per maximum comitium, ne ferunto."

The grand assembly of the people—the assembly by cen-

[1] Cicero, *De Leg.*, ii, c. 23; *De Orat.*, i, c. 43, 44; *De Re Pub.*, ii, c. 36, 37: iv, c. 4.

[2] Cumin, Introduct., p. 5; Mears, Introduct., p. lvii; Goodwin, p. 8.

[3] Amos, p. 13.

turies—alone has the right to judge capital offences of a citizen.[1]

Table IX. *Fr. 5.* "De eo qui hostem concitaverit quive civem hosti tradiderit." And Marcianus I, xiv, Inst. D (48.4), "Lex xii tabularum iubet eum qui hostem concitaverit, quive civem hosti tradiderit, capite puniri."[2]

A law of the twelve tables commands that he who incites an enemy against his country, or betrays a citizen into the hands of the enemy, shall be punished with death. This was treason, or "Perduellio, the term for all acts whereby a man within the state showed himself an enemy (Perduellis) of the established constitution. In the oldest trial for a capital offence on record, the Perduellion suit of Horatius, the execution contemplated was by flogging."[3]

Table VIII. (de delictis). *Fr. 26.* "Ne quis in urbe coetus nocturnos agitet."

Seditious meetings by night in the city are forbidden. This also was treason, and the penalty was death.[4]

"Incestum pontifices supremo supplicio sanciunto."

Against incest, let the chief priests give sentence of the extremest penalty of the law.[5]

Table IX. *Fr. 3.* "Ne iudex arbiterve ob rem iudicandam pecuniam accipiat."

No judge or arbiter shall receive money for his judgment (under penalty of death).[6]

Fr. 4. "De quaestoribus parricidii et de provocatione."

Of inquisitors of murder and right of appeal. Quaestores

[1] *See* Cicero, *De Legibus*, iii, 19, 44. *De Re Publica*, ii, 36. "Majestas," says Cicero, "residet proprio in populo Romano."

[2] Schoell, pp. 152–3.

[3] Ihering, p. 53.

[4] Porcius Latro, *Declamatio Contra Catilinam*, cap. 19.

[5] Cicero, *De Leg.*, ii, 8, 9. This is mentioned among old laws, but not as a fragment of the XII Tables.

[6] Aulus Gellius, *Noct. Attic.*, xx, 1, 7, and Cicero, *In Verrem*, i, 13.

parricidii were appointed by the Roman assembly to try murder cases,[1] but there was always the right of appeal to the people from the death sentence.[2]

Table VIII (de delictis). *Fr. 24.* "De homicidio" (concerning homicide).[3] "Indicat lex Numa Pompilii regis, si quis hominem liberum dolo sciens morti dint, parricida esto."

If any one kill a freeman wilfully and maliciously, let him be deemed a parricide.[4]

Table VIII. (de delictis). *Fr. 25.* "Qui malum carmen incantassit—malum venenum."

Incantations and wicked drugs.[5] M. Ortolan: *Explication Historique des Institutes,* thus interprets: Death for him who uses wicked enchantments or gives poison.

Fr. 23. "De poena falsi testimonii."

The punishment of false testimony. And Aulus Gellius, *Noct. Attic.*, xx, i, 53: False witnesses were hurled from the Tarpeian rock.

Through all the years of the Republic, and long after the Empire was established, the deep-seated reverence and affection of the Roman people for these ancient customary laws is plainly manifest. A storm of popular indignation greeted the unsuccessful attempt of Caius Gracchus, in 123 B. C., to change these customs by withdrawing the cognizance of murder and poisoning from the popular assemblies, to entrust it to permanent judicial commissions. Not till the next century was this very necessary reform actually carried out.

[1] *Digesta*, i, 2 (2, 23). *De orig. juris.*

[2] Cicero, *De Re Publica*, ii, 31.

[3] *See* Pliny, *Nat. Hist.*, xviii, 3 (3), for the death penalty inflicted on the man slayer; and Festus—"Parricidii quaestores."

[4] The word "Parricida" is most probably a contraction of parenti-cida—the murder of a relative. In earlier ages this was doubtless the only form of homicide which the Romans punished with death. Festus records the extension of this penalty to all murderers.

[5] Pliny, *Natur. Hist.*, xxviii, 2 (4), and *Digesta*, l, 16. *De verbor. signif.*

The Romans did not possess a permanent criminal tribunal of any sort until the first Quaestio Perpetua was appointed in 149 B. C., and this dealt with only a few political offences.[1] Sulla's legislation, early in the first century B. C., "covered the whole field of criminal law."[2] Thus we see how long and jealously the Roman people guarded their sovereign power and right of direct social punishment for crimes as against any other authority whatever, even one delegated to their own appointed judges. Indeed, it was this failure of the Roman people to develop a true criminal law, which finally degraded Roman criminal procedure into a weapon of partisan politics and made it completely void of principle. Criminal trials became mere party broils, and to this, more perhaps than to any other cause, may be traced the decline and fall of the Roman Republic.[3]

Spartans.—Very little is known about Spartan criminal procedure, but the popular assembly tried political offenders, being assisted in its judgments by the Ephors. A king, on trial before the High Court, composed of twenty-eight Senators, five Ephors and the other king, could, if condemned, appeal to the assembly of all Spartans.[4]

Athenians.—We are much better informed concerning the organization of justice in Athens than in Sparta. From remote antiquity the council of the Areopagus (Ἄρειος πάγος) met on Mars Hill, outside the city wall, to try traitors, homicides and the sacrilegious, where the city could not be defiled by the presence of such men. The judges were taken from the nobility, but they judged in accordance with ancient customs of the race. As yet there were no written laws. Under Draco the tribunal of the fifty-one Ephors became the great criminal court, and Solon made further changes. But always —and this is an important fact—the accused criminal had

[1] Extortion by Colonial Governors, etc. *See* Lex Calpurnia de Repetundis.
[2] Cherry, p. 74. [3] *See* Maine and Hearn. [4] Letourneau, pp. 330–2.

the right of appeal to a superior tribunal, composed of from 500 to 1000 or even 1500 jurors, chosen every year, by lot, from the mass of the population. This was the celebrated Heliæa (Ἡλιαία), essentially a popular tribunal, and there was practically no appeal from its sentence. The Heliasts bound themselves by terrible oaths to judge according to the customs and decrees of the people, never to pronounce in favor of oligarchy or tyranny, to be strictly impartial and to receive no presents. In time the high courts of the Areopagus and the Archons were practically replaced by the Heliaea.[1] The Athenians punished desertion to the enemy and other forms of treason with death. This was also the penalty for sacrilege and the profanation of mysteries. The bodies of such criminals could not be buried in the territory of the republic and their goods were confiscated.[2] Even the children of a traitor might legally be put to death. An Athenian guilty of gross crimes against nature was publicly disgraced and lost his rights of citizenship. Under Solon pecuniary fines were very largely introduced.

Slavs.—The primitive Slavic folkmotes included the common people, and were convened, not periodically, but as often as some question of state arose requiring public discussion. In early times the decisions of the people were unanimous. This meant that the minority, if it could not convert the majority to its way of thinking, was forced to acquiesce in the common decision. Any one who refused assent during the meeting was beaten with rods. Opposition to the vote of the majority, after the assembly, was punished by the loss of the dissentient's property, which was often destroyed by fire, unless he was ready to redeem it by a sum of money, varying according to his rank.[3] The statute of Vinodol shows that the early laws of the southern Slavs were

[1] Letourneau, pp. 334–345, and Maine, p. 360.

[2] Du Boys, pp. 175–7.

[3] Kovalevsky, p. 123.

codified in 1288 from old customs preserved in memory. Even to-day the regular tribunal of the Russian (Volost) villages, giving judicial decisions in civil suits and misdemeanors among the peasantry, is not bound to follow the prescriptions of law, but those of custom.[1] "Cases of high treason were referred to the popular assembly" at Novgorod, "just as they were in Poland and Bohemia." Whenever the Posadink—the supreme judge elected by the people—had to decide a case to which no existing law applied, he must consult the assembly of the people."[2] About the end of the 9th century, the Drevlians are related by the chronicle, to have on one occasion "thought in common with their prince Mal," and decided "to slaughter the son of Rurik, Egor." The prince evidently consulted the folkmote, and with its help arrived at the decision.

Germans.—Among the Teutons both legislative and judicial power were entirely in the hands of the people, and upon all matters of importance the king or chiefs had to seek the verdict of the folkmote. Thus we read in Tacitus, *Germania*, cap. 12: "It rests with the council of the freemen to accuse and hold over a man the peril of a capital charge. They distinguish between crimes and minor offences (delicto). Traitors and deserters they hang on trees. Cowards in battle and those who will not serve in war, together with men stained by abominable vices, they plunge into the mire of the morass, smothered under hurdles. For slighter offences the punishments are in proportion. Those convicted are fined in horses and flocks. Part of the fine goes to the king or to the state, part is paid over to him who is avenged, or to his near relatives."[3] With the Germans, again writes Tacitus, "good customs avail more than do strong laws elsewhere." Social abhorrence of the coward and the traitor are

[1] Kovalevsky, p. 105. [2] Charter of Pscov., 1467; Kov., p. 144.

[3] These fines were evidently compositions and the offences torts.

plainly manifest in the epic Beowulf. The social morality of that day stamped these actions crimes, while their opposites, courage and fidelity, were held up for honor and imitation as the peculiar virtues of the Germanic peoples.

Teutons and Celts.—Kings and leaders were elected by the people among both Teutons and Celts. When, without such election, some one ventured to assume "ever so limited a command, with a view to possess it for life," it enraged the people "to such extent that they avenged the outrage by his death." Thus in the case of Orgetorix among the Helvetii:[1] "Orgetorix having plotted to seize the royal power, they (the Helvetii) compel him, according to their customs, to plead his cause from chains. If condemned, the punishment must follow, that he be burnt with fire."[2] A literal translation best expresses the inevitable character of the doom to be inflicted in obedience to ancestral usage.

The Germans, writes Cæsar, hold robbery to be no disgrace, if the act is committed beyond the territory of one's own state.[3] This was an act of war, and praiseworthy. But when the deed is committed within the tribe, "those taken in theft, robbery or other offence are offered as human sacrifices, pleasing to the immortal gods. However, as a supply of this kind is wanting, they also offer innocent victims."[4] This shows punishment for torts, crimes or sins, in the name of religion, and also fewness of the offenders.[5] The Druids were apparently the repositors of the ancient penal customs of the Teutons. They possessed great power, especially in punishing sins, and the ban of excommunication was their heaviest penalty.[6]

The evidence seems to warrant the conclusion that among

[1] Cæsar. *De Bello Gallico.*, Book I, sec. iv.

[2] *Ibid.*, Book VII, sec. iv, and Tacitus, *Annales*, ii, 88, for the case of Arminius.

[3] Cæsar, Book VI, sec. xxiii.

[4] *Ibid.*, Book VI, sec. xvi.

[5] *Ibid.*, Book VI, sec. xvii.

[6] *Ibid.*, Book VI, sec. xiii.

European Aryans at the dawn of history, the people were everywhere sovereign. These free and sovereign peoples habitually punished a few most harmful acts, not as harms to an individual, but as crimes against society, and jealously guarded their ancient customs of social trial and social vengeance. Society alone declared what acts were criminal. Society alone punished men for their crimes. Society, by manifesting strong disapprobation, and by inflicting social vengeance, converted certain acts into crimes, and the perpetrators of such acts into criminals. Crime is a social product.

CHAPTER VI

THE ANGLO-SAXONS IN ENGLAND. 449 TO 1066

HITHERTO our study has been of the origin, nature and earliest forms of crime, and we have found true social punishment for wrongs against the commonweal among primitive Aryans and all other races of men. Now we shall study the growth of crime and its usefulness, in relation to social progress; following the history of the Anglo-Saxon people, among whom crime has had its largest development.

When the Angles, Saxons and Jutes abandoned[1] their old homes in Germany to conquer and possess the lands of fertile Britain, they doubtless brought with them their ancient penal customs, laws of tort and habits of punishing criminals, described by Cæsar and Tacitus. Living far from Roman influence, by the cold Northern Sea, they probably had no knowledge whatsoever of any legal customs not Germanic, and clung as tenaciously to their ancient usages and liberties as did their descendants, the English, in later years. The brief Saxon law of the continent, put in writing about 800 A. D., but reflecting customs of the centuries before,[2] is apparently little modified by the law of Imperial Rome, and the Danes and Scandinavians who invaded England in the 8th and 9th centuries had, if possible, a yet more archaic type of German legal custom. Wild men of

[1] Kentish traditions of the conquest state that part of the lands occupied by the Angles and Jutes before their emigration were long after left untilled and ungrazed. The invaders brought with them their wives, their children, and their cattle, just as in later times the Northmen carried both wives and cattle to Iceland, Greenland and Vineland. Traill, i, 132.

[2] Brunner, i, 347–349.

the woods, fierce rovers of the waters, sailing up the rivers and estuaries of eastern and southern Britain in their dragon ships, killing, pillaging and burning as they went; it must have seemed to the civilized inhabitants of the coasts as if the flood-gates of barbarism had been let loose upon them. Gradually, the invading bands pushed their enemies further and further into the west, where they became known as Welshmen (*i. e.*, foreigners), but the struggle was a long and hard one, lasting for more than one hundred and fifty years, and it resulted in the thorough Teutonizing of Britain, the supplanting of Christianity by heathendom and the disappearance of Roman law courts before the ferocious blood feud and the wergeld of the German forests.

We have almost no information regarding the Pagan period of Anglo-Saxon England; but existing evidence of the 7th and 8th centuries fully warrants our belief that the Anglo-Saxon penal customs and courts of justice were identical with those of Germany.[1] The first of the Kentish Codes—Aethelberght's, about 600 A. D.—consists of ninety short paragraphs, mostly relating to money compositions which the courts *allow* for very carefully defined personal injuries. Contemporary German codes contain practically the same offences and fines, and the laws of nations nearest of kin to the Angles and Saxons in Germany coincide with these laws of Aethelberght's the most closely.[2]

In the laws of Hlothar and Eadric (Kent 675) 8th paragraph, we read: "If any man make plaint against another and meet him at (cite him to) the *methel* or the *thing*, let the defendant always give security to the other and do him such right as the Kentish judges prescribe to them."[3] Both

[1] The Dooms of Anglo-Saxon kings have been pronounced by one scholar after another purest specimens of old Teutonic law. Traill, i, 172.

[2] Thorpe, p. iii, preface.

[3] *Ibid.*, p. 13.

the names and procedure of the old Germanic law courts are thus found in existence in Kent.[1] The Dooms of Alfred clearly distinguish between two courts: the folk gemot, or district court, held every four weeks, and the Gemot of the Ealdorman, formerly the Assembly of the State, which met twice a year. These are the time-honored tribunals of the German forests.[2] From the simplicity of life, the wide field allotted by ancient custom to individual and kindred vengeance, as also from the weakness of the ancient tribal state, the courts could punish very few acts as crimes, but treason, desertion from the army, cowardice and incest must have brought destruction upon offenders in heathen England as well as heathen Germany.

With time and social progress, however, private vengeance and the blood feud lost their rude usefulness, and became more and more social evils. Slowly and very cautiously the right of vengeance was curbed and limited by social pressure. Even in Homer's age, among the Greeks, some wise and honored chief occasionally acted as arbitrator in serious disputes, preventing revenge by his award of a composition for the harm done, voluntarily paid and voluntarily accepted.[3] At first, vengeance alone was honorable and composition disgraceful. Gradually composition became more permissible—then honorable. Social influence favored this modification of ancient custom, using the desire for gain as a substitute for the pleasures of revenge, but the individual's right of choice between vengeance and composition long continued.[4] Society at length compelled the injured man to seek arbitration and composition first, before vengeance on

[1] Adams, p. 9. [2] Alfred, ii, 22, 34, 38; Thorpe, pp. 34 and 37.

[3] See The Famous Shield of Haphæstus.

[4] "*The Iliad* (ix. 632–636) distinctly mentions both the duty of vengeance and the customary acceptance of the compensation. But the avenger of blood was under no compulsion to forego his feud. The State was simply a mediator." Hearn, p. 442.

the offender, thus giving time for passions to cool. Yet later, the adjudged compensation, if offered, must be accepted in most cases and finally in all. Such was the evolution of the tort.[1] "It was evidently the policy of the state to check these bloody quarrels, which continually deprived it of the services of its most active and warlike citizens." The method adopted was "making the best terms it could for the wrong-doer." "Accordingly it proceeded to determining the amount of composition for every injury. This learning of the wergeld, or the Eric—that is, the man-price —formed the largest portion of the law of Teutons and Kelts."

But the laws found in early Teutonic Codes of the fifth and sixth centuries are not laws of crime, neither did they include all the penal customs followed by early Teutonic society. The oldest rules of vengeance were not recorded in written laws. What we find are records of *deviations* from the most archaic customs — social checks and modifications of the cherished right of individual vengeance for private injury — laboriously established as customary laws of tort by social pressure. For the most part they are tariffs for bodily and other injuries, regulated, not by the gravity of the offence, but by the provocation to vengeance. Here are no provisions for the social punishment of criminals, that is, of offenders against the state; and no rules defining the penal authority of parents. We know well, however, that both the assembly of the freemen and the father in his family possessed the right to judge and used the right to punish. Probably unwritten social customs prescribed punishment for a few acts as sins against the gods,[2] but, in general, murder, theft and most other

[1] Hearn, p. 442–3

[2] Cæsar, vi, sec. 16.

harmful acts were not then crimes. We shall see how they became crimes in the progress of the centuries.

Long continued warfare in a foreign land has always raised up a king among Teutonic peoples. At first he was purely elective, and possessed little power, except when leader of the host. But the Anglo-Saxon kingdoms were for centuries like camps in a hostile territory. All adopted a military organization, and social necessity induced a gradual consolidation of power in the king's hands; for thus military strength and efficiency were greatly increased, and the people more firmly bound together for domestic peace.[1] This was the social requisite for survival. The strongest, most warlike, most united states rose to dominance; the weak disappeared from history. By the end of the sixth century, the victorious Angles and Saxons had established many petty kingdoms in Britain. Some, the westernmost, were growing yearly stronger and larger at the expense of their old Celtic enemies, while others were now entirely surrounded by Germanic territory, and could expand only by victories over those of their own race. Such wars at once began, and soon became the chief source of Anglo-Saxon weakness, the main obstacle to social progress.

Christian England.—Two strong forces made towards the union of these warring states into a single nation: one, enduring, the Christian Church, which formed an ever-tightening bond of union between Anglo-Saxon peoples; the other, the royal power, when held by some strong, victorious king, and usually passing with his death. The history of England, up to the Norman Conquest, may be regarded as a long struggle for national unity — a struggle never really successful, except temporarily, under pressure of foreign invasion. The Church was entirely victorious in its long warfare against heathendom, and its power was very

[1] Kemble, ii, 23.

great.[1] During the Danish invasions all the English were united for a time under Edward the Elder (in 924) and again under Edgar (958-975). Feudalism was gaining ground. The Anglo-Saxons were advancing, though slowly and painfully, in the right direction; and social progress (new life) was, as we shall see, speedily safe-guarded by the creation and enforcement of penalties for acts newly deemed criminal. The Codes show us the increase of penalties for acts against the Church, the person and power of the king and his officers. These penalties were socially made and enforced, thus making the acts true crimes. Under weakling kings we see a reversion to individual vengeance; under strong kings an increase of penalties and crimes. New crimes took the direction of offences against the new life of society and its upward progress.

Among Anglo-Saxons, the king, like every other man, was subject to the ancient legal customs of his race; the people were themselves the judges and found judgment in their own courts, with which the king had no right to interfere. Even an appeal to the king was a legal offence, punished by fine, unless justice had actually been denied in the ordinary courts. This law is re-enacted in the dooms of king after king until after the Norman Conquest.[2] Although the king was at the summit of the social order, yet he had his price (wer-gild), and his death could be compensated for like the homicide of any other man. Not until Alfred's time did treason against the king's person become punishable with death and bótless. But, as head of the state, the king was defender of the public peace, and as such possessed certain rights with judicial and penal authority, in which he was confirmed and supported by the people. Thus he was

[1] Stephen, ii, 397.

[2] Athelst, i, § 3, Thorpe, pp. 85–86; Edgar ii, § 2, Thorpe, p. 112; Cnut, ii, § 17, Thorpe, p. 165; Wm. the Conq., i, § 43; Thorpe, p. 209.

empowered to inflict fines upon officials and even private individuals, for neglect of duty menacing the public welfare. He might even sentence to banishment and outlawry for continued breaches of the peace, if the wealth and power of the offenders seemed to put them beyond the reach of the people's courts.[1] Early Germanic society was organized upon a basis of frith, *i. e.*, peace; and every violation of the peace was regarded as a wrong or injury to some one.[2] Every man's house was his castle and sacred, resting under his protection, his peace.[3] Whoso broke this peace incurred his vengeance, and later, when vengeance was very generally replaced by composition, the offence became a tort, for which damages were awarded in civil action before the gemot, by verdict of the people.[4] The king's peace was very naturally the most sacred and far-reaching peace. We know, from a law of Aethelstan, the exact extent of the mystic circle round the king's habitation.[5] It was "3 miles and 3 furlongs and 3 acres breadth and 9 feet and 9 palms and 9 barleycorns." At the three chief festival seasons of the year, and during the week of his coronation, the king's peace was extended to the whole people, and any breach of this peace was punished as a direct injury to him, in the people's courts. The king could also "give" his peace to individuals by his word and will, by his "hand," writ, or seal. Violations of the protection thus given brought a greatly increased punishment upon the offender — sometimes by large fines, sometimes by placing life and limbs at the king's mercy, or exposing the culprit to the dread social doom of outlawry. The people stood behind the king in all these dooms, and with him enforced the penalty.

[1] Aelthelst, iii, § 3, Thorpe, p. 92; Aelthelst, iv, § 1, Thorpe, p. 94.

[2] Adams, p. 263.

[3] Maitland and Pollock, ii, 452.

[4] Edw. and Guth., § 6, Thorpe, p. 73; Alfred, ii, § 42, Thorpe, p. 40.

[5] Aethelstan, iv, § 5, Thorpe, p. 95.

This is very important; for it was largely through the extension of the king's authority to punish for breaches of his peace—all unauthorized revenge being so considered—that individual vengeance, or fines ("bóts") for damages, became replaced by true social punishments for crime.[1] Non-payment of fines decreed by the courts, whether "bóts," recompense to the individual harmed, or "wíte" fines, paid to the court or to the king,[2] was punishable by outlawry, under all systems of Germanic law; and this was one of the earliest legal penalties for disobedience imposed by society—"the connecting link between private penal law and true criminal law."[3] The man who would not accept the people's verdict was put out of the law's protection. Any one could kill him with impunity. He was declared untrue to the folk ("tiht-bysig" and "folkungetryue") and to the old folk peace.[4] The outlaw was an enemy to the whole folk ("ûtlah wio eall folc");[5] and because he was an enemy to the people and the king, any one who harbored or aided him became a criminal and forfeited his possessions.[6] Gradually the old folk peace came to be considered as the king's peace, for the king could restore the peace to an outlaw ("frioian") or inlaw him again ("inlagis").[7] In outlawry we see the whole state putting itself in war against the criminal who will not abide by the laws, and this is the essential fact in all punishment for crime—social vengeance against the man who wrongs society as a whole. Among Anglo-Saxons the outlaw was excommunicated by the Church, and his position was utterly dismal.

[1] This change was not completed till long after the Norman conquest.

[2] The "wite" was originally regarded as a payment for the trouble of conducting the suit.

[3] Cherry, p. 85–6. Also Maine, pp. 170–174.

[4] Ethelred, i, 4, Thorpe, p. 120. The peace-breaker was "inimicus regis et omnium amicorum eius." See Athelst., ii, 20, § 7.

[5] Aethelr., i, 1, § 9.

[6] Ine, § 30; Cnut, ii, §§ 13, 78.

[7] Athelst., ii, 20, § 3; Cnut, i, 2, § 4.

The Church.—While persistent warlike needs were strengthening the power of the king, the Church of Christ was steadily converting the heathen Anglo-Saxons, and from the very first allied her fast-growing influence with the royal power, in the upbuilding of a centralized government. This was most natural, for the conversion of the English kingdoms began in most instances with the conversion of the king and his court. Under Archbishop Theodore of Tarsus in 673, all the Christian Bishoprics in England were united into a single Anglo-Saxon Church.[1] This unity of religion and of church organization was a strong influence toward political union also, but the inveterate Teutonic tendency to split up into little petty states long prevailed. Probably the Anglo-Saxons were well used to bodily penalties for sin, under the stern heathen worship of the Druids. At any rate, Christian bishops found little difficulty in inducing kings and wise men, with the consent of their people,[2] to proclaim heavy fines for offences against the Church, and later on to punish sins as crimes against the state. Such laws greatly strengthened the power and authority of the Church,[3] and at first this was greatly to the benefit of society. Through the aid of the king the Church multiplied religious laws and penalties. In return it aided him in many ways:[4] his growing power being secured by laws punishing, as

[1] Traill, i, 160.

[2] The preamble to the Kentish Laws of Whitraed (Thorpe, p, 16), close of the 7th century, declares that an assembly (Gemot) of great men, including the king and priesthood, "decreed, with the suffrages of all, these dooms, and added them to the lawful customs of the Kentish men."

[3] "Probably the clergy were never more powerful in any time or country than they were in England before the Norman Conquest. Civil and ecclesiastical legislation went hand in hand. Nearly every set of secular laws enacted by any of the early English kings was coupled with an ecclesiastical code, or contained ecclesiastical provisions: the bishop and the earl sat side by side in every county court. Heresy and schism were alike unknown." Stephen, ii, 397.

[4] Kemble, ii, 26–7.

crimes against the state, treason and other offences against his person and authority; giving him power of life and death in many instances, and enabling him to stiffen penalties and change torts into true crimes. All the Anglo-Saxon codes show this strong influence of the Christian Church, an influence rapidly increasing and intrenching itself behind these laws, punishing sins and failure to pay the Church her dues.

About the year 600, very soon after the establishment of Christianity in Kent, King Aethelberght caused the ancient dooms of his people to be put in writing.[1] This is the earliest Anglo-Saxon code which has come down to us. At the head of the 90 dooms is a single paragraph relative to the Christian Church; decreeing heavy fines for theft of property belonging to the Church or her servants, and for violation of Church right of sanctuary. The offences are regarded as torts, with heavy penalties, because of the majesty of God. Of the other dooms, 58 relate to attacks on the person; 11 to attacks on property; 13 to fornication or aggressions on women; 2 to adultery; and 5 are declaratory of rights. All are laws of tort and probably the equivalent of the penal customs brought by the Anglo-Saxons from Germany, relating to offences of an individual to a fellow man. Crimes against the state are not once mentioned in these dooms; neither are sins mentioned; but some unwritten criminal laws did exist, for a few actions had long been punished by society as crimes. The 90 "dooms" contain almost no corporal punishment, no imprisonment, and no death penalty that might not be compounded for. They present a great tariff of fines, which had come to be deemed punishment, rather than the purchase-price of forgiveness, an indulgence to the offender, the meaning they originally bore. As moral ideas developed

[1] Traill, i, 165.

under Christian influence, fines were regarded as a most insufficient punishment for weighty offences, and forfeiture to the king was introduced. Very probably, also, the old money fines were not thought sufficient to repress disorder.[1]

With time, Church and king became more and more united in support of centralized government, administrative, legislative and judicial, as opposed to a diffused and weaker system of local self-government and large personal independence. "The great struggle," writes Kemble, "assumed *the new form of offences against the state*," and state energies were more and more directed to punishing as crimes acts formerly regarded simply as unfortunate harms to an individual.[2] Offences of an especially serious character, or such as were altogether too prevalent, were made "bótless," and the state itself inflicted the penalty. From strong King Alfred's reign non-finable offences are multiplied,[3] and even injuries for which compensation was still socially permissible, were threatened with punishment at the will of the king.[4] Moreover, the king possessed large powers of pardoning.[5] By the dooms of Ine of Wessex (688–725), fighting in the king's house is punished by the loss of all property, and death or life at the king's pleasure.[6] In this reign the dooms confer considerable power upon the Church; a few sins are punished by fines, but almost no crimes are mentioned. Offences are still generally regarded as torts. In the Kentish dooms of Hlothar and Eadric (673–686) no crimes and no sins against the Church are mentioned. All are laws of tort.[7] Of the twenty-eight dooms of Whitraed King of Kent (690–725), the first four relate to

[1] Kemble, ii, 50. [2] *Ibid.*, ii, 50–1.

[3] Adams, p. 277–8.

[4] Alfred, ii, § 6, Thorpe, p. 30; Cnut, ii, § 36, Thorpe, p. 171.

[5] Alfred, ii, § 7, Thorpe, p. 30; Ine, § 36, Thorpe, p. 54; Cnut, ii, § 13, Thorpe, p. 164.

[6] Ine, § 6, Thorpe, p. 46. [7] Thorpe, pp. 11–15.

the Church, giving it "freedom from imposts" and otherwise strengthening its authority, and a very large proportion relate to composition for sins, such as Sunday labor,[1] offerings to devils,[2] and eating flesh on fast days.[3] Doom 26 shows a development of the king's power to regulate punishment for theft. There are no true crimes mentioned.

During King Alfred's noble reign (871–901), there is a very marked increase in the power of the king and of the Christian Church, as manifested and safe-guarded by penal and criminal dooms. The Code opens with forty-eight dooms of Almighty God, beginning with the Ten Commandments. Death is the penalty decreed for very many sins.[4] Of the seventy-seven secular dooms, most reproduce the customary tariff fines for personal and other injuries; but No. 42 is very important, for Alfred was strong enough to enact a true criminal ordinance, forbidding private vengeance until after compensation had been sought in the popular courts of justice.[5] To enforce this doom needed a mighty king, well supported by public opinion. At the end of Alfred's ecclesiastical ordinances, and again by No. 4 of the secular dooms, "treason against a lord" is declared to be "bótless," *i. e.*, made a true crime, unatonable by money fine, and death and forfeiture of goods are decreed against it.[6] This is a great change from ancient custom, and was probably effected through the influence of the Church, for the doom is decreed on the authority of the Bible.[7] The ecclesiastical ordinance reads as follows: "Many Synods assembled . . . . among the English race, after they had received the faith of Christ, of holy bishops and also of other exhalted 'witan.' They then ordained, out of that

[1] Whitraed, §§ 9, 10, 11, Thorpe, p. 17. [2] *Ibid.*, §§ 12 and 13, Thorpe, p. 18.
[3] *Ibid.*, §§ 14 and 15, Thorpe, p. 18.
[4] Alfred, i, 14, 30, 31, 32, Thorpe, pp. 21–24.
[5] Alfred, ii, 42, Thorpe, p. 40. [6] Thorpe, pp, 28–9. [7] *Ibid.*, p. 26.

mercy which Christ had taught, that secular lords, with their leave, might, without sin, take for almost every misdeed, for the first offence, the money-'bót' which they then ordained; except in cases of treason against a lord, to which they dared not assign any mercy, because God Almighty adjudged none to them who despised him, nor did Christ, the Son of God, adjudge any to him who sold him to death; and he commanded that a lord should be loved as one's self."[1] But King Alfred, notwithstanding these most important innovations, wished it understood that his dooms were but a compilation of the good laws long in force among his people, namely, the dooms proclaimed by Ine of Wessex, Offa of Mercia, and Aethelberght of Kent. As he himself tells us: "I then, Alfred, king, gathered these together and commanded many of those to be written which our forefathers held, those which seemed to me good; and many of those which seemed to me not good I rejected them by the counsel of my witan . . . . for I durst not venture to set down in writing much of my own."[2] The dooms of King Cnut and of William the Conqueror give similar rec ognition and royal enforcement of the ancient customary laws.[3] Thus we see how carefully and very jealously the people guarded their ancient penal customs, when even their wisest and strongest kings had to introduce most necessary changes as it were by stealth, and with the greatest care not to awaken too strong public indignation.[4]

[1] Alfred's *Dooms*, Thorpe, p. 26. [2] *Ibid.*

[3] Cnut, ii, 1, Thorpe, p. 161; Wm. the Conq., i, Thorpe, p. 201.

[4] "Men lived according to their customs, long before these customs were touched by the state. The state commenced its control by undertaking to enforce these customs, and it was only at a late period that it ventured gradually to alter them." The English judges to-day, "professing to expound only, and to develop, not to make the law, employed no legal fiction, but simply stated the very truth." (Hearn, p. 402–3.) "It needs but little reflection to understand how much more of the *security* and *comfort* of our daily life we owe to the action of custom than to the protection of law." (Hearn, p. 407.)

Gradually the nation was educated to new ideas, the laws were hardened, and the king's authority steadily increased, innovations being made, chiefly, by the plea that unauthorized vengeance was a violation of the king's peace. "Not, however, till long after the Conquest, was the king able, by means of this plea, to attract to himself the whole criminal jurisdiction, and finally put an end to private warfare and private revenge."[1] This progress and development is marked in the penal law of the Anglo-Saxons by the transfer of many acts from the category of torts to that of crimes; the essential difference being that society now punished as an offence against itself, acts formerly punishable only by request and prosecution of the person harmed. Besides such transfers, the laws declared many sins to be crimes, and other deeds were for the first time made criminal, largely in the direction of offences against the growing power of the king, which, as we have seen, was most necessary for the social welfare. The imposition of a social penalty necessarily implies offenders to be punished, and with each newly-created crime an increase in the number of criminals. But were these laws enforced? For if not, then the actions they aimed to punish were not crimes. Records from Anglo-Saxon times are scanty. The age was one of violence and blood-shedding. Might was very generally regarded as making right. The laws bore far more heavily on the poor and weak than on the strong and powerful. A noble could murder and be quit for a fine, he could steal once or twice and his money would free him; but slaves, women and men of low degree were branded, mutilated, killed, even burnt alive, for theft and other petty offences. As to the means for the enforcement of the laws: "There was not a single person in the realm (outlaws excepted) who did not, either directly or indirectly, give some kind of

[1] Cherry, p. 82.

security to the state for his good behavior."[1] Throughout the land men were organized in tithings, or groups of ten, each collectively responsible for the right conduct of its members. After the Danish conquest, in the early eleventh century, the peace-pledge, or custom of "reciprocal warranty" was clearly defined and rigorously enforced, in the attempt to repress assassination and other forms of violence. The townsman who entertained a guest even for a single night must be responsible for any evil he might do. There was watch and ward upon the highways and at the gates of the city. Yet human life continued to be held very cheap and property was secure only to the strong. Under powerful kings a stern determination to suppress violence is plainly manifest in the laws, and there is reason to believe the actions declared to be crimes were very frequently punished with outlawry, if in no other way. In modern times the criminal usually remains within the protection of the law, and the state cannot punish him unless it secures his person or property. In Anglo-Saxon days outlaws were numerous, and deprivation of all legal safeguard was the most common form of social punishment for crime. As we have seen, it was no light penalty.

Edward the Elder, Æthelstan, Edmund and Edgar, with the counsel of their witan, were strong and masterful legislators,[2] developing a centralized government, under pressure of frequent Danish invasions. In the dooms of Æthelstan (924–940), the rights of the Church are strongly secured. The ordeal is constantly in use. True criminal laws become more numerous, many sins being punished as crimes. Treason, incendiarism, secret murder, false coinage of money, denial of justice and support of thieves, applying to the king for justice before seeking it in the people's courts, failure to attend gemot or to join in attack upon the king's enemy,

[1] Pike, i, 59.
[2] Traill, ii, 168.

false witness, witchcraft, perjury and marketing on Sunday are socially punished by death, outlawry, forfeiture or heavy fine to the king, by mutilation, imprisonment and loss of social standing.[1] By Edmund's dooms (940–946) the right of private feud was yet more closely limited. None but the homicide shall bear the "faehth" (deadly feud). All his kindred shall be exempt. And if any one of the kindred of the slain take vengeance on any other than the real perpetrator, then "let him be foe to the king and all his friends and forfeit all that he owns."[2] Unchastity of ecclesiastics was punished by forfeiture of worldly possessions and of a consecrated burial-place, unless bót was made to God. Fornication and adultery among laymen brought exclusion from consecrated ground at death, unless a fine was paid to the Church. Perjurers and those who will not pay Church tithes are to be excommunicated,[3] and this ban of excommunication was re-enforced by heavy secular penalties, fines and confiscations, during Edgar's reign. Church tithes must be paid at appointed seasons. He who will not pay becomes a criminal as well as sinner.[4] Sunday must be observed on peril of the full "wite" (fine to the king) in the doom book.[5] These laws show a great increase in Church authority, due in great measure to Archbishop Dunstan, then the greatest man in Church and State.[6] King Edgar (959–975) begins his dooms with an ordinance that the hundred gemot shall meet every four weeks "and that every man do justice to another."[7] By this time the cattle thief had become a true criminal, so far as laws could make him one, and all must unite in his pursuit and punishment. He

[1] Æthelst, i, 3, 4, 6, 7, 10, 14, 20, 24, 25, and iv, 6; Thorpe, pp. 85–90, and 93–5.

[2] Edmund, *Secular Dooms*, i, Thorpe, p. 105.

[3] Edmund, i, 1, 2, 4, 6, Thorpe, p. 104–105.

[4] Edgar, i, 3 and 4, Thorpe, p. 111–112.

[5] *Ibid.*, i, 5, Thorpe, p. 112

[6] Freeman, i, 63.

[7] Thorpe, p. 109.

who will not pursue must pay a fine to the king, and for the fourth offence, forfeit all that he has and become an outlaw.[1] This law and Doom 7 of the Secular Law, relating to an old offender and a man "untrue to the people," show popular trial, conviction and execution of the law against true criminals.[2] Death is the penalty for the "notorious thief," and him "who is found plotting against his lord," unless the king pardon them. The king wills "that every man be worthy of 'folk-right' (the common or customary law of the land), as well rich as poor, and that righteous dooms be judged to him."[3] And again: "I will that secular rights stand among the Danes with as good laws as they best may choose."[4] "No man must apply to the king in any suit, unless he at home may not be worthy of law or cannot obtain law;"[5] showing that all men were subject to the old customary laws, sprung from the will of the people and owing their chief authority to social support. The king in theory simply sanctions and defends, yet by Edgar's time the old Teutonic dooms have been so modified that half the laws relate to crimes. In Athelberght's dooms we found not one.

But in the long reign of Æthelred the Unready (978–1016), especially after Dunstan's strong hand was removed by death, there was a speedy reversion to composition and laws of tort, under a weak king, in troublous times. Offences ceased to be punished as crimes and consequently the number of criminals must have decreased, while society was retrograding. The numerous ordinances, for the most part, only pray and instruct; there are many repetitions and but few commands with penalties. When any penalty is mentioned, it is almost always the "bót," or fine for tort,

[1] Edgar, i, 2 and 3, Thorpe, p. 110.

[2] *Ibid.*, ii, 7, Thorpe, pp. 113–4.

[3] *Ibid.*, ii, 1, Thorpe, p. 112.

[4] See Supplement to Edgar's *Dooms*, 2, Thorpe, p. 116.

[5] Edgar, ii, 2; Thorpe, p. 112.

awarded to the individual harmed. Thus, in the dooms ordained at Wantage, any breach of the peace, excepting that given by the king's own hand, is to be compounded for by "bót" only.[1] Murder and homicide can thus be paid for by "bót" to the kindred of the slain, and no "wíte," or fine for breach of the king's or folk peace is exacted.[2] How very different from the banishment ordained for all "frith" (peace) breakers by King Aethelstan and his witan.[3]

Under Cnut, the great Dane, more English than the English, the old folk laws are again proclaimed and enforced, "God's justice" is exalted, and there are many ecclesiastical ordinances. Many offences are again changed from torts into crimes; new crimes are created and wise distinctions made. Death or banishment are the penalties decreed against witches, diviners, perjurers and adulteresses, against outlaws and man-slayers, notorious thieves and public robbers, unless they amend their ways.[4] Sheltering an excommunicated person or an outlaw, and cowardice in fleeing from military service bring death and forfeiture of goods.[5] "House-breaking and arson and open theft and open morth (secret homicide), and treason against a lord are, by the secular law, 'bótless.'"[6] Edward the Confessor was a weak king, and during his reign very little was added to existing penal legislation, but he confirmed the old dooms of his people, which have ever since been known in England as the good laws of Edward the Confessor.

In conclusion: Anglo-Saxon history reveals a progressive increase in the number of actions declared to be criminal by the laws; and since outlawry was easily enforced against all but the strongest, it is probable that society, though weakly

[1] Æthelred, iii, 1, Thorpe, p. 124.
[2] *Ibid.*, i, 5, Thorpe, p. 122.
[3] Aethelstan, iv, Thorpe, p. 93.
[4] Cnut, ii, 4, 6, Thorpe. p. 162.
[5] *Ibid.*, ii, 67, 78, Thorpe, pp. 176. 180.
[6] *Ibid.*, ii, 65, Thorpe, p. 176.

organized, frequently succeeded in inflicting this, or some other penalty for offences it deemed most heinous. Anglo-Saxon states were busy turning torts into crimes, making sins crimes for the benefit of the Christian Church, and other actions criminal for the safeguarding and upbuilding of the royal power. Every new action socially punished as crime necessitated an addition to the existing body of criminals and an increase in the amount of crime. For criminal laws are not established by a community unless there are, at the time, enough offenders to make the need for repression distinctly felt. By earliest Anglo-Saxon dooms, the man who by a passionate blow killed his serf or little son, was no more a criminal than the modern father who punishes his child for disobedience. Ordinary homicide and theft became crimes only when society recognized and punished these acts as wrongs against itself, and ceased to think of them simply as unfortunate harms to an individual, for which pecuniary damages might be sought in civil action. As fast as society declared penal offences to be bótless, it added to the existing number of crimes and therefore of criminals also. Crime is a social product, and was increasing throughout the Anglo-Saxon centuries, keeping pace with the growing power of the two great factors, the king and the Christian Church, making for strong national unity and internal peace—the greatest needs of the Anglo-Saxon peoples.

New criminal laws safeguarded each advance in the right direction; but these laws were abrogated and crimes decreased when society was retrograding, as in Aethelred's days, by a return to laws of tort and individual vengeance.

New crimes took the direction of greatest resistance to the new life—the upward development—of the people; for they were acts in opposition to the power of the king and of the Christian Church, the two strong forces making toward centralization and unity. The needs of the times demanded the creation and enforcement by society of these new prohibitions,[1] which were therefore neither accidental nor whimsical, but inevitable consequences of increasing complexity of social life, of growth in knowledge, intelligence and social morality.

[1] *Crimes—Heathen Anglo-Saxons.*—Treason, cowardice, incest (death). *Christian Anglo-Saxons.*—Treason, cowardice, incest (Edgar, ii, 34, Cnut, 37, Alfred). Non-payment of fines decreed by court (outlawry); continual breaches of the folk peace (outlawry); harboring or aiding outlaws (forfeiture and outlawry); all unauthorized revenge (fines); an appeal to the king for justice before seeking it in the people's court (fines); denial of justice and neglect of duty menacing the public welfare; treason against the person of the king or a lord (death); many sins punished as crimes; the notorious thief, cattle thief and public robber; house-breaking, arson, and secret homicide; false coinage; witches, diviners and adulteresses. In Edgar's time one-half the dooms relate to crimes. In Aethelberght's, not one criminal law is found.

CHAPTER VII

ENGLAND UNDER NORMANS AND PLANTAGENETS. 1066–1307

THE whole Anglo-Saxon period of English history was marked, as we have seen, by a long struggle for national unity, unsuccessful because of the lack of a strong central government. The inveterate Teutonic tendency to split up into little warring, independent states, proved too strong for the increasing power of native kings and of the Christian Church, and required the strong arm of a foreign conqueror and a succession of despotic rulers, resolute to enforce law and order in their dominions, before the people of England could become a united nation. Such a government England obtained in her Norman kings, who succeeded, during the next century and a half, in building up, with the aid of the common people, a strong, united kingdom. Suddenly, in the reign of John, we find that the Normans had become Englishmen, the English had become united. This great work of nation building was accomplished mainly through the unification and enforcement of more equal law (mostly criminal), by the extension of the king's peace and royal justice over all the land. The problem, in the words of Henry II., was how to make "all men equal under one strong law." First the feudal nobility, then the king himself, then the Christian Church, had to be curbed and brought under this law: the mould in which a strong nation, a free people and a constitutional kingship were run. It was no easy problem this; and the great game required many moves and many curious combinations of attack and defence, before the king was checkmated and the people won. But not the commons only; for in the long struggle, the clashing factions were united into a great, free nation; the vanquished found themselves the victors, and the beaten king was more powerful as a constitutional monarch than any of his despotic ancestors, for he could rely on the support of all his people, now that "that which touches all has become the concern of all," under more equal law, more equal justice and representative, parliamentary government.

From the conquest of England (1066) to the loss of Normandy (1205), the chief constitutional fact was the union of king and people against the feudal nobility. The long conflict meant the extension and enforcement of a true criminal law, among men who had hitherto been, in large part, a law unto themselves and their dependents, because social justice could not reach so far. To secure military efficiency and some degree of order and stability, feudalism, with its multitude of petty tyrants, was a social necessity upon the continent of Europe. Even high-handed misrule was far better than anarchy, when anarchy meant destruction. But in England the time was come for better things—a time when all the clashing forms of private half-justice and tribal legal-custom should be gathered up and united into one common law, enforced over all the land by the might of king and people. From the very first Anglo-Saxon penal law was aristocratic in its tendencies. "Not only did it consecrate the barriers between classes, making a distinction between those who were 'dearly born' and those who were 'cheaply born,' but it raised those barriers by impoverishing the poorer folk."[1] It taught all men to consider justice as a means of revenue for the individual and for the state, so that no one thought of giving justice for nothing; and it set a price upon almost everything. The laws were very fragmentary, and the various tariffs clashed. The free people

[1] Maitland and Pollock, ii, 458.

were themselves the judges and could administer only a simple, unprogressive customary law, which became more and more unfitted to meet the complex requirements of more active Norman times. "The great need" of England, after the Conquest, was undoubtedly (as Maitland states) that the ancient system of money compositions, bót and wer and wíte, should give way before a system of true punishments.[1] Tort must be changed into crime, for the social welfare so demanded. This change, in its historic setting, meant the unification and enforcement of a strong criminal law over all classes; it meant in great measure the building of the nation; it meant also the rapid increase of crime and criminals. In the process we shall find the ancient rights and liberties of Englishmen preserved, strengthened, amplified. This is how it happened.

William the Norman was undoubtedly a dictator, but he was a dictator under constitutional forms. He came to England as the legitimate successor to the throne. Though a usurper, he had himself elected and crowned king by the Witan, after the death of Harold, and took the kingly oath to preserve and maintain the laws and liberties of the English people. But he had other and weighty reasons for maintaining local self-government and the judicial and penal authority of the people's courts. Normandy was a feudal principality. England was but half feudalized. William wished to secure for his new kingdom the military strength and centralized authority of the feudal system, while avoiding its chief danger—already painfully apparent to him in Normandy—the massing of too great power in the hands of the leading feudatories. While abundantly rewarding all his followers, he yet scattered the estates of his greater barons throughout England, thus largely limiting their power. Also, he sought the support of the people, appearing as their de-

[1] Maitland and Pollock, i, 51.

fender against the rapacity of the Norman nobility, and maintaining the jurisdiction of the old courts—the hundred and the shire—with their time-honored laws and customs of self-government. He maintained likewise the old English yeomanry, the fyrd or national militia,[1] made it dependent upon his summons, and caused every householder in England to swear loyalty to him personally, as against any other lord whatsoever. In this way he preserved the roots of popular liberty, and gained for himself and his successors the strong support of the people in the long hundred-years struggle to curb the Norman baronage, a struggle ending in the almost complete destruction of the old nobility.

For the first time England had secured a really strong and stable central government. What the people loved in their Norman kings was the good peace they made in the land; a peace unexampled elsewhere, allowing agriculture and industry to thrive as they had never done before, and making England a storehouse from which the distracted nations of Europe purchased the necessaries of life. Under Anglo-Saxon rulers the protection of the king's peace had been either local or temporary. William I. extended his peace to all his subjects, English as well as French, and this protection meant far more than of old, for William put down the robber, murderer and ravisher with a strong hand. Such security had never been known in England as during his latter years of peaceful reign, and "as the stern avenger of crime, even the conquered learned to bless him."[2] In the words of the old chronicle: "No man durst slay other man, had he never so mickle evil done to the other." "Stark he was to those who withstood his will, but he was mild to the good men who loved God." And it passed into a proverb that a man "who in himself was aught" (*i. e.*, who had any confidence

[1] Traill, i, 235.

[2] Freeman, ii, 170; and *Anglo-Saxon Chronicle*, Anno 1087.

in his own manhood) "might go in safety through William's realm with his bosom full of gold."[1] Royal justice was, however, the exception during all the Norman period. The Conqueror kept his oath to maintain "the good laws of Edward the Confessor," and these old customs of the English were promulgated and confirmed many times by his descendants, and enforced, as formerly, by the people, through the local courts of the hundred and the shire, whether communal or seigniorial. Probably the Normans brought with them to England but few crystallized legal ideas and institutions. "Written laws they had none."[2] After the Conquest, William introduced the celebrated murdrum, or murder fine; for the lives of his followers must be protected, and if the community could not produce the man-slayer, it must itself be held responsible and pay the fine. This was called the law of Englishry. Every man found murdered was considered a Frenchman till the contrary was proved: a presumption very advantageous to the king's exchequer, and showing the strong tendency to make money out of justice in those days. But there was surprisingly little new legislation of any kind. Under William Rufus there were no new laws, but he repressed the feudal nobility as sternly as did his father, and when they rebelled against him, owed his crown to the valor of the conquered English.[3] In this reign the "race of feudal lawyers" begins "to creep into light." Later on we shall watch them modifying antiquated laws to meet new needs.

Despite the many crimes and vices of Henry I., "the Lion of Justice," he is described by impartial men and eyewitnesses as "the almost perfect model of a king." Why? He was a despot, doing good, and just what England needed. In his hands the sword of justice was sharp, and it

[1] *Anglo-Saxon Chronicle*, Anno 1087.
[2] Traill, i, 275; Maitland and Pollock, i, 72–3.
[3] *Anglo-Saxon Chronicle*, Anno 1088.

is written that all men, great and small, French and English, had to bow before it. "Durst none man misdo with other in his time." A special law decreed death by hanging for all thieves and robbers, and we know that this penalty and many others were frequently enforced, even against the king's own followers.[1] Henry I. extended the rights of the crown beyond the limits set by his charter (1100) and "evolved a law for his tenants-in-chief, which was perhaps the severest law in Europe."[2] However, when Henry died, "little had yet been done toward centralizing justice," and in the woeful days of Stephen it looked as if English law would break into a hundred local customs, if it survived at all.[3] Then, for the first and last time, the Norman nobility gained complete control of the kingdom, and horribly did they misuse their power. The Chronicle has left us a most vivid picture of this time of utter lawlessness: "When every rich man his castles made . . . . . and filled them with devils and evil men." "If two men or three came riding to a town all the township fled for them and weened that they were reavers."[4] Many acts, formerly crimes, became no longer criminal, as is almost always the case when society is sick and degenerating. "Every man who had the power

[1] For many centuries theft and robbery, "in their coarsest form," were punished with death. Stephen, iii, 128. "Rex Anglorum Heinricus pacem firmam legemque talem constituit, ut, si quis in furto vel latrocinio deprehensus fuisset suspenderetur." Flor. Wig., Anno 1108, ii, 57. One reason for this extreme severity may have been the great social need of fostering the accumulation of property. There was comparatively little wealth in the world then, and what existed was very largely in the hands of the nobility and clergy, whose influence was dominant in the making of the laws.

[2] *Anglo-Saxon Chronicle*, Annis 1124 and 1125, for legislation concerning theft and coining, abuses of royal purveyance and bad money. Also Eadmer, *Hist., Nov.*, p. 94; Wm. of Malms., *Gesta Regum*, ii, 627. For legislation concerning measures see *Gesta Regum*, ii, 641. See also Maitland and Pollock, i, 73.

[3] Maitland and Pollock, i, 87.

[4] *Anglo-Saxon Chronicle*, Anno 1137.

did that which was right in his own eyes."[1] Robbery ceased to be a crime, for the great and powerful of the land mostly lived by spoliation as their acknowledged right. The picture is not of men waging war. "Every man who had the means to build himself a castle made it the centre of general havoc, of spoil for the sake of spoil, it would seem of torture for the sake of torture." There was no regard for sex, rank or calling.[2] The human fiends who did these deeds were not criminals, for society had ceased to punish such acts as crimes and seemed in the very throes of dissolution. For the certainty and severity of punishment are indices of the degree of social displeasure, or, in other words, of the idea of criminality, occasioned by an act. In times of national disorganization and anarchy, social energies are paralyzed or directed into other channels than that of justice. Wrongs remain unpunished, and this lack of punishment causes in many minds the total loss, or serious weakening, of the idea of criminality formerly associated with the act, and this the more easily in proportion as the conduct has only recently been made criminal. Thus society degenerates. For some reason, the punishment of malefactors becomes less sure than formerly. Then, their bad actions, grown common and frequently leading to success, waken less and less of the idea of criminality in the minds of the community. What the poet sings of vice is largely true of crime:

> "Yet seen too oft, familiar with her face,
> We first endure, then pity, then embrace."
>
> Pope, *Essay on Man*, Epi. ii, line 217.

Sometimes social degradation takes the reverse course, and apathy or blindness to the evil in bad acts precedes their freedom from punishment as crimes; but for enduring social progress to higher civilization, both a keen and sensitive so-

[1] Freeman, v, 242.

[2] *Ibid.*, v, 284.

cial disapproval of acts dangerous to national welfare and a strong and sure enforcement of prohibitory laws are necessary. Weakness in one generates weakness in the other. Crime ceases to be punished. Crime ceases to be crime.

> "After the nineteen winters of King Stephen,
> A reign which was no reign, when none could sit
> By his own hearth in peace; when murder common
> As nature's death, like Egypt's plague, had filled
> All things with blood; when every doorway blushed,
> Dashed red with that unhallow'd passover;
> When every baron ground his blade in blood;
> The household dough was kneaded up with blood;
> The mill-wheel turned in blood; the wholesome plow
> Lay rusting in the furrow's yellow weeds,
> Till famine dwarft the race." [1]

But all this was changed when Henry II. came to the throne. Lord of half France, as well as all England, his power was very great, and he was most resolute that all men, great and small, should be equal before the law. His first work was the destruction of two hundred castles of the robber barons, and the whole of his thirty-five years' reign was employed in strengthening, extending and enforcing royal justice. "From this time," writes Stubbs, "the reign of law may be said to have begun in England." "Perhaps no king ever did more lasting good to his people.[2]"

In the reign of Richard I. all things were salable, and some of the larger cities purchased their liberties from the king—a most important step in upward social progress. Despite the continuous absence of the sovereign, and the heavy taxation made necessary by his foreign wars, England prospered greatly. Already the freest and most orderly nation in Europe, it was fast becoming the wealthiest nation also.[3] Since the imposition of scutage under Henry II., the

[1] Tennyson, *Becket*, pp. 57, 58. [2] Traill, i, 261.

[3] The population of England was small at this time, not more than 1,500,000 to 2,000,000 inhabitants, concentrated in the south and east. The vast majority of the people were farmers. Traill, i, 362, 367, 452.

nobility had become country gentlemen, and were much more trusted and popular among the people. The reign of John made this plainly evident, when clergy, baronage and people all united to curb the detestable tyranny of an utterly vicious king. He had quarrelled with the king of France, and lost Normandy forever; with the pope, and been humbled in the dust; with all his people, and the result was Runnymede and Magna Charta, extending criminal law over the king himself. The opportune death of John preserved the throne for his infant son, Henry III.; but he soon proved himself a thoroughly weak sovereign, ruled by his favorites, who were hated by the people. There were but two acts of statute law in all his long reign—a reign filled with attempts to enforce Magna Charta upon an unwilling king, whose power for evil there seemed no practicable way to limit. The genius of Simon de Montfort began the solution of this great problem—how to make the king subject to the laws—by the creation of a Parliament, in which nobles, clergy, knights of the shire and burgesses from the towns united to represent the entire nation. Edward I., the pupil and conqueror of Simon, took up the work he had begun, and, under better auspices, pushed it to a glorious completion in the model Parliament of 1295, thus establishing upon a firm basis the English Constitution.[1] But to return to the growth of royal justice.

Under the wise rule of Henry II., "the king's own court flung open its doors to all manner of people, became a bench of professional justices, and appeared periodically in all the counties of England."[2] Henry concentrated the whole legal system of the nation around these judges expert in the law, put the Frankish inquest at the disposal of all his subjects, caused many actions to be removed into the king's court, and ordained that the inquest should be used in crim-

[1] Stubbs, *Select Charters*, Introduction. [2] Traill, i, 277.

inal procedure for great offences, upon a "large scale and as a matter of ordinary justice," by both sheriffs and royal justices.[1] The king could thus win both power and money. "He could control and he could starve the courts of the feudatories." His justice was so much better than theirs that the people, small folk as well as great, sought it gladly.[2] But they had to pay for it. How? By fines, fees and amercements. The way of justice in those days was tangled in a most intricate web of ceremonial rules, which were most strictly observed. A slip, a stammer, in uttering the set form of words, would spoil everything and give the suit to the adversary, unless the error was discounted by a fine paid to the state. He must indeed have been a bright and skillful man who expected to pass through a legal suit without one or more such fines. This evident intention to make a revenue from justice, as a substitute for taxation, must be borne in mind, when estimating the possible criminality of those on whom the multitudinous small fines were imposed. "Only by slow degrees, and in a haphazard way, do any inquiries about ordinary and non-official crimes that are less than felonies steal their way into the articles" of the inquest.[3] In the past, even gravest misdeeds had been regarded chiefly as a means of revenue to the person harmed, his right of vengeance being surrendered for a money composition. The arbitrators, or judges, also, had to be recompensed for their services in securing the pardon of the guilty man. The actions were not crimes, but torts. During Nor-

[1] The Frankish inquest is one of the very few legal institutions which we are practically sure was imported from Normandy; but it has in it the germ of trial by jury—the most distinctively English feature in the English law of the middle ages. Maitland and Pollock, i, 72.

[2] The intrusion of the king's judges into the popular courts really preserved the popular element by causing it to take a new form, one better suited than the ancient one for the needs of civilization. Freeman, v, 458.

[3] Maitland and Pollock, ii, 520.

man times, while the great offences were slowly being changed into crimes, the old procedure was still in use for minor offences, the "delites" mentioned in Magna Charta.[1] This branch of ancient penal law was "wide and indefinite to the last degree," and was much "used for oppressive and corrupt purposes."[2] The punishments inflicted were mainly small money fines, called amercements — three-penny amercements being common. In the reign of Edward I. we learn that "the causes for fines were now very numerous, and the king preferred a power of inflicting many small penalties to that of demanding heavy sums in a few grave cases."[3] "Every tort, nay every cause of civil action, was a punishable offence;" every defeated plaintiff could be amerced for a false claim, "every mistake in pleading brought an amercement. Most men in England must have expected to be amerced at least once a year," for the English were very fond of litigation.[4] A few cases are on record when real crimes were punished simply by amercement to the king,[5] but the very great majority of the men fined in this way, cannot, by the widest stretch of the name, be considered criminals. The king was evidently seeking revenue, therefore he developed this profitable system of fines, which, because customary, would not excite the indignation or opposition caused by a tax. The royal justices collected a very large sum total for "putting in mercy" communities neglecting to make "suit" or "hue and cry," that is, to perform their police duties. Thus the justices in Eyre who held sessions at Gloucester in 1221, "raised some £430 by about 220 fines and amercements, the profits of

[1] See article 20 of *Magna Charta*.

[2] Stephen, ii, 192–8.

[3] Maitland and Pollock, ii, 516; *Northumberland Assize Rolls*, pp. 92, 94.

[4] Maitland and Pollock, ii, 512, 517–8.

[5] See *Northumberland Assize Rolls*, pp. 92, 94, where two men, convicted of rape, were fined 1 mark, and at once set free on finding security.

minor offences, chiefly the offences of communities."[1] Probably the major part of these fines were collected from whole neighborhoods of law-abiding citizens, as the times go; so that, unless we hold almost all Englishmen to have been criminals, we must regard these amercements chiefly as a means of revenue to the king, in extension of the ancient custom of recompensing arbitrators and judges for their services.

Henry II. laid, broad and strong, the foundation for all future English justice. In his reign began the process by which the custom of the king's court became the common law of England.[2] This court based its judgments mainly upon the ancient dooms of the Anglo-Saxons, which feudal lawyers had translated into Latin as best they could, early in the twelfth century. In their translation it was almost inevitable that the old dooms should be modified to suit a new age, and also they added something drawn from foreign sources.[3] Since the Conquest, the king's court had been a French court, and its hands were very free. The old English laws were almost unintelligible to it, and by the twelfth century these "laws dealt with crime in a hopelessly old-fashioned way." There was no written Norman code, and as a result the court was very largely a law unto itself.[4] Naturally, the royal justices were careful to preserve whatever in the old dooms strengthened the power of the king, as against the feudal baronage, and whatever poured money into the royal treasury, like the ancient system of petty fines and amercements. Through the latter half of the twelfth and all of the thirteenth century, the extension of the king's peace, by the decisions of these royal justices, and the building up of a new case law, or law of precedent, went rapidly forward. Every action of trespass or assault in the

[1] Maitland and Pollock, ii, 555; and *Gloucestershire Pleas.*

[2] Traill, i, 277. [3] *Ibid.*, i, 276–7. [4] *Ibid.*, i, 277–80.

king's court presupposed a breach of the king's peace, and Glanvill, the earliest writer upon English law, informs us that even in his day some four or five words about the peace of our lord the king enabled an accuser to "place an assault outside the competence of the local courts."[1] In Bracton's time appellors were both permitted and encouraged to use such a form of words, which had become "the almost invariable preamble of every charge of grave crime."[2] Thus all serious forms of delinquency then known were gradually brought under the jurisdiction of the king's court, and the king's peace made "an all-embracing atmosphere."[3]

Felony was at this time becoming a name for the worst, the botless crimes. Larceny was the last of the great offences to become a plea of the crown under cover of a phrase charging the thief with breaking the king's peace.[4] In Glanvill's day it was still half tort, an actio dupli, for which the plaintiff might recover twice the value of the stolen property.[5]

Side by side with this extension of the king's peace went the increase in the reserved pleas of the crown. Through-

[1] "Nisi accusator adiciat de pace domini Regis infracta." Glanvill, i, 2–4. For the great importance of these words, see the *Select Pleas of the Crown*, pl. 21, 31, 88, 172.

[2] Maitland and Pollock, ii, 461–2; Bracton, f. 138, f. 144, etc.; *Select Pleas of the Crown*, pl. 104.

[3] In an accusation for wounding and robbery, the form of words was as follows: "Whereas, the said Alan (was) in the peace of God and of our Lord the King, there came the said William, feloniously as a felon, and in *premeditated* assault inflicted a wound on Alan, (and) robbed him of his chattels." Maitland and Pollock, ii, 461.

[4] Bracton. f. 150 b.

[5] Glanville, i, 2, xiv, 8; and Laws of Wm. I, *Select Charters*, c. 5.

"We must, however, except the crime of theft, which belongs to the sheriffs of counties, and is discussed and determined in the county courts. It also appertains to sheriffs in case of neglect on the part of Lords of Franchise, to take cognizance of scuffles, blows and wounds, unless the accuser subjoin to his charge that the offence was committed against the king's Peace." Glanville, i, 3.

out Anglo-Saxon times, we have seen that there were certain worst offences which were unemendable and bótless, that is, could not be paid for in money, no matter where they occurred, whether in or outside of the limits of the royal peace. Such actions were true crimes, and their number was steadily increasing, as society came to regard more and more offences as too heinous to be punished only by a fine; too dangerous to be left to the capricious, uncertain prosecution of the person injured. Such causes came to be known as the Reserved Pleas of the Crown, and came rightly within the jurisdiction of the king's own court. In the reign of Cnut we get the first list of these reserved pleas. "These are the rights which the king has over all men in Wessex and in Mercia." Breach of the king's special peace (grith or mund-bryce); hámsócn (attack on a man's house); forsteal (ambush); flymena-fyrmth (the harboring of fugitives from justice, outlaws); and fyrd-wite (neglect of military duty).[1] The list looks comprehensive, but "in reality it covers very little ground," for every man has his own peace.[2] Domesday book shows us "the old laws still at work," in William's time. Pleas of the crown are few.[3] The customary punishment for some of the worst crimes is still outlawry. Many acts (to us serious crimes) are still regarded as torts, for which a money equivalent should be paid to the sufferer.[4] In the Leges Henrici, we find another list of the reserved pleas. Already they extend beyond the dooms of Cnut and laws revealed by Domesday Book. Bótless crimes are treason against one's lord; breach of the Church's or king's special peace when some one is killed in the affray; open-morth (aggravated homicide);

[1] Cnut, ii, 12–15.

[2] Maitland and Pollock, ii, 451.

[3] D. B., i, 252, 238 b.; i, 179, 269 b.; i, 172.

[4] D. B., 56 b.–154 b.; i, 26–i, 172.

housebreach, arson,[1] and open theft. Other crimes are emendable with a very heavy fine, 100 shillings: breach of the king's own peace, obstruction of the king's highway, hámsócn, forsteal and the harboring of outlaws. Mere wilful homicide is still a tort, and no crime, but can be paid for, as of old, to the kindred of the deceased, whose right of vengeance is allowed, if the sum is not made over to them. The ancient system of bót and wer and wíte lingered on in Normandy, when extinct in England; and we are told that Henry II. made good his claim to homicide, robbery, mayhem, arson and rape, in his continental dominions, as crimes especially belonging to him.[2]

In direct opposition, seemingly, to this policy of extending and enforcing the king's own peace and justice, is the ancient feudal custom, extensively followed by England's Norman rulers, of granting out rights of private jurisdiction to such as would pay handsomely for them. Yet this at least implied that such rights centred in the king, and were his to sell or to withhold. Slowly the idea gains ground that the monarch is "the Fountain of Justice," and that none can rightly judge or punish who is not the king's duly authorized representative. Then, fortunately, the language used in these old private grants of jurisdiction became unintelligible, so that Angevin lawyers could maintain that they "conferred but lowly and impracticable rights." [3]

Suddenly, in the latter half of the twelfth century, the

[1] Arson, an old crime, *Leges Henrici*, 12, § 1. Mentioned by Cnut as bótless. Cnut, ii, 64. Among the felonies. Bracton, f. 146 b. Punishment was death by burning. Britton, i, 41. See a case in King John's reign, when this penalty was inflicted. *Gloucestershire Pleas*, pl. 216. But the fully developed common law substituted hanging. The thing burnt must be a house (1220). *Select Pleas of the Crown*, pl. 203; Britton, i, 41. This crime was one of the first in which intention was distinguished, indeed, had to be. Bracton, f. 146 b.

[2] Ed. de Gruchey, p. 195; *Ancienne Coutume*, c. 85; quoted by Maitland and Pollock, ii, 453.

[3] Maitland and Pollock, ii, 454.

whole unwieldy system of penal compositions disappears as if by an enchanter's wand. In its place we find a simple, bold scheme of justice, with large vague outlines. Less than a dozen crimes, or "felonies," with wide, crude definitions, "place life and limb in the king's mercy." Ordinary wilful homicide is now punished with death. This is an entirely new crime. Vengeance and compensation are alike denied to the kinsfolk of the slain.[1]

The crimes mentioned by Glanvill are:

1. Treason, "as the death of the king, or a sedition moved in the realm or army." (The word treason itself is not used.)
2. Homicide.
3. Concealment of treasure trove.
4. Arson (incendium).
5. Robbery.

[1] Maitland and Pollock, ii, 458.

Homicide, murder and manslaughter. The laws before the Conquest treat homicide "almost entirely as a wrong;" and "its development after that event was very slow." Stephen, iii, 27-8. There was practically no distinction between different kinds of homicide; the only approach to such before the Norman period, consisting in the introduction of the word "morth-slaying,"—homicide by stealth, not openly or fairly. A little later comes "murdrum," distinguished at first only by idea of secrecy—unknown offender. *See* Glanvill's definition. Later, wilful murder became the name for "an aggravated kind of felonious homicide, which was excluded from the benefit of clergy, contrasted with the felonious, but 'clergyable' crime of manslaughter." Stephen, iii, 40, 43-5. In Bracton's day, those deemed murderers were usually punished with death. Bracton, ii, 406 and 290. Britton states the penalty as death and forfeiture. Britton, i, 35. The Year-Books show the great prevalence of homicide as compared with other offences. The sphere of justifiable homicide became very narrow indeed. Society was evidently putting on pressure to crush out this dangerous evil. "Even a four-year-old child hardly escapes death for killing Robert (aged two) by misadventure." *Northumberland Assize Rolls*, p. 323; *Select Pleas of the Crown*, pl. 70, 114, 188; (21 Edward, 1 Stat., 2). This reminds us of the modern Chinese, who flay alive a three-year-old child for the horrible crime of accidentally killing his mother. (Instance, near Shanghai; account of a missionary.) The act, not the intent, constitutes the crime.

6. Rape.
7. "Generale crimen falsi."[1]

He disposes of minor offences in a very few words, merely stating that he does not intend to treat of thefts and other judgments which pertain to the sheriffs in the people's courts. When Bracton wrote, early in the thirteenth century, in the reign of Henry III., English "criminal law consisted of eleven known offences, crimes or felonies, nearly all of which were capital, and an unspecified number of misdemeanors."[2]

The felonies were:

1. Laesa Majestas.
2. Falsum.
3. Concealment of Treasure Trove.
4. Homicide.
5. Wounding.
6. Mayhem.
7. False Imprisonment.
8. Robbery.
9. Arson.
10. Rape (including abduction).
11. Theft.

There were a few other true criminal offences beside the felonies, punished by discretionary fines, which had taken the place of the old pre-appointed wites, paid to the king, as head of the state. Sometimes terms of imprisonment were added, but these were very often intended simply to secure the payment of the money fine. Misconduct of royal officials, tampering with some royal prerogative, infringing, even slightly, any royal right, and riot, were acts thus punished. Notice how hard these penalties must have borne

[1] Under which head are included: de falsis chartis, de falsis mensuris, de falsis moneta.

[2] Stephen, ii, 201–2 and 219.

upon the wilful and turbulent Norman nobility, whom the king and people had united to suppress, or curb, by social punishment. Maintenance — armed anarchy, interfering with the due course of justice—was just beginning to be noticed in the reign of Edward I. Later, this offence became very important, and it was not finally suppressed until Tudor times.[1] The writ of trespass (for forcible entry) was in the time of Henry III. and Edward I. taking a foremost place in the scheme of actions. The Northumberland assize rolls contain many tales of deliberate rapine and pillage, by armed bands. These were largely "wrongs done by gentlemen, who at the head of their retainers ravaged the manors of their neighbors."[2] But such acts were not crimes. They were harms to an individual, punished, when possible, by heavy damages. The state did not take the initiative, nor prosecute on its own account. In the thirteenth century, "protection against fraud was yet in its infancy."[3] All the minor forms of force and fraud were but little noticed—regarded merely as torts—compensated sometimes by damages, assessed by a tribunal, instead of by the old pre-appointed bót. And ancient law had practically no punishment for those who tried to do harm but did not succeed in doing it.[4] All immoral conduct came within the jurisdiction of the ecclesiastical courts, of which more anon.

Such great changes in English criminal and penal law certainly amount to a revolution; but, like most great revolutions, it had been prepared for gradually. Many causes —social and economic—had been long at work; but among them we may single out one which seems almost sufficient in itself to account for the utter breakdown and disappearance of the old penal customs. The introduction of the Norman monetary system had doubled or trebled the

[1] Stephen, iii, 234 and 238.

[2] Maitland and Pollock, ii, 525.

[3] *Ibid.*, ii, 533.

[4] *Ibid.*, ii, 507.

amount of the Anglo-Saxon fines — the bót and wer and wite. The wer of the poor ceorl, or villanus, had become £4; that of the theign £25;[1] and money was worth many times then what it is now. Few men could pay the large sums demanded in composition for their offences, and there were two alternatives — either to "flee for it," and become an outlaw, or to be sold as a slave.[2] The outlaw forfeits everything; life and limb and all that he possesses. He becomes a criminal, even though his original offence was only a tort, for he has refused to abide by the law of the land, and is now a public enemy. In this way very many men were made criminals, and fell into the king's hands. He could choose their punishment, whether death or mutilation, branding as bad and dangerous men, or it might be exile or loss of goods. No new legislation was necessary. The Norman kings were not fast bound by ancient custom in this respect. William I. preferred mutilation to the death penalty. His son, Henry I., hanged thieves taken in the act,[3] and from other offenders would sometimes accept and sometimes refuse a money composition.[4] Henry II. "hanged homicides and exiled traitors," and in his reign the loss of hand or foot was common. Very gradually during the thirteenth century, hanging came to be regarded as the fitting penalty for all felons. It is most probable that the royal judges had large discretionary power in such matters. Certainly, there was no direct legislation causing the change. But "a man who had forfeited everything for his crime could not complain if a foot was taken instead of an eye, or he was hanged instead of being beheaded.'[5]

[1] Leg. Hen., 70, § 1, 76, § 4; Leg. William I., c. 8.

[2] Maitland and Pollock, ii. 458.

[3] Flor. Wig., ii, 57.

[4] Wm. Malmesbury, *Gesta Regum*, ii, 641.

[5] Maitland and Pollock, ii, 460.

What effect had all these changes upon the amount of crime in England? For Norman days, we have, of course, no criminal statistics and but fragmentary historic records. Therefore it is impossible to prove the increase or decrease of crime by figures. We must seek the natural or inevitable results of new laws and changed conditions, enforcing such arguments, whenever possible, by historic evidence. In this search we should bear in mind two facts, revealed by a careful study of modern criminal statistics and of history in every age, namely: 1. That increased social disapprobation and repression of some form of conduct constantly results in the changing of torts into crimes, or in the creation of a crime from some action hitherto unpunished; 2. The enforcement of a new social prohibition, or of some old law hitherto unused, always means an addition to the nation's crime and criminals. Laws which seem to many as unjust encroachments upon old liberties will naturally provoke many offences among a sturdy and liberty-loving people, innately rebellious at restraint.

Main lines of social progress during the Norman age took the direction of greatly increased royal power and the unification of a more equal, more progressive system of law, enforced over all the land by the might of king and people. Readers of the earlier pages of this chapter may have been able to trace the way in which this social progress was promoted and maintained by the transfer of many actions, hitherto unpunished, or punished only as torts, into the category of true crimes; but, as the evidence is fragmentary and largely indirect, it will be well to state it more clearly. Norman kings were very stern in putting down the turbulent feudal nobility, and the people very zealously supported them in this most necessary work for social welfare. This means that the laws decreeing criminal punishment for any infringement of, or tampering with, some royal prerogative or right, for rebellion, robbery, riot, and possibly for maintenance (in Edward I.'s reign), were probably enforced, as they could not have been in Anglo-Saxon times, and as we know they were not during the later era of the new feudalism. The enforcement of these laws must have made many criminals among the nobles and their warlike followers, whose long resistance ended in their almost complete destruction, although wars against them were few. As Freeman writes: Henry I. "at least taught the highest and proudest of his nobles that there was a power in the land higher than their own. Where he reigned, rebellion and private war were not rights to be boasted of, but crimes against the law, which the law knew how to punish."[1] This severity was certainly not lessened under Henry II., and in earlier years William I. and William Rufus curbed their noble feudatories with a strong hand.

Treason, in Norman times, was a very elastic crime with vague limits, capable of indefinite expansion in developing the power of the king. The *Mirrour of Justices* (page 21), in the thirteenth century, shows this plainly. Beside the primitive treasons, aiding the nation's enemies,[2] betrayal of the person of the king, the army or the realm,[3] flight from battle[4] and a few coinage and forgery offences,[5] the crime of treason ("majestas") now included: Plotting or imagining the king's death, disinheriting the king of his realm, ravishing the queen, the king's eldest daughter, "or nurse, or king's aunt heir to the king," and also, adds the unknown author of this book: "The crime of majestas, or offence against the king, is neighbour to many other offences; for all those who commit perjury, whereby one belies one's faith to the king, fall into this offence." A large number of other treason-

[1] Freeman, v, 164 and note.
[2] Tacitus, *Germania*, c. 12.
[3] Glanvill, i, 2; Bracton, f. 118b.
[4] Cnut, ii, 77; Leges. Henr., 13, § 12.
[5] Aethelst., ii, 14; Cnut, ii, 8.

able crimes are also specified, all relating to dishonesty or misconduct of public officials, or assumption by them of too great power.[1] The law of Englishry must have made punishment for secret murder much more frequent and more certain. The knives then worn by all Englishmen were prone to stab on very slight provocation, and the killing of a Frenchman after the Conquest must have been an honorable and praiseworthy act at first among the conquered English. But the heavy fines, rigorously collected from each community failing to arrest and deliver over the man-slayer to justice, were probably quite sufficient to change social approbation or sufferance of such conduct into social disapprobation and criminal prosecution. Secret killing, therefore, was probably a crime in Norman days, and from the temper of the English there must have been many criminals. The Year Books for the Plantagenet period support this belief, for a large proportion of the cases mentioned relate to prosecutions for homicide;[2] showing also the great prevalence of homicide as compared to other offences in Norman times and to the same offence in modern England. The nation has been very successful in its long struggle to crush out this form of crime.[3] William the Conqueror punished very

[1] *The Mirrour of Justices*, pp. 16–19.

Treason—In Norman Times.—Piracy by one of the king's subjects on another was held to be treason. Stephen, ii, 246. By 21 Edward III. (1348) "an appeal of treason lay for killing of malice prepense a person sent in aid of the king in his wars with certain men at arms." See case of Sir John Gerberge. Hale, i, 80–1. "In the following year John at Hill was attainted of high treason for the death of Adam de Walton: 'nuntii domini regis missi in mandatum ejus exequendum.'"

[2] *Year Books*, and Stephen, iii, 34.

[3] *Murder.*—The original murdrum was a very heavy fine, 46 marks: 40 to the king, 6 to the kinsfolk: exacted from the hundred where the man (supposed to be a foreigner), was slain. In some cases the fine was exacted even for an accidental death. Bracton regarded this as an abuse. Surely we cannot accuse all the hundred men as being criminals. The murder fine was abolished in 1340. *See* 14 Edw. III., Stat. 1, c. 4. *Also* Maitland and Pollock, ii.

severely the ravishing of women, probably a very common offence in a land filled with foreign soldiery.[1] There is very little case law on record, but after the Conquest rape was probably bótless if the woman pressed her suit,[2] and the second Statute of Westminster (1285) made death the penalty for all cases of this offence, even though the woman did not wish to sue. This is a good example of the change from tort to crime.[3] It is said that William Rufus would permit none to break the laws but himself, and we know that Henry I. sternly inflicted the death penalty upon robbers and thieves taken in the act.. As the Old Chronicle tells us: "In his reign Ralph Bassett did a fine day's work in Leicestershire, for he hanged forty-four thieves, an exploit without a precedent."[4] Freeman believes that King Henry I. succeeded in "bringing all men, of whatever race and whatever rank, within the grasp of the royal authority," and that this "common subjection of Normans and English to the kingly power, when the kingly power alone represented law and right, did more than anything else to bind Normans and English into one nation."[5] The work was accomplished mainly by the extension and enforcement of criminal law, and the increase of the nation's criminals. It was all made possible by the support the people—the body of the nation —gave the king. Was not the process a most necessary, a most educational one? Does not civilization advance by converting tort into crime?

In the utter anarchy of Stephen's reign crime practically ceased, for society was either powerless to punish, or desired for the time nothing better than unlimited license.

[1] By castration and blinding. See *Anglo-Saxon Chronicle* (Anno 1087); also Maitland and Pollock, ii, 489.

[2] Leg. William I., c. 18; Henry, 13, § 6.

[3] Stat. West, ii, c. 34; Britton, i, 55; Coke, Third Institute, pp. 180, 433.

[4] *A. S. Chron.* (Anno 1124), p. 376.

[5] Freeman, v, 166.

But in the reign of Henry II. the robber barons again became criminals, for social justice was enforced against them. The aid of the people made the triumph of law and order permanent. The increase in the reserved pleas of the crown, coupled with great improvements in legal procedure, rapidly changed tort into crime, rapidly multiplied criminals. From this time society was called "upon a very large scale and as a matter of ordinary practice" to indict its criminal members, and we learn that more and more offences were included in this charge. The initiation of a penal action was no longer left to the individual harmed or to his next of kin. If the sufferer dared not or did not wish to prosecute, society would bring the action for him. "From this time onward a statement made upon oath by a set of jurors representing a hundred, to the effect that such an one is suspected of such a crime, is sufficient to put a man upon his trial."[1] Society accepted and supported this system of criminal procedure and held itself responsible to the king for the prosecution of its criminal members. This was very important in creating true criminal offences. Society, and not the individual harmed, became the prosecutor, and society inflicted the punishment for the sake of the general welfare. People were being trained to think of the accusation, prosecution and punishment of offenders as of great social importance—to consider the wrong done to society rather than the harm to the individual. The introduction of this indictment procedure must have led to a large increase in the number of prosecutions. It made punishment much more sure. It changed tort into crime. It must have greatly increased the amount of crime and the number of criminals. Those indicted were at once sent to the ordeal —"the judgment of God." But we find an increasing skepticism with regard to this form of trial, and note that those

[1] Traill, i, 291.

who passed the ordeal were nevertheless banished from the kingdom as dangerous suspects, forbidden to return on pain of death. Practically all who went to the ordeal, therefore, were punished as criminals.[1] Henry II. included larceny among the crimes named at the inquest, and this was the last of the early great offences to become a plea of the crown, under cover of a phrase charging the thief with breaking the king's peace. By the 13th century ordinary wilful homicide had become legally a crime, punishable with death, and the limits of justifiable manslaughter were then so narrow that a child of four years hardly escaped death for the accidental killing of another, aged two.[2] Death by a passionate blow was frightfully prevalent in those days, and society was slowly wakening to the idea that this was socially dangerous, and should be punished as serious crime. Probably the nation was not yet sufficiently convinced of this to enforce the penalty frequently and so make the action truly criminal, but pressure was certainly being exerted in this direction by the most intelligent portion of the community.

The forest legislation of the Normans has not yet been mentioned, for it is somewhat doubtful whether violators of these laws should be classed among the criminals, or merely as offenders against the king as an individual. Forest laws were no new thing in England, but in Anglo-Saxon days every man could kill wild beasts upon his own land. William the Conqueror made hunting a royal monopoly, the exclusive privilege or business of the king and a few special friends. Forest laws were very cruel and very strictly enforced. Wealthy Englishmen seem, at first, to have been

[1] Form of the inquest in criminal cases: "Do you suspect any of murder, robbery, larceny, or the like?" "This question was addressed by royal officers to selected representatives of every neighbourhood, and answered upon oath." Traill, i, 291.

[2] *Northumberland Assize Rolls*, p. 323.

special sufferers. Doubtless the chase was one of their greatest pleasures, which they were loth to relinquish. In the reign of William Rufus fifty such men at one time went to the ordeal to prove their innocence.[1] William of Malmesbury declares that the forest tribunals punished with equal severity rich and poor, Normans and Englishmen.[2] Henry I. is praised by the chronicler for keeping the hunting throughout his entire kingdom under his own hand.[3] "Peace he made for man and deer," and he saved England from "the curse of a little Nimrod in every manor." Probably there was much good in this. At any rate the forest legislation of Henry II., that great and wise sovereign, was but little less severe than that enforced by his grandfather. But all through Norman times outlaws received much public sympathy, because of the brutal harshness of these forest laws, which, breaking up as they did the favorite sport of a sturdy and obstinate people, must have caused many offenders among both Normans and Englishmen. Can we rightly call these men criminals? *Crime is any act punished by society as a wrong against itself.* The forest laws and tribunals "avowedly stood outside of the common law of the land—existed only for the king's personal pleasure," and were ruled only by his personal will.[4] Yet the people, in general, supported their Norman kings, and with good reason, for one tyrant was far better than many. It was better to groan occasionally under royal punishment for forest violations than to suffer the anarchy which must surely come if the wilful nobility and gentry were left unchecked to their own devices. Forest laws fell "far more heavily on the great men than on the bulk of the people,"[5] and as a means for extending the king's power,

[1] Eadmer, *Hist. Nov.*, p. 48; Freeman, v, 124. [2] Wm. of M., ii, 501.

[3] Henry of Huntingdon (221 b.), after H.'s death; and William of Newburgh, i, 21.

[4] Freeman, v, 455. [5] *Ibid.*, v, 164; Henry of Huntingdon, 221 b.

unifying law, and curbing the haughty baronage, forest tribunals must have been very effective and socially beneficial. This would explain their persistent use under Henry II., whose whole reign was devoted to the extension and enforcement of more equal justice. For these reasons it seems right to count offenders against forest laws among the nation's criminals, and surely their number must have been at times very great.[1]

The evidence seems to warrant the belief that there was much more crime in Norman than in Anglo-Saxon England; that the amount of crime greatly increased under strong, able kings, when the nation was prosperous and advancing, and very greatly decreased under weak sovereigns, when society was sick almost unto death. The increase of crime was due, in large measure, to the amount of outlawry occasioned by heavier money penalties; to improvement in legal procedure, turning torts into crimes; to the enforcement of true social punishment for actions hitherto practically unpunished, or punished only as harms to an individual. New crime largely took the direction of acts antagonistic to the growth of royal power, or to the unification and extension of royal justice over all the land—the two main lines along which national welfare then demanded upward progress.

Although history surely proves the wise enlargement and much more sure enforcement of criminal law in Norman England, as compared with the centuries before the Conquest, yet this only throws into darker relief the weakness of social justice and the consequent small amount of crime in that earlier period. Even under Norman kings the criminal law was exceedingly inefficient. Murder, highway robbery and other crimes of violence were of common occurrence, and, "whatever the law might wish, the male-

[1] Benedict, i, 92, 94; Stubbs' Preface to Benedict, ii, lxxxiii; *Select Charters*, p. 149; Freeman, v, 682.

factor's fate was like to be outlawry rather than any more modern punishment;"[1] while the records reveal an alarming number of evil-doers who escaped all punishment for their misdeeds. Upon the presentment rolls of the jurors we find continually the same sad story: Malefactors came by night to the man's house and slew him and all his family, and robbed his goods. "We do not know who they were; we suspect no one."[2] Life in Norman days must have been lamentably insecure, despite the boasts of the chroniclers. Murderers, thieves and robbers were rarely hanged, and the "hue and cry" after them was an utterly insufficient social protection. Men who had tracked cattle thieves to the county boundary generally turned home again, saying, "Let Gloucestershire folk mind Gloucestershire rogues." The justices in Eyre, who visited this county in 1221, after a long time in which criminal law had lain dormant during civil war, were told of three hundred and thirty acts of homicide, beside other offences. The best they could do in support of law and order was to hang some fourteen men, mutilate one and issue one hundred sentences of outlawry. But this again adds weight to the belief that wrong ceases to be crime when society is disorganized and at war within itself. In more peaceful times the proportion of criminals punished was much greater, although their punishment was still mainly outlawry. Thus, in 1256 the Northumberland justices heard of seventy-seven murders, for which four men were hanged and seventy-two outlawed, and seventy-eight other felonies, for which they hanged fourteen people and outlawed fifty-four. Reports from the same county, in 1279, revealed sixty-eight murder cases, for which two men were hanged and sixty-five outlawed, and one hundred and ten other

[1] Maitland and Pollock, ii, 555.

[2] Traill, i, 295.

felonies for which twenty suffered death and seventy-five were declared "lawless," having "fled for it."[1]

We must remember that in the thirteenth century, mere wilful homicide was just beginning to be made a crime; that the people generally were very much addicted to knifing and other passionate blows, which were considered too highly natural to be really criminal, even until the nineteenth century; that robberies were very often the work of gentlemen raiders, and, in this form, not yet thought to be dishonorable acts.[2] In ancient law robbery is open, theft secret. Bracton (f. 150 b) has to argue that the robber is really a thief, so much more detested was the covert than the open injury. In the same way, morth-slaying (homicide by stealth) was made a crime centuries before passionate manslaughter ceased to be the natural and honorable way of settling differences. This feeling has come down to our own day in the practice of duelling and fist-fighting, and it is only recently (since 1803) that desperate, unsuccessful attempts at homicide, with cuts and blows, have become really criminal.[3] Doubtless the enforcement of justice was much more difficult in wild Northumberland and other northern and western counties of England, than in the more thickly settled and civilized farming regions of the south and east. Probably outlaws were very generally driven into the west and north, and their escape from any other form of social punishment

[1] *Northumberland Assize Rolls.*

[2] See Case of Sir John Gerberge, Hale, i, 81.

[3] *Larceny.*—"In the thirteenth century manifest grand larceny was a capital crime, and all grand larceny was becoming capital. But it is most probable that throughout the Norman period only the thief, both manifest and great, was absolutely beyond all hope of emendation." See Maitland and Pollock, ii, 496.

"Folks are saying that the limit of twelve pence allows a man to steal enough to keep himself from starvation for eight days without being guilty of a capital crime. They are also boasting rightly or wrongly that the law of England is milder than that of France." See Cambridge Gloss on Britton, i, 56.

was rendered easy by the church right of sanctuary, which was fast becoming a public nuisance.[1]

Benefit of clergy saved another set of reprobates from the punishment they richly merited, but as yet this privilege shielded only clerks ordained into the holy orders of the Church. William the Conqueror had separated the courts spiritual from the courts temporal; in this way securing a free field for development of criminal law and royal justice among the laity. This was wise and statesmanlike, but it led almost immediately to the exemption of churchmen from all temporal jurisdiction, which became one of the most crying evils of the later Middle Ages. The Church courts held by compurgation, so that half a dozen or a dozen friends could swear a man free from all punishment for his misdeeds. The Church might draw no drop of blood, but it could sentence to life imprisonment, stripes, degradation, penance, etc. In practice these last two penalties were, with few exceptions, the only ones inflicted, even for the basest deeds of murder and adultery. "One clerk ruined the honor of a family and tried to murder its head. Another put poison in the sacramental cup."[2] The only punishment was two years' deprivation from office. Henry II. struggled hard to curb this dangerous benefit of clergy, but the people sided with the Church, and after the murder of Becket, the royal "Customs" were entirely abandoned, and churchmen and the offenders against them were left to the mild reproofs of their priestly judges. Sins of heresy and sorcery, incest and bigamy, fornication and adultery, came entirely within the cognizance of these ecclesiastical courts, which were very generally regarded by the people as the shield of the widow and the orphan, and in general, of the most unprotected portion of the community, from the hideous punishments of mutilation common in that age. No doubt this mild jurisdiction

[1] Traill, ii, 297.

[2] *Ibid.*, i, 260.

was useful in preserving many of the better educated men when any education was rare. Thus it placed a premium upon the acquisition of some little knowledge, and it was useful also as a protest against those inhuman punishments for crime. But the abuses of the system (practically preserving churchmen of every grade and all men who could read from the possibility of becoming criminals) became so markedly dangerous in later years, that in the time of Edward I.—"the age of triumphant Catholicism passing into decline"—it became possible, at last, to introduce the most necessary reforms, and begin to make the guilty clerk suffer as a criminal for his evil deeds.

Thus, true criminal law was extended and enforced by the king and people over the feudal baronage and the Christian Church, and by all orders of the people over their despotic kings. We shall see this great work of making all men equal under the law continued throughout the centuries, progressing, as it always will progress, so long as England is advancing into greater knowledge, wiser intelligence and truer social morality; but this work, this progress, means an ever larger number of social prohibitions, and, so far as history teaches, an ever greater volume of the nation's crime and criminals.

CHAPTER VIII

PARLIAMENTARY GOVERNMENT AND THE NEW FEUDALISM.

1307–1485

THE fourteenth and fifteenth centuries of English history present the rise, trial and failure of a great constitutional experiment—the rise of Parliament to sovereign power and the attempt to make it the direct instrument of government. Upon the rights and precedents then established was erected the firm system of constitutional government and national liberty won and secured during the seventeenth, eighteenth and nineteenth centuries. The rise of the House of Commons to the foremost rank in Parliament, the control of the executive by the legislative, and most of the minor developments of Lancastrian and Yorkist reigns were in line with the true upward growth of the national life, as later history abundantly proves. Why then did this first experiment in government by representatives of the people prove such a complete failure at the time, even though the failure was fruitful of future good?

1. "The nation had not yet learned the qualities needed for such a high stage of self-government."

A few of the new social prohibitions which the House of Commons tried to establish will perhaps suffice to make this manifest. Villains shall not send their sons to school. No one under the degree of freeholder shall keep a dog. Laborers must accept the low wages fixed by Parliament and must not leave their place of residence to seek employment elsewhere.

2. There were inherent defects in the representative system of that time.

The changes which fostered the growing power of the House of Commons, and induced it, nay, almost compelled it, to take a commanding position in the government, were many and important, actually throwing out of gear the old political machinery. Ever since Magna Charta, the baronage, clergy and people had united to curb and limit the too despotic power of the king. The barons of the thirteenth century had outlined the system by which the king was to be controlled; and the genius of Edward I., accepting the growth of the constitutional idea, had created the model Parliament from the three estates of his realm, harmonized the wishes of a mighty king with those of a determined people, and established a balance of executive and legislative powers by which the king was stronger, as a constitutional ruler, than any of his despotic ancestors, for he could rely on the support of all his people, now that "that which touches all" had become "the concern of all." But it required a wise and strong king to maintain this balance of power, and after Edward I. England had a succession of boy kings, shadow kings, or kings who owed their crowns to Parliament; while the hundred years' war with France and the constant royal need of money made the crown more and more dependent upon Parliament, and especially the House of Commons, which held the purse. Grants of money were made dependent upon the redress of grievances by the king, and most of the many limitations of despotic royal power during this period were thus paid for.[1] The work of limiting the authority of the crown went rapidly onward. Before the close of the fourteenth century two kings of England had

[1] Stubbs, ii, 599–600. All that was won by Parliament in its long struggle against royal despotism was won for the Commons, and the decision of many great questions passed irrevocably into their hands.

been dethroned by Parliament,—here is true social punishment for the head of the state. In the person of Richard II. royal power had sunk to its lowest ebb; and, after 1376, it became established that not only the great ministers of state, but the courtiers of the royal household and even the king's mistress, were responsible for their conduct to Parliament and the nation, and that no amount of personal service to the king could save his haughty and law-scorning followers from trial and conviction as criminals before the bar of the House of Lords upon impeachment by the Commons.[1] "Great as were the offences of Edward II., Stapledon the treasurer and Baldeck the chancellor were the more immediate and direct objects of national indignation. They were scarcely less hated than the Dispensers and shared their fate."[2] The "Good Parliament" (1376), impeached Lord Latimer, Lord Neville, Richard Lyons, Alice Perrers and many of the dishonest courtiers of Edward III., and from this time Parliament became "the grand jury of the nation, the sworn recognitors of national rights and grievances," punishing criminal wickedness in high places.[3] The impeachment of Michael de la Pole (1386) and of Sir Simon Burley and his companions (1388) was the work of the House of Commons, which later impeached Archbishop Arundel for his conduct as chancellor. Richard II. insisted that the laws were "in his own mouth and breast," and repeatedly broke the statutes of the land. Parliament deposed him and gave his crown to another, showing its power by changing the succession. This act closed the long struggle between constitutional government and the old idea of royal prerogative. The nation had asserted and maintained its right and might to punish as criminals all who did not obey the laws, even the king and his greatest ministers.

[1] *Rot. Parl.*, ii, 323–330 and 355; Stubbs, ii, 593.
[2] Stubbs, ii, 592.
[3] Stubbs, ii, 593; *Rot. Parl.*, ii, 323–330, 355; iii, 156–8, 241.

During the fourteenth century every department of government—legislative, executive, judicial—came directly or indirectly under the control of Parliament. The great bulk of new legislation was initiated by the lower house, as will appear from a comparison of the Rolls of Parliament with the Statute Book,[1] and the Commons were simply indefatigable in suggesting remedies for the many dangerous abuses prevalent in the courts of justice.[2] In 1351, 1352 and 1353 were passed the Statutes of Provisors, of Treason, of Praemunire, each of them vindicating national rights as against royal prerogative.[3]

Under the Normans, treason was essentially a crime against the king, so heinous that mere death was far too light a punishment. Its limits were undefined, and it had gradually been stretching out to cover many minor offences. Now, at the prayer of the people, "high treason was defined, and this act remained a bulwark of the subject's liberties" till the development of constructive treasons under the Tudors. One new treason, however, was created: "The making war against the king in his realm." [4] It seems most strange to us that so great a social evil should not have been made a crime until the middle of the fourteenth century; but when feudalism was at its height, making war against the king was an acknowledged right of the baronage, under certain conditions.[5]

The Statutes of Provisors and Praemunire dealt with the relations of England to the papacy. Henceforward there were to be no appointments by the pope to English benefices, and no appeals to him from the ecclesiastical courts. These acts were confirmed and enlarged many times, in 1364, 1377, 1390, 1393; but a system of division of spoils between the

[1] Stubbs, ii, 604. [2] *Ibid.*, ii, 639–40.

[3] Provisors, 25 Ed. III., Stat. 4; and Traill, ii, 147.

[4] Statute of Treason, 25 Edw. III., Stat. 5, c. 2. [5] See Stubbs.

crown and the papacy had come about, and the repetition of the statutes only registers their failure.

The reign of Richard II. was a "fruitful time for declaring and enhancing of treason in Parliament;"[1] such conduct becoming more and more crime against the state, rather than the person of the king. Parliament asserted its right to decide upon new points of possible treason as they arose.[2] In 1381 it was made treason "to begin a riot and rumor" against the king and his realm.[3] There were appeals of treason in 1387–9 and 1399, for "leading Richard to misgovern the country."[4] In 1397, Richard II. induced Parliament to declare it "high treason to attempt the reversal of the acts done in that session."[5] The reign of Henry VI. saw a few more treasons added to the list—some of them rather ridiculous.[6] Lifting of men or cattle out of England by Welsh marauders was thus made high treason by (20 Henry VI., c. 3) 1441. There were constant attainders of treason by Parliament during the Wars of the Roses.[7]

Until late in the fourteenth century the Commons felt themselves too weak to stand alone. They were but humble petitioners. The lords and higher clergy were their national leaders, and on them they still relied. But from the reign of Edward I., a widespread revolt against clerical influence in political and social life begins to show itself. The higher clergy were becoming ever more and more worldly and subservient to king or papacy. The lower were fast losing every trace of the last revival of religion. The people ceased to acknowledge church leadership in matters political and judicial, and tried hard to end the clerical jurisdiction over the laity.[8] "The church courts were the Church's worst en-

[1] Hale, i, 263. [2] Stubbs, iii, 536. [3] 5 Rich. II., Stat. 1, c. 6.
[4] Stephen, ii, 251–2. [5] 21 Rich. II., c. 20; and Stubbs, iii, 537.
[6] 2 Henry VI., c. 21 (1423), 8 Henry VI., c. 6 (1429). [7] Hale, i, 271.
[8] For an early evidence of this see the Petition of the Commons (1344): "That no motion made by the clergy to the injury of the laity might be granted without examination before the King and the Lords."

emy, and their abuses were among the first marks of the attacks of the new learning;" their immorality, their cost, their long delays.[1] In the attempt to reform these courts and strictly limit their jurisdiction, the "laicizing" movement of the age was strongest, but the majority of lords spiritual in the Upper House of Parliament, prevented much success. Rioting and mob violence against bishops, priors and their servants, witness to the changed public sentiment; as do also the great and growing reluctance to pay tithes and the marked falling off of religious foundations.[2] The suppression of the Templars (1307–8), the increasing dislike of the friars and of the "unbridled multitude" of the religious, are signs of the coming revolt, not only against the abuses of mediæval religion, but against that religion itself.[3] Yet even in her decline the influence of the Church penetrated into every corner of society, in politics, education, and care for the poor.

The high nobility had also earned the distrust of the people, when the Lords Ordainors failed to realize the strong new trend of the national life, and insisted upon governing for the people instead of by the people. This mistake enabled even the weak Edward II. to reassert his authority and to define the rights of Parliament as against the hated Ordinances. But the nobility refused to heed the warning so plainly given. They became more and more selfish and reactionary, retiring from the great work of upbuilding constitutional liberty to fashion a new system of feudalism, which soon became the great disruptive force of the age, and a deadly peril to justice, order, and national well-being.

The two greatest safeguards of liberty are sure and equal

[1] Traill, ii, 26.

[2] See Canterbury riot (May, 1327) against clerical privilege. Ilchester riot, 1348. The appointment of the first lay chancellor in 1340.

[3] Traill, ii, 25.

justice, and some successful form of constitutional government. The first of these safeguards is well-nigh indispensable. The age we are considering was undoubtedly one of great constitutional progress, but it was also one of increasing lawlessness, of intimidation and corruption of courts of justice, of the protection of malefactors by the high and mighty of the land, both in Church and State. The Church of the fourteenth century was hopelessly corrupt.[1] Both public and private morality seemed falling to lower and lower depths.[2]

The middle and laboring classes were not so ignorant as has been generally supposed. Some knowledge of reading and writing must have been quite common among them,[3] for even the villains could send their children to the monastery schools.[4] But such knowledge did but increase the number of wrong-doers who could escape punishment as criminals by securing benefit of clergy and trial in the ecclesiastical courts.[5]

It was a time of general disorganization. There was much luxury, much misery and little sympathy. "Vice was rampant and taken for granted. There was no unity of public interest, no singleness of political aim, no heroism of self-sacrifice. The clergy were neither intelligent enough to guide education nor strong enough to repress heresy."[6] Warwick, "the king-maker," with his army of 30,000 liveried hirelings, and other great lords, with their ruffianly followers, enriched by foreign wars and grown more wealthy than the Crown, overawed king, Parliament and courts of justice, and might was fast becoming synonymous with right. "All that

[1] Th. Rogers, p. 165.

[2] Stubbs, ii, 654.

[3] Stubbs, iii, 627; Th. Rogers, p. 165.

[4] 7 Henry IV, c. 17 (1405–6); *Rot. Parl.*, iii, 602.

[5] 25 Edw. III., Stat. 3 (old), Stat. 6 (new); "An Ordinance for the Clergy" (1350); Stephen i, 461.

[6] Stubbs. ii, 655.

was good and great in mediæval life was languishing even to death," writes Stubbs;[1] and when Henry VII ascended the throne, in 1485, there were but few signs of returning health.

It was in such a time that the first great attempt at government by Parliament, *i. e.*, by representatives of the people of England, was made. Despite the growing disorder, injustice and immorality, the middle classes of the fifteenth century were prosperous as never before. The nobles were busy with their own feuds, and flocks, herds and fields of grain were not much disturbed, even during the Wars of the Roses. Commerce flourished in the towns. The disorderly elements of the age circled round the feudal lords, and while protected by them, warred against each other. It was a time of the strong yeoman and his stalwart sons, the thrifty burgess and his trusty apprentices, and it was the representatives of such men—burgesses from the towns uniting with knights of the shire—who now took the lead in Parliament, and attempted to press back the advancing flood of anarchy. The troubles and weaknesses of the age forced a rapid development of constitutional government, but put a fiercer strain upon parliamentary institutions than they were then able to bear. The Commons of England had grown strong, but had not yet learned how to use their strength wisely. They were still the slaves of the blindest prejudice. The shire-moot, the basis of the representative system, was falling into decay, and the Lords were able frequently to return their own servants to Parliament. There was absolutely no assurance that the statutes passed by one Parliament would be enforced by the next, an evil which cabinet government has since remedied. Consequently, the House of Commons seems always seeking a champion among the great lords, who believed their power, wealth and even personal safety dependent upon the maintenance of the bands of ruffians who disgraced them,

[1] Stubbs, iii, 632.

and whom Parliament and the people were trying to punish as criminals.

"The livery of a great lord," writes Stubbs, "was as effective security to a malefactor as was the benefit of clergy to the criminous clerk."[1] The supporters of maintenance and livery were too powerful for the government.[2] Through the long list of statutes enacted against them, we can see these practices growing stronger and stronger,[3] and the evil was by no means confined to the great lords alone. How important an element of disruption lay in this custom of livery and maintenance during the latter Middle Ages may be judged from a statute of Richard II. aimed, however, only against small offenders, that declares: "Divers people of small revenue of land, rent, or other possessions, do make great retinue of people, in many parts of the realm, giving them hats and other liveries . . . . taking of them the value of the same livery, or percase, the double value, by such covenant and assurance that every of them shall maintain other in all quarrels, be they reasonable or unreasonable, to the great mischief and oppression of the people."[4]

Unfortunately the nation did not succeed in punishing as criminals the liveried hirelings of the great lords, and it permitted the extension of benefit of clergy to many evil-doers far outside the pale of holy orders. Consequently we cannot

[1] Stubbs, iii, 552.

[2] *Rot. Parl.*, ii, 10, 62, 166, 201, 228, 368, for petitions against maintenance.

[3] Edw. I., Stat. Westmin., i, cc. 25, 28, 33; 1 Edw. III., Stat. 2, c. 14 (1326); 4 Edw. III., c. 11 (1330); 20 Edw. III., cc. 4, 5, 6 (1346); 1 Ric. II., c. 4 (1377); 7 Ric. II., c. 15 (1383).

Closely connected are statutes of liveries. 1 Ric. II., c. 7 (1377); 16 Ric. II., c. 4 (1392); 20 Ric. II., c. 1 (1396). This last act also confirmed the Statute of Northampton: 2 Edw. III., c. 3 (1328), "which enacted that no one should go armed except on certain specified occasions."

For the great importance of making maintenance and livery criminal offences, See Stubbs, iii, 50–2; Stephen, iii, 236–9.

[4] 1 Richard II., c. 7 (1377).

rightly call the man who slew another in his lord's feud a criminal, any more than the malefactor who escaped punishment through the laxity of the ecclesiastical courts. The Commons perceived the nation's danger, and tried repeatedly to make both maintenance and livery crimes; to punish the anarchic lords as well as their evil dependents. But the lawless forces of the age proved themselves too strong for the yet unhardened institutions of representative government, and it required the strong arm of a despotic king, following up the self-destruction of feudalism in the Wars of the Roses, to crush out organized anarchy and restore law and order to the nation.

Parliamentary government failed, though supported by the body of the nation, because it was not strong enough to punish as crimes actions then most destructive of social welfare. It failed to maintain order and to enforce equal justice. The forces of armed anarchy, of reactionary class privilege, and of injustice prevailed. How hard the House of Commons strove to safeguard the upward progress of the nation to constitutional liberty by the creation of new crimes and the reformation of the courts of law, will be seen from even a casual examination of the legislation attempted.

But not only did Parliament prove itself too weak to punish acts rightly criminal at this stage of the nation's development. It was guilty also of attempting to stamp out as crimes new modes of life which the social welfare demanded. Statute after statute was passed to drive back the working classes into that condition of serfdom from which they were but just emerging. Every effort to establish a competitive system of wages was declared criminal,[1] and these statutes were re-enacted many times.[2] "Attempts

[1] See Statutes of Laborers, (23 Edw. III.) and (25 Edw. III., Stat. 2), 1349–50 fixing rates of wages and tying laborers to their existing place of residence.

[2] 12 Ric. II., cc. 3–10, (1388), etc.

to evade or neutralize" such laws were also made highly penal.[1]

It seems hardly fair to charge the landowners and middle classes, who were then supreme in Parliament, with intentional self-seeking in this matter; for they tried repeatedly to fix the price of provisions and other goods (as well as laborers' wages), thus preventing a rise in value of produce which would have been most advantageous to themselves.[2] It was the new competitive system which they dreaded and deemed highly dangerous; but their attempts to dam it back by penal statutes were as futile as an attempt to dam back the sea. Repressive measures only added wide-spread social discontent to the other misfortunes of the country. Parliament could not see that its laws were foredoomed to failure. More and more severe penalties were decreed—outlawry, branding, imprisonment instead of fine for even smallest infractions of the statutes. "To enforce these laws universally was of course impossible, but in many instances the landlords did not flinch from the attempt," and Parliament kept encouraging them constantly and adding new penalties.[3]

Doubtless, it was from ignorance that Parliament tried to make competitive prices criminal, as it was from weakness that it failed to punish maintenance, livery, organized ruffianism and legal injustice as crimes. But for both these reasons parliamentary government well merited its overthrow. It had fallen upon evil days, and while good in

[1] See 3 Hen. VI., c. 1, (1425), in which confederacies of masons were forbidden to meet in their general chapters under ban of felony for the officers who called them together, and imprisonment, fine and ransom for others.

[2] See laws regulating prices, keeping them down after the Black Death. They were laws of tort, an overcharge being punished by double the price received to the party "damnified." See Ordinance of June 18, 1349 (23 Edw. III., c. 6), and Statute of Laborers, 1351.

[3] Traill, ii, 146.

itself and destined to rule the future, it was not strong and wise enough in its callow youth to meet the needs of the times. A long period of royal despotism was necessary before it could grow to manhood; but that despotism was the choice of the people, was supported by them, and the people prospered under it; while all through the period of Tudor sovereignty there was abundant evidence, in Parliament and in the nation at large, that the spirit of constitutional liberty was not dead, but only sleeping.

If the theory of this book is correct, we should find in this age of social disorganization, injustice, immorality and growing anarchy, a decrease rather than an increase in the amount of crime when compared with centuries immediately preceding. The evidence is of course fragmentary, but on the whole it seems to warrant this belief. The Year-Books from the reign of Edward I. to that of Henry VII. show that the written law of crimes varied little from the days of Bracton to Tudor times. It consisted still of "a few vague definitions of the greater crimes," while Stephen believes "it hardly provided for the minor offences at all, except by the vague and arbitrary system of fining . . . . which seems to have been *greatly restricted* and to have fallen much *into disuse* during this period."[1] "Statutes creating new offences were not very numerous," and related chiefly to "crimes of violence, especially crimes directed against the public peace and the administration of justice, treason, riot, maintenance, livery, forcible entry and extortion of officers."[2] But these statutes, for the most part, rather aimed at the creation of crimes than actually created them, for the laws could not be enforced. Justice was delayed and thwarted by royal writ (contrary to the charter) and by the solicitations of great lords and ladies "who maintained the causes not only of their own bona fide dependents,

[1] Stephen, ii, 203. [2] *Ibid.*, ii, 203.

but of all who were rich enough to make it worth their while."[1]

If the criminal quality of an action depends upon its punishment by society as a wrong against itself, then actions which society customarily leaves unpunished, for whatever cause, are not crimes, no matter how bad they may be in themselves, no matter how many laws are enacted to suppress them. Only when society both wills to punish and succeeds in inflicting punishment upon a considerable proportion of offenders, does the evil action become a crime.[2] In the fourteenth and fifteenth centuries the laws against maintenance and livery were not, and could not be, generally enforced, and consequently the lords who broke the laws were not criminals any more than would be the supporters of a successful revolution; as for example the American Revolution of 1775. For the same reason the ruffians and malefactors whom their lords preserved from well-merited social punishment cannot rightly be called criminals, and the enlarged benefit of clergy must have shielded many more such, both in and out of holy orders.

Outside these acts of private war and legally or forcibly protected evil-doing, there was peace in the country at large, and in the cities, "judging by our own standard, very little crime, . . . very few cases are reported in the city records."[3] Hanging was the punishment for murder, burglary, highway robbery and gross theft, but in the city of London Rolls and Letter Books of the first half of the fourteenth century there are practically no heavy offences recorded, save one case of highway robbery, for which the man was hanged.[4] Assault

[1] Stubbs, ii, 640.

[2] The amount of social punishment required to make an action criminal cannot be expressed by percentages. It must be sufficient to establish a reasonable expectation in the minds of the community that offenders will be brought to justice.

[3] Traill, ii, 270.

[4] *Ibid.*, ii, 120.

cases were somewhat frequent, but "till late in the seventeenth century the most violent crimes against the person were treated simply as misdemeanors, punishable with fine and imprisonment."[1] This, to us, extraordinary leniency, shows that society for many centuries regarded such acts as highly natural and hardly criminal. When punished at all they were generally treated as torts, not crimes. In 1311 the Londoners made a clean sweep of common "roarers, roisterers, bruisers, night-walkers against the peace, and users of false dice."[2] There were also a considerable number of other misdemeanors in fourteenth century London, punished usually by confinement in the pillory or stocks. Some of these acts are now regarded as most serious crimes; for example, certain kinds of forgery and child-stealing. The laws of that period abound in regulations of the pettiest details of business. Light weight bread, bad dough, and many other little business frauds were frequently punished, by pillory, fines and forfeiture of the goods, a large part of the mulct going to the party who brought the suit. Thus the offence partook largely of the nature of a tort.[3]

The evils of forestalling and regrating were made the subject of very many statutes. Forfeiture and imprisonment were decreed against such conduct, but the laws themselves "recite" how former statutes "have been found deficient."[4] From the reign of Richard II. there were acts against unlawful games and gaming, with penalties of imprisonment and

[1] Stephen, iii, 109 (for evidence).

[2] Riley, *Memorials*, p. 86. Elmer de Multone and several other "roarers" were indicted about this time.

[3] (12 Edw. II., c. 6) for "assize of wine and victuals;" (13 Rich. II., Stat. 1, c. 8) for assizes of bread and ale; (51 Hen. III., Stat. 6) bakers transgressing assize. (11 Edw. III., c. 3), (25 Edw. III., Stat. 3), and many other statutes regulate butter and cheese, clothes, etc. (½ mulct to party suing). (7 Hen. IV., c. 7) arrow heads; (23 Hen. VIII., c. 4, § 2) beer and beer barrels.

[4] 5 and 6 Edw. VI., c. 14.

increasingly heavy fines, given in part to the person suing. Some of these laws were intended to foster the practice of archery, deemed necessary for the safety of the nation, but how well they were enforced we do not know.[1] Sumptuary laws, "against the outrageous and excessive apparel of divers people," in all grades of social life are very numerous. Offenders were to "forfeit to the king all the apparel they have worn against this ordinance," thus presenting to our minds a picture of the king of England as dealer in second-hand clothes.[2] Later, money penalties were added, but the laws could not be enforced, and successive statutes for centuries relate how "the commons of the realm, men and women, have worn and daily do wear, excessive" and inordinate array.[3] Finally an act of James I. repealed all this mass of useless legislation, vainly intended to make the wearing of expensive clothing criminal. Other misdemeanors punished by the Londoners were, pretending to be a physician, practicing sorcery, magic or soothsaying, being a procuress or a common scold, and counterfeiting the licensed begging poor.[4]

Beside civil court misdemeanors, there were a multitude of more or less common offences regarded as sins and coming under the jurisdiction of the ecclesiastical courts, whose judgments were notoriously mild, though their procedure was thoroughly inquisitorial. Among the most important are heresy, blasphemy, neglect of church services and ecclesiastical ceremonies, contempt of the clergy, and neglect by the clergy of clerical duty,[5] perjury, defamation, witchcraft,

[1] (Ric. II., c. 6), (11 Hen. IV., c. 4), (17 Edw. IV., c. 3), and one each under Hen. VII., Hen, VIII., Ph. and M., Chas. II. and Anne.

[2] 37 Edw. III., c. 8 to c. 14.

[3] 3 Edw. IV., c. 5.

[4] Riley, *Memorials*, p. 385.

[5] A very common offence apparently. See Stephen, ii, 404–5.

breach of faith, drunkenness, common bad language and every form of incontinence. Most of the business transacted by these courts was unimportant from the criminal standpoint. Out of 1854 cases cited before the ecclesiastical courts of the city of London, from 1496 to 1500, "one-half were charged with the crime of adultery and others of like nature."[1] The punishments were excommunication, penance and imprisonment, by writ from the king's chancery.[2]

On the whole the London of that age does not seem to have been a very criminal place, if we accept the Londoners' own standard of criminality. Of course the population was small, not more than 40,000 to 50,000 people; while the total for all England was only about 2,500,000. Some of the offences taken cognizance of by the canon and the common law in fourteenth century England were very far from being crimes. Thus, perjury was practically unpunished. Our ancestors could perjure themselves with impunity. "It was," writes Hallam, "one of the most characteristic vices of the Middle Ages." The only perjury punishable by the old common law was that of jurors, who were also at that time witnesses; and for several centuries the Year Books contain no reference to this offence. All other perjury was regarded as sin, an offence in ecclesiastical courts alone. But to be known as "a common swearer before the ordinary," by the absurdly antiquated system of compurgation still in use in these courts, was quite sufficient to brand a man as a common liar. It does not seem just, therefore, to call perjury a crime in those days.[3] As to

[1] See Hale.

[2] The coercive jurisdiction of the ecclesiastical courts was recognized and confirmed by the legislature a number of times. For the 14th century, see (9 Edw. II., Stat. 1), 1315; (15 Edw. III., c. 5); (31 Edw. III., c. 11).

[3] Hobart, "Searl *vs.* Williams," p. 291, states that the old common law procedure had made perjurers of "witnesses, compurgators and jurymen," and that "the judge himself was not clear." Hobart declares that 18 Eliz., c. 7. utterly abolished purgation, whereby "sundry perjuries and other abuses were avoided."

other offences common and severely punished later, we know that libel then attracted very little attention,[1] while the most violent harms to the person were very little regarded. There was a remote possibility of their punishment with fine and imprisonment, as misdemeanors,[2] but they were so very common and seemed so natural that people probably thought of them more as they have, till very recently, thought of drunkenness, rather than as serious offences. As for attempts to commit crime, they were practically unpunished until Tudor times.[3]

Summary. The fourteenth and fifteenth centuries were a period of marked constitutional progress, but of great degradation and weakness in the administration of justice, of increasing anarchy and corruption, of moral decay. Parliament to some extent succeeded in safeguarding the new development of government by the people, by holding the king and ministers of state rigidly responsible to the nation for their actions, and punishing them as criminals when they broke the laws. The representatives of the people fully realized the necessity for suppressing organized anarchy and making justice sure and equal, but their government was too weak to enforce the many statutes aimed at these abuses. The laws remained dead letters, and consequently the acts they were directed against were not crimes. Parliament attempted to punish, and to some extent probably succeeded in punishing as criminal the rise of the working classes to individual liberty, the introduction of competitive wages and competitive prices. In so doing it opposed the nation's true development. Thus, for many reasons, parliamentary government earned its downfall. But, despite successful anarchy and in-

[1] Coke mentions but two cases after his exhaustive study of the records. Stephen, ii, 302.

[2] Stephen, iii, 109.

[3] In 1340 Englishry was abolished. Sac (14 Edw. III., Stat. 1, c. 4).

justice, and indeed to a large extent because of it, there was little crime in England. The middle classes of the nation prospered as never before. Flocks and fields of grain remained safe, and commerce flourished in the towns; for the feudal nobility were busy with their own feuds, and the lawless men of the age were largely attracted to their service, by love of license, lust of gain and assurance of protection. The failure of parliamentary government to make these men criminals, was followed by the self-destruction of feudalism in the Wars of the Roses, and the board was swept clean for a despotic monarchy, strong enough to enforce law and to secure order.

CHAPTER IX

TUDOR ENGLAND. 1485–1603

THE Tudor government of England was not an unlimited absolutism, like the governments of France and Spain, during the same century.[1] Rather, it was a needful despotism, supported by the people, because necessary for the social welfare, but greatly limited by laws against which it was constantly chafing, and which it was strong enough frequently to break through and constantly to bend to its will.[2] Both the legislative and the judiciary were painfully subservient to the executive under Tudor administrations. Executive power was summed up in the king, and a large share of legislative and judicial power also.[3] But no law, intended to be permanent, was made in sixteenth century England without the consent of Parliament, and the courts of law were at least free in theory, however much they were controlled in fact.[4]

The nation's greatest need was strong law, enforced by a despotic king, putting down the civil feuds of the turbulent nobility, punishing criminals regardless of the maintenance or livery of any lord, reuniting the people and holding them firmly together until time had healed the old wounds of civil war and private feud. To secure this, the nation was willing to relinquish, for a time, some measure of its old constitutional liberties.[5] There are times, writes Montesquieu, when the Goddess of Liberty should be veiled; and this was

[1] Hallam, i, 276.
[2] Traill. ii, 459, and iii, 16 and 26.
[3] Judicial power through the Court of Star Chamber.
[4] Hallam, i, 278.
[5] Traill, ii, 456–7.

one. Parliament became the willing tool of the king, and the courts of law were almost equally swayed by his dictation. Yet a government that ruled by intimidation had no army at its command and was entirely without power to enforce its will.[1] The people supported the king, for he made good peace in the land and built up the wealth and prosperity of the middle classes, the backbone of England. Doubtless it was better that Parliament should for a time "register the acts of a despot," than that it should fall into the ignominy and contempt that had seemed awaiting it. The acts it registered were great acts, many of them, and they were all done "by the authority of Parliament." In the severe treatment meted out to the nobles and rich land owners the people fully acquiesced.[2] Indeed, the nobles richly merited punishment at the nation's hands. Grown rich in foreign wars, powerful in Parliament and social life, they should have been the natural leaders of the people in their struggle for liberty, as they had been for centuries. But they preferred to retire from leadership and use their might to terrorize king, Parliament and people, and make a mockery of justice by maintaining miscreants of every type; building up a new and dangerous feudalism upon a basis of glittering chivalry, and plunging the nation into civil war for their own selfish purposes. Parliamentary governments of the fourteenth and fifteenth centuries had failed in their attempts to punish the barons and their lawless dependents as criminals.[3] Both Parliament and people recognized this failure and accepted the necessity for a despotic monarchy, as alone able to suppress armed and organized anarchy and restore order—the greatest need of the age.[4]

A statute of the fourth year of Henry VII. shows the

[1] Hallam, i, 46–7; Traill, ii, 456. [2] Traill, iii, 30.
[3] (3 Hen. VII., c. 1.) Quoted on page 201.
[4] (3 Hen. VII., c. 2), 1487; (4 Hen. VII, c. 12).

widespread disuse of laws and extortions of sheriffs prevalent. "The king, our sovereign lord, considereth how daily within this realm his coin is traitorously counterfeited; murders, robberies and felonies are grievously committed and done; and also unlawful extortions and misdemeanings of sheriffs and many other enormities and unlawful demeanings daily groweth and increaseth within this his realm, to the great displeasure of God, hurt and impoverishing of his subjects and the subversion of the policy and good governance of this his realm." The statute further relates how that sufficient good laws have been made for repressing these mischiefs, but that they are not enforced by the justices; for "if his subjects complain to these justices of the peace of any wrongs done to them, they have thereby no remedy, but by many of them rather hurt than helped and the said mischiefs do increase and are not subdued." Therefore punishments are decreed against offending justices, etc. Accordingly, the people rallied round the crown, and while seeking its protection became at the same time its greatest support. Again, as in early Norman days, king and people united to put down the turbulent feudal nobility.[1] But not only was the old nobility humbled, crushed and prostrate under the heel of the king; the clergy also shared the fate of the barons "with whom they had latterly identified themselves."[2]

For centuries the Church had been losing its hold upon the people. The Reformation was prepared for slowly. The Lollard movement, the Renaissance, the increasing worldliness of churchmen, their greed of wealth and sus-

[1] First it was king, Church and people against the nobles. Next barons, Church and people curb the overweening power of the king. Now again it is king and people putting down the new feudalism, but they unite to put down the old ecclesiastical order as well. See Hallam, i, 64, and Traill, iii, 19, 27. Notice that the people were always on the side of true progress, while all the other forces were at some time opposed.

[2] Traill, ii, 458; Hallam, i, 81.

pected immorality, above all their dependence upon a foreign authority, all united to develop distrust and dislike in the minds of a nation now beginning to think more freely and independently upon matters of religion. Spiritual life and energy seemed to have left the Church, although her material power was never greater in England than at the close of the fifteenth century. Her services were never more faithfully attended. Her courts never had a wider jurisdiction. But more and more people were persuaded that fraud and corruption pervaded the established church (see Hallam, i, 84), and it was this belief, far more than theological reasoning, which prepared the way for the great revolution in religious opinions, the separation from the communion of Rome; and made the larger part of the nation acquiesce silently in the dissolution of the monasteries, the confiscation of their estates, the humbling of the secular clergy and the limiting of ecclesiastical jurisdiction.[1] The Church had failed to reform herself from within, and must therefore be reformed from without. Not only had she fallen from her old position of leadership in the struggle for constitutional liberty; she had become a positive drag upon the upward progress of the nation; and in nothing was this more apparent than in the ecclesiastical courts, where antiquated procedure and priestly jealousy of interference had made a mockery of justice, and shielded many malefactors from well deserved and socially necessary punishment as criminals.[2] The Church courts had made justice and punishment most uncertain, even for murder and highway robbery, and this not for priests and bishops alone, but for the great multitude of men in minor orders, offenders against all clericals, and even for those who could barely read or repeat a verse of the Psalms of David. Uncertainty of justice is an evil far worse and more insidious than mis-

[1] Hallam, i, 72 and 100; Traill, iii, 27.

[2] Hallam, i, 58.

takes and cruelty under the name of law. If the first and greatest safeguard of popular liberty—sure and equal justice —was to prevail in England, ecclesiastical jurisdiction had to be greatly limited. This great work was begun and largely carried out under the Tudors.[1]

The nation's greatest need, therefore, during this period was internal peace and order—the evident means thereto was the enforcement of strong law by a despotic yet popular monarch. How the Tudors succeeded, where parliamentary government had failed, in punishing as criminals the anarchic nobility and their lawless followers, in reforming the Church, and making justice more equal and sure by limiting the jurisdiction of the Church courts, we shall see in following the statutes, proclamations and legal procedure by which this most important work was accomplished. We shall find punishments growing heavy and sanguinary, and many of the powerful in Church and State brought low and punished as criminals. Laws of treason are multiplied, and treason again takes the direction of offences against the person and will of the king. Constructive treasons are developed. Many crimes are created by the king's desire, some of them opposed to popular liberty. But on the whole the Tudors did great good and deserved to be supported by the nation. The suppression of the anarchic nobility by the expansion of

[1] There were other reasons why the Church had to be purified and despoiled of her wealth. One-fifth of all the landed property of the realm was in the hands of the Church, which never lost, and always gained. Methods of farming in use on Church estates were hopelessly old-fashioned and unproductive. Lavish and unwise charity was filling the land with lazy beggars of church doles. There would have been great practical difficulties in the way of the new learning and of religious reformation, if the abbots had been permitted to hold their seats in the House of Lords, for the lords temporal were outnumbered by the lords spiritual, whose tendencies were strongly couservative and reactionary. The sharing of monastic spoils raised up a new landed aristocracy and strengthened their hands to resist later the despotic monarchy of the Stuarts, a most necessary work for English liberty. See Hallam, i, 74, 79, 80. For the people supporting the king in the severance from Rome, see Hallam, i, 64.

treason laws and the enforcement of old criminal statutes against maintenance, livery, etc., was accomplished mainly during the reign of Henry VII. through the court of Star Chamber.

The criminal jurisdiction of the Privy Council had existed from remote antiquity, and despite the remonstrances of Parliament in the fourteenth and fifteenth centuries, and three statutes (1350, '54, '68) which seem intended to abolish it, the Council continued to hold its "sittings in the starred chamber," and its powers of jurisdiction were increased, for it met a felt need of the nation, remedied defects and omissions of the common law, supplemented its meagre provisions by the gradual creation of new crimes, and was strong enough to enforce its authority where the ordinary law courts failed. Thus it may be said with truth that both the king and his arbitrary court faithfully represented the nation, and did its will, in the extension and enforcement of the criminal law, and the resulting multiplication of criminals.

"The praise of trial by jury as a bulwark of individual liberty is a familiar topic. It is less commonly known, but is certainly no less true, that the institution opened a wide door to tyranny and oppression by men of local influence over their poorer neighbors. In feudal times the influence of a great landowner over the persons who were returned as jurymen to the assizes was practically almost unlimited. . . . The offence which was long known to the law as maintenance, or perverting justice by violence, by unlawful assemblies and conspiracies, was the most frequent and most characteristic offence of the age. One of its commonest forms was the corruption and intimidation of jurors. Signal proof of this is supplied by the repeated legislation against this offence."[1] Henry VII. and his Parliament struck directly

[1] Stephen, i, 171–2.

at this evil—the most dangerous then existing—by a statute passed in the third year of Henry's reign (3 Hen. VII., c. i.), 1487, which describes both the nature of the offence and the means to be employed for its correction, and confers large authority upon certain members of the court of Star Chamber to proceed against all violators of this, or former statutes, and to punish them forthwith as criminals. The preamble and first section of this statute read:

"The king our said sovereign lord remembereth how by unlawful maintenance, giving of liveries, signs and tokens, and retainders by indentures, promises, oaths, writings, or otherwise embraceries of his subjects, untrue demeanings of sheriffs in making of panels and other untrue returns, by taking of money by juries, by great riots and unlawful assemblies, the policy and good rule of this realm is almost subdued, and for the not punishing of these inconveniences, and by reason of the premises, little or nothing may be found by inquiry" (*i. e.*, by inquests or juries) "whereby the laws of the land in execution may take little effect, to the increase of murders, robberies, perjuries, and unsureties of all men living, and losses of their lands and goods to the great displeasure of Almighty God. Therefore it is ordained for reformation of the premises by authority of said Parliament, that the chancellor and treasurer of England" (etc., naming the other members of the court) "upon bill or information put to the said chancellor for the king or any other against any person for any misbehaviour before rehearsed, have authority to call before them by writ or by privy seal the said misdoers, and them and other by their discretion, by whom the truth may be known, to examine, and such as they find therein defective to punish them after their demerits, after the form and effect of statutes thereof made, in like manner and form as they should and ought to be punished, as if they were thereof convict after the due order of the law."

It is very evident that these special powers conferred upon the court of Star Chamber were designed to restore law and order and secure the punishment of the turbulent nobility and their lawless followers. In later Tudor reigns, the chief importance of this court lay in the jurisdiction it developed over libels and several other offences, unmentioned in the statute of Henry VII., because not then recognized as really dangerous to the social welfare, or not as yet believed to be even criminal. The Star Chamber, so justly hated and abolished later for its tyranny, was undoubtedly of very great service to sixteenth century England, in restoring order and in supplying socially necessary punishments for "forgery, perjury, attempts and conspiracies to commit crimes, and many forms of fraud and force, which the old common law left practically unpunished," and which, therefore, remaining unpunished, were not crimes.[1] "This court," writes Coke, "doth keep all England in quiet."[2] Bacon describes it as "one of the sagest and noblest institutions of this kingdom."[3] It impoverished the haughty baronage by heavy fines. Thus, the Earl of Rutland was fined £30,000 for his share in the Earl of Essex insurrection. The Earl of Oxford paid a fine of £15,000 for keeping his retainers in livery; "a practice," writes Hallam, "mischievous and illegal, but too customary to have been punished before this reign."[4] The expansion and enforcement of treason laws is reported to have made treason the most profitable branch of Henry VII's revenue.[5] Indeed, the whole history of the administration of justice under Henry VII. is filled with records of fines and forfeitures, by which the old nobility were so thoroughly intimidated and impoverished, that when Henry

[1] Stephen, i, 177, ii, 229 and 470; Hudson, pp. 104–107.

[2] Coke, Fourth Institute, p. 65; and Hallam, i, 52.

[3] Bacon's *Works*, v, 54; also Rushworth.

[4] Henry VII. See Hallam, i, 15. [5] Traill, ii, 463.

VIII. ascended the throne there was no strength left in them.[1] Henry VII. was exceedingly anxious for this result, and he destroyed their ancient class privileges as ruthlessly as did his son the vested interests and legal rights of the clergy.

While humbling and putting down the upper classes in the state, the Tudors were zealous in uplifting the middle and lower orders. All through the sixteenth century these sovereigns posed as social reformers.[2] They created a new nobility from the wealthy rural landowners; they legislated for the benefit of the rising commercial class; they investigated the wages question and the relations of labor and capital.[3] Their policy transformed England from a poor and thinly peopled country into a rich, energetic and powerful nation. Under them the middle classes slowly grew into that enduring and disciplined strength which successfully asserted and maintained rights of individual liberty, equal justice and constitutional government against the Stuart kings. But the times were not yet ripe for this reassertion of popular sovereignty. Sixteenth century England was in the throes of a great new birth—a transformation, wrought out through much suffering, which replaced feudalism with commercialism, and Romanism with individualism.[4] The nation craved growing room, and for this kings were needed who both could and would cut the old bonds right and left, yet hold the social life together till the new order had become customary and its restraints natural. Not till toward the close of Elizabeth's reign did Parliament begin to reassert its authority.[5] But then the Tudor despotism had done its work, and its usefulness was in the past.

[1] Hallam, i, 47. [2] Traill, ii, 462.

[3] See Commercial Treaties with Flanders: "Intercursus Magnus" (1496), and another treaty (1506), favoring the English so greatly that the Netherlanders called it the "Malus Intercursus."

[4] Traill, ii, 459. [5] When Elizabeth relinquished the monopolies in 1601.

Meanwhile, the old Statute of Treasons (25 Edw. III.) was thought utterly insufficient to protect the person and power of the king, during the critical times from the beginning of the Reformation (1533), till the end of the century. The nation was very busy during all this period, creating new crimes—new treasons—safeguarding its new life. Especially is this noticeable during the reign of Henry VIII., when there were no less than nine acts creating such offences; and history shows how ruthlessly these laws were enforced for the suppression and execution of the king's enemies, whom the nation, in the main, regarded as its enemies also. Four of these acts proclaimed and defended the position of the king in his struggle for supremacy with the pope of Rome.[1] They were terrible laws, making the speaking of treasonable words treason; the obstinate refusal to take the abjuration oath against the pope, high treason; and even concealment or flight beyond seas to escape the penalties of royal proclamations concerning religion, high treason.[2] Stephen believes these laws necessary. The Tudors had to strike terrible blows against their adversary and his adherents, and victory was hard won even then.[3] Without the support of a very large body of the people it could never have resulted. But "catholicism, without the pope was," writes Traill, "the latent wish of most Englishmen," and this was what Henry VIII. practically gave. "He struck the true average, and that average backed him" and won his cause.[4] Sacerdotalism as a form of government perished out of England. The Reformation was "the social victory of the great lay classes over the clerical estate."[5] The question, "Who is to

[1] (26 Hen. VIII., c. 13), 1534; (28 Hen. VIII., c. 10), 1536; (31 Hen. VIII., c. 8), 1539; (35 Hen. VIII., c. 3), 1543.

[2] Parliament gave to royal proclamations in this reign the same force "for the time in them lymitted" (1539), as it gave to its own acts. Benefit of sanctuary was taken from all traitors in 1534.

[3] Stephen ii, 258. [4] Traill, iii, 49. [5] *Ibid.*, 51.

rule?" was answered forever. The nation had chosen the line of its religious development. Those who refused to follow were regarded as enemies of Church and State, and were to a large extent punished as criminals. We cannot enter here into a discussion of the necessity or usefulness of the Reformation. Let it suffice that England has prospered since. But as to the fact that the cutting loose from Rome led to the enactment of many new criminal laws protecting the new religious development, and a rapid increase of criminals in the land, there can be no doubt.[1] Bishop Fisher and Sir Thomas More were beheaded on a charge of high treason for denying the ecclesiastical supremacy of the Crown (Act of 1534);[2] and a considerable number of abbots and less distinguished men shared their fate. By the attainder of these abbots some of the larger monasteries were held forfeited to the king, contrary to all law.[3] In Edward VI.'s reign many people were sent to prison for hearing mass, and other similar offences;[4] but the persecutions fell mainly upon high ecclesiastics and noble victims, as later in the reign of Mary.[5] Under Elizabeth we learn from a Jesuit source, that "persecution in England was 'monstrous great.' Five priests have been executed; four hanged, drawn and quartered; the fifth stoned."[6] Even the most secret exercise of the Romish ritual was severely punished. The penalty for saying mass was 200 marks; for hearing it, 100 marks, together with one year's imprisonment for all con-

[1] Bishop Burnet, *History of the Reformation*, i, 351, and *State Trials*, i, 469, for many scores of men and women beheaded as traitors for their religious belief.

[2] *State Trials*, i, 385 and 395.

[3] The abbots of Reading and Glastonbury, and others, suffered death upon the scaffold. Hallam, i, 72.

[4] (2 and 3 Edw. VI., c. 1), 1548; Strype's *Cranmer*, pp. 333–4, for Papists, and p. 335 for Anabaptists (1550).

[5] Strype's *Cranmer*, pp. 308, 322, 324, 329.

[6] Strype's *Annals* (Elizabeth, 1587 and 1593), and Lingard, viii, 164–183.

cerned; and after the Spanish Armada the "execution of priests and other Catholics became more and more frequent, and fines for recusancy were exacted as rigorously as before."[1] Between 1588 and 1603, 110 Romanists, "61 clergymen, 47 laymen and 2 gentlewomen suffered capital punishment for some or other of the spiritual felonies and treasons which had been lately created."[2] Dissenting Protestants, as well as Roman Catholics, were punished as criminals. The first instance of this was in June, 1567, when a religious meeting at Plumbers' Hall was broken up and 14 or 15 dissenters sent to prison.[3] An act of 1593 (35 Eliz., c. 1), bore very heavily upon both Romanists and Independents. Many of these last fled to Holland to escape imprisonment, and two of their number, Barrow and Greenwood, were executed for spreading seditious writings.[4] During the Roman Catholic reaction under Mary, 277 "heretics" were burned to death.[5] Mere possession of books "filled with heresy and treason," made the possessor a rebel and liable to execution under martial law.[6] This was probably more tyrannous than any act of Henry VIII.

Returning from this discussion of increased criminality due to religious development, let us consider the other five treasons, created by act of Parliament during the reign of

[1] Strype's *Annals*, iii, 187; Hallam, i, 163; and (23 Eliz., c. 183).

[2] Lingard, viii, 355–6. Elizabeth's ministers always claimed that no one was executed for his religion—that every punishment had in view the safety of the state. But see case of Mayne, 1577. Hallam, i, 148 and 164.

[3] Strype's *Life of Parker*, i, 481–2.

[4] Punished under (23 Eliz., c. 2), 1580. See also hanging of Thacker and Copping, Anabaptists, in 1583, for denying the queen's ecclesiastical supremacy. Strype's *Annals*, iii, 186, and Lingard, viii, 183-185.

[5] Strype, iii, 473; Hallam, i, 105; Lingard, vii, 285, states the number as "almost 200."

[6] See royal proclamation in last year of Mary's reign. Hallam, i, 42–3, and Strype, iii, 459.

Henry VIII., and those who suffered under them.[1] These laws aimed to secure the succession to the throne, and made it high treason to attempt to alter the settlement of the succession, to assert the validity of certain marriages of Henry VIII., or to deny the validity of certain other marriages. Test oaths were provided by these laws and it was high treason obstinately to refuse to take them. The act of 1536 even made it treason to refuse to "declare their thought and conscience," in answer to questions on the oath. Such laws were of terrible severity, yet the Wars of the Roses and the evils of a disputed succession were fresh in all minds, and the nation had no wish to renew the experience. Both houses of Parliament united in sending to the scaffold many innocent and some guilty victims of Henry's jealousy, or hatred, and "new political offences were created in every Parliament against which the severest penalties were denounced."[2] The insurgent lords and their followers, implicated in the great northern rebellion (1536), were proceeded against by martial law, after the king's promise of a general pardon. Thirty-five of the leaders, high in Church and State, were condemned, and hanged, beheaded, or burned.[3]

Henry VIII. overawed the whole nation by his strength of will and greed of blood, but he exasperated his people also, and when Edward VI. ascended the throne the new treason laws were all repealed.[4] Nothing remained treason

[1] The statutes are: (25 Hen. VIII., c. 22) 1534; (28 Hen. VIII., c. 7) 1536; (32 Hen. VIII., c. 25) 1540; (33 Hen. VIII., c. 21) 1542; (35 Hen. VIII., c. 1) 1543.

[2] Hallam, i, 33. *Victims of "constructive" and other treasons*: De la Pole, beheaded 1513; Edward Stafford, Duke of Buckingham, 1521; Henry Courtney, Marquis of Exeter; Thomas Cromwell, 1540; Margaret, Countess of Salisbury, 1541; the Earl of Surrey, Queen Anne Boleyn, Queen Catharine Howard, and others who suffered with her. See *State Trials*, i.

[3] *State Trials*, i, 477, and Bishop Burnet, i, 351 *et seq.*

[4] (1 Edw. VI., c. 12), 1547.

except a denial of the king's ecclesiastical supremacy and offences under 25 Edward III. But the new administration scrupled not to bend the laws to secure attainder of treason by Parliament, as in the conviction of Lord Seymour, when the accused was not even permitted to be heard in his own defence.[1] In 1549 treason was extended by act of Parliament to cover mere rioting.[2] Queen Mary at first brought treason back to the limits assigned by 25 Edw. III., but after the Spanish marriage new treason laws were enacted, much like laws of Henry VIII. and Edw. VI. It was also made treason to pray God to shorten the life of the queen.[3] During Elizabeth's reign, and especially after the pope's Bull of Deposition and Mary Stuart's captivity in England had exposed the queen to serious dangers, many acts creating or renewing old treasons were passed by Parliament for her protection and the safety of the realm.[4] A statute of the year 1584 made it high treason for any Jesuit, or seminary priest, born within her majesty's dominions, "to come into, be, or remain in any part of this realm," and for any subject educated in any foreign college or seminary, not to return to England and take the oath of supremacy within six months after proclamation made in London. These laws undoubtedly put many men in constant danger of their lives as traitors to the state, and the one hundred and ten Roman Catholics put to death during the last fifteen years of Elizabeth's reign prove that the penalties were enforced.[5]

[1] *State Trials*, i, 483. This most iniquitous precedent of Henry VIII.'s reign was negatived by law a few years later—the same act also creating some new treasons. See 5 and 6 Edw. VI., c. 11, § 9 (1551–2).

[2] How many offenders under treason laws then: how few to-day! This old crime has been largely done away with by the most successful and civilized nations.

[3] 1 and 2 Phil. and Mary, c. 9 (1554–5).

[4] Such are (1 Eliz., c. 5) 1558, (13 Eliz., c. 1) 1571, (23 Eliz., c. 1) 1580, and (27 Eliz., c. 2) 1584.

[5] Some of those who suffered under the treason laws of Elizabeth were: Thomas

But beside the multiplication of crimes of religion and constructive treasons, another great class of crimes was created, or very largely developed, by decisions of the Star Chamber; decisions afterward accepted by the court of King's Bench as forming part of the common law of England.[1] "Perjury, forgery, gross public acts of indecency, conspiracies to commit crimes, or indeed to do anything unlawful," and, to some extent, political libels were thus made crimes.[2] Only by very slow degrees was perjury in all its forms made criminal by the court of Star Chamber. The first statute imposing a temporal penalty for this offence was not passed till 1540.[3] As for attempts at crime, hitherto unpunished by the laws, excepting very rarely "under the name of assaults or the like,"[4] Hudson writes, in his *Treatise on the Court of Star Chamber:* "It is the great and high jurisdiction of this court, that it punisheth errors creeping into the commonwealth, which otherwise might prove dangerous and infectious diseases—yea, although no positive law or continued custom of common law giveth warrant to it." As examples Hudson mentions, "attempts to coin money, to commit burglary, or poison, or murder." [5] As late as 1573 there was no legal punishment for even the most desperate attempts at murder.[6]

Howard, Duke of Norfolk, (1571), *State Trials*, i, 95, 97–8; John Felton, *ibid.*, i, 1086; Queen Mary of Scotland, *ibid.*, i, 1161 (1586); Earl of Northumberland, *ibid.*, i, 1112 (1585); Earl of Arundel, *ibid.*, i, 1250 (1589); Sir Christopher Blunt and five others, *ibid.*, i, 1410 (1600); Dr. Wm. Parry, *ibid.*, i, 1096 (1584); Thomas and Christopher Norton, *ibid.*, i, 1083 (1570); and very many others tried and executed with great cruelty, *ibid.*, i, 1158–78, etc.

[1] Stephen, ii, 224 and 229.

[2] Stephen, ii, 470.

[3] (32 Hen. VIII., c. 9, § 3); and see Stephen, iii, 244 and 247; and (5 Eliz., c. 9.)

[4] Stephen, ii, 223.

[5] Hudson, p. 107–8. Instances of such crimes are the attempt by Frizier against Baptista Baseman, in 5 Elizabeth (1563), and that attempt of the two brothers who were whipped and gazed in Fleet street, in 44 Elizabeth (1602).

[6] Stephen, iii, 110–111.

Thus we can see how busy was the court of Star Chamber in creating new crimes (and necessarily also criminals), in a direction which has since become generally recognized as a proper and necessary field for social punishment. In our own age "all attempts whatever to commit indictable offences are misdemeanors, unless by some special statutory enactment they are subject to special punishment."[1]

Libels attracted but little attention till the days of Elizabeth, when the court of Star Chamber was at the height of its power. The great intellectual movement of the age, and especially the invention of the printing press, gave a greatly increased importance to political writings, and thus increased social intelligence led to the development (the necessary development) of new crimes. Prosecutions for libel in the court of Star Chamber included: "Libels against the king's person and nobles," and "scandalous letters."[2] The trades of printing and bookselling were closely regulated by ordinances of the Star Chamber (1585).[3] Most men were forbidden to print at all, under penalty of a year's imprisonment; and even the the selling of books, printed contrary to ordinance, was punished by three months in gaol.[4] It was a crime to publish or even to possess any book or pamphlet in favor of the Romish faith.[5]

From very early times some forgeries were penal offences

[1] Stephen, ii, 224.

[2] Peter Breveston. Sir Wm. Hale's case against Ellis. *Notable cases are:* Stubbs (1579), who lost his right hand for the publication of his "Gaping Gulf;" and Udall, convicted for writing a book against the queen (1589); see also case of Penry. Some libels were very possibly punished as treasons in earlier times. See Stephen ii, 302.

[3] See also (1 Ric. III, c. 9); and (25 Hen. VIII., c. 15). The punishments were fines, to crown and party suing.

[4] Hallam, i, 239.

[5] Strype's *Grindal*, p. 124; and Appendix, p. 43. Also a proclamation dated February, 1589.

at common law, but they were punished, if at all, as torts, by damages paid to the individual injured.[1] Early in the history of the Star Chamber, we find many forgeries of all kinds punished not as torts, but as crimes against the state,[2] although it was not till 1562 that the important statute (5 Eliz. c. 14) was directed "against the forging of evidences (false deeds) and writings." This act recites the great evils resulting from the "small, mild and easy" punishments hitherto inflicted, and decrees very heavy damages, mutilation and perpetual imprisonment, for any person who forges "any false deed, charter or writing sealed, court-roll or the will of any person or persons in writing," or "who shall give in evidence any such charter, deed or writing, knowing the same to be false or forged." An act of Queen Mary's reign[3] (1553) made treasonable the counterfeiting of foreign coin passing current in England by the queen's consent, and also the forgery or counterfeiting of the queen's sign manual, privy signet, or privy seal. Many other statutes from time to time created new coinage offences, and decreed penalties for some as treasons and others as felonies or misdemeanors.[4]

In 1530 poisoning was made high treason. The first statute punishing fraudulent bankruptcy was passed in 1542 and was followed by another in 1570.[5] The creation of this new crime was made socially necessary by the extension of the credit system (due to the growth of trade), which opened a new field for dishonesty; but the penalties decreed were at first very light. On the other hand, unfortunate debtors were treated almost like criminals; but they cannot

[1] By (1 Hen. V, c. 3), 1413, a fine to the king was added. Forgery of certain seals was high treason.

[2] Hudson. *Star Chamber*, p. 65.

[3] (1 Mary, Sess. 2, c. 6).

[4] Stephen, iii, 179.

[5] (34 Hen. VIII., c. 4) and (13 Eliz., c. 7).

be classed with criminals, for imprisonment was inflicted only at the suit of the injured creditor, and not by the state directly.

In 1545, the statute 37 Henry VIII. c. 6 created many new crimes under the class "malicious injuries to property." The preamble to this law of Henry VIII. is interesting, for it shows that the legislators thought malicious injuries to property something entirely new in the land. It reads: "Whereas divers malicious and envious persons . . . have of late invented and practised a new and damnable kind of vice." Of course the social evil in such practices was just becoming apparent, and the result was the creation of some new crimes; but very little attention was paid to such offences until the reign of George I.[1]

Very severe statutes against vagrants, "sturdy rogues" and vagabonds were enacted at frequent intervals throughout the Tudor period, and many of these "poor Toms" were whipped at the cart tail through the streets, stocked, branded or imprisoned; but vagrants were so numerous that probably thousands of them continued their wanderings without ever hearing unfavorably from the laws against them.[2] Harsh game laws continued to make hunting a monopoly of the wealthy land owners.[3] There were laws against usury, but they were utterly ineffective, and at last interest up to 10 per cent. was legally distinguished from usury, in 1545.[4] The last general statute decreeing punishment against regrators and forestallers was 5 and 6 Edw. VI., C. 14, passed in 1552. Prosecutions for these offences lasted even into the nineteenth century, but the mischievous laws were very com-

[1] (43 Eliz., c. 7), 1601; and Stephen, iii, 188.

[2] Traill, iii, 241–3, 250–2, 356, 360.

[3] (11 Hen. VII., c. 17), 1494, and other statutes.

[4] (3 Henry VII. c. c. 5 and 6) and (37 Henry VIII. c. 9).

monly not enforced.[1] Many sumptuary laws were placed upon the statute books during Tudor reigns, but they were ineffectual.[2] Multitudinous acts for the proper care of highways appear from the time of Henry VIII., but the laws were not well enforced.[3] Forcible entry, or the taking possession of lands and property by force, was very common, and certainly not a crime in Tudor times and the centuries immediately preceding. The king's own actions often clearly countenanced such conduct in his followers. Yet there were many statutes against the offence, which was generally considered as a tort, with double or treble damages to the plaintiff, if he could collect them.[4] Piracy was very far from being a crime in the Elizabethan age, despite 28 Hen. VIII. c. 15. High-born gentlemen regarded it as an honorable profession, and a sure road to fame and fortune. Government encouraged these sea rovers, and the English nation applauded.[5] The African slave trade was started about 1562 by Sir John Hawkins, and excited no moral abhorrence. Even Queen Elizabeth shared in the profits of Hawkins' second voyage, and the Guinea or African Company was incorporated to carry on the business.[6] Not until modern times has growing social morality and intelligence made such acts highly criminal.

Benefit of Clergy.—Early in this chapter it was made clear that the greatest need of England at the beginning of the Tudor period was the restoration of order, by the sure and

[1] (5 and 6 Edw. VI., c. 14), recites that former statutes "have been found deficient." And see Stephen, iii., 201.

[2] (1 Hen. VIII., c. 14), and many later acts; and Traill, iii, 388.

[3] See (5 Eliz., c. 13, § 1), which relates the "inefficiency" of the statutes. There were four other highway acts during this single reign.

[4] (8 Hen. VI., c. 9); (4 Hen. IV., c. 4); also laws of Ric. II., Henry VIII., Eliz. and Jas. I. See Pike's *History of Crime in England*, for abundant evidence relating to forcible entry.

[5] Traill, iii, 473–5, 539–40.

[6] *Ibid.*, iii, 541.

more equal enforcement of justice, under a strong, despotic king. We have seen how the anarchic feudal nobility and their followers were punished as criminals by the court of Star Chamber, and have watched the multiplication of treasons, felonies and some misdemeanors in an age of rapid change and social development, political, intellectual, religious and industrial. But the statutes limiting ecclesiastical jurisdiction, remedying some of the grossest defects of antiquated law, extending and equalizing the operation of justice, and thus largely increasing the nation's criminal class, have not yet received attention. The privilege of clergy consisted originally in the right of men in holy orders ("*habitum et tonsuram clericalem*") and offenders against them, to be tried for their misdeeds in ecclestiastical courts alone. By the reign of Henry VI. it had become established that the clerk must be convicted in the lay courts before he could claim his clergy.[1] But a statute of 1351 extended benefit of clergy to "all manner of clerks, as well secular as religious, which shall be from henceforth convict before the secular justices;" and the judges interpreted this to mean, "every one who could read, whether he had the clerical dress and tonsure or not."[2] How many malefactors this must have saved from punishment as criminals, and what a farce it made of justice, the following description[3] of an ecclesiastical trial by the antiquated system of purgation shows:

"The trial was held before the bishop in person, or his deputy, and by a jury of twelve clerks, and there first the party himself was required to make oath of his own innocence; next, there was to be the oath of twelve compurgators, who swore they believed he spoke the truth; then wit-

[1] Stephen, i, 460.

[2] *Ibid.*, i, 461; Peere Williams, iii, 447. 25 Edw. III, Stat. 3, old form, or 6, new form, 1351.

[3] From R. *vs.* Burridge (1735); Peere Williams, iii, 447.

nesses were to be examined upon oath, but upon behalf of the prisoner only; and lastly, the jury were to bring in verdict upon oath, which usually acquitted the prisoner, otherwise, if a clerk, he was degraded or put to penance."[1] Hobart speaks of purgation as "turning the solemn trial of truth by oath into a ceremonious and formal lie."

As has been seen, the House of Commons in the fourteenth century repeatedly urged the reformation of the ecclesiastical courts, and the exclusion of all the laity from their jurisdiction, but the only result seemed to be the enlarging of church privilege, and the screening of more evil doers from justice. What Parliament had failed to do the strong arm of the Tudors at once began to accomplish. In 1487,[2] it was enacted that every person convicted of a clergyable felony should be branded on the brawn of his thumb with an "M" for murder, or a "T" for theft, and that any such branded person again claiming benefit of clergy should be denied it, unless he were actually in orders, and if ordained, unless he furnished proofs from the Ordinary within a day specified by the judge.

Up to this time there were but few felonies at common law. Coke's "Third Institute" only mentions seven, namely, homicide (including murder and manslaughter), rape, burglary, arson, robbery, theft and mayhem. Death was the penalty for all these crimes, except petty larceny (theft under 12 pence) and mayhem; but any man who could successfully plead his clergy escaped hanging and probably all other punishment worthy the name, thus happily belonging to a class of men who could with difficulty make themselves criminals, unless indeed they insisted on becoming traitors; for high treason was probably never clergyable,[3]

[1] A paraphrase by Stephen. See also Searle *vs.* Williams; Hobart, pp. 289, 291 (1620).

[2] 4 Henry VII., c. 13.

[3] Hale, ii, 330–331; and 25 Edw. III., Stat. 3 (1350).

though all the felonies were originally subject to this saving clause.[1]

As late as the reign of Henry VII. there were apparently but two forms of felony excepted from benefit of clergy—namely highway robbery and wilful burning of houses.[2] In 1496, a statute, 12 Hen. VII., C. 7, took away this privilege from laymen "prepensedly murdering their lord, master or sovereign immediate" (thus committing petty treason); giving as a reason that "many and divers unreasonable and detestable persons, lacking grace, wilfully commit murder" . . . . . "in trust to eschew the peril and execution of the law by the benefit of their clergy."[3] This was the first of a series of statutes which, during the next century, made justice more equal in the land, and must have largely increased the number of criminals. In 1512, persons committing murder in churches, on highways, etc., were deprived of clergy.[4] In 1531, petty treason, "wilful murder with malice prepensed," robbing churches or other holy places, certain other kinds of robbery, and some forms of arson, were declared non-clergyable for all laymen. Clerks in orders, guilty of these crimes, were to be imprisoned for life, unless —note how easily they escaped punishment even yet—"they could find two sureties in £20 each for their good behaviour."[5] In 1536, piratical offences were excluded from clergy.[6] In 1547, benefit of clergy was taken away in all cases of murder, certain cases of burglary and housebreaking, highway robbery, horse stealing and robbing churches.[7] In 1565 "felonious taking of money, goods, or any chattels, from the person of any other, privily without his knowl-

[1] Stephen, i, 463. However, the Church did not always interfere to save even clerical offenders from severe punishment at the hands of the temporal courts. See Traill, ii, 475.

[2] Hale, ii, 333.

[3] See Case of Grăme.

[4] 4 Henry VIII., c. 2.

[5] 23 Hen. VIII., c. 1, §§ 2, 3, 4.

[6] 28 Hen. VIII., c. 15, § 3.

[7] 1 Edw. VI., c. 12, § 9.

edge," was excluded from benefit of clergy. The courts interpreted this to mean above a shilling in value.[1] In 1576, "any manner of rape or burglary" was declared "without any allowance of the privilege of clergy;"[2] but the sections of this statute relating to burglary were very unskillfully framed. Abduction and forced marriage of heiresses was made a simple felony, with benefit of clergy, which must have practically negatived the law, by 3 Hen. VII., c. 2.[3] This offence seems to have been regarded as quite in the natural order of things.[4] 39 Eliz., c. 9, 1597, declared former statutes "insufficient," and decreed the death penalty without clergy.

From this legislation it is evident that the severity of the criminal law was greatly increased under the Tudors, for the terrible laws which had hitherto reached, for the most part, only the utterly illiterate and low-born, were now to be applied to the punishment as criminals of the educated, the powerful, the priestly classes of the nation, as well as to all men who for some slight knowledge of reading had been classed among the clerks, or servants of the Church.[5] But these statutes were so special and so variously worded that many loopholes still remained through which men could plead and obtain benefit of clergy. In this way, doubtless, many malefactors continued to escape the just reward of their deeds.[6]

To sum up this change in the laws: By the close of the sixteenth century death was the penalty decreed for the following crimes whether the offender could read or not:

[1] 8 Eliz., c. 4.

[2] 18 Eliz., c. 7.

[3] Also 4 and 5 Ph. and Mary, c. 8.

[4] See Pike.

[5] Women, not being eligible for holy orders, could not plead benefit of clergy. Mark the inequality of justice.

[6] This evil was not remedied until (3 Will. and Mary, c. 9, § 2), 1691, and (1 Anne, Stat. 2, c. 9). As the number of those who could plead benefit of clergy increased, the crimes to which this privilege extended became fewer and fewer.

High treason, petty treason, piracy, murder, arson, burglary, housebreaking and putting in fear, highway robbery, horse stealing, stealing from the person above the value of a shilling, rape and abduction with intent to marry. For all persons "who could not read, every kind of felony, including manslaughter, every kind of theft above the value of a shilling, and all robbery were capital crimes.[1]

Of how this system worked in practice we have but scanty evidence. It is probable that serious crime was very prevalent in the country districts, but not nearly so common in the cities. In 1514 the royal treasure-wagons were attacked and robbed upon the road, and eighty men were executed for the crime. The disorder and suffering of the times, the large amount of unemployment, created a great multitude of vagabonds and idle rogues, whom the oft-repeated penal statutes charge with "contynuall theftes," "robberyes and all evill actes and other mischiefs;" driven to such actions often, as the Act of 1533–4 declares, by their "myserye and povertie." Whether from public sympathy for such unfortunates, or for some other reason, the terrible penalties against vagabonds were very negligently enforced, as the statutes themselves bear witness. Thus the preamble to 1 Edw. VI., c. 3, 1547, states that former laws had accomplished almost nothing for the suppression of vagrancy, because of the "folishe pitie and mercie of them which should have seen the godlie Lawes executed." It is very doubtful whether mere vagabondage can be considered a crime in that age. In the cities—London for example—there does not seem to have been a very great amount of serious crime. A fearful murder, like that of Arden of Feversham (1551), created, apparently, just as much excitement as it would to-day. No criminal statistics of convictions or executions were kept till long afterward. But many of the

[1] Stephen, i, 467.

depositions and other records of the courts of Quarter Sessions, held at Exeter Castle, have been preserved. They begin in 1592.

"At the Lent Assizes of 1598 there were one hundred and thirty-four prisoners, of whom seventeen were dismissed with the fatal S. P., it being apparently too much trouble to write sus. per. coll. Twenty were flogged; one was liberated by special pardon and fifteen by general pardon; eleven claimed benefit of clergy, and were consequently branded and set free." "At the Epiphany Sessions preceding there were sixty-five prisoners, of whom eighteen were hanged. At Easter there were forty-one prisoners, and twelve of them were executed. At the Midsummer Sessions there were thirty-five prisoners and eight hanged. At the Autumn Assizes there were eighty-seven on the calendar and eighteen hanged. At the October Sessions there were twenty-five, of whom only one was hanged. Altogether there were seventy-four persons sentenced to be hanged in one county in a single year, and of these more than one-half were condemned at Quarter Sessions."[1]

Hamilton believes there was a special crusade against criminals in Devonshire at this time; but if each of the forty English counties averaged twenty executions in the year, or a little more than a quarter of the number of capital sentences in Devonshire in 1598, this would make a yearly average for all England of eight hundred criminals who paid the death penalty for their offences. The population of the country at this time was about 4,000,000, and it is quite possible that one in every 5,000 of the inhabitants was sent to the gallows every year. At all events, the number was notoriously very great. As Coke writes in the conclusion of his Third Institute: "What a lamentable case it is to see so many Chris-

[1] Hamilton, *History of Quarter Sessions*, pp. 30–1, compiled from Exeter Records.

tian men and women strangled on that cursed tree of the gallows, insomuch as if in a large field a man might see together all the Christians that but in one year throughout England come to that untimely and ignominious death, if there were any spark of grace or charity in him, it would make his heart to bleed for pity and compassion." Coke points out three remedies: Education, laws to set the idle on work, and "that forasmuch as many do offend in hope of pardon, that pardons be very rarely granted." Evidently there had been a very great change since the fourteenth and fifteenth centuries, when the great lords overawed or corrupted the courts of justice for the protection of their guilty followers, and the ecclesiastical courts shielded another large section of Englishmen from punishment as criminals.

Murder.—The history of the death penalty for murder well illustrates this change. It was not until Tudor times that a clear legal distinction was drawn between murder and homicide, and "unlawful killing with malice aforethought" was excluded from benefit of clergy, thus making that portion of the criminal law bear equally upon all men.[1] How necessary was this change which the increasing intelligence and moral sense of the nation demanded, a few facts will clearly prove, but it must have largely increased the number of serious criminals.

"Till 1487 any one who knew how to read might commit murder as often as he pleased, with no other result than that of being delivered to the Ordinary to make his purgation, with the chance of (its) being delivered to him 'absque purgatione.' That this should have been the law for several centuries seems hardly credible, but there is no doubt that it was. Even after 1487, a man who could read could com-

[1] The statutes which by degrees intraduced this important change are: 12 Henry VII., c. 7 (1496), which applied to petty treason; 4 Henry VIII., c. 2 (1512); 23 Henry VIII., c. 1, §§ 3 and 4 (1531); 1 Edw. VI., c. 12, § 9 (1547).

mit murder once with no other punishment than that of having M branded on the brawn of his left thumb, and if he was a clerk in orders he could, till 1547, commit any number of murders apparently without being branded more than once."[1]

The passionate blow unintentionally causing death was probably too common, and seemed too highly natural among the higher classes, to be socially regarded as criminal in those days of unrestrained temper. It was simply a misfortune—an unfortunate accident. When the laboring classes were tied to the soil, the master who killed his serf in a fit of anger was certainly very far from being thought a criminal. So long as the social mind confused mere homicide with wilful murder, it was not ready to punish, or at any rate not to punish severely, the revered clergy or any member of the governing classes for such an act. Naturally the weight of the upper orders went to maintaining this good old custom of practical immunity. It was good not to be a criminal, and hang for it. But with the laboring masses all was very different. They should have learnt by long centuries of oppression to curb their tempers and not strike deadly blows. It was not good for society to let them get into so bad a habit. Consequently, the low-born, ignorant man-slayer paid with his life for the life he had taken. But when knowledge of reading became diffused among the common people — how then? The middle classes were attaining to power. People were thinking more clearly and intelligently. The upper classes had become discredited. Murder was distinguished from homicide, and the law was made equal for all men. Every murderer was henceforth (in theory at least) a heinous criminal, and his punishment was death.

[1] Stephen, i, 463–4.

CONCLUSION

England in the sixteenth century had great need of strong law, strongly enforced against all men, and this is what her Tudor sovereigns gave her. But all the great nations of Europe, and not England alone, then felt the need of a dictator. It was an age of great religious, political, intellectual and social upheaval, when the old feudal state was passing into the modern nation. Everywhere we find concentration of power in the hand of a despotic and often of an absolute monarch, strong enough to hold the nation firmly together and crush the growing forces of anarchy and confusion. It was a period of rapid growth and of very greatly increased crime and criminals. In England this flood of criminality largely took the direction of acts:

1. Against the life and person of the king: treasons, libels, etc.

2. Against national unity and the majesty of the law: statutes of maintenance and livery, etc., for the suppression of the anarchic feudal baronage and their followers, were now first enforced.

3. Against the established religion: heresy, præmunire and other laws, new and old.

4. In violation of the new laws, making justice more equal for all men, by excluding many serious crimes from benefit of clergy.

The criminal law was terribly severe in Tudor times, and punishments were largely enforced. Out of 387 persons presented for trial in a single county, Devonshire, in one year (1598), 74 were hanged. This is not far from one-fifth of those presented. The amount of what was regarded as serious crime seems to have been great — very much greater than at present, in proportion to the population.

Does this negative the idea that crime increases as society develops to a higher stage of civilization, and that such increase is possibly a necessary factor in upward social progress—new criminal laws safeguarding new growth?

Not at all. The facts support the theory, for they show a very large increase in the amount of serious criminality, resulting from the operation of new laws or of old laws now first successfully enforced, at a time of rapid growth, when the English nation was at length entering into, taking possession of, and safeguarding that larger life, truer liberty, more strong and equal justice, for which it had long been preparing.

Social progress is not regular and equal, year by year, century by century. It comes by leaps and bounds—a sudden development, an almost fierce expansion, followed by a long period of quiescence or seeming retrogression, a time of silent preparation. Like a crustacean, shedding its old shell, which in a few hours seems ridiculously small, it expands rapidly for a brief season until the new sheathing hardens round it, and then for a year it stores its powers, preparing for another crisis, another period of apparently sudden growth.[1]

The sixteenth century, in England, with its greatly increased criminality, followed upon a long period of moral degradation, corruption and intimidation of justice, and of decreasing crime. While the new feudalism was triumphant there were but few statutes creating new criminal offences, and most of these could not be enforced. In the seventeenth century we reach another period of violent upheaval and civil war, when but little was added to the criminal law, and consequently there were but few new crimes in England.

But was there more crime in the sixteenth century than in

[1] Criminal law is in some respects like the crustacean's shell. It hardens round the nation and safeguards the social life, but in time it becomes too small and must be broken through and extended to permit new growth, while casting a more ample protecting shield around the larger life.

our own day? Certainly not. The nation made a strong attempt at that time to stamp out certain forms of most serious crime by the infliction of severe punishment. On the other hand many bad crimes were then practically unknown, for the social mind had not yet created them, by stamping such actions with public disapproval and punishing them as crimes. Doubtless in Tudor England there were more murderers, highway robbers, etc., than in the England of to-day, and the wholesale hangings probably rid the nation of a large part of its brutal criminal degenerates. Society then and since has been to a great extent successful in stamping out these old deeds of serious and often passionate crime. Modern man has learned to keep the peace and curb his temper, thanks to strong law and the hanging of bad human stock. In every progressive and truly prosperous nation we should expect to find, and I believe very generally do find the laws successful, and old crimes gradually diminishing.[1] But crimes of fraud have to-day taken the place of crimes of violence, and society is now engaged in its struggle against the fraudulent criminals its business and social developments have called into existence.[2] Some serious forms of crime thus show decreasing criminality, while other serious crimes have been coming into existence, and the enforcement of the laws against them has increased the number of criminals.

It is not, however, upon the doubtful weighing of decrease and increase among serious crimes that the proof or failure of our theory depends. The modern age is an age of misdemeanors, and the Tudor age was not. There is the truth in a nutshell. The nation was so occupied with great changes in Church and State, the legislature and the courts

[1] Modern criminal statistics confirm this.

[2] Some of these crimes are fraudulent bankruptcy, and forgery in writing, of various kinds.

of justice so busy with new heresy, new treason and new felony, that there was little time or thought for the creation of petty misdemeanors, safeguarding the minor needs of social life. It was a time for stern laws and terrible punishments, if the English were to be held firmly together, changed from a feudal state into a modern nation, the Church reformed, justice equalized, anarchy crushed, order established. One hears little of misdemeanors in those days. Of course they existed and were punished to some extent by the pillory, imprisonment, branding and fines; but the old system of fines had fallen greatly into disuse,[1] the gaols were mostly for the detention of debtors and those awaiting trial, and there was then no prison system in England. The trained police force is a modern institution. One important reason why hanging, branding, flogging and mutilation were so frequently inflicted, was because no other system of punishment for serious crimes had yet been devised. Either death must rid the nation of the malefactor forever, or branding or mutilation must mark him, so that all may know him for a criminal and be on their guard.

In modern England, according to the census of 1891, there is one police officer for every 714 of the population, a grand total of 40,596 men employed to perserve order and bring offenders against the laws to justice. A great multitude of so-called police-court offences have been created, and the police force is very largely engaged in the arrest and prosecution of perpetrators of these and other misdemeanors, most of which were unknown in the sixteenth century. Thus, under the Elementary Education Act, there were 82,745 persons convicted and punished each year, from 1889 to 1893, inclusive. Under the head of police regulations the annual average for the same period was 77,980. Other misdemeanors are cruelty to animals (11,855), offences in re-

[1] Stephen, ii, 203.

lation to dogs and diseases of animals (7,095), vaccination acts (2,312), railway offences (3,554), stage and hackney carriage acts (9,478), offences against sanitary laws (8,822). It is this multitude of petty transgressions—of ever-increasing misdemeanors—punished by the modern state, and unknown to the laws a single century ago, which swells our criminal lists. We have more criminals than our ancestors to deal with, but it is because society is growing better, more sensitive to right and wrong, more interdependent, that this is true, and not because we are growing worse or more rebellious against law.[1]

[1] [See page 15). The offenders punished for modern misdemeanors are as truly criminals as are murderers and robbers, for all are punished by society for wrongs against itself.

CHAPTER X

ENGLAND UNDER THE STUARTS. 1603–1714

THE sixteenth century was a period of rapid development and expansion, the seventeenth one of painful introspection and civil strife. Enormous powers had been granted the Tudors:

1. To restore order and enforce the laws, especially against the anarchic nobility.

2. To separate the English Churchfrom Rome and to reform ecclesiastical abuses.

3. To defend the nation against threatened invasions.

After the Armada, the work of the Tudors was practically accomplished. Their dictatorship was supported by the people, and on the whole they used their discretionary powers well. They made no attempt to define their authority, but were content to plead social necessity. Not so their successors. James I, "the wisest fool in Europe," immediately sought to define the prerogative, and claimed, by divine right, an absolute authority above all human law. In this he was supported by the Established Church, which also maintained the duty of passive obedience to the king.[1]

Through Tudor reigns, the middle classes had grown strong, wealthy and intelligent, and neither people nor Parliament had relinquished the ancient belief that a king of England was such by the will of the people, was responsible to the people, and must obey the nation's laws. All the Stuart period is filled with the struggle of Parliament (es-

[1] Rushworth, i, 422–3; Hallam, i, 415.

pecially the Commons) to curb the royal prerogative; a struggle resulting in the beheading of one king, the dethronement of another, and the establishment of a new line of Protestant sovereigns. But the conflict was religious as well as political. Indeed, it is hard to determine which element was the more powerful. Puritans were dominant in the House of Commons; they were the great supporters of constitutional government and popular liberty against the arbitrary and contemptuous despotism of the Stuart kings; but their antagonism to bishops, ceremonies, ritual—all that reminded them of the Romish Church—filled them with religious zeal and fed the fires of opposition. These two great problems, the extent of the royal prerogative and the question of state religion, confront us throughout the entire seventeenth century, and were already prominent when James I. ascended the English throne. A hearty welcome from a strong and united nation greeted him; but both James and his son utterly failed to understand the English people and the strong, new development of the old constitutional idea. Deeply convinced of their divine right to rule the nation as they thought best, and supported, not only by the High Church prelates[1] and nobility, but also by many decisions of the judges,[2] they thought that the vexatious opposition to their beneficent government proceeded chiefly from a few turbulent members of the House of Commons, and would cease with their suppression.[3] But Parliament after

[1] Rushworth, i, 422–3; Hallam, i, 322–3.

[2] *State Trials*, ii, 371 (Case of John Bates); Hallam, i, 318. Mr. John Bates was prosecuted for "refusing to pay a duty on foreign currants, imposed by a mere act of the crown." The Court of Exchequer "unanimously supported this taxation by prerogative." See Hampden's case, *State Trials*, iii, 825.

All the judges of Westminster Hall, with but two exceptions, gave judgment in favor of the legality of ship money. Monopolies, loans and benevolences also received some legal sanction during this period. See *State Trials*, ii, 372.

[3] See Rushworth, iv, 482, for attempt of King Charles I. against the five members of the House of Commons.

Parliament took up the same grievances, and made money grants conditional upon their redress.[1] Neither king nor Commons would yield, and the Stuarts, in desperate need of money, resorted to all manner of illegal taxation to obtain it. Refusal to pay was met by conviction and punishment at the hands of judges, bribed or terrified into subservience to the crown.[2] Never before, in English history, had corruption been so widespread, so brazen-faced.[3] The decision of the judges in Darnel's, or the five knights' case, gave the king the right of arbitrary imprisonment, and practically annihilated the 29th clause of Magna Charta; *i. e.* "No free man shall be taken and imprisoned unless by lawful judgment of his peers, or the law of the land."[4] The Court of Star Chamber and the High Commission Court became the deeply-hated instruments of royal tyranny and extortion,[5] and were finally swept away by the Long Parliament in 1640, when "ship money, tonnage and poundage, and all impositions levied without consent of Parliament were declared illegal."[6]

Civil war brought victory to the constitutional party, the execution of King Charles as a traitor to his country, and the establishment of Presbyterianism as the state religion. But the melancholy tyranny of the new discipline, the unrest, insecurity and uncertainty of the times, brought inevitable reaction and the restoration of Charles II. His reign was noteworthy for its "good laws and bad government," for the triumph of vice and sensuality, for the terrible persecutions of non-conformists. Renewed despotism under James II., in

[1] See discussion of the Bates case in Parliament, 1610, and many subsequent petitions and remonstrances.

[2] See Pym's speech against Strafford in the Commons. Rushworth, iv, 200.

[3] Hallam, i, 358.

[4] *State Trials*, iii, 1.

[5] Rushworth, ii, 475; Hallam, i, 349–50; ii, 9–10, 31.

[6] Rushworth, iv, 88; Traill, iv, 14.

his attempt to reintroduce the Roman Catholic religion, contrary to the laws of the land, brought the great revolution of 1688, the dethronement of the king, and the final establishment of a constitutional and Protestant monarchy. There were three successful revolutions in less than half a century; and as either party rose to power, it used the strong arm of the law to punish, as the worst of criminals, those who attempted to overthrow the established order of society. Punishment of traitors, libelers and non-conformists was frightfully severe, and constantly enforced.[1] Even after toleration had been granted to all Protestant sectarians, in the reign of William and Mary, penalties against Roman Catholics were made more severe.[2]

Criminal statutes were ready weapons against political and religious enemies within the state: weapons which each triumphant party was compelled to use for the safe-guarding of the new social development for which it stood. Many of these penal laws were of temporary service only, and have since been repealed. Some aided the nation's upward progress, some were reactionary and retrogressive, but all were intended to support the true life of society as seen by that part of the nation then supporting the government; and the criminals of the seventeenth century are mainly political and religious offenders against these statutes, similar laws of previous reigns, and the multitude of prohibitions created or resurrected by decisions of the Court of Star Chamber and the High Commission Court.

Early in the seventeenth century the House of Commons reasserted its long disused right of impeachment, and Parliament became once more a high court of justice, holding the powerful ministers of state responsible to the nation for their stewardship. Shameless corruption had made its way through all departments of official life during the reign of

[1] *State Trials.*

[2] 1 Will. and Mary, c. 9 and c. 15.

James I. Lord Chancellor Bacon was convicted on impeachment by the Commons, and fined £40,000 for receiving bribes from suitors.[1] The Earl of Middlesex, Lord Treasurer, was unanimously convicted of bribery and other offences.[2] Other impeachments were those of Mompesson and Michell, both convicted and punished; Field, Bishop of Llandaff, censured for bribery, and Sir John Bennet, judge, for corruption in office.[3] Under Charles I., Mainwaring was impeached, fined £1,000, and declared ineligible for any dignity in the Church, for proclaiming the absolute authority of the king in his sermons; but Charles quickly pardoned him and advanced him to a bishopric.[4] In 1640, Strafford was impeached and executed for high treason [5] against the state, and later Archbishop Laud shared his fate.[6] Evidently Parliament was very earnest to put down official corruption, and defend the constitutional rights of Englishmen against the supporters of royal despotism. The end of the great tragedy witnessed the trial and execution of Charles Stuart, King of England, as a "tyrant, traitor, murderer and public enemy." [7]

The supporters of the Divine Right of Kings were still more active in punishing their political and religious opponents as criminals. Both executive and judicial authority were largely in their hands, and through the Court of Star Chamber, with its branches, and the Court of High Commission, they used their powers mercilessly.[8] The Earl of Oxford, Sir Edward Coke, Sir Robert Philips, Mr. Pym, and a few other members of Parliament were sent to the Tower or other prisons during the reign of James I., "on pretence of having spoken words against the king," or other similar

[1] *State Trials*, ii, 1088 (1620).
[2] *Ibid.*, ii, 1184 and 1250 (1624).
[3] *Ibid.*, ii.
[4] Rushworth, i, 423; *State Trials*, iii, 335.
[5] Rushworth, viii, and iv, 267–9.
[6] *Ibid.*, iv, 202.
[7] *State Trials*, iv, 1128.
[8] Rushworth, ii, 475.

offences.[1] Under Charles I. the Earl of Arundel was sent to the Tower for a marriage displeasing to the king, and Sir John Eliot, Hollis, Selden, Long, Hobart, Stroud, and other eminent members of the Commons, were committed, some to the Tower, some to the King's Bench prison, and their papers seized, "for notable contempt and for stirring up sedition, in a warrant under the King's Sign Manual."[2] "The court was unanimous in declaring they had jurisdiction, although the alleged offences were committed in Parliament."[3] Refusing to contribute to a "benevolence" for the king was made a crime by decisions of the Court of Star Chamber, early in the 17th century. Thus, Mr. Oliver St. John was fined "£5000 and imprisonment during pleasure" for such a refusal and for putting legal reasons for his action into a letter.[4] Later, Mr. Richard Chambers was fined £2000 and sent to prison for a like offence.[5] Many other gentry were thus imprisoned, while common people who refused to aid the king by contributing to a "general loan" were impressed for service in the navy.[6]

The utter tyranny and contempt of the High Commission Court for the laws and liberties of Englishmen were glaringly shown in the case of Mr. Fuller, lawyer, imprisoned till he died for moving the release from prison of two Puritans, committed by this court for refusing to take the *ex-officio* oath. Fuller's plea was that "the High Commissioners were not empowered by law to imprison or to fine any of his majesty's subjects." This was punished as "an unpardonable crime."[7] The State Trials of this period furnish many

[1] Hallam, i, 368.

[2] Rushworth, ii, 79; *State Trials*, iii, 235 and 293; Hallam, ii, 2. Eliot was also fined £2000, and died in prison.

[3] Hallam, ii, 5.

[4] *State Trials*, ii, 899.

[5] *Ibid.*, iii, 373.

[6] Rushworth, i, 426 (1626); Hallam, i, 383 and 416.

[7] Neal, ii, 39 (1610); Fuller, iii, 243.

instances of the utterly illegal punishments of both men and women. Thus, Lady Shrewsbury was fined £20,000 and discretionary imprisonment for refusing to answer damaging questions,[1] and Peacham was found guilty of high treason (compassing the king's death) for merely having in his possession a sermon, never preached nor intended to be preached, severely censuring the king and government.[2] He "was examined before torture, in torture, between torture and after torture" (Jan. 19th, 1614) for this offence, and, though no confession was secured, he was condemned, but not finally executed.[3]

The principal offences within the jurisdiction of the court of Star Chamber were: maintenance, riot, forgery, perjury, fraud, libel and conspiracy; but this court also established its right to enquire into and punish "every misdemeanor," especially those of public importance, "for which the law, as then understood, had provided no sufficient punishment,"[4] The decisions of this court created many new crimes; some of them very wrongly chosen because the acts punished were helpful to the public welfare, but others the true crimes of the age because thoroughly injurious to social life, at that stage of its development. Thus, "corruption, breach of trust, malfeasance in public affairs," and all "attempts at felony" were non-indictable by the common law, and practically not crimes until the Star Chamber made them so.[5] The evil that it did largely perished with it, in 1640, but the good work accomplished by its authority was permanent and

[1] *State Trials*, ii, 769. [2] *Ibid.*, ii, 869.

[3] *Ibid.*, ii, 871. See also cases of Arabella Stuart (Winwood, iii, 201, 279); Whitlock (*State Trials*, ii, 765); Thomas Owen (*Ibid.*, ii, 879), and Williams, convicted of high treason for predicting the king's death in 1621. Also, Sir Walter Raleigh (*State Trials*, ii, 1.)

[4] Hallam, ii, 31.

Hallam, ii, 31. The highest officers of state had been held responsible by Parliament for malfeasance in office during the fourteenth and fifteenth centuries.

well worthy of a great court of justice. But this work, both good and bad, meant the rapid increase of social prohibitions and the multiplication of crimes and criminals. When we examine the numerous cases tried before this tribunal,[1] we find that the bulk of them were misdemeanors—many of them political—such as libels, conspiracies, breaches of the public peace and assaults with violence. The money penalties inflicted were enormous. Thus, Allington was fined £12,000 for marrying his niece; Sir David Fowlis, for opprobrious words against Lord Wentworth, £5000 to the king and £3000 to the party libeled.[2] Sending a challenge to the Earl of Northumberland was punished by a fine of £5000. For saying the Earl of Suffolk was a base lord, £4000 were awarded to him and £4000 to the king. Bishop Williams' sentence for concealment of a libelous letter was £5000 to the king, £3000 to the archbishop, and imprisonment during pleasure.[3] Soap-boilers, for not complying with the king's illegal monopoly, were fined £1500, and again £1000.[4] Besides crushing fines and life-long imprisonment, the punishments for more humble criminals were bloody whippings, pillory, slitting of the nose, cutting off the ears, branding of the cheek or forehead—all inflicted with extreme cruelty. The revival of the ancient forest laws and other statutes long disused, was simply for the purpose of exacting money to supply the urgent needs of the king. Monstrous fines were imposed on trespassers. Lord Salisbury was fined £20,000, Lord Westmorland, £19,000, and Sir Christopher Hatton, £12,000. The Earl of Southampton was nearly ruined by forest boundary decisions. For certain alleged breaches of

[1] See Rushworth and *State Trials*.

[2] *State Trials*, iii, 586.

[3] *Ibid.*, iii, 770.

[4] See also cases of Leighton, Lilburn, Prynne, Burton, Bastwick, and a multitude of others recorded in Rushworth, ii, 57, 469, 471, and *State Trials*. For the Council of the North, see prosecutions of Sir David Fowlis, Bellasis and Maleverer. (Rushworth.)

their charter rights, the Star Chamber imposed a fine of £70,000 on the city of London, and the money was paid.[1]

History reveals the drawing of an even larger proportion of criminal cases into these royal courts of extraordinary jurisdiction, with the evident intention of magnifying the king's power (by giving royal proclamations the force of laws, etc.), and punishing his political and religious opponents as criminals, while at the same time securing a considerable revenue by fines and forfeitures, and habituating the nation to a criminal jurisdiction, less restrained and more closely dependent upon the will of the king.[2] The Council of the North and the Council of Wales (branches of the Star Chamber) are said to have "deprived one-third of England of the privileges of the common law," and the wide sweep of the criminal jurisdiction exercised by the Star Chamber itself has just been evidenced.[3] Laud "absolutely governed the Church through the High Commission Court," but thought the punishments imposed on the refractory, both clericals and laity, inadequate.[4] The ordinary courts of common law must have been completely overawed and half paralyzed during the first half of the seventeenth century.[5] Juries returning verdicts disagreeable to the government were liable to a summons before the Star Chamber, which reprimanded, fined, or imprisoned them, thus creating a new class of criminals. Records of the courts of Quarter Sessions in Devonshire and Bucks counties[6] show that the criminal cases left for their decision were comparatively few and generally unimportant.

Ecclesiastical Offences. The Court of High Commission

[1] Hallam, ii, 27.
[2] *Ibid.*, ii, 34.
[3] *Ibid.*, ii, 99.
[4] *Ibid.*, ii, 46.
[5] See the "emphatically threatening words" of Wentworth, Earl of Strafford, to some justices of the peace, "that the king's little finger should be heavier than the loins of the law." Rushworth, viii, 149, 154.
[6] Hamilton, *History of Quarter Sessions*.

was created by an act of Queen Elizabeth to try religious offences "according to the known boundaries of ecclesiastical jurisdiction;" [1] but in the seventeenth century it assumed the power to imprison and to fine the laity, and became more and more tyrannical in its illegal practices.[2] Many Puritan clergymen were deprived for non-conformity under James I. and Archbishop Bancroft, the number being variously estimated at from three hundred to forty-nine.[3] In the very beginning of this reign, persecutions of the Papists were renewed with rigor. 1 Jas. I., c. 4, 1603–4, decreed new penalties against recusants, and forbade them to educate their children according to their religious faith. The administration of the laws was made exceedingly severe. The jails were filled, and a few men were put to death.[4] "Recusants in the middle classes of life were ground to the dust by repeated forfeitures." In Hereford county alone "four hundred and nine families suddenly found themselves reduced to a state of beggary." [5] Under Archbishop Laud, prosecutions for non-conformity were renewed with great severity. Those who objected to "his novel ceremonies," or dared to preach on the Calvinistic side, were "harassed by the High Commission Court as if they had been actual schismatics." [6] Thirty of the "precise" or puritanical clergy were excommunicated and deprived in the single diocese of Norwich for refusing to read in their churches a proclamation called the "Book of Sports." This was enforced as a test of Puritanism throughout all England, and several hundred Englishmen about this time exiled themselves to the coast of Massachusetts to be free from persecution and serve God in a savage land.[7] On the other hand, Charles I. favored his

[1] Hallam, ii, 98. [2] Neal, ii, 244–6. [3] Hallam, i, 394.
[4] 7 Jas. I., c. 6, 1609–10; Hallam, i, 405; Lingard, ix, 41, 55.
[5] Lingard, ix, 41, 53–6. [6] Hallam, ii, 55; Neal, ii, 236–9.
[7] Neal, ii, 228.

Roman Catholic subjects, "winked at the domestic exercise of the Catholic religion," and did not enforce the fines and imprisonments for recusancy which the laws demanded. Only one Romish priest was executed before 1640, and the number of Romanists pardoned during the first sixteen years of Charles' reign is said to have been 11,970 in but twenty-nine counties. The large and increasing number of converts to the Romish faith—some of them men and women high in royal favor—excited great alarm throughout the nation. Clarendon tells us that "they (the Papists) were looked upon as good subjects at court, and as good neighbours in the country; all the restraints and reproaches of former times being forgotten." Evidently Romanism was not a crime in this reign.[1]

When the Puritans came into power, Parliament subscribed the covenant, and a severe persecution of the Anglican Episcopalians followed. The private estates of all clergy who had helped King Charles were confiscated by an ordinance of April 1, 1643. But when the Covenant was imposed as a test of conformity to Presbyterianism and the established government, about 1600 beneficed ministers, probably more than one-fifth of all in the kingdom, were ejected from their churches for refusing to sign it. The Puritans made a large variety of sports criminal: such as wrestling, shooting, bowling, ringing of bells for pleasure, masks, wakes, church-ale, games, dancing or other pastime. All persons were forbidden to be present at such on the Lord's day, under heavy penalties.[2]

Cromwell seems to have desired the establishment of religious liberty, but the English nation was not yet ready for

[1] Clarendon, i, 116 and 142 for Sec'y Windebank releasing papists; Neal, ii, 226; Hallam, ii, 58 and 66–7. There were from 250 to 360 Jesuit priests in England, 180 other regulars, and five or six hundred secular priests. Hallam, ii, 61.

[2] Traill, iv, 167.

so radical a change, and after the Restoration, Parliament reached a height of religious intolerance never seen before nor since in England; as the Corporation Act of 1661, the Act of Uniformity, 1662, the Conventicle Act, 1664, and the Five-Mile Act, 1665, abundantly prove. The Act of Uniformity, 13 and 14 Car. II., c. iv, § 3, decreed that every beneficed minister, fellow of a college and even schoolmaster must unfeignedly agree to all the contents of the book of common prayer. About 2000 Presbyterian clergymen were deprived for non-compliance with this act, on St. Bartholemew's day, in the year 1662.[1] The act for suppressing seditious conventicles punished attendance at such by three months imprisonment for the first offence, six months for the second, and seven years transportation for the third, "on conviction before a single justice of the peace." The gaols were soon filled with both ministers and laymen.[2] Statute 17 Car. II., c. 2, known as the Five Mile Act, was horribly severe. By far the greater number of non-conformist clergy refused to take the subscribed oath, and were driven from their homes into the wilderness.[3]

Twelve years after this date, in 1677, capital punishment for heretics was abolished by law. Apparently the English people were beginning to tire of religious persecution. But regarding the original social necessity or great usefulness of punishing sins and non-conformity as crimes, Stephen writes: "If scepticism had been accepted as a basis of legislation, say at and after the barbarian conquests, it is difficult to see how western Europe could ever have ceased to be barbarous. Or, if the same view had prevailed in the 15th, 16th and 17th centuries, it is difficult to see how the oppressions of the clergy could ever have been removed."[4]

Turning from religious offences back to political and other

[1] Neal, iv, 326 and 335; Baxter, *Life*, part 2. p. 384.
[2] Hallam, ii, 347.
[3] Hallam, ii, 351.
[4] Stephen, ii.

crimes, it appears that during the civil war "the gown had to yield to the sword, and the laws were comparatively silent in the midst of arms."[1] Under Cromwell, military despotism overrode the common law. Rebellion among the people and the resistance of Parliament to his authority compelled such action, yet, on the whole, the country was wisely, if despotically, governed. The kingdom was divided into eleven districts, and over each was placed a colonel or major-general[2] "bitterly hostile to the royalist party and insolent towards all civil authority." How many criminals (probably mostly political and religious) were punished by these military judges we have no means of knowing; but proceedings at common law were frequently interrupted,[3] and for all men alike the times were "troublesome" and "distracted."[4]

Charles II returned to his throne amid the joyful acclamations of his people. The declaration from Breda gave a free and general pardon "to all his subjects" not specially "excepted by Parliament;" but this boasted forgiveness amounted to very little in practice. Thirteen of the regicides were put to death.[5] Sir Henry Vane was executed on a charge of high treason, in violation of the king's promise, and a straining of the law.[6] Colonel Hutchinson died in prison, and many other officers of the old army were illegally incarcerated for years—Wildman, Creed and others. The law of high treason was made more strict during the king's lifetime,[7] and the State Trials bear ample witness to the utter brutality and hateful partiality of the royal judges, Scroggs, North and Jones, during this reign. "Never," writes Hallam,

[1] Hamilton, p. 127. [2] Thurloe, iii, 701.

[3] Thurloe, iii, 78, 265, 296–7, 359–60, 568.

[4] For instances of Cromwell's arbitrary government and violations of law, see case of Maynard, Twisden and Wyndham, sent to the Tower; Gerard and Vowel, executed in 1654; Slingsby and Hewet in 1658. *State Trials*, v, 518, 871, 883.

[5] *State Trials*, v, 947. [6] *Ibid.*, vi, 120. [7] 13 Car. II., c. 1, 1661.

"were our tribunals so disgraced."[1] Yet the Court of Star Chamber and its branches, swept away in 1640, were not restored, and "the Ecclesiastical Courts were reduced to a dignified impotence."[2] The practice of rebuking, fining and imprisoning jurors for returning verdicts against the direction of the court was given up and declared illegal. English common law was virtually completed, and since the Restoration the adapting of law to the growing needs of society has been mainly the work of Parliament and the Courts of Equity.[3]

The brief reign of James II is notable for his arbitrary reassumption of despotic power to accomplish his great desire, the restoration of the Roman Catholic religion.[4] His intemperate zeal soon united the majority of Englishmen against him, and on the prosecution and acquittal of the bishops (June, 1688),[5] the Anglican clergy finally renounced their doctrine of passive obedience to royalty, and strongly supported the popular movement before which James fled.

With William and Mary England entered upon a great period of reform, both in the policy of government and in the social life of the people. The first step taken was the establishment of legal toleration for Protestant non-conformists. Although Papists were expressly excluded, there were almost no more persons punished for their religious beliefs and observances.[6] Religious crimes practically disappeared and political offences rapidly decreased.[7] A few new

[1] Hallam, ii, 423.

[2] Traill, iv, 362. For evidence of the early usefulness of these despotic courts, see the resentment shown by Yorkshire men over the suppression of the Council of the North, which had proved itself "a bridle on the stout nobles." Traill, iv, 222.

[3] Traill, iv, 363.

[4] *State Trials*, xi, 1315. Proceedings against the Univ. of Cambridge.

[5] *Ibid.*, xii, 183.

[6] Stephen, ii, 492, and Hamilton, pp. 253 and 258.

[7] *State Trials*, xii.

treason statutes were enacted, but these were in their nature essentially temporary, though necessary safeguards of the new social life. Thus, in 1698, by 9 Will. III., c. 1, it was made treason for the followers of James II. to return to England without special license; and in 1701, by 12 and 13 Will. III., c. 3, corresponding with "the pretended Prince of Wales" was declared treason. In Queen Anne's reign there were several similar acts.[1]

But in the sweeping away of this great mass of political and religious offences, crimes did not cease. Criminal punishments were merely transferred from the field of religion and politics, to be used against conduct which had largely ceased to be criminal since the restoration of the house of Stuart.[2] William and Mary strongly urged the enforcement of laws against swearing, immorality, drunkenness, and other lewd and disorderly practices which had universally spread themselves by neglect or connivance of the magistrates. But, on the whole, it was from the people, rather than from government, that the movement for social purification came. Voluntary associations of citizens took up the work. Five hundred disorderly houses were suppressed in London alone before 1699, and the movement showed extraordinary success elsewhere.[3]

Religious and political crimes, and the enforcement of penalties against them by courts of extraordinary jurisdiction, have filled most of this chapter; but there were other criminal tribunals, ordinary courts of common law, which though much weakened and tyrannized over by a centralized administration of justice, by military despots and dictatorial judges, yet continued to hold sessions and decree punishments. These will now be considered, but unfortunately the

[1] 1 Anne, c. 17, 1702; 3 and 4 Anne, c. 14, 1705; 4 Anne, c. 8, 1705; 6 Anne, c. 7, 1709; 7 Anne, c. 4, 1709.

[2] See 4 Will. and Mary, c. 8.

[3] Traill, iv, 593–4.

records that have come down to us are very incomplete. The best evidence is furnished by the records of the Court of Quarter Sessions preserved at Exeter Castle, for the county of Devon, and the records of the neighboring county of Bucks.

In the records of Quarter Sessions during the reign of James I. there is much evidence of the corruption and extortion practised by all ranks and degrees of officials. Charges were frequently "preferred and proved" against constables and rate-collectors, bailiffs, "clerks of the market," and other similar persons; and the justices even sent a letter to the Chief Justice, in 1604, requesting that one Collacott be made an example of for his notorious corrupt practices; but nothing is said as to the actual infliction of punishment on these offenders—a very significant silence. On the other hand, directions for more strictness in prosecuting recusants arrived from the council of the king, and convictions became very frequent.[1] Men were committed to prison for baptizing a mare and a dog, and other petty offences and sins. The game laws also appear to have been quite strictly enforced.[2] The penalty for drunkenness was five shillings, "at which it remained until our own times;" but this fine did not prevent, and was probably not much enforced, for intoxication was disgustingly customary, even at the royal court. Vagrants fairly swarmed in England during the first quarter of the 17th century. The justices neglected to enforce the laws for branding them, nor were the people willing to lay information against them. Evidently neither vagrancy nor drunkenness can be considered crimes in that age, for society refused to inflict punishment. Under Charles I. we find frequent sentences to the pillory for "cozening the people by telling fortunes."[3] Witchcraft, charm and sorcery were punished by a year's imprisonment. Humphrey Moore, for

[1] Hamilton, pp. 74–5. [2] *Ibid.*, pp. 89 and 111. [3] *Ibid.*, p. 113.

"being a very lewd and dangerous fellow" and for "false accusation," was sent to the House of Correction. Those who attended "revels, maypoles and the like" were to be punished as "idle and lewd people." Most of the offences punished by Quarter Sessions during the reigns of the first two Stuart kings were very insignificant, showing how large a proportion of the serious crimes was drawn into the jurisdiction of higher courts. There were many complaints of outrages by soldiers quartered in the country, but no punishments could be inflicted.[1] At the winter Assizes of 1630 there was an extraordinarily long calendar of prisoners, and seventeen of them were hanged, but this can be accounted for by the prevalent distress, caused by dearth and the high price of food. It is evidently not a customary number of criminals. During the civil war "the justices were out a colonelling," and legal business was almost at a standstill.

Under the Commonwealth most of the cases tried at Quarter Sessions related to petty sins. There are "literally hundreds of such indictments of this period" for the single county of Devon.[2] As the cavalier poet sang:

> "Those gospel-walking times,
> When slightest sins are greatest crimes."

Swearing was a crime very strictly punished. Every oath was counted. A single specimen was fined 6s. 8d., but the charge was reduced to 3s. 4d. for a quantity. Among the "oaths" thus fined were "upon my life;" "on my troth;" saying "God's life" in conversation, and "God is my witness," in court.[3] By a Devonshire order we learn that every woman who had ever borne an illegitimate child and remained unpunished, was to be committed for trial. The sentence was generally three months' imprisonment, but sometimes

[1] Hamilton, p. 114. [2] *Ibid.*, p. 159.

[3] For Sabbath breaking and many other offences, see Hamilton, pp. 153–162.

"to be whipt." Twenty-two such cases are on record for a single sessions.[1] The laws against sturdy beggars, rogues and vagabonds, remained, however, unenforced. The death penalty was decreed against adulterers, but there was great partiality in prosecuting. Less than 5 per cent. of those indicted in Devonshire were males. Fines of from £5 to £500 were inflicted for "traitorous words" against the Lord Protector.[2] Deducting the petty sins punished as misdemeanors, by fine and imprisonment, the calendars of Quarter Sessions are decidedly short; but we do not know how many offenders were disposed of by the Judges of Assize and by the Major Generals.

Entries in the Devonshire records during the reign of Charles II. relate chiefly to the persecution of Protestant non-conformists, and to the imposition of the hearth tax.[3] Intolerance seems to have been the essential qualification for a justice of the peace in those days. Epitaphs of the time, relating the virtues of the deceased, tell how he was "Ecclesiæ Anglicanæ, vindex acerrimus." The records of Quarter Sessions do not show how many were punished for their religion by imprisonment and transportation, for when such penalties were inflicted, the nature of the offence was rarely mentioned. But one-third of all the fines, imposed for non-conformity, had to be paid in at Quarter Sessions, and some record of accounts collected has thus come down to us. In Devonshire, 1665, but one case is mentioned: Roger Murkle, attending conventicle, fined "x s.," and on refusal to pay, committed for one month. In the strongly Protestant county of Bucks (from 1678 to 1682) there were many indictments against Popish recusants, and about 1682 many scores of Protestant "absenters from church" were

[1] Hamilton, p. 160.

[2] See cases of James Nynoe, Mary Farye, and John Hinxlie.

[3] Hamilton, pp. 173, 177–200.

indicted, but very many of the offenders, both Papists and Protestants, were not arrested.[1] Thieves, wandering peddlers and other small offenders were publicly whipped in Bucks, and sometimes the penalty was worse than the crime.

Under James II. the business of Quarter Sessions continued much the same. The justices dealt for the most part with petty offences, gaming, vagabondage, etc., and there were but few punishments inflicted.[2] After the Monmouth rebellion (1685), there was renewed prosecution of non-conformists, and several ministers were executed,[3] but Judge Jeffries had visited Exeter in 1685 and "left little work for the county (Devon) justices to do," except for the high sheriff, who cared for the hanging and quartering of the rebels.[4] Twenty-six rebels were executed in Devonshire, and at least 233 in the county of Somerset; while 400 were condemned at Taunton and 700 at Wells, in the "Bloody Assizes." Whipping and transportation was the punishment for most.

After the coronation of William and Mary there were no further persecutions for conscience sake in Devonshire, but in Bucks "Popish recusants" continued to be presented for trial, although not in very large numbers. Some gentlemen were sentenced but not punished. In 1691, thirty Papists were fined from £20 to £40 each. A new act against swearing and other disorderly practices (1695) was strictly enforced in Bucks (1697–8). The fine per oath was 2 s., but 4 s. if the man was convicted a second time.

Under Queen Anne, the business of Quarter Sessions (Devonshire) was strictly local, confined to the old familiar

[1] Hamilton, p. 222.

[2] Mr. Northmore, assistant deputy sheriff of Devon, writes to the sheriff, just before the Monmouth rebellion, "here hath been very little or no business;" in other words, very few hangings, etc.

[3] Richard Evans, Mr. Vincent, and Mr. Robert Wolcombe. See Hamilton, p. 241.

[4] *Ibid.*, p. 227.

routine work. There were constant orders against vagrants, which the constables neglected to enforce.[1] Paupers in this reign are said to have numbered nearly one-fifth of the population; but it is impossible to regard them as criminals, despite the many penal statutes against them. Gaol fever and slow starvation rid the land of many of its prisoners, but few of these prisoners were vagrants.[2]

The reader may possibly have noticed how few statutory additions to the criminal law have been mentioned in this chapter. The explanation is that few such statutes were enacted. "Criminal law," writes Stephen, "varied little from the time of Elizabeth to the end of the 17th century."[3] After each revolution the party in power supported its government by decreeing the pains and penalties of high treason against its adversaries; but every government that comes by force must do this in self-defence. The Statute of Stabbing, 1 Jas. I., c. 8, 1603-4, was probably intended to restrain the frequently fatal affrays between Englishmen and the Scotchmen who had followed James to London. The utter indifference of society in that age to crimes of violence against the person, especially when death did not result, is truly astounding. Stephen believes that as late as 1603 "a person who killed another on the sudden, even without provocation, or on any slight provocation, was guilty of manslaughter only.[4] In 1679, when Giles and several others did their best to assassinate Arnold, stabbing and cutting him dangerously in many places, the hardest sentence the judges could inflict under the laws was fine, imprisonment and pillory. This great defect in English law has been

[1] Hamilton, p. 268-9.

[2] At the end of the seventeenth century the population of England was 5,500,520. See Traill, ii, 394.

[3] Stephen, i, 466.

[4] See evidence furnished by this same Act: 1 Jas. I., c. 8; and Stephen, iii, 48.

gradually remedied, and two of the earliest statutes in this direction were 22 and 23 Chas. II., c. 1, § 6, 1670–1, and 9 Anne, c. 16. Fraudulent bankruptcy was first punished with any severity by 21 Jas. I., c. 19, § 6, 1623–4. The penalty was pillory for two hours and the loss of one ear. The expansion of trade and the greatly increased use of credit led to the passing of this act, and also the important Statute of Frauds, in the reign of Charles II. Obtaining property by false pretences was not made a statutory misdemeanor until the 18th century. 1 James I., c. 7, § 3, 1603–4 added branding for rogues and vagabonds, to the whipping and imprisonment commanded by 39 Eliz., c. 4, § 3; and a number of severe game laws were enacted in 1604, 1609, 1670 and 1706.[1] 11 Will. III., c. 7, shows the inefficiency of the old statutes against piracy, states that offenders had very much increased, and proceeds to harden the law against them; but it was long before they were punished to any extent. New forms of crime, well known in modern days, greet us in 8 and 9 Will. III., c. 32, 1697: an Act "to restrain the number and ill-practice of brokers and stock jobbers;"[2] and in 9 Anne, c. 30: "For desolving the present and preventing the future combination of coal owners, leightormen, masters of ships and others to advance the price of coal." The penalties were fines from £20 to £100, part going to the person suing. This statute was made perpetual by 1 Geo. I., Stat. 2, c. 26, and was evidently deemed socially necessary.

Summary.—Two bitterly antagonistic political and religious parties were striving to develop English national life in opposite and contradictory directions throughout the seventeenth century. Growth in either direction was mainly political and religious. The new social prohibitions, created

[1] See *Statutes of the Realm*.

[2] Several other acts against these evils soon follewed.

during this century, were likewise political or religious, in essence or in application, and necessary social weapons of the times. History reveals a very large amount of serious criminality, political and religious, other forms of crime being relatively infrequent. Crime was evidently taking the direction of greatest resistance to the new life of society, although that life was, for the time being, double-headed.

CHAPTER XI

Modern England.

THE history of seventeenth-century England, that bitter century of civil strife, closes with a double compromise—in religion, toleration; in politics, a limited monarchy. A despotic and persecuting Church, whether Anglican or Presbyterian; the divine right of an absolute king; the military tyranny which was the practical outcome of a vision of democracy; all these ideas are of the past and the result is peace. England, alone, of all the great European nations, wanted no continental dominions. She was forced, against her will, into the Protestant League against France, by the support that nation gave to the exiled James. But after the Peace of Utrecht, England was made the special guardian of that peace, and it was largely through the efforts of Georgian statesmen that the next twenty-five years of European history were, on the whole, peaceful years. No doubt their aims were essentially selfish, but these led them to guard the throne of the Revolution and all that meant to England. They struggled for peace abroad and for the sanctity of treaties, they struggled for peace at home and for the maintenance of their own power, and they were successful. Since the revolution of 1688, the internal peace of England has continued practically unbroken.[1] Parlia-

[1] The brief Jacobite risings of 1715 and 1745 were crushed in Scotland. Many of the leaders in these rebellions were tried and condemned for treason, but only five were executed. In 1715 nearly 1300 rebels were imprisoned, but not more than 28 put to death, while 29 were transported for seven years. After Culloden military vengeance was let loose upon the fugitives. In 1803 Colonel Despard and six accomplices were executed for treason; and modern instances of treason

ment has assembled every year and its deliberate wishes have been obeyed. Legal changes have come to be more and more the result of statutes.

Under Walpole's long ministry (1721 to 1742), cabinet government was firmly established, and the sovereign lost the right of veto, which has never been exercised since the reign of Anne. The continued rule of peace was most advantageous for the nation, and secured a great material development which carried England triumphantly through the European wars of the century. But to maintain himself in power, Walpole established an "organized system" of parliamentary bribery. Corruption became open and utterly shameless. Horace Walpole publicly boasted of his father's great and statesman-like use of public money, called "secret service money," for bribes;[1] while the bursting of the South Sea Bubble disclosed great frauds and widespread corruption of members of the Lords and Commons.[2] Self-

by levying war are insurrections, such as those of Frost, 1840; Smith O'Brien, 1848; and the Fenians, 1867. The crime of treason, once so fearfully common, has almost ceased to be upon the soil of England. The last statute upon this subject was (11 and 12 Vic., c. 12), 1848, which reduced many old treasons to the rank of felony. This law has been enforced several times.

[1] H. Walpole, i, 204, 320, 332; Doddington's *Diary* (15 March, 1754), p. 240–1.

[2] Bribery at parliamentary elections is said (Hawkins, i, 415), and see 12 Ric. II., c. 2, and 5 and 6 Edw. VI., c. 16, to have been punishable at common law, but this seems doubtful. See Stephen, iii, 252. The first statute directed against this offence was 2 Geo. II., c. 24, 1729. Section 7 imposed a fine of £500 upon "every voter who asked, received or took any money or other reward," and every person who bribed any other to vote or to abstain from voting. This law left unpunished "all payments for having voted and all corrupt practises, except giving or promising money or other rewards, and all gifts to other persons than voters;" yet it remained unaltered for eighty years. See Stephen, iii, 255. Acts 49 Geo. III., c. 118, 1809, and 5 and 6 Vic., c. 102, § 20, 1842, remedied these defects. 17 and 18 Vic., c. 102, 1854, is the law now in force, and makes bribery a misdemeanor. 35 and 36 Vic., c. 60, 1872, extends this law to cover municipal elections. It is safe to say that these forms of bribery were not made crimes by the enforcement of punishments until well on into the nineteenth century. See Preamble to 5 and 6 Vic., c. 102, 1842.

love and a cynical contempt of mankind took possession of the higher classes, and this same spirit showed itself among the masses in increasing lawlessness and admiration of successful criminals.[1] Coaches were plundered in broad daylight every day for weeks together. The mail from Bristol to London was robbed five times in as many weeks. Thefts, foot-padding, and street assaults were every-day affairs, and "the newspapers were full of lists of 'lost,' that is, stolen property, and of accounts of the insecurity of the streets."[2] People believed that highway robbery was a special evil of their own times, and Luttrell's *Diary*, and other writings of the latter seventeenth and early eighteenth centuries, show its alarming prevalence. Luttrell's six volumes are simply filled with accounts of highwaymen, executions, etc. Thus an entry for December 22d and 23d, 1690, reads: "The 22d, thirteen persons were executed at Tyburn for several crimes; as also a woman at Newgate, and a notorious highwayman in Fleetstreet." "The 23d, Sir John Jonston, condemned for stealing Mrs. Wharton, went up in a mourning coach to Tyburn, and was executed for the same."[3] Yet the highwaymen, hanged at Tyburn, were but humble imitators of robber knights and successful men of old who loved brigandage and rapine, and often lived by such, but nevertheless were not criminals.[4]

There was undoubtedly a strong outcry in the eighteenth century over the terrible increase of crime. The whole structure of society was said to be disintegrating. But history shows this cry very often repeated. We have heard the same in our own day. Doubtless there was and is some

[1] See stories of Jack Sheppard, burglar, hanged 1724; Jonathan Wild, king of thieves and receiver of stolen goods, hanged 1725; Dick Turpin, highwayman, hanged 1739.

[2] Traill, v, 145.

[3] Luttrell, ii, 147–8.

[4] See Reign of Stephen.

element of truth in this idea, though it is but a half truth, and needs careful winnowing. There seems, however, to be good historic evidence that murder, robbery and theft had diminished rather than increased in England, if we compare the eighteenth century with earlier years.

This is well illustrated by the history of "forcible entry." Very slowly indeed the idea of private property in land prevailed over the old savage notion that "might makes right:"

> "The good old rule, the simple plan,
> That they should take who have the power,
> And they should keep who can."[1]

In a Roll for the twelfth year of William III. (1700), "no less than eleven cases of violent seizure or detention of land are mentioned. A century and a half earlier it would have seemed impossible that the number could in any year have been brought so low; a century and a half later the thought of asserting a claim to a manor by force would hardly have occurred to any one but a madman."[2] "Forcible entry was practically extinct before the first half of the eighteenth century was completed, and has never been revived in its ancient form."[3] Here we have three stages in the development of forcible entry. For many centuries it was certainly not a crime. A man's own strong right arm must defend his property, or revenge him on those who seized it, in private war. Slowly the law came to his aid. Early statutes treat forcible entry, for the most part, as a tort, with double or treble damages to the party grieved, and the possibility of fine, ransom, or a year's imprisonment, at the pleasure of the king. Generally, the rightful owner of the property and

[1] Wordsworth.

[2] Pike, ii, 259 *et seq.*, for abundant evidence of the prevalence of such seizures, and note also the old saying, "Possession is nine points of the law."

[3] Pike, ii, 260. For early statutes against, see (5 Ric. II., Stat. 1, c. 7), (4 Hen. IV., c. 4), (8 Hen. VI., c. 9) and also laws of Hen. VIII., Eliz., and Jas. I.

his friends were expected at least to help, by force of arms, in the ejection of his enemy. By the eighteenth century, forcible entry had become a crime against the state, and with advancing civilization, the laws have been successfully enforced, and this form of crime has ceased to exist.

In the year 1348 (not at all an anarchic period of English history), the coroners' inquests for Yorkshire return eighty-eight verdicts of "felonious homicide," all relating to grown persons. At that time Yorkshire could not have had more than one-eighth or one-tenth of its present population, and Pike concludes, from his investigation of these and other coroners' inquests, that murders in the middle of the fourteenth century were at least sixteen to eighteen times as frequent as in our own day.[1] "The farther back we look," writes Pike, "the more theft, robbery and homicide we find," and in the eighteenth century there were no more such evil acts than usual.[2] But such acts were at first not crimes at all, but torts, or mere misfortunes. The moral intelligence of the nation regarded them in an entirely different light from what it does to-day. Slowly developed into crimes as society became wiser and stronger, such actions again ceased to be punished as crimes, and were considered most natural and even honorable with each relapse into comparative anarchy, as in the reign of Stephen, or among the turbulent nobility of the fifteenth century.

How then account for the strong popular belief in the increase of crime early in the eighteenth century? The nation had just passed through ninety years of turmoil, suffering and violence, and the evils bred in those dark days naturally expressed themselves in later lawlessness, increased no doubt by the prevalent selfishness and cynical disregard of

[1] As late as 1600 the population of Yorkshire did not exceed one-sixth what it was in 1873, when Pike's *History of Crime in England* was written. See ii, 468.

[2] *Ibid.*, ii, 339 and 370.

virtue and honest dealing. There is no denying that crimes of violence were very numerous. But newspapers were just securing a wide circulation, and it is most probable that "the popular outcry about the increase of crime was to a large extent the work of news writers." [1] When we consider the era of peace introduced by the bloodless revolution of 1688, the popular crusade against vice which immediately succeeded it, the enlarging business interests of the nation, the increase of wealth and of quiet happiness in country homes, is it not most probable that people placed a higher value than formerly on the security of life and property, and were more alarmed and incensed by acts of criminal violence at a time when newspapers were bringing the frequency of such misdeeds more glaringly before their eyes? The result would naturally, almost inevitably, be a demand for increased severity of penal laws and a firm enforcement of their penalties, and this is what we find. The English were resolved these actions should be serious crimes in fact as well as on the paper of the statute books. Accordingly, after some experience in the blessings of peace and security came the severer punishment of peace-breakers. The new internal peace was safeguarded by the creation of a multitude of felonies punished with death without benefit of clergy. "From the Restoration to the death of George III.—a period of 160 years—no less than 187 capital offences were added to the criminal code," [2] and between 1760 and 1810 sixty-three statutes decreed new capital crimes. The death penalty was inflicted for even the most petty offences, as for example, stealing in a shop to the value of five shillings, stealing from a dwelling house, or on shipboard to forty shillings. As Mr. Burke sarcastically observed: "If a country gentleman can obtain no other favor from government, he is sure to be accommodated with a new felony

[1] Traill, v, 351.

[2] May, ii, 552.

without benefit of clergy." Paley justified this extreme severity to all grades of criminals by "the necessity of preventing the repetition of the offence."[1] In 1798, offences committed on the high seas were for the first time declared equally criminal with the same acts on shore.

For years these terrible statutes were very largely enforced. Men were hanged at Tyburn, every Monday, by the dozen and the score, and many thousands were transported to the colonies in America and Australia, in commutation of the death penalty. Between 1787 and 1857, no less than 108,715 criminals were thus shipped off to Australia. This was the ordinary punishment for felons, under sentence of death,[2] but the Capital Punishments Society reported, in 1845, that more than 1400 people had suffered death between 1810 and 1845, for crimes since then no longer capital;[3] and this was long after the revolt against such cruel punishments was under full headway. Official *Accounts and Papers*, Vol. 22, 1822, give the number of convicts sent out of the United Kingdom from January, 1816, to January, 1822, as 16,373. The numbers by years are as follows:

1816.	1817.	1818.	1819,	1820.	1821.	1822.
1441	2228	2986	3163	3630	2639	286

The Statistics of Prisons in the same volume bear witness to the increased criminality and increased social pressure against evil-doers, during the early years of the nineteenth century. It gives "an account of the number of persons committed to the different prisons in England and Wales for trial at the assizes and sessions held for the several counties, cities, towns and liberties therein." Signed "H. Hobhouse, Whitehall, 20th May, 1822."

[1] See Paley, *Moral and Political Philosophy*, book vi, chap, ix. Quoted in May, ii, 554.

[2] Pike, ii.

[3] *Report of 1845*.

Year..........	1811.	1812.	1813.	1814.	1815.	1816.	1817.	1818.	1819.	1820.	1821.
No. of persons.	5337	6576	7164	6390	7818	9091	13932	13567	14254	13710	13115

Crimes Against the Person. The extraordinary lenity shown by the English for even the worst and grossest offences against the person continued till the beginning of the nineteenth century. The Coventry Act had made it felony to cut with intent to disfigure. In 1722, the Black Act, 9 Geo. I., c. 22, made it felony "wilfully and maliciously to shoot at any person." 11 Geo. II., c. 22, and a later statute punished wounding "with intent to hinder the export of corn," and wounding seamen in the ordinary discharge of their business. But the first general act on this subject was 43 Geo. III., c. 58, 1803, Lord Ellenborough's act. This statute has 79 sections and "is as elaborate and complete as the early law was crude and imperfect."[1] The death penalty was decreed against all desperate assaults upon the person, including worst attempts to commit murder. Hitherto such attempts were not regarded as serious crimes. At most they could be punished only as misdemeanors at common law, with pillory, fine and brief imprisonment.[2] 9 Geo. IV., c. 31, § 11, added attempts to drown, suffocate or strangle, to the capital felonies punished under the act of 1803. And it was again greatly extended by 24 and 25 Vic., c. 100, 1861, which is the law now in force. By 7 Will., 4 and 1 Vic., c. 85, the death penalty was restricted to attempts to murder by poisoning, stabbing, cutting or wounding with that intent, and in 1861 these also were made non-capital crimes. Evidently, in this peaceful nineteenth century, England has been very earnestly engaged in turning injuries to the person into serious crimes.

Malicious Injuries to Property. The history of malicious injuries to property shows how great a number of actions

[1] Stephen, iii, 113.

[2] *Ibid.*, iii, 114 and 116.

have been made criminal since the thirteenth century, as particular forms of mischief became noticeably harmful to society. But one offence of this kind was known to the common law, arson ("bernet"). Special statutes have been passed from time to time through the centuries, making other malicious injuries criminal. The first such was the Statute of Westminster, 13 Edw. I., Stat. 1, c. 46, and relates to the throwing down of enclosures. Certain injuries to trees and a few other things were punished by statutes in the reigns of Henry VIII.[1] and Charles II., and the wilful destruction of ships was declared criminal by 22 and 23 Chas. II., c. 11, § 12, and 1 Anne Stat., 2, c. 9; but there was exceedingly little legislation of this kind until the reign of George I. The Black Act of 1722, (9 Geo. I., c. 22), punished with death malicious injuries to trees, cattle, fish ponds, hay stacks, etc.—offences much the same as those punished by Henry VIII. with a fine of £10. Many statutes of George II. and George III. decreed death for malicious conduct, hitherto unpunished.[2] Even the cutting of hop-binds growing on poles in a hop plantation was thus punished, during the eighteenth century. 7 and 8 Geo. IV., c. 27, repealed and consolidated a very large number of these special statutes, and was re-enacted by 24 and 25 Vic., c. 97, the law now in force. The most important new crimes of this class added during the nineteenth century, come under the head of malicious injuries to railways, telegraph and telephone lines Punishments have become much less severe, and the death penalty has been entirely abolished.

Piracy was not a crime at the beginning of the eighteenth century, for it was not punished to any extent, and successful pirates were greatly admired by the lower classes.

[1] See 37 Hen. VIII., c. 6.

[2] See 3 Statutes of Geo I.; 5 Statutes of Geo II.; 11 Statutes of Geo. III.

Pirates and privateersmen were much confused in the public mind. Many prominent nobles united in a business venture, fitting out the pirate Kidd to catch other pirates; instead of which work he preferred to rob merchantmen.[1] Wrecking was made a capital offence by 26 Geo. II., c. 19, and piracy was at last extinguished as a profession and, with wrecking, became punished as a crime, by the close of the eighteenth century.[2]

The terrible severity of the eighteenth and early nineteenth century laws doubtless freed England from a large amount of very undesirable criminal stock, but it made the land a human shambles, and wonted the people to thoughts and acts of violence and bloodshedding, thus fostering the very lawlessness which the punishments were intended to repress. Hanging seemed to many men an honorable death to die; the march to the gibbet was often a triumphal procession, and the weekly executions a free theatrical entertainment. Reaction came, for the wholesale executions and banishments did not seem to lessen crime. A more humane spirit was growing up within the nation, and it began to seem an awful thing to punish petty larceny with death. This spirit is plainly evident in the decreasing willingness to inflict the death penalty in the eighteenth century, and much more noticeably in the nineteenth. The proportion of capital convictions to executions in the home circuit, which included the counties of Hertz, Essex, Kent, Sussex and Surrey, from 1689 to 1814, were as follows: [3]

Proportion of	*Convictions*	*to*	*Executions.*
1689 to 1718	38	to	20
1755 to 1784	46	to	13
1784 to 1814	74	to	19

[1] Pike, ii, 263 and 268–9.

[2] *Ibid.*, ii, 371.

[3] See evidence presented to the select committee for the investigation of capital punishment, 1819. Selections in *Annual Register*, 1819–20, p. 338. The figures from 1718 to 1755 were not given.

The select committee for the investigation of capital punishment (1819) reported as follows concerning the three capital felonies: Privately stealing in a shop to the amount of five shillings; Privately stealing in a dwelling house to forty shillings; Privately stealing from vessels in a navigable river to forty shillings. "Numerous and respectable witnesses have borne testimony, for themselves and for the classes whom they represent, that a great reluctance prevails to prosecute, to give evidence and to convict, in the cases of the three last-mentioned offences, and that this reluctance has had the effect of ***producing impunity*** to such a degree that it may be considered as among the temptations to the commission of crimes."[1] Old professed thieves much preferred to be tried on a capital charge, from the greater chance of escape.[2] Some crimes, "not of atrocious nature," but punishable with death, were, so Judge P. Colquhoun believed, "never brought under the review of magistrates at all."[3] Sometimes he had even been "obliged to threaten imprisonment to prosecutors who had refused to enter into recognizance," so great was their reluctance to prosecute. Even when criminals were brought to trial, juries insisted on returning verdicts greatly under the value of property stolen, to avoid capital punishment. The public conscience was evidently in revolt against the infliction of the death penalty for such crimes as Colquhoun mentions: "Forgery, shop-lifting, larceny, burglary without entering the house, horse stealing, cattle stealing, sheep stealing, frame breaking, house breaking in the day time, highway robbery with acts of violence on the person, and various other *minor offences*."[4] Right Hon. Sir A. Macdonald believed that "more offenders

[1] See Report, *Annual Register* (1819–20), p. 342. This evidence was given largely by London traders, clerks and officers of criminal courts, magistrates, gaolers, etc., and "their testimony was perfectly uniform."

[2] *Annual Register*, p. 360. [3] *Ibid.*, p. 355. [4] *Ibid.*, p. 355.

escape justice from flaws and informalities in this country than in any other," and that "out of about two hundred and thirty felonies that exist by the present laws, it is seldom that more than from a dozen to twenty of them, when committed, are capitally punished."[1]

It may be doubted whether the enforcement of these ferocious laws during a large part of the eighteenth century really had the desired effect of reducing crime; but at any rate the public mind at first believed in them and was not revolted by their cruelty. Statutes, hangings and transportations evidence the increased public detestation of acts against the security of life and property. Some of these acts were made crimes for the first time, in fact, if not in theory (thus increasing the number of criminals), and many others were made much more heinously criminal. Probably the increased severity and sureness of punishment had some good results. Certainly the decrease in murders was very great, judging by the records of the "home circuit," from 1689 to 1814, and there was no added hesitation in punishing the convicted murderer with death.

The whole number of convictions for murder.	*Total of executions for same.*
1689–1718=123	87
1755–1784= 67	57
1784–1814= 54	44

"When we consider the large increase of population during a prosperous period of one hundred and twenty-five years" (so reads the Report), "and also that a considerable city had grown up during this time on the south bank of the Thames"—it is probably "no exaggeration" to say that in this part of England (a district not over favorably situated in this respect) "murder has abated in the proportion of three if not four to one."[2] The convictions for murder in

[1] *Annual Register*, p. 350–1.

[2] *Ibid.*, p. 338.

London and Middlesex from 1755 to 1814 also seem to support this belief. For the thirty years from 1755 to 1784 there were seventy-one convictions, while from 1784 to 1814 there were but sixty-six convictions. The investigation of the select committee of 1819 (already referred to) convinced them that "In general, murders and other crimes of violence and cruelty have either diminished or not increased; and that the deplorable increase of criminals is not of such a nature as to indicate any diminution in the humanity of the people."[1]

Society was thus apparently successful in decreasing the amount of the most serious crimes of violence by the enforcement of terrible laws. The great mistake was in attempting to punish petty offences with the same severity. But whether useful or harmful on the whole, most of these eighteenth century statutes certainly outlived their usefulness, and it became painfully evident that the nation was choosing its punishments badly, and that many acts rightly criminal had ceased or almost ceased to be crimes. Accordingly, the early nineteenth century is filled with repeals of old criminal laws and the enactment of milder statutes, under which society immediately began to increase her criminals, by bringing to justice those classes of offenders whom she had latterly refused to prosecute. The committee of 1819 found that certain laws had "not been carried into effect in Middlesex for more than a century, in the counties round London for sixty years, and in the extensive district which forms the Western Circuit for fifty."[2] In 1805 there were but 4,605 persons committed for trial for all indictable offences. In 1854 this number had increased to 29,359, and the figures had grown continually larger in the years between. A like increase is shown by statistics of summary convictions since 1857; an increase which has become truly

[1] *Annual Register* (1819–20), p. 338. [2] *Ibid.*, p. 339.

appalling in recent years, unless we see clearly that it means life on a higher plane of social morality, rather than an increase in the bad and destructive elements of society.

During the first half of the eighteenth century wealth and knowledge increased not slowly, and in the second half began a large development of trade and agriculture. Toward the close of the century the nation entered upon a period of "vehement life," and the nineteenth century has been throughout an era of unexampled prosperity and expansion. Population has multiplied rapidly and wealth even faster, but till 1833 the evils of the factory system were at their worst, the land was full of ignorance and over-worked women and children. With the great development of trade and commerce, increased heinousness naturally attached to fraud, forgery and other acts injurious to new business methods. Many such acts, not formerly punished as crimes, or regarded as simple misdemeanors only, became capital offences.

Forgery.[1] The reign of George III. (1760–1820) teems with forgery statutes, due to the commencement of the national debt, the invention of bills of exchange and the establishment of the banking system.[2] From 1824 to 1830 more than forty kinds of forgery were punishable with death. In 1837, all, with two exceptions, ceased to be capital offences.

[1] Forgery was vaguely recognized as a crime by common law from very early times; but in practice it was generally made a tort, remedied by civil action, until comparatively modern times. For statutes see 1 Hen. V., c. 3; and 5, Eliz., c. 14. By 1 Hen. V., c. 3: "The party grieved may sue and recover his damages," and "fine and ransom at the king's pleasure." 5 Eliz., c. 14, awards "double damages to the party grieved . . . . and pillory, loss of ears, forfeiture of profits of lands, and imprisonment. The introduction to the *Report on Forgery*, by the Select Committee on Criminal Laws of England (1824), shows how the idea of forgery as a crime was gradually enlarged. See pages 4 to 6.

[2] *Pictorial Hist. of England*, vii, 612; 13 Geo. III., c. 79; 18 Geo. III., c. 18; 33 Geo. III., c. 30; 35 Geo. III., c. 66; 37 Geo. III., c. 46; 37 Geo. III., c. 122; 41 Geo. III., c. 39; 41 Geo. III., c. 57; 43 Geo. III., c. 139.

The penalties were at first largely enforced. Thus, Thomas Shelton, clerk at the Old Bailey, giving evidence before the investigating committee of Parliament in 1819, states with regard to forgeries: "Bankers were extremely rigid formerly" in prosecuting for these offences. "Generally persons convicted of forgery were executed, and indeed it was almost universally the case."[1] "Forgery," writes Pike, "was very lightly regarded in early England, but was recognized as a crime of highest magnitude when trade became large. A great number of forgers were sentenced to death before the law was modified."[2] "No part of the criminal law of the latter part of the 18th century," writes Stephen, "was more severe in itself, or was executed with greater severity than this."[3] But, during the seventeenth century (a period of civil strife), the law of forgery remained unaltered. According to the life of the people, so vary the nation's criminals. The forgery of "deeds, wills, bonds, bills of exchange and promissory notes or endorsements on them," was made felony without benefit of clergy by 2 Geo. II., c. 25, soon after the celebrated trial of Hales (1729) for forging endorsements on promissory notes.[4] The statute 5 Eliz., c. 14 did not make this criminal.[5] The necessity for the safeguarding of forms of paper money, now coming generally into use, led to the passing of many new social prohibitions, creating new and serious forms of crime. Thus, death was the penalty decreed for the forgery of bank notes

[1] See Report in *Annual Register* (1819), p. 346–7. [2] Pike, ii, 335.

[3] Stephen, iii, 182. For other statutes on this subject, see 15 Geo. II., c. 13, § 11, and consolidation act of 1830 (11 Geo. IV., and 1 Will. IV., c. 66). "Mr. Hammond, in the title 'Forgery' of his 'criminal code,' has enumerated more than 400 statutes which contain provisions against the offence." *Pict. Hist. of England*, vii, 612.

[4] See 17 *State Trials*, pp. 162–296.

[5] See also 7 Geo. II., c. 22; and 18 Geo. III., c. 18, protecting corporations, etc.; for extensions of same law.

and everything of that nature, the uttering of forged bank notes, the making or possession of paper suitable for such forgery, or of instruments suitable for that end.[1] From 1830, the year of the first consolidation act,[2] the punishment for forgery became less severe, and in 1837,[3] the death penalty was abolished for this offence, with a very few exceptions—done away by the consolidation act of 1861.[4] Of course the forgery of postage stamps is a new crime, for they did not exist till the reign of Victoria. The law of 1861 contains many elaborate provisions on this subject.[5] Personation as a means of acquiring certain kinds of property was not recognized as a crime till after the trial of Orton for perjury for declaring he was Sir Roger Tichborne. 37 and 38 Vic., c. 36, 1874, made this crime a felony, punished with penal servitude for life as maximum. Wilful falsifying of any account, or omission to make an entry in such account, by any clerk, officer or servant was not a crime till 1875.[6] This was greatly needed, as will appear from the following case. "A clerk in charge of a branch of a county bank overpaid his own account to the extent of £1500. When the inspector came round, the clerk transferred £2000 from the account of one of the customers to his own, the result being that he appeared to have a credit balance. He was prosecuted and held to have committed no legal offence. His overpayment of his own account was only an unauthorized loan to himself. His transfer of the £2000 was effected without forging the customer's

[1] For statutes on this subject see 15 Geo. II., c. 13; 13 Geo. III., c. 79; 41 Geo. III., c. 39; and Stephen, iii, 182.

[2] 11 Geo. IV. and 1 Will. IV., c. 66.

[3] 7 Will. IV. and 1 Vic., c. 84.

[4] 24 and 25 Vic., c. 98.

[5] There are yet some extensions of the English law of forgery needful. At present it is probably not a crime to forge "letters to prove the existence of a contract." Stephen, iii, 185.

[6] 38 and 39 Vic., c. 24.

check, and by a mere entry in the bank books."[1] It is plainly evident that England has been very busy creating new social prohibitions along this line of the national growth, and that new crimes were taking the direction of greatest resistance to that growth.

From 1802, we find a very great number of statutes relating to trade, navigation, ship-owners, mariners and fisheries. Such laws began in the reign of Edward III., but as late as 1760 there were only thirteen in existence. At the death of George III., the number had increased to seventy-nine.[2] As Pike states: "Trade and the devices for its propagation were continually outgrowing the primitive laws." "The extension of the list of felonies, in the eighteenth century, was, in one aspect, a sign of progress;" for "every new development of trade brought a new form of fraud," or "a new adaptation of old forms."[3] Commercial progress made possible the South Sea Bubble and many other swindles of the age, and "left a permanent impress on the statute book." A law (23 Geo. II., c. 13) aimed to prevent the seducing of artificers into foreign lands, and there were many more labor laws and many offenders against them. There were acts to punish the adulteration of new imports, such as the "Tea Act" of 1777. With the increased use of coal came many schemes for defrauding purchasers, which induced the passage of the "Coal Meter Act" in 1767. The growth of textile manufactures was accompanied by very severe laws against short measure. But the eagerness of eighteenth century legislators to increase the severity of the criminal laws soon exceeded both the needs and the desires of the nation.

Early in the nineteenth century it was manifest that

[1] Stephen, iii, 186. See also extension of forgery to protect children, in factory act of 1833. 3 and 4 Will. IV., c. 113, § 28.

[2] *Pictorial Hist. of England*, viii, 635.

[3] Pike, ii, 448 and 393.

society would no longer enforce such severe penalties, and that whole classes of evil doers, such as fraudulent bankrupts and fraudulent dealers of all kinds, were free from prosecution, and had almost ceased to be regarded as criminals, to the great danger of business interests, and the social standard of morality. Thus, Mr. Basil Montague, giving evidence before the select committee on capital punishment in 1819, said that since 1732, when the death penalty was decreed against fraudulent bankruptcy by 5 Geo. II., c. 30, § 1, "with nearly 40,000 bankrupts I doubt whether there have been ten prosecutions; I believe there have been only three executions; and yet fraudulent bankrupts and concealment of property are proverbial, are so common as to be supposed almost to have lost the nature of a crime."[1] Edward Foster,

[1] Extracts in *Annual Register* for 1819, pp. 356–359. Fraudulent bankruptcy was first punished with any severity by 21 Jas. I., c. 19, § 7, 1623, which decreed pillory for two hours and the loss of an ear. This remained the penalty till 1732, when 5 Geo. II., c. 30, § 1, made the offence capital. Throughout the eighteenth century, however, this important offence was certainly not a crime, for "the excessive severity of the law prevented its execution," and this despite repeated statutes against it. Since 1819 the law of fraudulent bankruptcy has been greatly elaborated. See 6 Geo. IV., c. 16, 1825; 12 and 13 Vic., c. 106, 1849; 24 and 25 Vic., c. 134, 1861; 32 and 33 Vic., c. 87, 1869. But the character of the offence has remained substantially unchanged.

Fraudulent bankruptcy, as legally defined in 1732, was much the same as it is to-day, only now the act is a crime, and then it was not. The punishments decreed became gradually much less severe and very much more frequently enforced. Stephen, iii, 231. 1 Geo. IV., c. 115, § 1, substituted transportation for life, or for not less than seven years, or imprisonment up to seven years for the old death penalty. 12 and 13 Vic., c. 106, 1849, created a new crime: "To destroy or falsify books," and to "obtain goods on credit under the false pretence of carrying on business within three months of bankruptcy, and with intent to defraud the creditor." This was punished with a maximum of three years imprisonment at hard labor. 24 and 25 Vic., c. 134, § 221, 1861, made penalties for fraudulent bankruptcy much lighter, while more carefully defining the acts punishable. 32 and 33 Vic., c. 62, 1869—the Debtors' Act—abolished imprisonment for debt, and "added a considerable number of new penal offences, consisting chiefly in omissions to comply with the provisions of the bankruptcy act." All these new offences are misdemeanors, with the exception of one felony, where a bankrupt

Esq., banker, stated before the same committee that "probably more than one-half" the cases of forgery are not prosecuted, because of the death punishment. This was true even for very aggravated forgeries, for large amounts (£1500 instanced) with no extenuating circumstances.[1] Severe laws against false weights and measures were frequent, but were powerless against offenders, who were very numerous and for the most part unpunished. The petty frauds of retail dealers were practiced on a larger scale by manufacturers and merchants.[2]

If this evidence is correct, and there seems to be no good reason to doubt it, then fraudulent bankruptcy and other forms of business fraud were not crimes in the latter eighteenth and early nineteenth centuries; for they were not socially punished, though notoriously common, and were deemed highly natural acts. The forty kinds of forgery, legally punishable with death, were certainly very dangerously near the non-criminal line, if indeed they had not crossed it. Evidently, a wide-spread reduction of penalties was absolutely necessary, if these dangerous evils were to be punished as crimes. A thousand bankers, from all England, united in a petition to Parliament against the extreme death penalty for forgery May 24th, 1830.[3] The report of the select committee of 1819 states that: "Your committee are

absconds with property. Punishments are decreed against "obtaining credit by false pretences," and "dealing with property intended to defraud creditors," by other sections of this same law. Not until 1857, by 20 and 21 Vic., c. 54, were fraudulent directors, trustees and other officers of public companies declared to be criminals, punishable under the law. "Experience," writes Stephen, "had shown these provisions to be necessary." See Stephen, iii, 233.

[1] See *Annual Register* (1819), p. 356. Also evidence of John Harmer, Esq., p. 359. Note the strong public sympathy in favor of James Bolland, swindler and forger, executed in 1772, and for Dr. Dodd, forger, both utterly unscrupulous rascals, who richly deserved their doom.

[2] Pike, ii, 393.

[3] See Mr. Braugham's petition, quoted by May, ii, 557.

of opinion . . . that in the present state of public feeling a reduction of the punishment in most cases of that crime (forgery) is become necessary to the execution of the laws, and consequently to the security of property and the protection of commerce; . . . and that this reformation is a matter of very considerable urgency."[1] Business developments and needs had induced the enactment, and in forgery cases the early enforcement, of laws so severe that the growing humanitarian spirit of the age had refused to punish under them; thus decreasing temporarily the number of criminals in the nation. But the common sense o the community, grown more intelligent as well as more humane, plainly perceiving that these actions should be crimes, caused the repeal of the old laws and the enactment of lighter penalties, which it could and did enforce, thus again swelling the volume of the nation's crime. But society, at this time, not only punished, and thus made criminal, many business offences long known to the laws. It branded other actions as crimes for the first time, by creating and enforcing statutes against them. "It is strange to discover," writes Stephen, "that until the end of the eighteenth century there was no law to punish embezzlement, no law to punish criminal breaches of trust until early in the nineteenth century, no law to punish fraudulent trustees proper until 1857, and no law to punish the falsification of accounts till 1875, except in a few special cases."[2] Evidently in lines of fraud and forgery society has been very busy creating new crimes and criminals, and this for the general welfare.

The humanitarian movement of the age further showed its strength in the increasing social pressure for legal remedy of worst abuses of the factory system, which had produced

[1] See *Annual Register* (1819), p. 343.

[2] Stephen, iii, 186.

terrible misery and degradation among the working classes. Such legislation meant the creation of many new social prohibitions and new crimes. It was high time. Labor was unorganized and powerless in the hands of greedy employers who ground the faces of the poor. A well-meaning system of out-door poor relief (begun about 1796) had reduced agricultural laborers to pauperism, and put a premium upon immorality and laziness. There was no system of national education, and great numbers of people could not even read and write. The Factory Act of 1833[1] was the first great forward step in the reorganization of industry, and this was followed by the Mines and Collieries Act of 1842, and other extensions of legal protection for workers.[2]

The early nineteenth century was "a period of great legislative reform, but of slow material progress."[3] The seeds of future good were planted, the harvest was not yet. The new Poor Law (4 and 5 Will. IV., c. 76) of 1834, has since resulted in a great decrease of pauperism and the restoration of manliness and self-respect to the rural population. The industrial legislation, just mentioned, and the legalizing of trade unions has done at least as much for the factory hands and miners. Commerce has grown, capital accumulated, the land has been covered with railroads. The better organization of labor has enabled it to secure a larger share in the wealth product of the nation. Free trade was at last established, and was followed by great reductions in the price of necessaries of life. "In 1842 the Customs Tariff embraced 1163 articles; in 1860 it comprised less than fifty, of which

[1] 3 and 4 Will. IV., c. 113.

[2] 5 and 6 Vic., c. 99; 23 and 24 Vic., c. 151, 1860; and 34-page report on the Factories Act in "*Accounts and Papers*," 1840, showing large amount of new criminality (hundreds of people), convicted, fined and imprisoned in the year 1839, for offences under this act. From 1889 to 1893 inclusive, the annual average of criminals punished under factory acts was 1662.

[3] Traill, vi, 229.

fifteen contributed nearly the whole revenue."[1] A mighty increase of wealth and population has resulted.[2] From 1821 to 1871 (fifty years), the population about doubled. It did the same between 1570 and 1801 (two hundred and thirty-one years). England has become a land teeming with great cities, a land of manufactures, trade and commerce. More than thirty million people live where three million dwelt in Norman times, and four and a half million in the golden age of Elizabeth. The increase of scientific knowledge and the great inventions of the eighteenth and nineteenth centuries have made this possible. England is the most wealthy nation in the world, in proportion to population. Her wise government and strong laws, enforced by the enduring energy of a persistently progressive and moral people, have made good peace in the land. England is probably to-day the greatest leader in the world's civilization—largely because she has succeeded in choosing her crimes wisely.

The franchise was extended in 1832 and again in 1867 and 1884–5, until now England has practically manhood suffrage. Education gradually became more general and finally, in 1870, a compulsory public school system was introduced. In 1873 there were 6693 persons tried for offences against the Education Act, and in 1892, 86,149. See how with social progress criminals are multiplied; for all of these petty offenders (if indeed it be a petty offence to keep a child in ignorance and dwarf its possibilities for usefulness) are punished as wrongers of society, and their acts seem to us more morally reprehensible, more criminal, than did cuts,

[1] The coming of free trade by no means did away with all offences due to the regulation of commerce. Bakers, brewers, butter dealers, coal dealers, millers, manufacturers of arms, apothecaries, knackers, pedlars, sellers of gunpowder, brokers, pawnbrokers, pilots, chimney sweeps, marine store dealers, manufacturers aud retailers of tobacco, etc., are all under strict police regulations, which, if broken, are punished by heavy fine or three months imprisonment at hard labor.

[2] May, ii, 573, *note*.

blows and other personal violence to our recent ancestors. The wide diffusion of knowledge, the lifting of the average of intelligence, above all the higher social morality with its expanding feeling of brotherhood and human sympathy, have caused in recent years an enormous multiplication of statutes creating misdemeanors (petty crimes), made necessary by the growing complexity of social relations and the increased interdependence of mankind. These statutes have been enforced. The judicial statistics of England and Wales show that in one year, 1896, the enormous number of 709,338 persons were proceeded against by courts of summary jurisdiction.[1] The very names of the offences prove that much of this great mass of petty criminality is essentially modern, and the statistics show how rapidly such crimes have been increasing in the last forty years. Thus we find, comparing the annual average number of persons tried in the five-year periods 1857–61 and 1892–96.

	Annual Average. (1857–61)	(1892–96)
Adulteration of foods and drugs	none	3,002
Cruelty to animals	2,400	12,725
Diseases of animals and offences in relation to dogs	none	15,969
Offences against the Education act	none	67,851
Highway acts	6,766	27,525
Drunkenness	84,358	175,628
Factory acts	395	1,769
Police regulations	45,159	86,292
Railways	1,018	3,891
Sanitary laws	4,357	7,446
Sunday trading	893	3,006
Stage and hackney carriage acts	5,949	8,292
Vaccination act	none	1,755
Gaming (*i. e.*, gambling) and other offences	2,804	20,103

The mutual rights and duties of men, women, children and animals are being more and more carefully prescribed and guarded by legal statutes, creating not mere torts (offences

[1] The penalties were of course slight—fine, brief imprisonment, and sometimes but a night in gaol and mere caution for first offenders.

at cival law), but new criminal offences. For society now believes that a great multitude of acts harmful, primarily, to the person, property or well-being of an individual citizen, or even stranger, should be punished as wrongs to the whole community—in other words, as crimes. The injury to one has become more and more a wrong to all, in the progress of civilization.

Our remote ancestors could not have punished such acts as crimes, even if they had deemed them criminal, which they certainly did not. When society had barely grasped the idea of private property, forms of crime could not be numerous. Men were more passionate then, more rebellious at restraint. The state was far less strong, less able to punish, and possessed no diffused army of policemen, ever ready to arrest and bring to justice offenders, small and great, against the laws. Drunkenness, for example, has been very widely punished as a misdemeanor only in recent years;[1] while the mass of police offences tried in criminal courts every month, require for their detection and punishment a very large and efficient police, and an extensive system of courts of summary jurisdiction, never possessed till modern times.[2]

[1] Drunkenness is said to have increased greatly in eighteenth century England. Certainly it was not criminal then. The moral sense of the nation was not opposed to it, and punishments were rarely inflicted. Later, in 1825, Sir Walter Scott writes; "Drinking is not now the vice of the times; sots are excluded from the best company." But while the upper classes were turning against the practice, gin drinking was very prevalent among the masses. See Report of Select Committee of House of Commons, 1834. After 1833 drunkenness became a criminal offence. No longer, as before, drunkards were "taken care of" by the police, and dismissed when sober without being entered on the charge sheet." Traill, vi, 636.

[2] The metropolitan police was established by law in 1829; the borough police in 1836; the county police in 1839 and 1856. In 1858 there was one constable to every 902 of the population. In 1873 the proportion was one to 795, and in 1891 (according to the census) England had a disciplined army of 40,596 police and constabulary, or one to every 714 of the population. The increase since 1881–2 has been 7,423, or 22.3 per cent. See Stephen, i, 194–200 for the ancient police of England and its utter inefficiency.

The various statutes which established this police force "created a large number of petty offences, all of which are punishable on summary conviction."[1] The Highway Act, 5 and 6 Will. 4, c. 50, bristles with penalties for offences of surveyors, collectors, cart drivers and owners, and other persons using, or injuring the highways. Every general or special railway act creates "many offences by servants of the railway, by passengers, and by other persons." A summary of offences against the public health and safety[2] includes: "Sewerage and drainage, privies, water-closets, etc., scavenging and cleaning, water supply; cellar dwellings and lodging houses; common lodging houses; houses let in lodgings; nuisances; offensive trades; unsound meat; infectious diseases and hospitals; highways and streets; and miscellaneous."[3] The list is quite sufficient evidence of the modern multiplication of police misdemeanors. Then there are offences under the explosive acts, gas works acts, the adulteration of bread, or food and drugs, and water works in towns.[4] The Customs Laws Consolidation Act decrees many penalties for revenue offences. The factory and mining acts, the companies acts and many others regulating special trades or businesses, all create new forms of crime, and a multitude of statutes punish cruelty to animals (a notable instance of the growth of our humanity),[5]

[1] See Stephen, iii, 264–5, (2 and 3 Vic., c. 47), 1839, sections 26–37 for offences on the Thames; sections 54–60 for street offences; 10 and 11 Vic., c. 89, 1847, sections 21–31. Section 28 alone specifies 30 misdemeanors.

[2] See Public Health Act.

[3] Oke's *Magisterial Synopsis.*

[4] 38 Vic., c. 17; 22 and 23 Vic., c. 66; 6 and 7 Will. IV., c. 37; 38 and 39 Vic., c. 63; 10 and 11 Vic., c. 17; 39 and 40 Vic., c. 36.

[5] The Annual Report of the American Society for the Prevention of Cruelty to Animals contains a history of the movement which the society represents. "The first statute passed in any country for the protection of cattle was introduced into the English Parliament in 1822. Previous to that, in 1811, when Lord Erskine made a speech in the House of Lords, demanding attention to the sufferings of

fishery offences, unlawful gaming, etc. The Elementary Education Act of 1870[1] and a later statute impose penalties on parents who do not send their children to school, and on employers of labor who disobey the regulations for the employment of children. Under this Education Act alone 82,745 people were punished every year from 1889 to 1893, inclusive. Under Police Regulations, the annual average was 77,980; under Drunkenness, 178,845; under Cruelty to Animals, 11,855; under Sanitary Law offences, 8,822.

Is not crime clearly a social product, and has it not been increasing with giant strides in this enlightened and humane nineteenth century? Is not this increase due to growth of intelligence and social morality, realizing the new needs of a rapidly progressing civilization, causing the enactment of new social prohibitions, and by the enforcement of these prohibitions increasing crime and making criminals? Doubtless society does not wish offenders against her laws; she would much prefer that all men prove obedient; but the times are in the future, far distant, more Christian centuries, when a new criminal law will find none to break it. Meanwhile, the most civilized and progressive nations have the

animals, he was met by a chorus of cat-calls and cock-crowing from that noble body which effectually drowned his words."

"In 1824 the first society for the prevention of cruelty to animals was founded in London. In 1840 the queen permitted the society to prefix to its name the significant and useful adjective 'Royal;' after that it had plenty of friends."

In 1888 a similar body was organized in New York by Henry Bergh. "His attention was called to the need of protection for animals by cases of unusual cruelty which he had noticed in Russia while Secretary of Legation. In 1888 there was not a law in any State protecting animals against cruelty. There are now 209 local societies in the United States, and there is not a State in the Union in which cruelty of whatever kind is not forbidden by law." See *The Churchman.*

"Only in countries like Spain, which are still governed by the antiquated metaphysical teachings and narrow moral theories of the mediæval hierarchy, has the jus animalium as yet found no place in codes of ethics or systems of jurisprudence." See Evans, p. 14.

[1] 33 and 34 Vic., c. 75, § 74; 39 and 40 Vic., c. 79, §§ 7, 11, 12.

most criminals, and more abundant crime as they ascend higher in the scale of social development.[1]

The increase of social prohibitions and of offenders against them in England, is but a type of what is happening in all the leading nations of the world. In the United States of America, the most highly developed, most progressive, best educated, most moral states have in general the largest percentage of criminals, while the smallest percentage must be sought for in the unprogressive and illiterate regions of the south, or in lately settled territories of the west.[2]

The Massachusetts legislature has often been called a manufactory of misdemeanors, and this state, always one of the foremost in our civilization, has, even by statistics of prisoners, almost the largest average ratio of criminals to population during the last five census periods. The record of criminal prosecutions in the lower courts of Massachusetts reveals the mighty rise in the flood of crime, and shows also that the great totals of her criminality are more than half due to the energetic attempt to punish drunkenness as crime against the state. But, subtracting the many thousand cases tried for this offence, we find that prosecutions for other misdemeanors reveal the same rapid increase in crime, from 26,679 in 1882, to 41,217 in 1894.

There is not a state in the American Union, however, which has not seen a large and generally progressive increase of criminality (judging by prison population) since 1850. Many of the young western states are to-day among the most rapidly progressive sections of the Union, and their last census returns (1890) show an astounding in-

[1] See next chapter.

[2] Official statistics in this country unfortunately relate only to prisoners, and give no returns of petty criminals, fined by the courts, under which class would come a very large percentage of the increasing criminality of the most highly developed and progressive states. See *United States Census*, Report on Crime.

crease in the proportion of prisoners to population. The same phenomenon is observable in some southern states.[1]

Increasing crime, therefore (due to the enforcement of new criminal laws, or of old statutes formerly unenforced), is a sign and till now a sure accompaniment of social betterment and growth to a higher plane of life, and does not imply social degeneration and decay, unless there is evident failure in attempts to crush out old and serious forms of crime, which should certainly show a marked diminution, if the nation is in strong and healthy life. Let us understand this clearly. Under static conditions—laws remaining the same and criminal prosecution the same (as we can imagine them in some utterly unprogressive community)—increasing crime would be an unqualified evil, would mean degeneration and threaten social death. But, in every truly progressive community, criminal law is being extended continually to guard and foster new relations and modes of life. Increasing prohibitions (if wisely chosen), and their enforcement, raise the average of intelligence and social morality among the lower masses of the people, by educating them through punishment to an understanding of new social requirements, an acceptance of new social duties; but, at the expense of an increased amount of criminality, due to the actions of rebellious social laggards. Increasing totals of crime, together

[1] See *United States Census*, Statistics of Prisoners, 1850 to 1890. These statistics include prisoners in the state prisons and penitentiaries, county jails and city prisons, workhouses and houses of correction, leased prisoners, military and naval prisoners, and insane prisoners in hospitals and asylums. The increase by States, from 1850 to 1890, has been as follows: (Ratio of prisoners to 100,000 population); Massachusetts, 1243 to 2335; California, 670 to 2813; District of Columbia, 890 to 2153; New York, 416 to 1912; Rhode Island, 698 to 1621; Maryland, 681 to 1441; Pennsylvania, 178 to 1234; Georgia, 47 to 1599; South Carolina, 54 to 1029; Arkansas, 81 to 1306; Mississippi, 76 to 913; Utah (census 1860), 199 to 1294; New Mexico (census 1860), 107 to 1335; North and South Dakota (census 1870), 212 to 538.

with a decrease under old forms of delinquency, and sometimes their entire disappearance, is exactly what history and statistics show for Great Britain, France, and so far as we have evidence, for other nations also.[1] But the decrease does not by any means counterbalance the increase under new forms of crime.

It is necessary always to remember that no action is a crime unless society actually punishes it as a wrong against itself. No amount of legal prohibition will suffice, unless the laws are enforced. For a nation shows its will much more by the enforcement of punishment than by the creation of laws, which may be the work of a few legislators, and contrary to the social wish. Only when the people stand behind and support the law, or inflict social vengeance by

[1] See succeeding chapters and Appendix I.

It may be interesting to mention here the names of some old crimes which have become practically obsolete in England, the necessity for punishment having almost ceased. There have been no offenders under laws for treason, seditious libel and tumultuary petitioning (act of 1661) for many years. (Stephen, ii, 373 and 376.) Forcible entry, in its old form, and piracy no longer vex society by land and sea. Usury ceased to be legally a crime in the eighteenth century, but a few wise exceptions have been made in the pawnbrokers and bill of sales acts, guarding the destitute, the ignorant and the foolish from the scoundrels who prey upon them.

Religious crimes, non conformity, heresy, witchcraft, etc., are no longer punished, for society has ceased to believe such acts rightly criminal. (See England under the Stuarts, page 240.) Freedom of religious thought and observance has been followed since 1832 by almost complete freedom of political discussion. (See many prosecutions for seditious words and libels (1704 to 1831) in *State Trials.*) "So far as press offences are concerned" the law of England "has almost entirely ceased to be enforced for a period of about 50 years." (Stephen, ii, 376.) Probably the law of newspaper libel has been relaxed entirely too much. (See Stephen, ii, 384–5, upon this subject.) It should be noticed that some of these old forms of crime—treason, piracy and forcible entry—are as highly criminal to-day as they have ever been. Society would punish such offences if they were committed. But religious non-conformity, heresy, witchcraft, usury, and some old political offences are no longer even forms of crime: a man may commit any number of such acts, and not be punished as a criminal.

lynch violence, do the actions aimed at become crimes. It is the social standard of right action, which determines for every age the crimes of that age. In the establishment of this moral standard, the man strong and influential in the nation naturally counts for more than one relatively weak and unknown. The power is distributed much as was the franchise in the Roman Republic; a small group of great men have as much power as a large group of small men.[1]

[1] The author planned as critical a study of French history, and of the growth of crime in France, as has been made for England, but the limits of this book and the time required for such a task prevented. A preliminary study showed that French history affords strong evidence for the truth of the theory here developed.

CHAPTER XII

HAS CRIME INCREASED DURING THE NINETEENTH CENTURY?

THE nineteenth century has been filled full with the transformation of industrial life—that greatest event of modern times—wrought out through steam, machinery, and electricity, so that the industrial arts of the eighteenth century are farther removed from those of 1900 than from those of the Roman Empire, or even Egypt under the Ptolemies.[1] The capital amassed during this single century amounts to a sum at least double all that has been accumulated and left by former ages.[2] A hundred years ago the annual output of the world's mines was estimated at £9,000,000 sterling, while between 1880–88 the average yearly value at the pit's mouth was £210,000,000.[3] The value of goods manufactured each year in Europe and the United States has increased from £650,000,000 sterling in 1800, to £4,618,000,000 in 1888.[4] So rapid has been the diffusion of the comforts and luxuries of life, and so radically have our ideas and ways of thinking changed, that we can realize only with great difficulty the extremely simple lives of our own grandfathers.

Nor has the march of education been less remarkable than the progress of industry and wealth. One hundred years ago reading and writing were rare accomplishments. Even as late as 1840 but two per cent. of adults in Russia could

[1] Compare the paintings representing trades on the walls of Pompeii and Egyptian tombs, with encyclopædia engravings of the 18th century, and the illustrations in modern popular science magazines.

[2] Seignobos, p. 681. [3] Mulhall, p. 398. [4] *Ibid.*, p. 365.

write, fourteen per cent. in Spain, sixteen per cent. in Italy, and twenty-one per cent. in Austria; while in France and the United Kingdom the proportions were forty-seven and fifty-nine, and in the United States and Germany eighty and eighty-two per cent. respectively.[1] The average number of children attending school has increased one hundred and forty-five per cent. during the forty-eight years since 1840; while the population of Europe has been increasing about thirty-three per cent.[2] Education has even been made compulsory by the most progressive nations.

The nineteenth century well deserves the name of the scientific age, for it is the great discoveries in Physics, Chemistry and the Biologic Sciences that have made it possible. It is an age of rapid concentration—of large things generally—great armies and mighty cities, great factories and joint stock companies, gigantic trusts and vast labor organizations. It is an era of strengthening democracy, of fierce competition and great inequality, but of broadening and deepening sympathy, charity and mutual helpfulness. It is preeminently an age of progress, and if the theory of this book is a true one, we should find rapidly increasing crime. Has crime increased throughout the nineteenth century? Is it increasing now? For the first time we can seek our information in full and reliable judicial records of the criminal classes, which unfortunately do not extend back beyond 1860 or 1870 for most nations; but enough is available to show the strong trend of both the anti-social and the social life in modern Europe.

Of course the judicial statistics of crime, whether dealing with the number of persons held for trial before the courts, with the number of convicted, or the number of prisoners, do not and cannot give any *exact* information as to the total

[1] Mulhall, p. 231. [2] *Ibid.*, p. 231.

amount of criminality in the nation. This would equal the entire number of those acts which the society intends to punish as wrongs against itself, and for which it inflicts a penalty when it discovers and convicts an offender. Many crimes remain hidden, and others, although known, remain unprosecuted and unpunished. Such do not appear in the statistics. But students are fairly well agreed that these judicial records give us at any rate the best index we have of a nation's crime, and may with safety be relied upon to furnish an approximately correct idea of the rise and fall, the increase or decrease, of delinquency. This probability is greatly strengthened if we accept the definition of crime adopted in this book; which would exclude from among the truly criminal offences all conduct which the nation practically leaves unpunished, either from unwillingness or inability to inflict the penalty. In other words, acts criminal in the eyes of the law, but protected or unprosecuted by society, are not crimes. Naturally such actions scarcely appear in the statistics, while the truly criminal conduct is largely recorded there. It has been found that the various forms of these numerical tables—especially the statistics of the accused and of the convicted—bear a certain proportionate relation to each other, which in general does not vary greatly. Thus both give practically the same results.

England. The first annual official record of the state of crimes (commitments for trial) in England and Wales was prepared in 1805, and the volume for 1841 reads: "From that time to the present there has been a progressive increase in the numbers committed. Until the peace in 1814 the increase was gradual, but commitments then increased so rapidly that they were nearly doubled in three years. This great increase was maintained until 1821," and two years later "an increase again commenced, which continued almost uninterruptedly for the ten succeeding years."

ENGLAND AND WALES.—THE TOTAL NUMBER OF PERSONS COMMITTED FOR TRIAL FOR ALL INDICTABLE OFFENCES.

		Proportion per 100,000 population.			Proportion per 100,000 population.
1805............	4,605	49.00	1817..........	13,932	
1811............	5,337	52.51	1818..........	13,567	
1812............	6,576		1819..........	14,254	113.45
1813............	7,164		1820..........	13,710	
1814............	6,390	72.88	1821..........	13,115	
1815............	7,818				
1816............	9,091				

In 1834 the statistical tables were enlarged, and a comparison of the totals for the next two five-year periods indicate another large increase in criminality, after which the annual numbers do not vary greatly until 1855–56. In the following year a great change took place in the judicial statistics; the records of the courts of summary jurisdiction appearing for the first time beside the tables of indictable offences. These latter statistics make a gigantic leap from less than 30,000 in 1854 to more than 53,000 from 1857 to 1861,[1] and after mounting yet higher in the years immediately succeeding, show, since 1886, a considerable diminution in the actual figures, while in proportion to population the decrease has been very great, and almost continuous since 1862–66. Practically all serious crimes are indictable, as are also many old minor offences.

ENGLAND AND WALES.—THE TOTAL NUMBER OF PERSONS FOR TRIAL FOR ALL INDICTABLE OFFENCES.

	Annual average for each 5-year period.	Proportion per 100,000 population.		Annual average for each 5-year period.	Proportion per 100,000 population.
1834–38........	22,174	148.54	1857–61......	53,158	270.02
1839–43........	28,058	174.95	1862–66......	59,715	285.94
1844–48........	27,027	158.98	1867–71......	58,480	263.15
1849–53........	27,431	151.80	1872–76......	52,148	219.18
1854............	29,359		1877–81......	57,234	225.58
			1882–86......	59,259	220.11
			1887–91......	56,280	197.83
			1892–96......	54,689	181.93
1836...........	20,984	140.56	1896..........	50,679	164.91

[1] See Appendix II.

Modern forms of minor criminality appear under the statistics of summary prosecutions, and have been continually increasing up to the present time. The total amount of all crime in England and Wales has also grown steadily larger, if the statistics reveal the truth. The number of persons held for trial in 1896 was 720,441, as against 389,502 in 1857. Notwithstanding the very rapid growth of population, crime seems to have increased even faster. The proportion per 100,000 averaged 2003.34 for 1857–61 and in 1896 it was 2344.34. We shall study these English statistics more closely later, for they will be found to throw much light upon the nature and the increase of crime in modern times. Moreover, their curious and strangely sudden changes demand an explanation.[1]

England and Wales.—Total Number of Persons for Trial before All the Courts and Tribunals Judging Criminal Offenders.[2]

	Annual average for each 5-year period.	Proportion per 100,000 population.
1857–61	394,394	2003.34
1862–66	446,537	2138.19
1867–71	509,317	2291.82
1872–76	607,989	2562.67
1877–81	648,193	2554.81
1882–86	683,936	2540.42
1887–91	684,381	2405.70
1892–96	690,130	2295.79
1896	720,441	2344.34[3]

France. The history of France during the nineteenth

[1] See Appendix III.

[2] See *Judicial Statistics of England and Wales*, 1898, vol. civ, p. 40.

[3] *Scotland.* The 29th Report of the *Judicial Statistics of Scotland*, 1897, gives the average number of criminal prisoners convicted each year in Scotland from 1846 to 1896. The total number has increased from 17,425 (average for five years, 1846–51) to 48,707 (1891–96), and 50,822 in 1896. The tables reveal a very great decrease in serious offences (punished by three or more years of penal servitude) and a tremendous multiplication of sentences for misdemeanors: the class "Imprisonment, with alternative fine or penalty," having increased persistently and rapidly from 3,397 (1846–51) to 38,327 (1891–96), and 40,893 in 1896.

century presents a confusing record of sudden revolutions, unexpected, unsupported, save by a small minority of the people, yet accepted by the nation at large as if it did not know its own mind and were willing to try any form of government offered it. Yet, upon the whole, progress has been persistently in the direction of democracy, with the diffusion of political power, property, education and intelligence among the masses.

The overthrow of the Emperor Napoleon I., in 1814, was followed by the restoration of royalty, but the "old regime" was not restored. "France preserved the social organization created by the revolution, and the administrative organization established by Napoleon."[1] The new government, which soon showed itself to be a "monarchy of the propertied classes," found the instruments of a centralized administration well fitted to its needs, and either did not wish, or did not dare, to attempt a return to the old outworn forms of a belated feudalism and its serfdom. "From 1814 to 1848, the domestic history of France is little but a record of political contests. The court, the high officials, and the wealthy middle-class people who alone possessed the power, ignored the needs of the people; and the people, excluded from the right of voting, had no way to compel a recognition of their needs."[2] They were densely ignorant and dependent, despite doctrines of legal equality. Strikes and even associations of laborers were criminal in the eyes of the law. "The great majority of the French people could not read," in 1821 there were 25,000 communes without schools, "and it was not until after 1833 that the state began to organize primary instruction. Church services were rarely attended by the middle classes, and religion seemed to have lost its hold upon the life of the people; nor did it begin to regain much influence until 1840. For the masses

[1] Seignobos, p. 106.

[2] *Ibid.*, p. 150-1.

it was an era of peace—almost of stagnation—and quiet agricultural existence. Outside of Paris there was practically no political life. Wealth increased, but there was little true social progress, for the government and the voting class opposed even necessary reforms. It was a time of rest and recuperation, of ignorance and inertia. As the criminal statistics prove, there was comparatively little delinquency, and much of what there was, consisted of ancient forms of petty theft from forest and stream, and of offences against the customs laws, that have since greatly decreased in number.

FRANCE.—TOTAL NUMBER OF PERSONS TRIED BY THE CORRECTIONAL TRIBUNALS FOR FISCAL AND FOREST CONTRAVENTIONS.

	Annual average for 5-year periods.		Annual average for 5-year periods.
1826–30	118,681[1]	1861–65	28,862
1831–35	138,752	1866–70	24,560
1836–40	111,235	1871–75	28,727
1841–45	102,385	1876–80	25,131
1846–50	95,966	1881–85	23,936
1851–55	89,810	1886–90	27,724
1856–60	57,470	1891–95	——

As what life there was in France during these 35 years was mainly political, so the new social prohibitions were political, and there were many offenders punished because of them. The government waged a ceaseless struggle against the Republicans, through the instrumentality of new laws, making criminal many acts against the power of the king and Chambers. In 1830, a law was passed against seditious placards; in 1831, against mobs; in 1834, against seditious cries. There was a new criminal statute against associations, and one forbidding the keeping of fire-arms in private houses. Over 2,000 Republicans were arrested, and 164 tried before the Chamber of Peers, "for attempts against the peace of the state," in one monster prosecution during

[1] Estimate.

1834. New press laws were passed, dealing with political offences of the newspapers, and the "Laws of September" made the condemnation of political offenders in general extremely easy.

Then came another sudden and utterly unexpected revolution in Paris (1848), accepted, as usual, passively by the rest of France. But its importance for the nation was very great, for it gave political rights to every Frenchman of legal age. It awakened the masses of the people from their lethargy. Their active interest in the national life commenced. They began to be educated politically. "At a single stroke the revolution took the power out of the hands of the property owners, converted France into a democracy, transformed all the conditions of political life," and attempted an equally radical transformation of industrial life.[1] For the Socialists at first rose to power. The revolution caused a business crisis, interrupting industry. Multitudes of the unemployed flocked to Paris, and the government resolved to find employment for them in national workshops. Seven million francs were distributed in wages to these men, but the plan was not successful. A great socialist insurrection followed, but was suppressed by the national guard with much bloodshed. "The prisoners were shot summarily, or tried and transported. Thirty-two socialist newspapers were suppressed by the government."[2] The socialist party was crushed out of existence. Then came the election of Louis Napoleon to the presidency by an overwhelming popular vote, followed three years later by the coup d'état and the establishment of the second empire. An enormous multiplication of crime followed, from 1850 to 1865, as revealed by the statistics. Why was it? The nation was awake again. It was filled with new life. It was progressing rapidly—politically, industrially and educationally. Napoleon III.

[1] Seignobos, p. 159.

[2] *Ibid.*, p. 164.

had to crush his enemies with a strong hand. There was no war. The army and the people supported him, placing in his hands practically unbounded power to inflict criminal punishment.

This was undoubtedly a time of political education for the French nation, and the diffusion of other knowledge was not neglected, for "colleges and ecclesiastical primary schools were founded all over France."[1] A large development of modern forms of industry, finance and trade began (1850–60), which brought with it a corresponding increase in certain opposing kinds of criminality. Joint stock companies were created, railroads were rapidly constructed, great financial establishments—the credit foncier, the credit mobilier—were founded, and the systematic transformation of Paris was begun. The statistics on page 328 show the rapid increase of criminal convictions for fraud, forgery, and other business offences.

Throughout the disastrous period of the Franco-Prussian war, the amount of crime punished by the French nation was relatively small, although a large part of the decrease is apparently accounted for by the absence of the statistics from the tribunal of the Seine. Notice the great drop in the total of police court contraventions, 427,010 (1866–70), as compared with 538,441, the average from 1861 to '65. The nation was probably too busy and distracted for the punishment of minor offenders.

After the war, renewed social pressure rapidly increased the number of those prosecuted, for both delites and contraventions; this upward tendency being strongly stimulated by the enforcement of the law of January 23, 1873, against public drunkenness.[2] The suppression of the Commune in

[1] Seignobos, p. 167.

[2] *Statistique de la Justice Criminelle en France*, Introduct. vol. (1880–81), page xciv.

1871 was followed by 13,000 condemnations of political criminals; 7,500 were transported to New Caledonia. Since then France has had no more rebellions or revolutions. The nation has certainly advanced very greatly in intelligence, industry and political stability since 1814.

Primary education was made gratuitous in 1881, and compulsory by a law of the following year, but the law does not seem to be enforced. However, a larger proportion of the population is recorded as attending school in France than in any other country of Europe, except Switzerland.[1] Trade unions were at last made legal in 1884. The ill-treatment of animals was made criminal by a law of July 2, 1850, and prosecutions for this offence have been greatly multiplied. These things indicate a higher and wiser standard of social morality. The totals of all crime have increased since 1826–30, from 319,263 to 684,017 in actual numbers, and from 1002 to 1784 for each 100,000 of the population. In general, this increase has been in the direction of greatest opposition to the new life, the upward progress of the nation; and has been called into existence, very largely, by the enforcement of new social prohibitions. Since 1875, although the amount of crime has grown somewhat, yet the totals have never again rivaled those from 1856 to 1865, when the masses of the people had awakened from their lethargic, oppressed and almost stationary existence under the monarchy, and the forces of the nation were progressing rapidly in many directions, usually associated in the development of a great modern, industrial and democratic civilization. In proportion to population, crime has even decreased slightly in most recent years. Is civilization rising or declining in France?

From 1856 to 1860 the proportionate amount of crime in France and England was almost the same, to-day the French

[1] See Mulhall

figures are far lower. England has increased her crime in proportion to population from 2003.34 to 2295.79, while France has been decreasing hers from 2062.00 to 1783.90. A comparison with other European countries—Austria, Italy and Germany—where both civilization and crime are believed to be advancing rapidly, will surely prove interesting and instructive. Meanwhile, let us look for a moment at the French statistics themselves, and question somewhat more closely, whether the great rise in the figures from 1851 to 1865 actually meant a corresponding increase in the nation's crime, or not.

FRANCE.—TOTAL NUMBER OF PRISONERS FOR TRIAL BEFORE ALL THE COURTS AND TRIBUNALS JUDGING CRIMINAL OFFENDERS.

	Annual average for 5-year periods.	Proportion per 100,000 population.		Annual average for 5-year periods.	Proportion per 100,000 population.
1826–30	319,263	1002.1	1861–65	715,011	1912.5
1831–35	348,866	1071.2	1866–70	597,850[1]	1570.5
1836–40	398,287	1187.5	1871–75	655,745	1816.3
1841–45	464,791	1357.8	1876–80	664,822	1801.4
1846–50	487,534	1377.1	1881–85	684,044	1815.8
1851–55	715,504	1999.6	1886–90	686,892	1797.3
1856–60	743,114	2062.0	1891–95	684,017[2]	1783.9

The judicial statistics of France are directly comparable for a much longer time than those of any other nation. A division of these 70 years into three nearly equal periods, makes possible an interesting comparison between the average amount of crime in the early and relatively non-progressive period, and the era of vehement life and development that followed.

THE TOTAL NUMBER OF PRISONERS BEFORE ALL THE FRENCH COURTS AND TRIBUNALS.

	Total persons held for trial.	Proportion per 100,000.	Persons convicted.
1826–50	403,748	1199.1	350,775
1851–75	685,445	1872.2	639,047
1876–95	679,944	1799.6	650,318

[1] Time of Franco-German war. Laws silent in the midst of arms; society disorganized.

[2] Statistics for four years, 1891–2 and 1894–5.

The explanation of the sudden flood of crime, as recorded in the criminal statistics of France, from 1851 to 1865, is three-fold. The first great cause was legal, the second judicial, the third, political.

First: A glance at the table on this page will show that most of this great increase falls under simple police court contraventions, which mount with astonishing rapidity from 258,690, the average for the five years 1846–50, to 463,254, and 530,311 for the next two quinquennial periods. The main reason for this is found in new laws, especially the law of June 8, 1851, upon the police of wagons and public coaches, which created many new forms of minor social prohibitions; and the enforcement of such laws by the energy of a widely extended national police force.

FRANCE.—TOTAL NUMBER OF PERSONS TRIED BY THE CORRECTIONAL TRIBUNALS FOR DELITES AND BY THE POLICE TRIBUNALS FOR CONTRAVENTIONS.

	Delites.	Police court contraventions.	Total of delites and P. contraventions.	
	Annual average for 5-year periods.	Annual average for 5-year periods.	Annual average for 5-year periods.	Proportion per 100,000 population.
1826–30......	59,340[1]	134,112	193,452	6c7.21
1831–35......	64,455	138,193	202,648	622.21
1836–40......	80,550	198,615	279,165	832.31
1841–45......	93,140	262,162	355,302	1038.co
1846–50......	125,448	258,690	384,138	1085.07
1851–55......	155,336	463,254	618,590	1728.73
1856–60......	149,950	530,311	680,261	1887.54
1861–65......	143,158	538,441	681,599	1823.14
1866–70......	142,005	427,010	569,015	1494.77
1871–75.....	160,128	461,818	621,946	1722.70
1876–80......	171,352	463,965	635,317	1721.45
1881–85......	188,903	466,823	655,726	1740.62
1886–90......	199,872	455,067	654,939	1713.65
1891–95......		443,578		

The second great cause was the coming of the practice of

[1] Estimate. Only total for all offences tried by the Correctional Tribunals given for this 5-year period.

correctionalization. Laws of August 7th and October 18th, 1848, permitted its introduction, and since 1855 this custom has been more and more generally observed. It consists in passing over the aggravating circumstances of certain crimes, in order to bring offenders before the correctional tribunals, which inflict a surer, though lighter penalty. This has proved to be in the interest of social welfare; for, prior to its introduction, juries oftentimes refused to convict, when the law demanded what seemed to them too heavy penalties. The change has been much the same as that wrought out in England by other means—*i. e.*, the repeal of ancient laws and the enactment of the Criminal Justice and Summary Jurisdiction Acts. Bad conduct, once largely left unpunished, has been made truly criminal. Society has grown both more eager and more able to prosecute and punish for crime. The increasing numbers and efficiency of the police are both an expression of this desire and a main cause of its fulfillment. The total of all crime, but especially of minor crime, has been very greatly increased in France, by strengthened social pressure and new social prohibitions.[1]

The third great cause, multiplying French criminality between 1851–65, was political. Napoleon III. crushed his political opponents—especially the Republicans—by making them criminals. The coup d'état of December 2d, 1851, established an autocratic empire, practically concentrating all power in one man, the emperor, though theoretically it was vested in a sovereign nation, which had no way to express its will but by plebiscite, voting yes or no. The masses of the people supported Napoleon III. and gave him the "sole initiative in law making" (1852), and almost unlimited power to punish, especially for political offences.[2] "The government depended on the army, which assured its

[1] See pages 289–90. [2] See law of 1858; also Seignobos.

power; on the commercial middle class, satisfied with being no longer troubled by politics; and, above all, on the clergy, who made the country electors vote for the official candidates." [1]

Immediately after the coup d'état, "the President proclaimed martial law in 32 departments, granted himself by decree (December 8, 1851) the right to exile all members of secret societies, and created mixed commissions (a general, a prefect, and an attorney) with power to judge without appeal. According to a document discovered in the Tuileries in 1870, there were 26,642 persons arrested, and only 6,500 released; 5,108 were made subject to police supervision, and 15,033 condemned (of whom 9,530 were transported to Algeria, 239 to Cayenne, and 2,804 confined in a French city). Eighty representatives, almost all Republicans, were banished." Napoleon "found himself absolute master of France." [2] Political life practically ceased. "The Republicans, deprived of their chiefs by exile or transportation, and persecuted by the police, had no longer any means of showing their opposition. Press offences were taken away from jury courts and given to tribunals of summary jurisdiction. It was unlawful to report press cases or sessions of the Chambers, or to publish false news—that is to say, news displeasing to the government. Even individuals were watched by the police, and a political conversation was enough to brand a person as a suspect under this administration, which, having no public exposure to fear, made arbitrary disposal of the liberty of all its subjects. The caprice of an agent might cause the arrest and detention of any one who seemed to him dangerous. The comedian Grassot was arrested for having been overheard to say in a café: 'This is like Sebastopol; one can't take anything.' A woman was arrested at Tours for having said that the

[1] Seignobos, p. 175. [2] *Ibid.*, p. 171.

grape blight was coming again; in releasing her the prefect threatened to imprison her for life if she spread any more bad news." All the classes in France were ordered to hold their exercises at the same hour, and the professors had to shave their mustaches, to "remove from their appearance, as well as from their manners the last vestiges of anarchy." To wear a mustache thus became a criminal offence for a professor.[1] After the discovery of the Republican plot of 1853, and three attempts to assassinate the emperor, the administration obtained the passage of the general security act (1858), which "gave government the power to detain, exile or transport, without trial, any person previously condemned for political offences; and to imprison or exile any person so condemned in the future." "Espinasse, a general well-known for his share in the coup d'état, was appointed minister of the interior to apply this law. He sent an order to each prefect to arrest a certain number of persons, using his own choice in the selection. According to Blanchard this number varied from 20 to 41; it was 'proportioned to the general spirit of the department.' Each prefect interpreted the order in his own way—some limiting themselves to men condemned at the time of the Republic, others taking those who seemed to them dangerous, chiefly workingmen, lawyers and doctors. The object was simply to intimidate the people."[2] Surely there is little further need to ask whether the statistics (1851–'65) reveal the truth, or, for what reasons crime increased so greatly in France, during the time of the second empire.

Austria. Great changes have been taking place in Austria-Hungary during the last forty years. Defeated in foreign war, the ruling aristocracy has been forced to admit the

[1] The great industrial and financial development beginning from 1850, and its effect upon the nation's crime, has already been mentioned.

[2] Seignobos, p. 176.

masses of the people to some share of political power. The constitution and laws of the land have been radically altered. A province has been lost and another gained. Politically, the change has been from a strongly centralized despotism to a representative and constitutional monarchy. In a country where, in 1840, but sixteen per cent. of the population could read and write, more than sixty per cent. now possess the means for more intelligent and broader life. The manufactured product of the nation has increased from an estimated yearly value of fifty million pounds sterling in 1800, to one hundred and forty-two millions in 1840, and two hundred and fifty-three millions in 1888.[1] The Empire of Austria-Hungary has been growing stronger, politically, intellectually and industrially; has been rapidly developing its type of civilization to a higher plane. During this progress and because of this progress, the amount of the nation's crime has multiplied enormously; for the nation has been very busy in the creation and the stern enforcement of new criminal laws, regulating and maintaining mutual rights and duties in the changed relations of life.

The Austrian Empire is a conglomerate of disunited nations, or fragments of nations, living side by side, owning allegiance to the same man, but preserving their distinctive languages, and to a great extent their native forms of administrative government. Originally these peoples had nothing in common. Until 1806 they were not even united under a collective national name—Austria. Soon after this date the government became firmly centralized and absolutist. None but the nobility possessed any political rights. The people were densely ignorant, and were forbidden even to think about affairs of state. What education there was "still excluded all modern subjects." A democratic revolution in 1848 came suddenly with a single riot, but was almost as

[1] Mulhall.

speedily suppressed. Absolutism was restored, resting upon the power of the nobles, and upon the despotic authority of the Roman Catholic Church. "The general assembly of the thirty-two Austrian bishops condemned political liberty as 'impious,' and all political life ceased in Austria for ten years." [1]

But after the disastrous Italian war of 1859, the absolutist system fell, for its credit was gone—the government could no longer borrow money, upon which its existence had for years depended. Popular interest could be re-awakened in public affairs only by admitting the people to some share in their decision. Very reluctantly this was recognized, and the next seven years were filled with political negotiations between the court and the nationalist factions, with attempts and failures in various forms of parliamentary government; until finally in 1867, after crushing defeats in the war with Prussia, a system of representative and constitutional government was firmly established for the dual empire. The statistics of crime during this time of war, disorganization and confusion (1859 to 1869) indicate few criminals for all offences, even for the most serious. Whether the disorderly elements were drafted off into the armies, or society punished so little as to make many evil acts really non-criminal; or whether malefactors continued as criminals, only to a somewhat larger extent unpunished, it is very hard to decide. At any rate the statistical tables for this period do not seem rightly comparable with those after 1870. The constitution of 1867 guaranteed complete religious liberty. Public schools were soon afterwards removed from the supervision and control of the Roman Catholic Church, and thrown open "to all citizens without regard to creed." The pope declared these laws "abominable" and "void for the present and the future," but they have been enforced nevertheless;

[1] Seignobos, p. 422–3.

and a very considerable degree of industrial liberty has likewise come in with the existence of political, educational and social rights. Manufactures, trade and commerce have rapidly developed, and Austria is no longer among the illiterate nations of the world. Radical change and upward progress have been the order of the last forty years, and in fostering and safe-guarding this healthy forward movement of civilization, many new social prohibitions have been found necessary, and, as the statistics show, the criminal population has increased with great rapidity. The tables are for Austria alone: those for Hungary not being available.

Lately, there has been a reaction—the government has become less liberal, less anti-clerical, more aristocratic and anti-democratic. The statistics of crime for the last five years show a slight decrease.

TOTAL CONVICTIONS FOR ALL CRIMINAL OFFENCES.

AUSTRIA.

	Annual average for 5-year periods.	Proportion per 100,000 population.	Census.
1871–75	303,381	1477.0	1870[1]
1876–80	416,042	2130.9	1880
1881–85	527,713		
1886–90	579,725	2403.0	1890
1891–95	568,677		

ITALY.

	Annual average for 5-year periods.	Proportion per 100,000 population.	Census.
1881–85	367,510	1291.3	1881
1886–90	467,249	1614.7	1891
1891–95	506,687		
1896–97	527,634		

Italy. The unity of Italy, like that of Germany, has been wrought out through victorious war, and by the federation of many little states around the strongest and most warlike of their number. From 1859 to 1871 Europe witnessed the

[1] Estimate.

binding together of two great scattered races, with their little princedoms, into two strong national groups, drawn together at last by the powerful attraction of kinship and mutual interests. As it was when history began, so nation building is still the work of war. Those races whose unconquerable love of liberty and independence made national unity and social growth for long most difficult, have established at the last the best and most progressive type of civilization—a truly active, well-balanced, moving equilibrium—by preserving the right and opportunity for individual development and socially useful variation; but always at the expense of an increasing mass of crime, utterly unknown among unprogressive tribal communities, and the barbaric empires of the world.[1]

Thus, since the establishment of the kingdom of Italy, the totals of its criminality have been advancing with giant strides; from 367,510 (1881–85) to 527,634 (1896–97). The reasons for this are manifest. The upbuilding and strengthening of a centralized parliamentary government, the enforcement of law and order after tumult, disorganization and confusion, the crushing out of old hereditary forms of organized lawlessness, and the rapid development of industrial and commercial life, especially in the northern provinces, have all called for the creation and strong social enforcement of new criminal laws, political, administrative, fiscal, industrial, social.

Sometimes the laws were already in existence, but the evils they were aimed at had never been made crimes. The struggles of the Italian soldiers and gendarmes against brigand bands in the mountain districts, have at times seemed almost like organized warfare. The national army has been a splendid school for the Italian people; a school

[1] See the chapter on Savages; on Peru, Mexico, etc.

"for national sentiment" and "also a primary school for raw recruits who enlisted without knowing how to read:" (64 per cent. in 1866.).[1] The diffusion of popular education in united Italy has been marked, although the compulsory education law has never been enforced, and the nation is not yet ready to punish as crime the rearing of children in ignorance. Yet in 1889, 47 per cent. of the population knew how to read and write; a very great improvement since the 14 per cent. of 1840.[2] The electoral reform of 1882 extended the right to vote by an educational qualification to 1,338,000 men, the total number of voters being increased at that time from 627,000 to 2,048,000. The Italians seem to be growing more democratic, more peaceful and orderly, more wonted to their national government.

Long and patient attempts to secure a reconciliation with the pope and induce him to renounce his claim to temporal power having proved unavailing, the new penal code of 1889 decreed imprisonment with hard labor for "any attempt against the unity of the state;" also "one year's imprisonment for any servant of the Church who should, in the performance of his office, criticise any action on the part of the government."[3] A large amount of other new legislation was also introduced by this code, which, as Signor Bosco writes, "not only made criminal acts formerly unpunished, and modified the juridical concept of certain offences, but introduced notable changes in the prosecution of some delites, increasing the ease with which the party injured can promote penal action."[4] Delites, including all serious delinquency, have accordingly increased about 30 per cent., and all crime by over 40 per cent., from 1885 to 1897,

[1] Seignobos, p. 360. [2] Mulhall. [3] Seignobos, pp. 368–9.

[4] As did the Criminal Justice Act, 1855, and the Summary Jurisdiction Act, 1879, in England.

while the growth of population is estimated at 12 per cent. for the same years.

Germany and Spain. The judicial statistics of Germany and Spain relate only to offences punished under the criminal code, and, in Germany, to a few other crimes recently created by special laws. Later chapters of this book will show the radical difference in the nature of the crimes most prevalent in these two countries. Meanwhile, a glance at the following table will reveal the enormous increase of delinquency in modern Germany—a state that has been advancing so very rapidly to the proud position of political, educational and industrial leadership upon the continent of Europe—and the almost stationary condition of criminality in Spain, where political disaster, economic distress, and the burden of uneducated ignorance and blind superstition have made of a once great nation an almost unprogressive, if not a degenerating people.

TOTAL CONVICTIONS FOR OFFENCES UNDER THE CRIMINAL CODE, ETC.

GERMANY.

	Annual average for 5-year periods.	Proportion per 100,000 population.	Census.
1882–85	337,290	745.7	
1886–90	362,220	773.0	1885
1891–95	428,823	867.6	1890
1896–97	460,292	880.4	1895

SPAIN.

	Annual average for 5-year periods.	Proportion per 100,000 population.	Census.
1883–85	84,188	504.1	1880
1886–90	91,846	532.5	1891
1891–95	89,923	521.4	1891
1896	81,118		

All the leading civilizations of Europe—England, Germany, France, Austria and Italy—reveal, in their judicial statistics, the same great forward movement of the flood of crime; not only in the actual amount of delinquency, but also in proportion to a rapidly increasing population.[1] Spain alone, the one laggard nation we have been studying, does not show increasing criminality. Four great states give the totals of convictions for all criminal offences. Placing the average number of those convicted per 100,000 of the population beside the estimated annual value of the manufactured product and the percentage of the people able to write, we get a rough idea of the relation between the industrial efficiency, the educational activity, and the amount of criminality in these nations.

	ENGLAND.	AUSTRIA.	FRANCE.	ITALY.
Average annual convictions for all crimes per 100,000 of the population (1871–1890)	2183.8	2125.9	1734.8	1464.5
Estimated value of the manufactured product (1888) in pounds sterling	£820,000,000	£253,000,000	£485,000,000	£121,000,000
Percentage of population able to write (1889)	90 per cent.	55 per cent.	85 per cent.	47 per cent.

The extraordinary amount of crime in Austria may be accounted for by the extremely rapid development of that nation—politically, industrially and intellectually—in recent years. From 1871 to 1875, the proportion of convictions for crime in Austria was far lower than in France—1477.0 per 100,000 population, as against 1722.4 for the latter country. In Italy also, as we have seen, the proportion of

[1] "Latest figures show increase of crime in almost all countries, especially in lighter crimes." Mayo-Smith, *Statistics and Sociology*.

[2] Statistics for ten years (1881–1890). Census figures of 1870–1 and 1880–1 used for calculation of proportions of crime. See Mulhall's *Dictionary of Statistics* for estimates of manufactures and percentages of ability to write.

convictions is very rapidly increasing, from 1291.3 for the period 1881–85, to 1680.1 for 1891–95; keeping pace with the nation's progress. Do not the most civilized and progressive states have the most crime, and more crime as civilization increases?

CHAPTER XIII

IS PUNISHMENT POWERLESS AGAINST CRIME?

Is civilization, then, a failure, as some would have us think? Are we losing our moral fibre, and becoming more and more degenerate in mind and body? Is the actively anti-social man—the true criminal—securing an ever stronger foothold in our midst? Is serious crime increasing steadily, and are our punishments powerless against its growth? "Why," writes Dr. Morrison, of her majesty's prison, Wandsworth, "are our penal methods so helpless and discomforted in face of the criminal population? Why do the combined efforts of legislators, judges, police and prisons produce so few practical results? Is it because the social disease with which these agencies are grappling is beyond the reach of human skill, and will continue to rage with unabated virulence so long as social life exists?[1] If so we may well tremble for the welfare of the state, and look with gloomy

[1] See "*The Female Offender*," Lombroso and Ferrero. Introduction written by W. D. Morrison, page vii. Dr. Morrison believes that if the "principles of penal treatment advocated by the criminal anthropologists"—classification, reformation, education—"were applied to the criminal population, it is certain that recidivism would diminish, it is certain that the habitual criminal would become a greater rarity, and, most important of all, *it is certain that society would enjoy a greater immunity from crime*." (See p. xx.)

Concerning this last statement the author regretfully finds himself compelled to differ even with so high an authority as Dr. Morrison; and this despite his firm belief in the great practical value of the "penal treatment advocated." For the amount of a nation's crime depends upon (1) the degree of civilization attained, (2) the rapidity of social evolution, necessarily calling into existence new forms of crime, and (3) the general attitude of the people toward the criminal law, and especially the new laws: obedience being more difficult to obtain where individual liberty is customary and highly prized, and restraint consequently more irksome forebodings toward the future. For, as General Brinkerhoff, President of the National Prison Congress of the United States, well says: "Other questions which agitate the public and divide parties are doubtless important. But the country can live and prosper under free trade or protection, under bimetallism or monometallism, under Democracy or Republicanism; but it cannot survive a demoralized people with crime in the ascendant. That crime is on the increase out of proportion to population is indicated in many ways, but for the country as a whole, the United States census is the most reliable guide."[1]

These are not isolated expressions of pessimistic opinion. In France, Germany, Italy, and other countries, distinguished

[1] *The United States Census—Report on Crime by Decades.*

Year.	Prisoners.	Ratio to population.
1850	6,737	1 in 3,442
1860	19,086	1 in 1,647
1870	32,901	1 in 1,171
1880	58,609	1 in 855
1890	82,329	1 in 757

"This rate of increase in a few States, we are glad to note, has nôt been maintained, and in one or two, for the higher crimes, it has even decreased a trifle; but, upon the whole, the swell has been continuous, like a tide that has no ebb." (General R. Brinkerhoff.)

Compare with these figures the statistics of prisoners in Orissa, India, under British rule since 1803, as revealing the relation of civilization to increasing crime.

In the Districts of Orissa "crime is much less frequent than in the more civilized parts of Bengal." "Cottack is the most civilized of the three Districts, and furnishes the highest proportion of criminals. Yet the average jail population was but 415 in 1868, or about one person to every 3,116 of the population. No European country could show anything like this immunity from crime which the worst district in Orissa enjoys. In Blasaor the proportion is one to every 3,375 of the population. Puré District, however, the seat of the so-called abominations of Jugannáth, would blush to own such an overwhelming criminal population. The proportion was, in the last year of which we have the returns, one criminal to every 6,000 of the population, and one female to every 100,000." "Strictly speaking, there are no criminal classes in Puré District—that is to say, no classes who live by preying on society." See W. W. Hunter, *Orissa*, ii, 135-6, Appendix, i, 21, and Appendix ii, 58. London, 1872.

specialists have voiced these same sad views. Crime is increasing rapidly, and our existing penal systems are powerless against it. Professor Von Liszt, an eminent German jurist, has felt himself compelled to this belief by his recent wide survey of these important problems. Have we really good cause for great anxiety and fear? What do statistics tell us concerning old and serious forms of crime? Is there a progressive increase among heinous criminals? It is certainly worth our while to investigate.[1]

England. The total number of persons arraigned for serious crimes before the high courts of England and Wales, from 1857 to 1896, were as follows:

ENGLAND AND WALES.—TOTAL NUMBER OF PERSONS FOR TRIAL AT ASSIZES AND QUARTER SESSIONS.

	Annual average for 5-year periods.	Proportion per 100,000 population.
1857–61	17,825	90.53
1862–66	19,758	94.61
1867–71	18,445	83.00
1872–76	15,096	63.63
1877–81	15,567	61.36
1882–86	14,303	53.13
1887–91	12,481	43.87
1892–96	11,816	39.31
1896	11,103	36.13

Social pressure against heinous criminals appears to have been exceedingly successful in England during the last half century. Serious crime has very greatly decreased, both in actual numbers, and yet more notably in proportion to the

[1] But international comparison should be avoided (except, perhaps, in the case of an offence like homicide), for the forms of crime judged by the higher criminal courts are far more numerous in some nations than in others, and this not alone on account of the varying degrees of criminal heinousness attached by different peoples to the same act, but also, and chiefly, because some nations, like the French, Italians and Austrians, have three different grades of criminal offences—serious crimes, delites and contraventions—while the English and Americans have but two—serious crimes and misdemeanors—and the Germans only one (so far at least as their statistics are concerned), all offences, grave and petty, being grouped together, as crimes against the person, property or the state.

population. The totals have grown steadily less and less since the early sixties, and the statistics for Ireland give exactly the same pleasing results.

IRELAND.—TOTAL NUMBER OF PERSONS FOR TRIAL AT ASSIZES AND QUARTER SESSIONS.

	Annual average for 5-year periods.	Proportion per 100,000 population.
1852–56	12,155.2	185.52
1857–61	6,071.0	99.52
1876–80	4,255.6	80.86
1881–85	3,683.2	73.11
1886–90	2,430.4	50.55
1891–95	2,133.0	46.15

But perhaps the United Kingdom stands alone in happy isolation as to this retreating march of serious crime?

France. The French national statistics extend from 1826, and, with care, are comparable safely throughout their entire length, a period of seventy years. Courts of Assize (Cours D'Assises) do not have jurisdiction over so large a proportion of criminal acts as do the Assizes and Quarter Sessions in England; for the French possess Correctional Tribunals (Tribunaux Correctionnels) dealing with delites, a class of offences midway between serious crimes and police court misdemeanors.

FRANCE.—TOTAL NUMBER OF PERSONS FOR TRIAL AT ASSIZES.

	Annual average for 5-year periods.	Proportion per 100,000 population.
1826–30	7,130	22.38
1831–35	7,466	22.92
1836–40	7,885	23.51
1841–45	7,104	20.75
1846–50	7,430	20.99
1851–55	7,104	19.85
1856–60	5,383	14.94
1861–65	4,550	12.17
1866–70	4,275	11.23
1871–75	5,072	14.05
1876–80	4,374	11.85
1881–85	4,382	11.63
1886–90	4,229	11.07
1891–95	3,984[1]	10.39

[1] Statistics for 1893 omitted (not obtainable).

French statistics evidently support the English. The totals of most serious crime show a persistent decrease in actual numbers, from more than 7,000 to less than 4,000 persons held for trial; while in proportion to population the diminution is far more than half, from 22.38 to 10.39, for each 100,000 inhabitants. This is encouraging. But do these figures tell "the truth, the whole truth, and nothing but the truth?" Many persons doubt the competency of statistics as witnesses at all times, but especially perhaps in criminal matters. Let us look very closely and critically, but I trust not wearyingly, at them for a moment, to get a glimpse of the strong currents at work beneath the quiet surface of this sheet of crime; and see whether, like a great Gulf Stream, some marked change in judicial procedure may not have borne silently away a large portion of these French criminals, simply to deposit them in other tables of statistics? What do expert statisticians think of the reliability of the evidence presented by these figures, so laboriously and carefully collected during seventy years of modern life? The great object is to find the truth, irrespective of any theory whatsoever, and truth is not always easy to discern.

Reasons for Decrease in the Totals of Serious Crime.

From 1826 to 1855 the average annual number of prisoners held for trial before the French courts of Assize did not vary greatly, but in proportion to population there was a sensible decrease, from 22.38 per 100,000 at the beginning of the period, to 19.85 at the close. After 1855, the totals decrease rapidly—a decrease accentuated in 1870 under the influence of war, when by far the lowest total, 3,501, was reached. [Laws silent in the midst of arms: society disorganized.] Then followed a reaction and somewhat larger numbers, falling again from 1875–80 and continuing to decline until the present time, when the figures again fall below 4,000, and continue there. The principal cause of the reduction since 1855 is the custom, more and more generally observed, of passing over the aggravating circumstances of certain crimes in order to bring offenders before the correctional tribunals, which inflict a surer, though lighter penalty. This practice, called "la correctionnalisation," has thus come about in the interest of the social welfare, because juries oftentimes refused to convict where punishments they deemed too heavy would surely follow under the law, and also to diminish the expenses of criminal prosecutions. By this practice France has accomplished much the same result as England by the repeal of old and cruel laws, and the enactment of lighter penalties. In both countries, the growing moral sense of the community demanded less severe punishment, if evil acts were to be punished as crimes. The reply to this demand, in milder criminal procedure, has brought to both nations increased criminal prosecutions before the lower courts; additions to the acts punished as crimes, and a consequent multiplication of criminals. Laws of 7th August and 18th October, 1848, permitted the introduction of this extra-legal "correctionnalisation" into the French courts. In the statistics for 1856–60 its great influence is plainly manifest. It has become a firmly seated judicial custom, and is said to be conducted with much discernment and justice. A law of 1863 has also contributed to reduce the number of prisoners (prévenus) tried before a jury, by placing certain crimes, such as cuts and blows, corruption, false witness in certain cases, and menaces within the jurisdiction of the inferior courts. But after making full allowance for correctionalization, French statisticians believe that the amount of serious criminality has certainly been diminished. The thirty years before this system of extenuating circumstances was introduced, show a very considerable decrease in proportion to population; and during the fifteen years 1881 to 1895, when the effects of the changed procedure and of the legislation of 1863 may be considered to have worked themselves out, the decrease has also been noteworthy, both in actual number of offenders and in proportion to population.

In England, as we have seen, the need of lighter punishments, if malefactors were to continue criminals, resulted in the direct legal transfer of large classes of offenders to the jurisdiction of the inferior courts. This change was introduced in 1855, and in 1879 its sphere of influence was very greatly extended. The effect upon the statistics was immediate; not diffused over a long period of time, as in France. Therefore we can the more easily and accurately make allowance for it, and may rest secure in the belief that English judicial statistics since 1858 reveal the truth as to the great decrease of serious criminality throughout the nation.

Germany does not separate her statistics of serious crime from those of minor offences. The great recent growth of her delinquency, as a whole, has already been noted, and its more searching examination later will reveal some interesting and important tendencies in the modern march of crime.

Austria and Italy have been passing through great political changes and developments since 1860. The progress in modern forms of industry and trade has also been noteworthy. In both nations the criminal population has been increasing with startling rapidity. Have serious criminals multiplied in like proportion? For Austria, apparently yes, at first sight. The totals mount rapidly from 1860 to 1880, only to be followed by an almost equally rapid fall during the ten years from 1886 to 1895, so that in proportion to population the Austrian statistics show a considerably less number of condemned for serious crimes for 1886–95 than for 1866–75. Delites are few in number in Austria, and almost half of the persons condemned by the high courts of the nation were sentenced to terms of imprisonment not exceeding three months, so that much of this criminality is really not serious. In Italy, on the contrary, where offences termed delites are much more numerous and increasing rapidly, the totals of most serious crime show a very great and persistent diminution.

AUSTRIA.—THE TOTAL NUMBER OF PERSONS CONDEMNED FOR (SERIOUS)[1] CRIMES.[2]

	Annual average for 5-year periods.	Proportion per 100,000 population.	Census.
1861–65	18,154		
1866–70	24,189	125.34	1870[3]
1871–75	27,304		
1876–80	31,428	142.03	1880
1881–85	31,475		
1886–90	28,834	121.70	1890
1891–95	29,328		

ITALY.—TOTAL NUMBER OF PERSONS CONDEMNED FOR SERIOUS CRIMES BY THE COURTS OF ASSIZE.[4]

	Annual average for 5-year periods.	Proportion per 100,000 inhabitants.
1875–79	6,830	23.355
1880–84	6,464	
1885–89	4,952	13.982
1890–93	3,297	

In *Scotland* the number of criminals sentenced to long terms of penal servitude has fallen to less than one-fifth during fifty years.

[1] Almost half these persons were condemned to terms of imprisonment not exceeding three months.

[2] See *Statistische Monatschrift* (1899), 25 Neue Folge, 4; Dr. Hugo Hoegel, pp. 378–9; and *Sulla Statistica della Delinquenza in Vari Stati d'Europa*, A. Bosco, p. 57.

[3] Estimate from 1869 census.

[4] See *Annuario Statistico Italiano* (1895), page 263.

SCOTLAND.—TOTAL NUMBER OF PERSONS SENTENCED TO PENAL SERVITUDE (FROM THREE YEARS TO LIFE PENALTY.)

	Annual average for 5-year periods.		Annual average for 5-year periods.
1846–51	432	1876–81	161
1851–56	337	1881–86	181
1856–61	237	1886–91	108
1861–66	207	1891–95	79
1866–71	210	1896	85
1871–76	163		

Spain. Delites, which have been rapidly increasing among the most progressive and highly civilized nations in recent years, are, in Spain, united in the statistics with more heinous crimes, and the two together show a decided decrease. Even when contraventions, under the code, are added to these figures of serious criminality, the result is a diminution since 1888. This does not bode well for the upward growth of civilization in the Iberian Peninsula.

SPAIN.—TOTAL NUMBER OF PERSONS CONDEMNED FOR BOTH SERIOUS CRIMES AND DELITES UNDER THE PENAL CODE.

	Annual average for 5-year periods.	Proportion per 100,000 population.	Census.
1883–85	22,853	136.84	1880[1]
1886–90	23,405	135.70	1891
1891–95	20,102	116.55	1891
1896	19,623		

Official records of the criminal classes reveal, therefore, a notable decrease in the total amount of serious crime among the most civilized and progressive nations of modern times. We know that justice is becoming more sure—the proportion of convictions to acquittals having very generally grown larger—while we have good reason to believe that the pursuit of criminals has become more keen and successful; and therefore, it is most probable that the great decrease recorded in the statistics is exceeded by the actual

[1] Estimate.

facts, could we obtain them. For, increased probability of arrest, and added likelihood of conviction, if guilty, would necessarily mean increased statistics of serious crime, if such existed. Social punishment does not seem to be powerless against delinquency.

But is it not possible that some crimes, and those perhaps the most dangerous, have increased; although this does not appear in the statistical totals, because of the diminution under other, less serious, forms? This is not the case. Certain old and most heinous crimes, such as treason and piracy, have almost disappeared, while others, murder, homicide[1] and most serious wounding (dangerous to life), etc., show a marked decrease. Meanwhile criminals have very greatly multiplied under relatively new and essentially modern forms of serious crime, such as the many kinds of business fraud, forgery and fraudulent bankruptcy.

The records of these offences tell a most interesting and instructive story to those who read aright: a story of changing crimes with changing times. Governments are now too powerful, too well protected by repeating rifles and breech-loading cannon to be overthrown by an angry mob, armed with the plunder of the gunshops. "It is surely not a mere coincidence that revolutions and insurrections, so frequent in Europe until 1848, should have entirely ceased since the transformation in arms."[2] A German socialist, Bebel, gave the true reason for this great change, when he said, in 1890: "I have already told what the result of a revolution would be, carried on by 200,000 men at most, in this epoch of repeating guns and Maxim cannon; we should be miserably shot down like sparrows." Armed rebellion has become too dangerous and too hopeless a form of crime to be indulged in. The traitor, as a criminal, has practically ceased to exist. Social pressure has been eminently successful against him.

[1] See next page. [2] Seignobos, p. 675.

THE TOTAL NUMBER OF CONVICTIONS FOR MURDER AND HOMICIDE, AND THE ANNUAL AVERAGE FOR FIVE-YEAR PERIODS PER 100,000 OF POPULATION.

	England.		France.		Austria.		Germany.		Italy.		Spain.	
		Per 100,000.		Per 100,000.		Per 100,000.		Per 100,000.		Per 100,000.		Per 100,000.
1861–65	159	7.87	573	15.33	296							
1866–70	146	6.56 (1866–75)	398	11.55 (1866–75)	411	20.74 (1866–75)						
1871–75	154		436		441							
1876–80	155	....	415	....	436	....	......	....	3231[1]			
1881–85	152	5.84	465	12.34	391	17.66	299[2]	6.61	2649	93.08	1113[3]	66.65
1886–90	134	5.13 (1886–95)	431	11.55 (1886–95)	368	15.42 (1886–95)	259	5.45 (1886–95)	2391	76.11 (1886–95)	940	44.70 (1886–95)
1891–95	133		455		369[4]		280[5]		2200		602	
1896	125	....	400[6]	....	......	....	......	....	2203[7]	....	824	
1897	......	....	......	....	......	....	......	....	1801[7]			

[1] Statistics for 1880.
[2] From 1882 to 1885.
[3] 1883 to 1885.
[4] 1891 to 1894.
[5] 1891 to 1894.
[6] 1895.
[7] Infanticide (averaging about 70 cases between 1886–95) has been included under homicide for the last two years.

The seas have been swept clean of pirates, for the vast development of international trade and commerce made this absolutely necessary, and the navies of the civilized world speedily accomplished the task. Modern weapons and powerful explosives have brought us peace at home and peace upon the ocean. Are we learning to love peace now for its own sake? Crime is certainly taking a less impulsive and passionate, a more crafty and cautious form. Men are learning to curb their tempers under the rule of law. Not only is the hasty blow that causes death, or danger to life and limb, more rare, but common wounding by cuts and blows—which seemed too natural and human and unimportant to be punished as crime until modern times—this also, with our growing sense of mutual rights and duties, in more peaceful times, has been made widely criminal; and for some nations, as in England and evèn passionate Italy, the large totals of such crimes show a decrease—a marked decrease in proportion to population. (See table on next page.)

Notice the very large amount of serious wounding in Austria, and Spain (where the numbers would seem far larger in proportion to the population), as compared with the small number of convictions for such offences in England, Germany and France. But in the last named country, the practice of correctionalization is probably responsible for the practical disappearance of serious wounding from the statistics; such offences being generally transferred to the jurisdiction of the correctional tribunals, and included among the lighter cuts and blows. Naturally, also, the increase in medical skill, and in the promptness of medical attendance among all civilized nations have contributed largely to decrease the number of wounds now dangerous to life and limb, and also the number of homicides, by putting many cuts and blows into a less heinous category of crime.

THE TOTAL NUMBER OF PERSONS CONDEMNED FOR WOUNDING.

	England.		France.		Austria.		Germany.		Italy.	Spain.
	Serious.	Light.[1]	Serious.	Light.	Serious.	Light.	Serious.	Light.	Cuts and Blows.	All wounding under the Code, mostly serious.
1861–65	103	54,901	61	18,856	1,934					
1866–70	85	57,998	51	20,520	3,206					
1871–75	103	62,070	41	19,946	3,907	36,084				
1876–80	104	58,722	31	22,741	4,227	45,678				
1881–85	62	55,654	28	25,677	4,462	57,048	554[2]	47,349[2]	62,770	6,827[3]
1886–90	35	50,922	19	26,987	4,704	62,847	597	53,497	65,084	6,868
1891–95	90	47,447	20	31,234	4,561[4]	64,342[4]	497	69,026	62,620	5,694
1896	92	43,021	....	....	....	....	....	....	63,520	5,823

[1] Including acts of violence and threats. [2] 1882–85. [3] 1883–85. [4] 1891–94.

Germany. A careful study of the great recorded increase of crime in Germany, under the less serious forms of wounding, political offences, fraud, delites of immorality and lust, reveals two most interesting facts.

First. That this multiplication of criminals is directly traceable to the rapid progress of the nation from a less to a more complex civilization; to the great wave of industrialism now sweeping over the land, crowding the population into factory towns and large cities, those centres of modern progress, culture, democracy and enlightenment; and to the consequent greatly increased interest of the masses in the political, social and economic problems of the day.

Second. That many minor cuts and blows are being changed, even now, in Germany, from mere torts, prosecuted or left unpunished at the pleasure of the person injured, into crimes, punished by society as wrongs against the nation. The old laws of tort, relating to such minor harms to the person, have not been repealed, but offences under them have only just about kept pace with the growth of population. The great increase in such cuts and blows has been placed by society, because of increasing need for repression, under the head of crime. Judicial and penal authorities, representing the nation, have been interpreting more rigorously the laws relating to perilous (gefährliche) wounds; which, although not really serious, are punished as true crimes under the Code. Under this head have been included not only cuts with a knife or other dangerous weapon or instrument, but even slight blows or injuries occurring in wordy quarrels or disputes, which frequently arise where many people are closely crowded together. It will be remembered that in the early years of the nineteenth century such conduct was not yet criminal in England. A clearer perception of what is necessary for the general welfare under new industrial conditions has occasioned this great change in both nations; bringing with it increased social pressure to stamp out these evil acts, creating new forms of crime and rapidly enlarging the number of criminals.

The German statistics show far more crime in the city than in the country. Thus, from 1891 to 1895, there were 1080 crimes per 100,000 inhabitants in the country districts, while in the cities (of more than 20,000 people) the proportion was about 1400. Moreover, the character of the delinquency is very different: in the city crimes of fraud and cunning, light wounds and rebellion against authority; in the country crimes of ferocity and malicious damage.

	Condemned per 100,000 population (1891–95).	
Crimes.	City.	Country.
Violence and outrages against authority	83	33
Light wounds	68	56
Outrages against chastity	12	4
Procuring	31	2
Serious theft	37	20
Simple theft	68	56
Unlawful appropriation	109	37
Fraud	63	32
Serious wounding	1.3	2.1
Less serious wounding	126	160
Malicious damage	36	40

The statisticians report that the great prevalence of light wounds in the German cities appears to be provoked by the crowding of the population, the change from a quiet agricultural life to a nervous industrial existence, and to the abuse of liquor; while greater participation in politics induces violence and outrages against authority, and increased delites against the state and public order.

The crowding of men and women together in factories, together with the increasing economic difficulty of establishing and maintaining a family, have occasioned a large increase in delites of immorality and lust, the figures having mounted steadily from little more than 3000 condemned in 1882–85 to over 4000 in 1891–95. Other crimes against the family (bigamy, incest and adultery) are also increasing, while the number of those condemned for procuring is mounting higher and higher; but this last is in part caused (as the official publications attest) by increasing social pressure to crush out this form of evil, through the more rigorous vigilance of the police.

From 1882 to 1895 fraud increased in Germany by fifty per cent., fraudulent bankruptcy by forty-five per cent., and forgery of deeds by forty-five per cent. Meanwhile all forms of theft, serious and simple, while varying from year to year, show at the end of the period a diminution in proportion to population, and a very slight increase in the actual number of criminals.

All these crimes are more numerous in the cities than in the country, as will appear by a glance at the table just given. When we note, for each manufacturing province and state of Germany, the great increase of crime among young men and women, as their number in the factories increases, can we doubt that the rapid growth of Germany into a great industrial civilization, with its accompaniments of factory and city life, is very largely responsible for the astonishing increase in the nation's crime, from 329,968 convictions in 1882 to 463,584 convictions, only fifteen years later, in 1897? Especially is this evidence convincing when we remember how very large a proportion of all criminals are young, and that the years sixteen to eighteen are probably the most critical period of a person's life, deciding for many whether the later career will be good or bad, socially useful or criminal.[1]

[1] Undoubtedly there are many other causes influencing delinquency in Germany and other great modern nations beside industrial development and the increase of city life. It is only wished to lay stress upon these very important causes at this time.

PROPORTION OF YOUNG MEN AND WOMEN EMPLOYED IN FACTORIES AND CONDEMNED FOR CRIMES IN GERMANY.

States and Provinces.	Young people of both sexes from 12 to 18 years of age employed in factories (per 10,000 inhabitants).			Young people of both sexes from 12 to 18 years of age condemned for crimes and delites (per 10,000 inhabitants.)		
	1885.	1890.	1895.	1885.	1890.	1895.
Prussian Provinces—						
Brandenburg, including Berlin	250	313	361	63	68	83
Prussian Saxony	280	316	419	55	59	66
Westphalia	462	550	620	33	36	39
The Rhine Country	447	535	615	36	38	50
Prussia	259	303	359	55	58	65
Bavaria	155	206	257	65	77	90
Saxony	797	1,014	1,084	56	66	81
Wurtemburg	284	344	408	45	48	53

But this industrial development and growth of cities in Germany—is it so very great and sudden as has been here implied? Surely we cannot doubt this either when we consult the facts.

The transformation in the life and product of the Germanic nation in fourteen years (1882 to 1895) seems almost magical. In 1882, of every 1,000 persons in the population, 188.8 were engaged in agriculture and 161.2 in industry. In 1895, but 163.8 were engaged in agriculture, while 195.7 were in industry—a veritable revolution. Notwithstanding the large growth of population, which increased by seventeen per cent. in these fourteen years, or from forty-five to fifty-two millions, "the agricultural class decreased by 724,148, while the number of operatives increased from 7,340,789 in 1882 to 10,269,269 in 1895, or by about forty per cent. Large manufacturing establishments, employing from fifty-one to many thousands of operatives, numbered 9,974 in 1882 and 18,955 in 1895. The annual output of coal has mounted from 59,118,000 tons in 1880 to 103,958,000 tons in 1895. The total product of pig iron has been doubled in these sixteen years: from 2,729,000 to 5,464,000 tons.[1] Meanwhile the growth of the city population of Germany has been more rapid than anywhere else upon the continent of Europe.

It is during such times of fundamental change, when old business ways are becoming unprofitable, and large new opportunities for gain arise; when family bonds are broken up, and the young and strong depart with hope into untried fields of labor; when old legal safeguards are no longer sufficient, and new laws have yet to be introduced, and men in haste for riches may hurt society and their fellow-men almost with impunity, without fear of criminal prosecution; when the new liberty is very dear and largely mixed or confused with license—it is precisely *then* that the social standard of right action is rapidly elevated and enlarged; society is educated by the perception of its own necessities; new forms of crime are most rapidly created to guide the strong new life into healthy modes of helpful development, and the multiplication of criminals goes on apace, and this in the wisest and most prosperous of nations.

But we must not think that the persistent increase of crime, under the special forms now prevalent in Germany, is a necessary and inevitable accompaniment of industrial civilization, at all times and in all its stages. This would be manifestly untrue, as is evident from the decrease of these same crimes of violence in England. It is rather the beginning of the new life, the formative and transition period, the time of most rapid development and sudden progress to a higher, more complex civilization, that occasions the multiplication of criminals. This was as true of England half a century and more ago, as it is true of Germany to-day.

[1] The figures for 1870 were 34,003,000 tons of coal and 1,391,000 tons (metric of 2,204 lbs.) of pig iron.

Lock up a healthy country boy in a city house and he will be irritable and ill-behaved at first. Time alone can wont him to his new and physically cramped surroundings. Yet the city education may make a more useful man of him, for the city is the chosen home of modern energy, science and skill, as well as the great laboratory of practical Christian charity, uplifting helpfulness and brotherly love. The English people have had time to settle down into the forms of industrial and city life, which are no longer new, strange and irksome to them. For the displacement of the population from the country to the city, from agriculture to manufacturing and trade, began in England one hundred years ago, and had its greatest development about the middle of the nineteenth century; while in Germany the transformation is far more recent and more sudden. English operatives now feel the benefit of the factory and mining legislation, and of many other protecting and educating laws, which have safeguarded individual life and liberty, increased happiness and the social well being, while greatly multiplying criminals. In Germany, such industrial and social legislation is being even now very rapidly introduced and extended. It is the period of sharp transition—of rapid growth—that hurts most. The stronger the nation, the more rapid the growth, the more independent and liberty loving the citizens, the larger the resulting criminality is apt to be.

But meanwhile, in the midst of all this growth of delinqency, many of the old and most serious crimes are, as we have seen, decreasing. Recent statistics of murder and homicide for the leading nations of Europe point to some very interesting conclusions, when compared with the rank of these nations in the modern industrial world, and the greater or less diffusion of education among them.

	England. 1.	Germany. 2.	France. 3.	Austria. 4.	Italy. 5.	Spain. 6.
Industrial rank (value of manufactures produced yearly in millions of pounds sterling, 1888).	820	583	485	253	121	85
Percentage of adults able to write (1889)	90%	96%	85%	55%	47%	28%
Convictions for murder and homicide per 1,000,000 of inhabitants (average for 10 years, 1886–95)	5.13	5.45	11.55	15.42	76.11	44.70[1]

Murder and homicide are the crimes of races backward in the diffusion of education, and the development of modern industrial life. They are crimes of the country rather than the city; crimes of a decaying civilization, or of the rough edges of an advancing civilization. Within low savage tribes such actions are not crimes. They are left to individual vengeance. No idea of moral wrong is connected with them at first; no sense of a common injury to society, awakening in the community the passionate longing for revenge. Until quite late in history, no distinction is made even between wilful murder and accidental homicide, and both are simply the private affairs of the families directly concerned. Very slowly, and long after the coming of Christianity among the Anglo-Saxons, did this people grow into the belief that murder and homicide are seriously harmful to the state, and should be punished as crimes. "Open morth" (secret homicide), was the first of these evil acts thus made distinctly criminal, and even then, it was probably the unfairness of the attack, more than the resulting death, that originally induced social vengeance; just as highway robbery remained even honorable, long after society had

[1] It is very doubtful whether the law is as strongly and widely enforced in Spain as in Italy, which may account for the smaller proportionate number of homicides recorded.

resolved to punish, and succeeded in punishing various forms of secret theft as crime.

Distinctive characteristics of the modern criminal are his insistence upon the right of private vengeance,[1] and his firm belief that might makes right, that to the victor belong the spoils, no matter how the victory is won. This was also the glory of the warlike hero of the "golden days," the robber baron of mediaeval ages, and to a large extent of the modern politician, with the creed that "politics is politics," and who is in "the business" for what he can "make" out of it, for himself and for "the boys," his heelers. This has been distinctly the creed of the Sicilians and Sardinians in our own time. Assassination, highway robbery and cattle stealing were certainly not crimes among them until very recent years. Everywhere was found the strife between classes; everywhere ignorance, superstition and suspicion, with the strong conviction that "there is no justice, but only a goad for the poor," and that "the best way is to act for oneself," for "summary and private justice is better than that of the government, which is slow, expensive and evil disposed."[2] Hence the dreaded Maffia: which is, properly speaking, not an association, with statutes and officers; but a moral union, a tacit consent, traditional among the peasantry, to maintain the rights of vengeance as they have inherited them, to impose upon the weak and to resist the strong—especially the government—not openly, but with concealed, impassive force. "They will follow a man for months waiting for a fitting time to strike, when an alibi can be proved easily. The whole country knows the author of the murderous deed, beholds the meshes in which justice is entangled, and when it fails they are all happy. Worse yet, murder was done in open day, on Sunday, on a public road, among a hundred

[1] Giddings, *Principles of Sociology*, p. 128.

[2] Alonzo, "*Maffi*" (1885).

persons. Nobody saw anything. No one knew what was going on. What was it? "Una Sparatina."[1]

Highway robbery is the perfected work of the sea coast Maffia, as cattle stealing is the specialty of the inland agricultural districts; with these go assassination and homicide; and all these deeds were not crimes until recently, for the Sicilian people not only did not punish such offenders, but even united to uphold and maintain them against the nation's laws.

Nor was it only in the islands—Sicily, Sardinia and Corsica—that such misdeeds were prevalent and unrebuked. They were common in many mountainous districts of the continent, in Spain and Italy, as well. Since the coming of a strong central government in Italy, great efforts have been made to crush out these ancient forms of evil. The country districts are filled with gendarmerie—the roads are patrolled. The assassin, the brigand, the highway robber, have been hunted down and punished by society. Their acts have been made crimes, and in northern and central Italy, where industry, commerce and education are rapidly developing, such offences are now few in number. But in Sicily, where the people, in blind ignorance and fear, have all along protected such men and opposed a social barrier to their public punishment, the task before the government is a very difficult one—not to be solved perhaps until the day of popular enlightenment, and of the coming of the modern industrial arts among them.

The number of homicides in Italy, as a whole, has decreased by more than one-third during the seventeen years from 1880 to 1897, and this large diminution is a marked characteristic of the recent movement of crime in Italy. In Spain also, the numbers show a considerable decrease, although it is very doubtful if the law is enforced as strongly

[1] *Ibid., Archivio de Psichiatria*, vi, 430–440.

there as in Italy. Among the other nations of Europe, murder and homicide have long since become very exceptional crimes, and they are decreasing still.

Many people associate the various forms of criminal delinquency with different races; as, crimes of passion and physical violence with the hot-blooded Latin race, and cooler, more calculating crimes with the nations of northern Europe. But, in reality, the character of a nation's crime depends far more upon the degree and form of social development attained, than upon differences of race and geographical position. These deeds of murder, brigandage and robbery, so very prevalent even now in parts of Spain and Italy, were no less abundant in England a few centuries ago. In the United States such actions are more numerous among the ignorant, degraded and brutal "white trash" and low negroes of the South, and in regions of abandoned farms in New England. They have accompanied the march of civilization westward, and are very prevalent on the frontiers, where social life is rough, and physical strength and ability to shoot well and quickly are more highly esteemed, and indeed far more necessary, than many of the quiet and more sober virtues of the Eastern States.[1]

In general, there are three distinct stages in the history of any action which becomes a crime:

First: The action is not a crime. It remains entirely unpunished, and no idea of moral evil is connected with it; or it is repressed only by individual and family vengeance, and is essentially a private affair.

Second: Society grows into the belief that such conduct is

[1] Crime at Cape Nome, the new gold region of Alaska. San Francisco, July 8th, 1900. (In New York "*Sun*," July 9th.) "According to a letter just received here, crime is rampant at Cape Nome. The writer of the letter, who is F. C. Graves, a prospector, states that 'murder is an every-day occurrence' and suicides 'average three or four a day.'"

bad for the general welfare. How? The act is recognized as an evil—perhaps a sin—at first, by the wiser, the more intelligent, more Christian portion of the community. Others are converted to this belief. Society resolves upon punishment, and gradually succeeds in inflicting it, thus making the action a crime and multiplying criminals; educating, by this means, the lower masses of the people into the feeling and the knowledge that such conduct is bad for them, bad for all, and wrong—in a word, raising the social standard of morality, advancing civilization through crime.[1]

Third: Where punishments are wisely chosen, and the nation strong and progressing in civilization, social pressure is generally successful in diminishing the number of offenders under this (now) old form of crime; and sometimes, with the growth of knowledge and changed conditions of life, this kind of criminal act disappears from the statistics. The nation has conquered—has progressed. This evil has practically ceased to exist. Life is on a somewhat higher plane. Man has become more truly social.

Curious light is thrown upon social conditions in thirteenth century England, by a discussion among the lawyers in the time of Bracton, whether the breaking of teeth could be punished as crime under the law. "Everything whereby a man is disabled from fighting is a mayhem. But what shall be said of him who has his teeth broken; if the breakage of teeth is to be adjudged a mayhem?" And the decision was: Yes, "if they are fore-teeth, . . . for teeth of this kind assist much to victory."[2] A man was important to the community as a fighting animal, and as such was to be socially protected. He who disabled his fellow man from active service to the nation in time of war, or in maintaining the peace and pursuing criminals at home, was to be con-

[1] Of course this is but one of the great means by which civilization progresses.

[2] Bracton, f. 145, b. 3.

sidered a criminal so far as the law could make him one. Breaking of the back teeth was not crime. A bruise, or swelling, from a stick or stone did not count; neither did what was then termed a graze. The wound must be of some very considerable length and depth—measured by inches—before the law courts would take any notice of it whatever. Pain and disfigurement hardly entered into the consideration at all. Such was happy England in the good old times—"the golden days." Have we not progressed somewhat? Now, the enforcement of a social penalty has made practically all assaults upon the person criminal. A man shall go about his business where he will, in safety, for the social welfare demands that this shall be so.

Turning now to crimes against property, we find that such offences, in all the great industrial nations of Europe, divide naturally into two main classes with strikingly different tendencies; the one class remaining stationary, or even decreasing slightly, while the other rapidly increases. The first class includes robbery, extortion and theft—old forms of crime. In the second are the many forms of fraud, forgery and fraudulent bankruptcy—essentially modern forms of serious delinquency. In general, the worst of the ancient offences, robbery, extortion and most serious theft, show a decrease, especially when the growth of population is considered; while the total of all thefts punished has remained practically the same for many years, in proportion to population, for the nations of Europe we have been considering. The figures quoted in these tables of special crimes are always those of convictions, which would be more likely than any other statistics of these offences to show an increase, if such existed.[1]

[1] Throughout the latter chapters of this book, wherever statistical evidence has been deemed necessary, the author has tried to select those tables which (with equal probability of truth) would be less likely than others to favor the conclusions he himself believes to be the true ones.

The Total Number of Convictions for Robbery and Extortion, and for the Most Serious Thefts.

	England.		France.		Austria.		Germany.		Italy.	Spain.
	Robbery and Extortion.	Serious Theft.	Robbery and Extortion.	Serious Theft.	Robbery and Extortion.	Serious Theft.	Robbery and Extortion.	Serious Theft.	Robbery and Extortion.	Robbery and Serious Theft.
1861–65	313	....	86	1,296	121	11,600				
1866–70	289	....	109	1,285	219	14,868				
1871–75	215	....	152	1,773	178	15,943				
1876–80	208	....	138	1,345	172	18,207				
1881–85	215	7,095	143	1,285	164	17,589	893 [1]	10,719 [1]	725	1,871 [2]
1886–90	227	6,599	184	1,288	133	14,350	869	11,512	562	1,729
1891–95	226	6,927	184 [3]	1,129 [3]	107 [4]	14,590 [4]	1,024	12,354	859	1,214
1896	202	6,470	....	....	....	....	....	....	1,254	1,356

[1] 1882–85. [2] 1883–85. [3] 1891–94. [4] 1891–94.

THE TOTAL NUMBER OF CONVICTIONS FOR BUSINESS FRAUDS AND FRAUDULENT BANKRUPTCY.

	England.		France.		Austria.	Germany.		Italy.	Spain.	
	Frauds.	Bankruptcy.	Frauds.	Bankruptcy.	Frauds and Bankruptcy.	Frauds.	Bankruptcy.	Frauds and Bankruptcy.	Frauds.	Bankruptcy.
1861–65	1,073	6	11,475	843						
1866–70	1,062	19	12,408	804						
1871–75	1,092	21	12,849	812	12,018					
1876–80	1,655	45	13,261	814	16,622					
1881–85	1,782	37	13,955	845	17,783	28,985[1]	680[1]	....	828[2]	3[2]
1886–90	1,696	24	13,972	826	17,050	32,832	784	8,875	918	1
1891–95	1,805	32	14,039[3]	823[3]	19,078[4]	42,788	987	10,791	799	2
1896	1,810	32	....	....	....	....	....	11,116	813	
1897	....	....	....	....	....	....	....	11,619		

[1] 1882–85. 1883–85. [3] 1891–94. [4] 1891–94.

At any rate the statistics prove that the leading civilizations of Europe have not been growing worse, so far as these ancient forms of crime are concerned. Social punishment has apparently been successful against them. But under fraud, forgery and fraudulent bankruptcy, modern forms of criminal offence against property, the totals of convictions are mounting higher and higher in all the strong industrial nations of to-day. The forms of these crimes are ever more numerous, for new laws are continually increasing them. Not many years ago such conduct was, for the most part, not yet criminal. They are characteristic offences of our modern industrial civilization, hardly found in such nations as Spain, which are laggards in this development. They are acts most strongly opposed to business security and prosperity, to the continued development of modern business methods; and therefore they have been made serious crimes, and many thousands of men criminals, since the coming of modern forms of trade and commerce, and the widespread introduction of credit instruments and certificates of indebtedness—those essentially modern forms of wealth investment.

Crime is essentially a social product, increasing with growth in knowledge, intelligence and social morality, along lines of greatest resistance to the new forces and forms of this higher social life. The upward progress of civilization has been even more strongly marked by the creation of new forms of

When a work has advanced thus far towards its completion, it is inevitable that certain central ideas should be firmly seated in the author's mind, and he wishes to guard as carefully as possible against biased judgment and any distortion of the evidence. However, in this connection, it should be said that a careful study of the Judicial Records preceded the writing of any chapter in this book, while the theory here presented was as yet unformed and nebulous.

These statistics may be found grouped in convenient form for reference in Prof. A. Bosco's *Sulla Statistica della Delinquenza in Vari Stati d'Europa* (1898).

crime, and the consequent multiplication of criminals, than by the successful punishment and diminution, or extinction of criminals under ancient forms of anti-social conduct. Great reforms have been introduced by criminal laws and made victorious by social punishment. In the next chapter we shall behold some of the records of these deeds, this social progress to better things. For the statistics of the criminal classes are like the sand and clay of the old, old earth, forming layer by layer, strata by strata:

......" Wherein the footprints of their age
Are petrified forever."

We must " not fear to follow out the truth
Albeit along the precipice's edge."
Surely, surely, we should have "no dread of what
Is called for by the instinct of mankind."

"The world advances, and in time outgrows
The laws that in our fathers' day were best;
And, doubtless, after us, some purer scheme
Will be shaped out by wiser men than we,
Made wiser by the steady growth of truth.

"Get but the truth once uttered, and 'tis like
A star new-born, that drops into its place,
And which, once circling in its placid round,
Not all the tumult of the earth can shake." [1]

[1] James Russell Lowell, *A Glance Behind the Curtain.*

CHAPTER XIV

THE TREND OF CRIME IN MODERN TIMES. A BRIGHTENING OUTLOOK

THREE of the most striking characteristics of life in modern times are its complexity, its speed, and its liberty of thought and action, as compared with all the previous ages of human history. We are all becoming specialists to-day, every man dependent upon his fellow-men for almost everything he needs and uses. The food we eat, the clothes we wear, the knowledge that fills our minds—these come to us from the four corners of the earth, through the hands and brains of multitudes of human beings, for whom we also labor. Even the religious cravings of our nature, those highest and most carefully guarded yearnings of man's soul, are nourished by the truth of God culled now from all the world. The man who makes the hundredth part of a watch, the twentieth part of a shoe or of a pin, the spinner, the carder, the weaver, the employer, must all rely upon the efficiency, the activity, the honest dealing of their fellow laborers to find a profitable market and secure a continuous demand for the goods produced. How very different, all this, from the conditions of life among savages, where each household—the economic unit—is sufficient, almost, unto itself. How very simple in comparison seems the life of the mediaeval hamlet, clustered around its protecting castle, where the indwellers produced for themselves nearly everything that was required, food, raiment, coats of mail, security and entertainment.

Modern man must depend upon his fellow man, must rely upon society as a whole, to an extent undreamed of even by our recent ancestors; for the struggles and the strikes, the business enterprises and speculations, the thoughts and the demands of men we have never known, living a thousand miles away, may destroy our means of livelihood and ruin our life's happiness, and the individual is powerless to defend himself. Are we therefore slaves, tossed to and fro and crushed by blind titanic forces, the offspring of what is known as civilization? Surely not. Where the strength and wisdom of the individual, the family, or the little association are insufficient, there the social might steps in to define and regulate the mutual relationships and duties of men, to defend the right, to educate the people, to promote upward progress toward the social ideal—the ideal of the national type—by wise laws and penalties, strongly enforced, creating crimes and multiplying criminals. The more sensitive becomes the social body, the nation, to rights and wrongs, great and small; the more far-reaching and contagious is the influence of evil conduct among the classes and the masses of the population, the farther must the strong arm of the criminal law be extended, for the social welfare demands that this should be so.

Higher evolution means great and increasing complexity, specialization, interdependence, and consequent sensitiveness of the social life. The harm to one individual becomes more and more the injury to all. Society recognizes this, and the extension of the field of crime, the field of prohibited action, goes on apace. Nor does the criminal law stop, in modern times, with negative commands; it adds positive orders as well. Not only, thou shalt not kill, but, thou must have thy children educated. Not one of the great, progressive civilizations has been able to escape from the necessity of increasing, very largely and persistently, its criminal statutes during the nineteenth century. Naturally, the most crying evils are first made crimes. Afterwards, the lesser evils become more noticeable, and their increasing number and heinousness demand public attention and punishment. It becomes criminal for taskmasters to degrade women and children to the level of the brute for mere money gain. Factory and mining legislation stamps out these great abuses of the new industrialism. The horrors of train wrecking cause intense public indignation and the enactment of ever heavier penalties. Embezzlement is made a crime. Society begins to punish fraudulent trustees, and those who seek to thrive by newly discovered forms of fraud and forgery. Common assault and battery becomes a misdemeanor; likewise drunkenness. The police of highways, wagons, wharves and docks assumes very large proportions. Sanitary and public health statutes are enacted and must be enforced. Public morality is protected. Perilous, but necessary occupations are made as little dangerous as possible, by safeguards compelled by law. Cruelty to children and to animals is made increasingly criminal. Public education becomes compulsory. Every important new invention enlarges sooner or later the field of crime. The harnessing of steam, electricity and compressed air for the service of men has greatly increased our criminality. How then? Is there anything essentially evil and maleficent in these great forces of nature? Surely not. But "their application to modern life opens up new sources of temptation and reveals new sources of danger. A host of modern inventions or manufactured articles having a market value constitute a new opportunity for the thief." The modern highway robber may get a message from the telegraph wire, "worth more to him than a well-filled purse." The stealing of power or light from electric lines by tampering with the meters, these are petty acts of crime easily and often committed. But not only has the theft of electricity been made criminal. Even its gift to certain persons and its acceptance by them are declared crimes in some communities. Thus, in Nebraska, officers or agents of telephone and electric light companies "are forbidden to give free or reduced rates to any city or village official," under penalty of heavy fine and imprisonment for all parties concerned. Where overhead electric wires crowd our city streets, kite-flying becomes a crime, for the strings, entangled in the wires, divert the current, causing loss of valuable power and interruption of business. In addition to the ancient crime of horse-stealing, we have, in modern days, the theft of bicycles and automobiles. Stealing of rides on railway cars is prohibited by many statutes, but ticketless tramps still travel at their leisure, despite the laws. Jumping on or off cars in motion is likewise prohibited, and it is a criminal offence for railroad companies to charge extortionate transportation rates, or to discriminate against individuals. The introduction of petroleum "blazes luridly in penal codes." The discovery of anæsthetics was a very great blessing to suffering humanity; but New York State has recently made the possession of such drugs, with intent to administer to any person, without the direction of a duly licensed physician, a felony, punishable by ten years' imprisonment at hard labor in state prison.[1] Laws prohibiting the adulteration of food, candy and milk are very numerous and necessary. Social pressure against gambling is increasing. Of liquor laws there are a legion. Cigarettes must not be sold or given to minors; and children must not frequent pool or billiard rooms, unless with the written consent of their parents. A multitude of other new social prohibitions could easily be mentioned here, but to what use? The reader will find them on every side of him in real life, yet they probably do not worry or

[1] Maximum sentence.

annoy him greatly. Many of them certainly create new crimes and multiply criminals, for the laws are enforced. Others, as certainly, do not have this result; for society does not, and sometimes does not wish to inflict the penalties. This tendency is shown in an extreme and somewhat ludicrous form at the close of an interesting article by S. J. Barrows upon "New Crimes and Penalties" in the United States.[1]

"What would Draco and Solon have thought of such laws, . . . after reading, as the writer has done, 30,000 pages of legislation in the forty-five states—all of it less than two years old? Suppose, for instance, that Draco took it all seriously, and imagined that all the laws we passed were meant to be enforced. Suppose they really were enforced, and that the Greek lawgiver should make a tour of the prisons and jails of the United States. Imagine him asking a score of convicts why they had been convicted."

"I," said an Alabama man, "have been sentenced to thirty days for jumping off a train while in motion." "I," said a Virginian, "rode a horse on the sidewalk through an unincorporated village, and am in prison for sixty days." "I," said another Virginian, "killed a partridge on the second day of February in Cumberland county, and am in prison for thirty days." "I," said a California woman, "am a nurse, and I neglected to report to a doctor that a baby's eyes became inflamed within two weeks after birth. I am in prison for six months." "I," said a Tennesseean, "'lobbied' with the legislature." "You mean bribed it?" asked Draco. "Oh, no, I just 'lobbied,' but I did not address my arguments 'solely to the judgment,' and so I am 'in' for five years." An Adonis from the same state curled his mustache: "I fell in love with a young lady at a Tennessee boarding school. In a rash moment I ventured to loiter on the op-

[1] *The Forum*, Jan., 1900, pp. 539–41.

posite side of the street, and I threw a kiss to her. Now I have thirty days to serve in the county jail."

"By Jupiter!" exclaimed Draco. "It is all very well for you to swear by Jupiter," said a man from New Jersey; "but I made the mistake of swearing by the name of Jesus Christ, and so I have two years to serve." "I," said a New York man, "tampered with an automatic ballot machine, and for the next five years I shall labor for the benefit of the state." "I," said another New Yorker, "was calling on a friend in the upper story of a sky-scraper, and I ventured to drop some of my advertising circulars down the letter-chute. Unfortunately, I had forgotten to address them. So I got five days." "I," said a New Jersey man bitterly, "did not drop my ad. into a letter-chute; I wish I had. I made the mistake of putting it up on the Palisades, and I am sentenced to three years for disfiguring the landscape." "As to advertising," said a lawyer from Washington, "I ventured to solicit divorce business by an advertisement in a newspaper, and now I shall read my newspapers in jail for the next six months." "I can go you one better," said a Pennsylvania criminal. "I thought it would be a compliment to my country to print my advertisement on a picture of the American flag. The court thought differently, and I am in seclusion for six months." "You ought to live in South Dakota," said a bystander. "I did the same thing, and I got off with a five-dollar fine." "But be thankful you do not live in North Dakota," said another criminal. "I ventured to organize a 'trust.' I thought I might promote trade by lessening competition; now I have ten years in which to reflect upon my conduct." "I," said a Wisconsin man, "sold some impure ice, and I shall spend the winter in the county jail." "Well! you have my company," said a Wisconsin baker. "I ventured to sleep in my bakery. My first offence cost me $50 a night; and the second $100 a night. For the third offence I had to pay $250 a night. And now, to even things up, I am lodging six months in jail, at the expense of the state." "It all happens in the course of business," said a Michigander. "I thought it was all right to buy an empty beer bottle stamped with the brewer's name. My mistake costs me ninety days in jail." . . . "Well, be thankful you don't keep a boarding house in Virginia," a Southerner remarked. "I failed to put up a sign which the law said must be in Roman letters not less than one inch square, 'Imitation Butter Used Here,' and now I am a jail-boarder myself for six months." . . .

Perhaps, to close the interview, which might go on almost indefinitely, we can imagine two prisoners from Tennessee saying: "Well, you are all low-grade criminals. You are nothing but misdemeanants; we have the honor to be felons." "You are, perhaps, murderers," said Draco, his face brightening at the thought of some crime with which he might be familiar. "Yes, we are both murderers. I murdered some fish with dynamite—a Greek word, you know—and am 'in' for three years. And my friend here murdered some trees without the consent of the owner, and he also is 'in' for three years."

Would Draco think the world had grown better, or that it had grown worse, and would he note it as an occasion for modern thanksgiving that the Americans live under milder laws?

One great difference, however, these ancient law-givers would find between their time and ours. The laws of the American people bear a very close and intimate relation to their life. Right or wrong, good or bad, they are not imposed by external authority or by an aristocratic class. They are made by the people themselves. Whether enforced or not, the laws embody the ethical sentiment of the American people, and reflect the spirit and the characteristics of American civilization.

What then? Is modern man becoming helplessly, and ever more and more firmly, bound around by the myriad twisting and constricting tentacles of a kind of social devil-fish—the criminal law—sucking the life and the individuality out of him, and preventing growth in almost every direction by increasing pressure and punishment? Is this the final outcome of our boasted civilization—that the individual shall be met at every turn by a prohibitory or a mandatory statute: Thou shalt not do this—Thou must do that—under penalty of the law; no, not even walk upon the grass, under pain of punishment as a criminal? Is not this sheer slavery, and is not savage liberty far better than such bondage?

Dryden once had a dream:

> "When wild in woods the noble savage ran."

But how painfully different was the truth. The free, untrammeled, primitive man, meeting with his fellows to form the "social contract" of Jean Jacques Rousseau, had absolutely no existence in real life. The farther back we trace human society, the more is the individual savage the slave of his superstitious fears, crawling in abject obedience under a mass of semi-religious or demoniac observances, compared to which the Aztec or Babylonish tyrannies were easy and pleasurable.

Liberty is very far from being a natural, original and fundamental right of man. On the contrary, its history shows a very slow and painful development. True liberty has been won by man for man in the progress of the ages, with the growth of civilization, and by the might of law. It is being won and amplified to-day.[a]

Do not let us confuse liberty with license. License is absolute freedom from restraint. A man may kill himself or his fellowman if he wills and has the power. Liberty

[a] Following, as the author believes, God's law of evolution for the uplift of mankind.

is also freedom; but freedom within limits, found necessary for the preservation of a like freedom for our brother man, and for the maintenance of the general welfare. It is precisely such liberty that we are developing in modern times: developing by means of law—criminal law. Think of it! Freedom of body, freedom of thought and speech, freedom of religious worship and belief—these are all modern achievements, guaranteed by law to-day. Political and civil liberty, the right to vote, the right to own property (especially for women); industrial liberty also—that is, the right to work (in general) where and when one wishes—these are forms of true freedom, struggled and fought for through the ages, established and still developing under the law to-day.

The key-note of the nineteenth century, writes Gladstone, the great English statesman, near the end of his long life, is "Hands off," "Strike off the fetters." Individual liberty, freedom of action and of thought, the opportunity to do that which seemeth best, have come to man far more fully in this than in any former age of the world's history. The unyielding, curiously cramping, despotic customs of savage races are not for us. Yes, strike off the fetters, the swaddling bands of infant societies, the hard, stern rules that hold and tame and socialize the brave, but cruel and passionate boyhood of mankind; for the leaders of the human race, the great Aryan civilizations, no longer need them, or most of them. They have grown strong through social discipline. They have learned through long centuries of drill in nature's school to walk upright, physically, mentally, and to some degree morally. It is no longer imperatively necessary, as in ancient days, to unite every available social force for the mere preservation of the social life against disruptive violence within the group and blood-thirsty enemies without, ever eager, ever ready to attack at the first evidence of weakness. The world is becoming a less cruel, a far safer place to live in. Not only are the rights of fellow-citizens enlarged, protected and respected, at least within the letter and beneath the shield of law, but there are international rights and duties, an international customary law as well. We shudder with horror when ambassadors, legations, women and children, or unarmed and wounded prisoners of war are slaughtered by the Chinese; but the masses of the yellow race regard all such as enemies, and think it right to kill them. The preservation of the Chinese Empire, the maintenance of its ancient religions and ways of life, they believe demand such barbarous actions. Our early ancestors held much the same ideas. Even Charlemagne, the great hero of early European Christianity, did not hesitate to slaughter thousands of brave, unarmed Saxons, who had voluntarily surrendered themselves, when he thought the welfare of the Frankish Empire and the spread of the Christian religion demanded it. Yet, as a rule, he was far more kind and generous to enemies than other conquerors of that olden time.

As the nations grow larger and more civilized the sphere of war is becoming gradually more exclusive. That is, organized hostilities are becoming practicable only between large social groups, and probable only for a comparatively few great causes. Meanwhile, the sphere of crime is becoming rapidly more inclusive. Men who formerly would have been enemies, because members of petty, independent, hostile groups, have become criminals to-day, through inclusion in a single commonwealth. The amount of war is decreasing; the amount of crime is increasing. Industry and commerce, Christianity and education, are strongly opposed to warfare, at any rate between the leaders of the world's civilization; but they are persistently demanding and securing new social prohibitions for the punishment of evils formerly disregarded. The brotherhood of men seems less visionary than of old, for the wide-spread flowering of Christian love in manifold forms of practical charity and wise, uplifting helpfulness, is truly marvelous in this our day. Even the rights of animals to kindness and the law's protection have been recognized and enforced by the humanitarian spirit of the age. Social morality is growing increasingly sensitive to little rights and wrongs. Small evils are being made crimes as well as great ones. The standard of right action, to which every citizen must conform at his peril, is being raised far higher than of old, and one result of this is seen in the largely increased volume of crime and criminals among the nations of modern Europe; while the success of this education through social punishment in moralizing and uplifting the people, is plainly manifest in the decreasing statistics for many old and serious forms of crime, and indeed for many ancient misdemeanors also.

The great nations of the earth have nothing to fear from their rapidly increasing totals of criminality. They but evidence the rise to higher and higher planes of social morality and intelligence, and reveal the care with which upward progress is being fostered and safeguarded by the creation and enforcement of new and wise criminal laws. Even the coming of freedom, that crown of the nineteenth century, makes necessary many new forms of crime. Personal liberty is a priceless gift, but it is also a most dangerous possession: dangerous both to the man himself and to the society of which he is a member. For unless the individual be well developed intellectually, morally and socially, liberty is very apt to degenerate quickly into license. Hence the absolute necessity for compulsory public education in our great modern civilizations. The ignorant weakling may drift very easily into minor criminality, while the rebellious social laggard will deliberately choose anti-social, selfish conduct, and believe he has the right to do so. Both the temptations and the opportunities for such action are becoming ever more numerous; and therefore, society, while enlarging the sphere of individual liberty and life in ways made possible by the advance of civilization, and now necessary for its continued progress, must defend itself by the large increase and stern enforcement of prohibitory statutes.

Probably the men of each generation think that the new laws of their age create for the most part only minor forms of crime. The more heinous evils have long ago been made criminal by their ancestors.[1] Undoubtedly we think this to-day. The typical crimes of our age are known as contraventions or misdemeanors; termed often minor offences, although some of these modern forms of delinquency are recognized, even now, as no less socially dangerous than many ancient forms of so-called serious crime.[2]

Yet, upon the whole, it is surely true that the new forms of crime are far less deadly to the social life than are the ancient forms. Thus, the traitor is somewhat more dangerous to the community than the forger; the murderer than the man who neglects to educate his children; the thief than the common drunkard.

On the other hand, new social prohibitions are far more numerous, and occasion more criminal acts, than do the

[1] Thus, when the field of crime was being greatly extended in England and Wales, by the summary jurisdiction of justices, and the energy of a disciplined army of police—two modes of increasing and widening social pressure—we read in the police returns for 1857 (*Accounts and Papers*, p. ix): "The offences with which this large number of persons were charged represent, in a great degree, the vices, rather than the crimes of the population. The offence first in magnitude is assault." Common assaults number 60,695; assaults on peace officers, 12,750; and aggravated assaults on women and children, 2,584. In 1896 the numbers under these three forms of crime are 59,051, 12,315 and 1,743. The decrease in proportion to population is, of course, far greater—from 403.44 (1857–61) to 237.90 (1896). Social pressure seems to be successful here.

[2] See chap. i, pp. 15–16, and Stephen, i, 489.

ancient penal statutes. In fifty years, from the beginning of the reign of Queen Victoria, no less than 5,344 enactments have been added to the statute-book;[1] and perhaps nothing in the old Laws of the Realm causes more surprise than the paucity of legislation, even until the nineteenth century. Is it wonderful that the amount of crime has so greatly increased when such a multitude of actions, formerly unpunished, have been made criminal under the law? Yet are not these prohibitory statutes, in the main, wise and called for by changes and developments in social life? Have we not grown to believe in the necessity of factory and mining legislation, in sanitary laws, in the prohibition of cruelty to children and animals, and in compulsory education? Every one of these great and wise reforms was introduced, in England and elsewhere, only after long and bitter opposition by a large and influential portion of the nation, and not alone by the uneducated.

All the leading civilizations of the world have been advancing along this same path; have been hastening, and enforcing this progress upon their people by the creation of a multitude of new laws and the rigorous punishment of offenders under them. In the German Empire, from 1882 to 1895, new legislation increased the number of delites, punishable under the Code, from 323 to 447, or by 38 per cent. The growth of population in Germany is very rapid, exceeding that of most European countries, and during this period it increased from 45 to 52 millions, or by 17 per cent.; but the number of forms of conduct punished as criminal under the Imperial Code increased more than twice as rapidly as the population. Do we wonder that the German statistics should testify to a very great and continued increase of criminality, "notwithstanding that education is so diffused, and the flowering of industry and commerce so

[1] Besant, p. 237.

rapid and successful that other nations, even though more rich, begin to fear being vanquished?"[1] Nay, it is because of these very things, this wonderful development, that new penal legislation is necessary; and thus the multiplication of criminals is at once both a result of this upward growth, and a cause of its continuance, and of the nation's prosperity. As the author, just quoted, tells us, in his valuable little pamphlet upon "The Statistics of Delinquency in Europe:" "The increase of delites (*i. e.*, new social prohibitions) in Germany, both those of the Code and those provided for by other laws, has been continuous and progressive. That these last have been more than tripled, during less than fifteen years, is due to the deliberate intention to extend imperial legislation specially concerned with the tutelage of the laboring classes; and it is but natural that infractions also should have increased, with the introduction of these laws upon the cleanliness and healthfulness of factories, upon workmen's insurance and the orderly arrangements of labor."

The growing mass of the criminal population of Germany is registered in the official records of the convicted, as follows:[2]

GERMANY.—THE TOTAL NUMBER OF CONVICTIONS FOR CRIME UNDER THE IMPERIAL CODE AND SPECIAL LAWS OF THE EMPIRE.

	For crimes against the Code.	For crimes against special laws.		For crimes against the Code.	For crimes against special laws.
1882..........	323,839	6,129	1890..........	372,160	9,290
1883..........	324,410	5,718	1891..........	381,816	9,248
1884..........	340,181	5,796	1892..........	410,828	11,499
1885..........	336,259	6,828	1893..........	414,657	15,746
1886..........	345,628	7,372	1894..........	427,657	18,453
1887..........	348,595	7,744	1895..........	433,697	20,514
1888..........	342,450	8,215	1896..........	434,359	22,640
1889..........	360,321	9,323	1897..........	439,535	24,049

[1] See Bosco.

[2] See *Statistik des Deutschen Reichs*, 1888, 1893, 1896–8.

The persistent coming of this social and industrial legislation—this legislation of social guardianship—is one of the most distinctive characteristics of the modern state. Not one of the great industrial civilizations of Europe has been able to escape from the necessity of creating such laws in ever larger amount. This is no less true of England, the home of free trade, where business interests have prospered so long and very greatly under doctrines of individualism and laissez faire that they have been exalted almost into a national creed—than it is true of Germany, where the opposite doctrine of paternal oversight and regulation, even of the minutest details of life, is accepted as a most important function of the government.

The effect of this new legislation upon the criminal population must be looked for under contraventions or misdemeanors, and especially under transgressions of special laws. The statistics of such offences are precisely those that show the greatest and most persistent increase for all the great nations of Europe. This new industrial and social legislation is, of course, but one of many causes influencing the rapid growth of criminality in modern times, but it is probably the very strongest and most important of the forces in operation, although in Austria, France and Italy political legislation also has been influential.

Thus Austria, since 1860, "has renovated most profoundly her constitution and political form, has lost and acquired a province, and—through the midst of a struggle, ever more active, between the nationalities and races that compose her population: a struggle in which ethnic and historic causes are associated with those of an economic nature—has progressed continuously."[1] One result is seen in the large increase of minor offences, administrative, fiscal and economic, which have been multiplied during twenty-five years (1871

[1] Bosco, p. 56.

to 1895) in the ratio of four to one. "The energy with which this nation has renovated, in large part, her ordinances, and enforced obedience to new legislation, is clearly manifested in these figures of the penal statistics:"[1]

AUSTRIA.—THE TOTAL NUMBER OF PERSONS CONDEMNED FOR CONTRAVENTIONS UNDER THE CODE AND FOR OTHER MINOR OFFENCES PROVIDED FOR BY SPECIAL LAWS.

	Contraventions under the Code.	Provided for by Special Laws.	Total of all these offences.	Proportion per 100,000 population.
	Annual average for 5-year periods.			
1871–75......	234,783	38,753	273,536	1331.7
1876–80......	316,152	66,913	383,065	1981.4
1881–85......	375,068	119,405	494,473	
1886–90......	383,196	165,790	548,986	2277.2
1891–94......	386,386	152,902	539,288	

Italy. "The principal traits of the movement of crime in Italy," writes Professor Bosco, "during the past 20 years, are these: The lessening amount of crimes of violence, especially of homicide; the increase in those of fraud and against the authority of the state; and the small variation in those against property—robbery and theft." There are, as Professor Bosco tells us, two distinct trends of delinquency in modern Italy: one toward crimes of violence, and one toward fraudulent and political crimes. "These are here associated together, although they are properly distinctive of two diverse moments of historical evolution. In the other great nations of Europe delinquency presents itself therefore in another manner than in Italy, with a much greater development of the second than of the first type of crime. We are approaching the condition of the other states."[2] The various regions of Italy differ very greatly in the degree and form of their civilization. In the northern states modern industrial

[1] Bosco, pp. 57–8.

[2] *Ibid.*, p. 16.

and commercial life is rapidly developing. Central Italy remains, as it has long been, essentially the home of art; while Sicily, Sardinia and Southern Italy are backward in civilization and somewhat resemble Spain, both in social conditions and in the character of their criminality. Therefore it is only natural that we should find in northern Italy crimes of fraud, and in southern Italy crimes of violence—such being the distinctive expression, in delinquency, of two different stages of social development.

ITALY.—THE TOTAL NUMBER OF PERSONS CONDEMNED FOR CONTRAVENTIONS UNDER THE CODE AND FOR MINOR CRIMES PROVIDED FOR BY SPECIAL LAWS.

	Annual average for 5-year periods.	Proportion per 100,000 population.
1881–85	146,449	514.58
1886–90	212,658	740.37 (1886–95)
1891–95	233,904	
1896–97	239,808	

Turning from the study of these three nations, Germany, Austria and Italy, that have recently been developing so rapidly, politically, industrially, and intellectually, it is sad to contemplate the backward condition of civilization in poor old Spain, once the foremost nation of all Europe.

Philip the Second forbade the education of girls, and ever since the women of Spain have continued to be exceedingly illiterate. In the entire population of both sexes, only 28½ per cent. know how to write. Religious faith is yet alive among them, but has degenerated into superstition and mere worship of externals.[1] Their entire social life seems organized within the narrow and worn-out customs of many centuries ago. With the exception of a single province, the development of industry is very slight. Although Spain possesses "some of the best iron fields in the world," she

[1] Bosco, p. 60.

"imports 30 per cent. of what is used in her foundries," paying nearly £700,000 a year for such material. The cultivated area of land is believed to have been much greater in former times than it is to-day. Ways of earning money are few, and the people are ground down by taxation. From 1832 to 1888 the average annual accumulation of wealth was probably not more than 27 shillings per inhabitant, while the taxation in 1887 equaled 35 shillings.[1] The nation has repudiated its debts many times, twice within the last sixty years, yet the excess of government expenditure over public revenues goes on increasing. Politics are thoroughly corrupt and organized upon the spoils system. Civil war and the insurrections of her grievously oppressed colonies have gone far to ruin Spain. Everywhere throughout the peninsula may be seen the mournful effects of the economic depression, which, through varying years, becomes ever more acute and serious.[2]

What effect has all this suffering, want and ignorance upon the nation's criminality? Is crime very prevalent in Spain as compared with other states of Europe; and in what forms does it manifest itself?

If we may believe the official statistics, the total of Spanish criminality is not only relatively small, but it is also sensibly decreasing at the present time, especially in proportion to the population. Both delites and contraventions under the Code, after beginning to increase from 1883 to 1890, a time of great improvement in Spanish affairs, industrially and politically, have since diminished during the later years of deepening economic gloom and of national defeat and depression.

[1] See Mulhall. [2] See Bosco.

SPAIN.—THE TOTAL NUMBER OF PERSONS CONDEMNED FOR DELITES AND CONTRAVENTIONS PROVIDED FOR BY THE PENAL CODE.

	Delites.	Contraventions.		Total Recorded Offences.	
	Annual average for 5-year periods.	Annual average for 5-year periods.	Proportion per 100,000 population.	Annual average for 5-year periods.	Proportion per 100,000 population.
1883–85	22,853	61,335	367.27	84,188	504.1
1886–90	23,405	68,440	400.83	91,846	532.5
1891–95	20,102	69,821		89,923	521.4
1896	19,623	61,495		81,118	

Spanish statistics do not take the slightest notice of crimes proceeded against under special laws, those forms of social prohibition which have become in other nations of Europe such very important aids and safeguards of modern industrial and social progress; but regard only the offences punished by the Code. Probably beyond its sphere of repression there are very few forms of conduct actually made criminal by social punishment; for a close examination of the statistics reveals among the contraventions (minor crimes), acts which are regarded as much more serious offences (true and proper delites) among nations more highly advanced in civilization. Thus, cuts and blows, causing sickness and incapacity for work during seven days, are placed by the Spaniards among the minor criminal offences. This apparently reveals less social antipathy to such conduct and a lower, more antiquated standard of social morality. We are forcibly reminded of the conditions that prevailed in England a century or more ago, long before the advent of laws of social guardianship and modern industrial regulations, when even serious assaults upon the person were very lightly regarded. If some of our serious crimes are in Spain but misdemeanors (in the eyes of the law), then many of our minor offences are probably not crimes at all there.[1]

[1] The Spanish criminal statistics should be theoretically among the best, for the methods of tabulation are excellent; but irregularities and gaps in the figures leave us in great doubt as to their reliability, so far as any accurate study of the

As to the nature and the forms of crime in Spain, the following passage from a book published in 1832 is almost as true now as then, and supplies an interesting commentary upon the relative amount and kind of criminality in the different nations of Europe, as seen by a French gentleman and eyewitness nearly seventy years ago.[1]

"The judicial statistics of Spain present a series of extraordinary phenomena. One finds assaults with violence, by open force, with murder or attempts at homicide, prodigiously multiplied. One would say that these are annals of some barbarous age; or those of modern peoples, such as the Albanians and Bosnians, who are deprived of the benefits of social order, of the light of instruction, and of the tutelary protection of laws.

But, by a sort of compensation, one hardly finds a trace of crimes the most common in countries arrived at a high civilization. Nothing is more rare than the counterfeiting of money, theft by swindling, fraud, forgery of documents public or private, poisoning, incendiarism, fraudulent bankruptcy and the delits which presuppose artifice and trickery. Thus, precisely contrary to that which happens elsewhere, property is in Spain much less exposed to injury than the person; and while in London, for example, one runs the risk every instant of being robbed in one way or another, in the Peninsula one runs no danger if he remains within the circuit of the towns, but if he goes beyond he must look out for everything."

amount of delinquency in the Iberian Peninsula is concerned. They probably give us, however, an approximately correct idea of the increase or decrease of the nation's crime; for we must always remember that forms of conduct remaining socially unpunished are not criminal. In most recent years the nation's money, time and energy have been almost entirely devoted to political disturbances at home, and to disastrous foreign wars. There has been little strength left, probably, for the enforcing of justice and the punishment of criminals.

[1] See *Statistique de L'Espagne*, par Alex. Moreau de Jonnès, p. 298.

"Among the causes that multiply crimes in Spain, it is necessary, without doubt, to count the absence of all popular instruction, which is able to facilitate, vary and increase the employments of the lower classes, to preserve them from idleness, to deliver them from the prejudices and propensities of barbarous times, and to enlighten them upon the danger of violating the laws. But, even while considering ignorance as a social calamity, we cannot accuse it, as some have done, of engendering all crimes, or even of being their principal, immediate and fruitful cause; for the judicial records of Europe teach us that those countries where there are committed each year the greatest number of delites, Southern Germany, Prussia, England and the Netherlands, are precisely those where education is the most extended and the best perfected. Certainly, it is not because the people there are better educated than elsewhere that crimes are more numerous, and one must even think, that without the education which these men receive they would be yet more vicious. But, when one consults the facts, he must resign himself to the conclusion that public instruction, despite its beneficent effects, does not possess the power with which it has been credited, of preventing crimes against the social order, and of decreasing their number in proportion to the extent of its diffusion among the people."

M. Jonnès rightly concludes, that to secure the disappearance of those crimes of violence which most trouble her, Spain needs, beside public instruction, "a code of judicial procedure and criminal laws which would reach the actual needs of the people of the peninsula; a repression vigorous and constant, such as that which, during the occupation of Italy by the French, delivered that country from thefts, murders and acts of brigandage which, perpetrated during more than a thousand years, seemed to have continued forever; a greater division of the soil, and the modification of the customs laws, which, by raising smuggling into a rich commerce, a regular profession, puts a large portion of the population in continual hostility against society," so that the contraband trade "should be considered in Spain as the school of crime."[1]

In 1830, out of a total population of 11,200,000, it was estimated that 300,000 people made their living by smuggling;[2] and the census of 1877 recorded 1,630,000 men—285 out of every 1,000 adult males—as *vagrants, smugglers*, etc. The contraband trade was surely not criminal in Spain during the first half of the nineteenth century, for it remained practically unpunished, and was strongly supported by a large portion of society. It was undoubtedly a school for crime, or acts of violence against the laws, for brigandage, highway robbery and minor forms of wounding were very likely not yet truly criminal, whatever the laws might read. The ignorant masses of the population, holding to their ancient customs, and regarding strangers as their natural prey, aided or connived at the escape of the law-breakers, and society as a whole seemed powerless to repress such deeds. Yet at this time Spain was believed to be one of the most Christian of nations, and drunkenness was almost unknown among her people.

Probably not more than 50,000 out of nearly 1,500,000 children of school age in Spain, were receiving regular instruction in 1830. "The census of 1803 indicated 29,900 students, or but one for 346 inhabitants. This was thirty-four times less than the proportion in Switzerland, Germany, England and the Netherlands, and twenty times less than in France in 1830." "The ignorance to which the lower classes in Spain are condemned," writes M. Jonnès, "makes them seem, to the nations of Northern Europe, like brutish people and savages." Notwithstanding the "admirable

[1] Jonnès, pp. 298–301. [2] Mulhall, p. 542.

temperance" of the Spaniards, and the strength of the "religious sentiment" among them, "one sees in our day a nation degenerate and declining, despite all the gifts with which Providence has endowed it."[1]

Although acts of violence were widely prevalent in Spain in 1830, the total amount of criminality must have been very small. The manifold forms of modern industrial delinquency were practically unknown, for the business development—the industrial civilization—which induces such acts, and makes necessary their punishment as crimes, did not exist in Spain then, and is scarcely found there even now. The social standard of right action was so low, owing to the dense ignorance of the people, and the state of brutish oppression in which they lived, that many ancient and honorable forms of rapine and bodily injury had not yet been made criminal by social punishment, because of the inert, or active, opposition of the masses, and the undeveloped and disunited condition of the social existence.

How comes it that Spain, this proud and virile nation, once the leader of the world's civilization,[2] whose land was the home of strength, culture and enlightenment—how comes it that she fell so low?

Surely one of the chief reasons is that for centuries she has persisted in choosing her crimes wrongly. Not only has the Spanish race failed to make criminal those violent and bloody actions which should have been the true and proper crimes of its stage of civilization, but it has ruthlessly and indefatigably crushed out almost every tendency to helpful variation—killing, torturing, or banishing every citizen who was suspected of thinking for himself in matters of religion, thus eliminating most of the progressive men of Spain, who could and would have led her to higher levels of social development, prosperity and enlightenment, if the nation

[1] Jonnès, pp. 303 and 305.

[2] In the sixteenth century.

had been willing to follow them rather than the leaders of the Inquisition.

As in Anglo-Saxon England, so also in Spain, the creation of a united nation, from many warring states, was accomplished mainly through the growing strength of two great socializing forces—the king and the Christian Church—working harmoniously together for the establishment of a centralized government; extending and securing their mutual authority, first by successful wars, and second by criminal prosecutions for acts deemed most dangerous to their power and continued prosperity. But in England, when either king or Church became dangerously tyrannical, the other great forces of the nation united to curb and limit the growing despotism—thus maintaining and enlarging individual rights and liberties, which would else have been crushed out, under the iron heel of a criminal law, framed, not to foster and defend continued social progress, but to enforce absolutism and to prohibit growth in any but this one direction. In Spain despotism was victorious. While the English people rose to power and greatness, throwing off the shackles of a feudalized ecclesiasticism and of the divine right of kings, the Spanish people sank into ignorance, superstition, and blind obedience to the constituted authority.

Nowhere else in the entire Christian world has "the whole purpose and strength of Church and State been so centralized as there, in the repression of what was regarded as a common evil threatening the life of both."[1] The yoke of this despotism was fixed triumphantly upon the nation's neck, and has remained there through long centuries, even until recent years, permitting progress only within very narrow limits. The strong Romanism of the Spanish people permitted and supported the Inquisition—that most power-

[1] *Johnson's Universal Cyclopædia* (1898), "The Inquisition," p. 598.

ful engine of a so-called "Christian" absolutism—consequently the tortures inflicted by the "Holy Office" were true criminal punishments, and the victims of the Inquisition the criminals of Spain. Lorente gives the figures for this one nation, down to 1809: burnt alive, 31,912; burnt in effigy, 17,659; imprisoned, tortured, etc., as penitents, 291,450; a total of 341,021. The Jews were expelled from the country in 1492, and much of the learning and ability of Spain went with them, although their wealth was largely confiscated. How many protestant "heretics" were driven out we do not know, but the number must have been very great. France and Italy also punished as heretics many thousands of their best citizens. The true value of the men and women thus made criminals may be estimated from the stimulating and educating influence of their presence among the nations—England, the Netherlands and America—whither some of them escaped; and from the large number of distinguished citizens who trace their ancestry to Huguenot refugees.

Until the French invasion in 1808, Spain was an "absolutist and ecclesiastical monarchy. The old assemblies of the estates (the Cortes) were no longer convoked. The descendants of the aristocracy, the Spanish grandees, had been thrust aside. The king had centralized all political authority in his own person, but he had ceased to exercise it himself; he left it to his court. It was the sovereign's immediate circle—his wife, his confessor, his favorite, or his wife's favorite—that governed Spain in the king's name. This little group was called the camarilla, or little chamber."[1]

The Church alone retained its ancient strength. "It retained its immense domains almost without taxes, its right to acquire property by mortmain, its convents and its ecclesiastical courts. It kept up the Court of the Inquisition, and its

[1] Seignobos, p. 286.

control of family relations, which gave it authority over the private life of all laymen. Its censorship of all publications made it supreme over the nation's intellectual life. There were thus in Spain but two real powers, the camarilla and the clergy. The Spanish submitted to this two-fold despotism without the thought of saving themselves from it, at least without the power to do so."[1] However, the Inquisition had gradually been losing its hold—its will was murderous, but its teeth were dropping out. In the eighteenth century torture was abandoned, and the death penalty was inflicted but two or three times a year.[2] As late as 1826 a Jew was burnt and a Quaker schoolmaster hanged in Spain by officials of the Inquisition. In 1851, the government of Isabella again "gave the clergy the control of education and a censorship of books, and put itself at the service of the ecclesiastical authority." So also from 1863 to 1868 Catholic absolutism and the camarilla were revived, and priests became once more the most influential men in the government. Not until 1869 did the Spanish nation dare "to inscribe religious liberty in a constitution,"[3] and then all her bishops, with one exception, refused to swear obedience. Religious toleration is now admitted in theory, but even to-day "public exhibitions or ceremonies of any other than the national religion are forbidden," and the placing of a Protestant notice or emblem on the outside wall of any building is criminal under the law.[4]

Was not the yoke of monarchical and ecclesiastical absolutism fastened firmly upon the Spanish people, and has not the effect of its criminal prosecutions been the crushing out of that independence of thought and action, and even of the desire to think and study for oneself, to which the great

[1] Seignobos, p. 287.
[2] *Ency. Brit.* (1881), "The Inquisition," p. 94.
[3] Seignobos, pp. 299 and 311.
[4] *Ibid.*, p. 316.

political, scientific, industrial and educational development of this modern age is due?

Spain has chosen her crimes wrongly, and therefore the grand and inexorable law that guides the progress of the world to better things has punished her. She has fallen into the decadence prepared by her own mistakes, while the leadership of the world's civilization has passed to other nations, among whom true liberty can grow and thrive, unless they also fall into the like error of punishing the social good and fostering the social evil.

There is more hope for Spain to-day than for centuries past. She has been compelled, like every other nation of Europe, to free herself from the crushing weight of monasticism. Universal suffrage has been established; a constitutional and representative government introduced. Spain is free at last from the heavy burden of colonies which she knew not how to govern wisely, which were almost always in revolt against her power, and a constant drain upon her resources and vital energy. Also, she has probably succeeded now in making criminal most of those ancient forms of violence, which in the first half of the nineteenth century remained very largely unpunished.

How widely different from the sad conditions we have just been studying are those prevalent in modern England; where the entire nineteenth century has been filled with a marvelous activity and development, industrial, social and political, material, mental and moral—England, where the great increase of population has been outstripped by the yet greater increase of wealth;[1] where education is now compulsory; where the wide extension of the franchise, the organization of labor, the coming of steam, compressed air and electricity, shorter hours of work, a larger money recompense for toil, with the diffusion of the comforts and

[1] Giffen, p. 110.

even luxuries of life, have all united to stimulate intelligence, promote national solidarity, and spread abroad among the people that strong feeling of brotherhood, which has induced the great practical humanitarian and truly Christian movements of the age. England, first of all the great European civilizations, recognized the rights of animals to kindness and the law's protection; and very many forms of wise educational, prohibitive or protective legislation for men, women and children have had their origin and widest enforcement here.[1] This nation, during twenty recent years, 1870 to 1890, has had the largest total amount of crime, in proportion to population, of any of the great nations for which we have reliable official statistics; and were it possible to compare such tables for a longer period in the past, there seems very little doubt but that the preponderance of English crime would be yet more pronounced and greater. (See page 300.)

The number of persons held for trial for all criminal offences before the courts and tribunals of England and Wales has nearly doubled within forty years, rising from 389,502 in 1857 to 720,441 in 1896. In proportion to population the growth has been from 2003.34 (the average from 1857 to 1861) to 2344.34 in 1896.

But this increase is not under all forms of crime, far from it. Old and most serious kinds of criminality show a greater and more continuous diminution in England than in any other great nation. The figures since 1856 read as follows:[2]

[1] Factory and mining legislation, for example. Spain has no laws for the protection of animals even now.

[2] See *Judicial Statistics of England and Wales*, 1898, vol. civ, page 40.

The remarkable decrease under most of these serious old forms of crime becomes more manifest if we compare the separate offences, or classes of offences (in proportion to 100,000 population), for two periods, 1836 and 1896—sixty years apart.

Murder has diminished from .49 to .19; manslaughter from 1.35 to .54; malicious wounding from 3.19 to 2.48, and assault from 4.69 to .66. Attempts to murder and felonious wounding show an increase from .81 to 1.05; but from 1834

NUMBERS FOR TRIAL FOR ALL SERIOUS OFFENCES IN ENGLAND AND WALES—ASSIZES AND QUARTER SESSIONS (1857 TO 1896 INCLUSIVE).

	Annual average for 5-year periods.	Proportion per 100,000 of population.
1857–61	17,825	90.53
1862–66	19,758	94.61
1867–71	18,445	83.00
1872–76	15,096	63.63
1877–81	15,567	61.36
1882–86	14,303	53.13
1887–91	12,481	43.87
1892–96	11,816	39.31
1896	11,103	36.13

Many old misdemeanors are decreasing also, and the enormous multiplication of criminals in modern England must be credited to the enforcement of the ever larger number of new social prohibitions with which the statute-books are rife. It is not necessary to take this upon the word of any man. Here are the judicial statistics—they shall speak for themselves:

to 1838 the average number under this head was .94 per 100,000 of population, The total number of persons tried for murder, wounding and assault, etc., has decreased, despite the rapid growth of population, from 1572 (1836) to 1512 (1896); or, in proportion to population, from 10.53 to 4.92.

Unnatural offences have decidedly decreased, while, on the other hand, rape, defilement and indecent assaults, etc., have multiplied greatly, from 1.25 to 2.94 per 100,000.

Serious offences against property, with violence—burglary, robbery, etc.—show a great diminution in proportion to population, from 8.74 (1836), 9.44 (1834–8), to 6.16 in 1896.

On the contrary, indictable offences against property without violence show a decided increase, from 108.33 to 146.08; but this is largely accounted for by the multiplication of criminals under embezzlement, fraud and offences in bankruptcy, larceny of post letters and other relatively modern forms of theft.

For malicious injuries to property the figures are 1.07 and .93. Forgery and offences against the currency show a notable decrease, from 2.41 to 1.07. Against treason and piracy laws there were no offenders during both periods, while under the head of riot the decrease is truly enormous—from 3.56 to .07.

The grand total of all indictable offences—which includes all serious crimes and many petty offences—has increased in proportion to population from 140.56 (1836), 148.54 (1834–38), to 164.91 in 1896; but this is entirely due to offences under the larceny group. Old serious crimes have decreased greatly.

Old Minor Offences Tried by Courts of Summary Jurisdiction in England and Wales.

		1857–61.	1862–66.	1867–71.	1872–76.	1877–81.	1882–86.	1887–91.	1892–96.	1896.
Simple larceny and other old indictable offences now tried summarily ..	Annual average number.	34,521	39,957	40,036	37,052	41,666	44,956	43,799	42,873	39,576
	Proportion per 100,000	175.35	191.33	180.15	156.17	164.22	166.98	153.96	142.62	128.78
Assaults...........	Total	79,424	90,513	92,273	90,300	86,540	83,550	76,941	72,268	73,109
	Per 100,000	403.44	433.41	415.21	418.55	341.09	310.34	270.46	247.06	237.90
Stealing and receiving animals, fruit, etc.	Total	4,713	5,007	5,833	4,767	5,333	5,392	5,293	4,655	3,967
	Per 100,000	23.94	23.98	26.25	20.09	21.02	20.03	18.61	15.49	12.91
Malicious damage ..	Total	15,661	19,327	21,820	22,731	21,748	21,471	19,178	18,135	17,369
	Per 100,000	79.55	92.55	98.19	95.81	85.72	79.75	67.41	60.33	56.52
Game laws—offences against..........	Total	7,947	10,216	11,720	11,621	11,876	10,640	9,509	8,874	8,884
	Per 100,000	40.37	48.92	52.74	48.98	46.81	39.52	33.43	29.52	28.91

These are ancient forms of criminality which have not been much enlarged by statutes in recent years; although the new crime of embezzlement is here included, after 1872, with the old indictable offences of simple larceny. However, the figures for this one crime are comparatively small, ranging from 731 for the period 1873–76 to 1,035 in 1892–96.

The great wave of social pressure against minor offenders which began in England about 1855–57, with the enlarged jurisdiction of the summary courts and the establishment of a disciplined police force throughout all the country, is very noticeable in the increased numbers of these statistics for several five-year periods after 1857–61. It is very probable that common assaults, and some other forms of delinquency here recorded, were not made really criminal, by determined punishment until that time. We know that prosecutions for simple larceny mounted then (1855–57), with a great jump, and it is probable that a similar increase took place under malicious damage and game-law offences, but we can hardly believe that the amount of social punishment in previous years had not sufficed to make such conduct criminal. The greater pressure simply made social disapprobation more distinctly recognized and felt. (See the argument in Appendix II.) Drunkenness, as we have seen, did not really begin to be made a crime until after 1833, although laws existed penalizing the offence.[1] Vagrancy, in some of its forms, is a very old crime, and the laws were somewhat strongly enforced against it, early in the nineteenth century. But recent statutes have largely changed the character of such delinquency, and the growing social pressure against gaming has made such conduct criminal and greatly increased the number of prosecutions under the vagrancy acts. The Education Act of 1871 introduced an entirely new form of crime

[1] See Page 272, Note 1.

into England, and large have been the additions to the nation's criminals because of it. Accordingly, the statistics for drunkenness, vagrancy and offences against the Education Acts tell a different story from that disclosed by the old and relatively unchanged forms of misdemeanor we have been considering—a story of greatly increasing crime. (See tables on succeeding pages.)

NEW OR RECENTLY DEVELOPED MINOR OFFENCES TRIED BY COURTS OF SUMMARY JURISDICTION IN ENGLAND AND WALES.

		1857–61.	1862–66.	1867–71.	1872–76.	1877–81.	1882–86.	1887–91.	1892–96.	1896.
Drunkenness	Annual average number.	84,358	99,880	121,669	185,862	184,099	185,847	176,101	175,628	187,258
	Per 100,000.	428.50	478.26	547.48	783.41	725.61	690.31	619.02	584.24	609.34
Offences against vagrancy acts	Average number.	20,132	22,685	30,464	26,915	37,355	40,849	42,422	49,499	52,487
	Per 100,000.	102.26	108.62	137.08	113.45	147.23	151.73	149.12	164.66	170.80
Offences against the education acts (Statutes of 1871 and 1876.)	Average number.	....	....	....	17,061	47,417	82,008	83,483	67,851	67,858
	Per 100,000.	....	....	....	71.91	186.89	304.61	293.46	225.71	220.81

MODERN FORMS OF MINOR CRIME. THE STATUTES CREATING OR ENLARGING THEM—AND THE TOTAL NUMBER OF PERSONS TRIED BECAUSE OF THEM.

Annual average for five year periods.

	1857–61.	1862–66.	1867–71.	1872–76.	1877–81.	1882–86.	1887–91.	1892–96.	1896.
Adulteration of food and drugs	…	…	…	1,029	1,324	1,552	1,919	3,002	2,951
Cruelty to animals. (Multitude of recent Victorian Statutes.)	2,400	3,627	5,136	7,065	9,167	8,803	10,149	12,725	12,919
Diseases of animals—Offences in relation to dogs. (Many statutes 1854 to 1894.)	…	…	1,743	952	1,185	2,375	6,717	15,969	26,797
Factory acts. (Laws of 1878 and 1895)	395	432	419	974	616	1,273	1,482	1,769	1,675
Gaming (gambling) and other offences. (32–3 Vic., c. 87, 1869, and later acts.)	2,804	3,107	4,822	7,108	9,242	10,429	12,174	20,103	22,823
Highway acts. (5 and 6 Will. 4, c. 50.)	6,766	10,472	15,262	15,850	19,528	19,286	18,913	27,525	34,276
Police regulations. (Laws of 1839, 1847, and many later.)	45,159	43,993	52,400	61,511	66,120	65,093	73,045	86,292	97,910
Prevention of crimes. (Acts 1871, 1879, 1885.)	…	…	…	193	428	592	505	369	364
Railway offences. (In every recent R. R. act.)	1,018	1,253	1,766	2,689	2,845	2,799	3,153	3,891	4,019
Revenue laws. (39 and 40 Vic., c. 36.)	2,065	4,066	8,114	7,170	11,094	11,305	13,413	12,330	11,306
Sanitary laws. (Public Health Acts of 1866 and 1874, and many since.)	4,357	5,129	7,898	10,172	11,507	10,416	9,867	7,446	7,284
Stage and hackney carriage regulations. (Many recent laws.)	5,949	6,921	7,352	7,154	6,650	6,978	9,287	8,292	6,791
Sunday trading. (Recent statutes.)	893	649	556	868	919	2,060	2,521	3,006	3,593
Vaccination acts. (Statutes of 1867 and 1871.)	…	…	…	1,205	1,779	2,560	2,622	1,755	1,715

Many of these offences could not possibly have been made criminal till within the last sixty-five years. All stand for conduct which we should expect to have punished with increasing energy by a great modern industrial civilization, advancing rapidly in knowledge, intelligence and social morality.

Meanwhile the total number of persons tried by English courts for all misdemeanors has steadily and rapidly increased, each five-year period showing a decided, and in every instance but two a large increase over the five-year period before it. The change, in actual figures, has been from 363,417 in 1857, to 709,338 in 1896; and in proportion to population from 1912.81 (the average for 1857–61) to 2308.21 in 1896.

England and Wales.—Total Number of Persons tried by Courts of Summary Jurisdiction.

	Annual average for 5-year period.	Proportion per 100,-000 population.
1857–61	376,569	1912.81
1862–66	426,779	2043.58
1867–71	490,872	2208.82
1872–76	592,893	2499.04
1877–81	632,626	2493.45
1882–86	669,633	2487.29
1887–91	671,900	2361.83
1892–96	678,314	2256.48
1896–	709,338	2308.21

"But," some one may say, "the English judicial statistics are not comparable throughout their entire length. You have confessedly no full and continuous record of misdemeanors until 1857. How do you know that the mass of minor criminality before that date was less in proportion to the population than it has been since? How then can you be sure that crime has been increasing during this century of rapid progress? Such questions are but right and must be answered, if you expect to establish more than a mere possibility."

With the close of Queen Victoria's sixtieth year of reign, the English statisticians made the most careful examination and comparison possible of the state of crime in England and Wales in 1836 and 1896. Doubtless they sought the truth fearlessly. But, if personal inclination could in any way have influenced their conclusions, the trend would probably have been toward the showing of a larger amount of crime in the earlier as compared with the later period, a time of great national exaltation and rejoicing. What do they tell us?

Summary Proceedings in 1836 and 1896.

"The most marked features of the figures for 1896 are, first, the large number of indictable offences dealt with summarily, and second, the large number of newly created criminal offences. In 1836 there were no cases at all corresponding to the 39,576 indictable cases disposed of at petty sessions in 1896, or to the 67,858 cases under the Elementary Education Acts, or to the 1,715 cases under the Vaccination Acts. Under other heads, such as Sanitary Laws, Adulteration, Intoxicating Liquor Laws, Military and Naval Law, Stage and Hackney Carriages, and Factory Acts, the law has been so much extended as to be practically new. Unfortunately no figures exist as to the total amount of work done by justices out of sessions in 1836, and it is not possible to frame a comparative table on the subject. A return was asked for by Parliament of the number of persons *committed to prison* on summary conviction during the year ending at Michaelmas 1835, but as in many places no proper records were kept at that time, cases being sometimes disposed of by magistrates at their own houses, the reports made by clerks to the justices are very incomplete.[1]

[1] See Parl'y Papers, H. C. (580), 1837.

The digest of gaol returns for 1836, however, professes to give the number of persons *received* in prison on summary convictions under different heads.[1] As the figures in these two returns, though incomplete, are of considerable interest, they are given below with the figures for 1896 that most nearly correspond to them." Notice the great increase under "Police Acts" and "Other Offences," which include most of the new forms of crime.

	1836.		1896.	
	Persons Committed to Prison on Summary Conviction.	Persons Received in Prison on Summary Conviction.	Persons Convicted and Sentenced to Imprisonment.	Persons Convicted and Fined or otherwise Disposed of.
Vagrancy Act, Offences Against	2,106	18,863	20,483	21,677
Assaults	757	8,991	10,016	32,237
Game Laws, Offences Against	779	3,229	302	7,304
Malicious Trespass Act, Offences Against. [Malicious Damages]	339	2,837	1,058	11,017
Larceny Act, Stealing Animals, Fruit, etc.	218	2,668	236	2,642
Revenue Laws	50	49	40	8,877
Metropolitan and other Local Police Acts	27	726	1,379	75,576
Servants and Apprentices, Offences by	218	....	....	....
Other Offences	186	13,015	31,838	331,970
Offences not Stated	26,962	....	....	....
Total	31,672	50,378	65,352	491,300

"It is to be noted that of 491,300 persons convicted in 1896, but not sentenced in the first instance to imprison-

[1] See Parl'y Papers (c. 89), 1837, p. 439.

ment, a considerable proportion, probably over 70,000, went to prison ultimately in default of paying their fines."

"It is probable that the 50,378 given as the number of persons received in prison on summary conviction during 1836, includes all persons committed by justices out of the sessions, whether they were technically convicted or no; the corresponding figure to which for 1896 would be 145,428. A comparison between the two figures illustrates the immense increase of the work done by courts of summary jurisdiction. While the number of offenders committed to prison (for serious crimes) on conviction on indictment has decreased about 54 per cent., that is to say, from 16,418 to 7,582, the number of those committed by summary process (minor offenders) has increased 188 per cent. The increase in the number of criminal offenders dealt with summarily *otherwise than by imprisonment* (by fines, etc.) has probably been *at least* as great."[1]

Meanwhile the population of England and Wales has enlarged, during this period of sixty years, by 105.9 per cent. Therefore, minor crime has multiplied much more rapidly than population—in the ratio of 188 to 105.9—according to the very conservative estimates of the English statisticians.

The author himself believes that the increase of crime in England since 1836 has been far greater than 188 per cent., on account of the strong modern tendency to substitute fines for imprisonment in the punishing of minor offenders.

A comparison of the penalties inflicted by courts of summary jurisdiction, in 1857 and 1896, reveals the strength of this tendency. In 1857, the total number of persons proceeded against summarily was 363,417 as against 709,338 in 1896. Of these, the justices convicted 233,759 in the earlier and 556,652 in the later year. Imprisonment was decreed for 63,061 persons in 1857, and 65,352 in 1896. But the

[1] See *Judicial Statistics of England and Wales*, 1898, vol. civ, pp. 29, 30.

number of those fined mounted from 143,463 in 1857, to 475,900 in 1896; and the total of those convicted and "disposed of otherwise than by imprisonment" rose from 170,698 in 1857, to 491,300 in 1896. Thus, while the figures for the imprisonment of minor offenders have remained practically the same, fines have been multiplied in number almost three and one-third times.[1]

The nature of the sentences imposed for indictable offences in 1836, when contrasted with those of 1896, point strongly to this same great preference for fines in the punishment of modern minor offenders.[2] Accordingly, if 188 per cent.

[1] *Judicial Statistics* (1857-58), pages ix and 16, and (1898) pp. 30, 36 and 77.

[2] The record of sentences imposed for all indictable offences (which include all serious crime and much minor delinquency) in 1836 and 1896, show that the amount of punishment by fines for indictable offences has very largely increased since 1836, while short terms of imprisonment (two years and under) have decidedly decreased; and this, although we are accustomed to consider brief imprisonment as a most characteristic feature of the modern English penal system.

In 1836 serious crimes were punished customarily with death, or transportation for life, fourteen or seven years. Out of a total of 14,771 persons convicted for all indictable offences that year, 3,611 were thus sentenced, while in 1896 only 400 of the most heinous criminals were punished by death, or penal servitude for over three years. The penalties for even grave offences have undoubtedly become relatively short terms of imprisonment in our time; and yet, in 1836, the amount of imprisonment (two years and under for all indictable offences) was 68,546 in proportion to 100,000 sentences, while in 1896 it was only 53,847. Meanwhile fine, whipping (for boys) and recognizances, which in 1836 were 2,051, 224 and 1,347 respectively (per 100,000 sentences), have risen to 20,253, 7,280 and 14,367 in 1896. [See *Judicial Statistics of England and Wales*, 1898, vol. civ, pages 22-3 and 42.] Therefore, the less heinous indictable crimes were punished in 1836 mainly by imprisonment under two years, and in 1896 largely by fine, whipping and recognizances.

This same strong tendency has extended, as we have already seen, to the punishment of offences tried summarily (1857 to 1896), and therefore the statement of the English official statisticians, that "the increase in the number of criminal offenders dealt with summarily, otherwise than by imprisonment, has probably been *at least as great*"—namely, 188 per cent.—as the number of those committed to prison, should be regarded as too conservative an estimate. The percentage of increase for minor crime in England and Wales from 1836 to 1896 is probably decidedly greater, and the increase of all crime at least as great.

correctly represents the increase of minor criminals "committed by summary process," (see report of English statisticians) then it is surely probable that the increase of "offenders dealt with summarily" by fines or "otherwise than by imprisonment" is far greater.

Naturally some regions of England are developing much more rapidly than others in wealth, prosperity and civilization. In this age when change of domicile is so very easy, and men and women of the energetic, marrying and child-rearing period of life are moving continually from place to place, in search of remunerative employment, it follows almost inevitably that the most prosperous and progressive regions in any country, the homes of modern industrial and democratic civilization, should be, in general, those where the population is rapidly increasing. A comparison between the growth of population and the growth of crime in the different counties of England and Wales will, therefore, be both interesting and important. Such a study has recently been made by English statisticians, and the results of their labors are given here, largely in their own words.

In the construction of the necessary tables, the estimated population of each county in 1836 and in 1896, together with the percentage of increase or decrease during the period, are contrasted with the number of prosecutions per 100,000 of population, for crimes against the person and against property, including forgery and coining.[1] But "the figures for individual counties are so small and so liable to be affected by purely local and accidental causes, that they cannot be safely used as a basis of comparison." Therefore, "the counties are grouped according to the rate of increase of their population since 1836." In general, for all England, the result shows greater delinquency in 1896 than for the

[1] Indictable offences, not including the miscellaneous crimes grouped in Class VI of the English statistics.

twelve-month sixty years before, even for indictable offences, which are here alone considered.

"The first group contains three counties (Huntingdon, Cornwall and Rutland) whose population has decreased since 1836. The decrease of crime in this group, as a whole, is markedly greater than the decrease of population; from 75.9 per 100,000 (average 1834–38) to 69.5 in 1896, while the number of inhabitants has grown less by 1.5 per cent."

In the second group also, consisting of thirteen counties, in which the population[1] has increased on the average only 18.4 per cent., the decrease in crime has been noticeable; the number of crimes per 100,000 being 137.4 in 1834–38 and only 126.2 in 1896.

Next we have a group of nine counties in which the population has increased at rates varying from 57.7 per cent. to 99.5 per cent., a growth less than the average for all England, which is 107 per cent.[2] In these, crime, as tested by the number of criminal prosecutions, shows a slight increase, from 141.4 (1834–38) to 143.1 (1896).

In the next twelve counties the increase of population has been large, varying from 102.9 per cent. in Sussex to 179.1 per cent. in Lancaster.[3] But crime has risen yet more rapidly, namely, from 141.6 to 173.6 per 100,000 persons.

"Lastly, we have the county of Durham, where the popu-

[1] Hereford, increase, 1.0 per cent.; Salop, 4.9 per cent.; Somerset, 5.7 per cent.; Wilts, 7.6 per cent.; Dorset, 16.5 per cent.; Norfolk, 17.7 per cent.; Cambridge, 20.1 per cent.; Westmorland, 20.1 per cent.; Suffolk, 20.4 per cent.; Oxford, 21.3 per cent.; Devon, 25.7 per cent.; Bucks, 25.8 per cent.; Lincoln, 39.6 per cent.—total, 18.4 per cent.

[2] Counties with increase of population 50 per cent. and less than 100 per cent.: Cumberland, Herts, Berks, Gloucester, Northampton, Bedford, Worcester, Leicester, Nottingham.

[3] Counties with increase of 100 per cent. and less than 180 per cent.: Sussex, Chester. Northumberland, Derby, Southampton, York, Warwick, Monmouth, Stafford, Metropolitan counties, Essex and Lancaster.

lation has increased by more than 303 per cent., and crimes have increased from 61.6 to 188.4 per 100,000."

In Glamorganshire, the only Welsh county showing a great enlargement of the population (439.0 per cent.), the proportion of crime has multiplied from 62.9 to 270.7. But throughout all Wales, except Pembrokeshire, crime has "largely increased" in proportion to the population; and this whether the number of inhabitants (per county) has decreased or increased.[1] "But," so states the report, "the very low proportion of crime recorded in Wales in 1836 is suspicious, and the actual figures are so small for all counties, except Glamorganshire, that it would be unwise to attach much importance to them."

"If we take the English counties alone, the figures at first suggest the conclusion that an increase of population leads to a disproportionate increase of crime, or in other words, that the number of crimes for every 100,000 of the population increases, speaking generally, with every increase of population. On closer consideration, however, such a conclusion seems open to much doubt." . . . In the Metropolitan Counties, in Essex, in Warwickshire and Cheshire, where the growth of population has been greater than the average for England as a whole, the proportion of crime has diminished. On the other hand, "in Cumberland, Notts and Westmorland, the increase in population has been below the average for all England, but the increase in the number of prosecutions has been far above the average."

"On the whole, it seems probable that where the increase of population is merely the increase of a pre-existing class

[1] Five Welsh counties show a decrease averaging 11.3 per cent.: Montgomery, Raynor, Cardigan, Brecon and Anglesey. Five show an increase averaging 23.9 per cent.: Pembroke, Flint, Merioneth, Carmarthen and Denbigh. Carnarvon shows a gain of 58.4 per cent. in population, and crime has increased from 37.6 to 91.4 per 100,000 people.

of the population, such as mining, industrial or shipping population, it has not been accompanied by a disproportionate increase of crime; but that where the increase of population has been due to a change in the character of their employment, a disproportionate increase of crime is likely to ensue."[1]

In other words, it is the beginnings of new life, the formative and transition period, the time of rapid early development and progress to a probably more complex industrial civilization, that occasions the multiplication of criminals.[2]

What conclusions, then, if any, are warranted by the evidence just given? The relation of the growth of crime to the increase of population is strikingly illustrated by the groups of English counties; but mere growth in the number of inhabitants is surely not the dominant cause multiplying criminals. In Wales, crime has increased out of all proportion to the slight increase of the population. This is true in many of the English counties also.

The criminal records used by the English statisticians in these comparisons include only indictable offences,[3] which show "an increase in the proportion of prosecutions to population" for all England, of but "about 10 per cent. since 1834–38." According to their own very conservative estimates, the growth of non-indictable crimes, tried by courts of summary jurisdiction, has been very much greater during this same period of sixty years: "the increase in the number of criminal offenders committed to prison, or otherwise dealt with by summary process," having "probably been at least 188 per cent," for England and Wales, while population has been increasing 105.9 per cent.[4]

[1] See *Judicial Statistics of England and Wales* (1898), vol. civ, p. 28–9.

[2] See chapter xiii, pp. 315–20. [3] Omitting miscellaneous crimes in Class VI.

[4] See *Judicial Statistics of England and Wales* (1898), vol. civ, page 30. This included, however, indictable offences tried summarily in 1896—39,576 out of a total of 709,338 crimes.

Now it is precisely these new forms of minor crime, within the jurisdiction of the summary courts, which have caused the great multiplication of England's criminals since 1836; and this increase of minor offenders is especially true of the industrial and city districts where the population is most dense and most rapidly increasing. Accepting the growth of England's minor criminality as "at least 188 per cent.," this average increase exceeds the growth of population in every separate county of England and Wales save two: Durham and Glamorgan. Meanwhile the amount of most serious crime has decreased about 54 per cent.: the actual figures being 16,418 and 7,582;[1] but these numbers are so small relatively that they could not greatly change the relative proportions of England's total delinquency in the two periods.

We may conclude therefore that the growth of crime in all England has outstripped the rapid growth of the population, but that this increase of crime is very unevenly distributed, the most prosperous and progressive industrial and city regions getting the most of it—especially those in which the character of employment has changed—while the relatively unprogressive counties, where population is declining or not enlarging greatly, show a much smaller increase of delinquency, or even in some instances a probable decrease.

Summary. The typical crimes of the most highly developed and successful nations of to-day are largely misdemeanors, caused by the fine legal adjustments made necessary by our ever more and more complex social life. Will this process continue forever? Will more delicate adjustments always be necessary and result in an ever-enlarging list of social prohibitions? Probably. But the rate of increase may not be as rapid in the twentieth century as it has been in the

[1] Offenders committed to prison on conviction on indictment in 1836 and 1896. *Judicial Statistics*, 1898, page 30.

eighteenth and nineteenth. There was so much to be accomplished, and so much has now been done, to guard the rights and foster the upward growth of each and all under the laws, that we may well hope our suffering and arduous labors will make the creation of new forms of crime less necessary for our great-grand-children; that this education through social discipline may gradually become less difficult, its lessons more easily and quickly learned. If this prove true, and if society continues to be successful in diminishing the amount of criminality under old laws, then the age of maximum crime will have been passed, and from thenceforth society will have a decreasing, rather than an increasing total of delinquency.

Indeed, there is some evidence that the flood of crime has even now reached its height in England, for the increasing totals of misdemeanors have since 1882–86 failed to keep pace with the yet larger growth of population; so that per 100,000 inhabitants England and Wales show a sensible decrease in crime, comparing 1882–86 with later five-year periods. The statistics of Austria and Italy, Germany, Scotland and Massachusetts, have no encouragement to give to this pleasing idea, but the French records may be thought to favor it. On the whole, it must be confessed that the happier time is certainly not yet fully come, and this book deals with the present and the past, not the future; with historical and statistical facts, not with prophesies of a coming era.[1]

[1] In England and France the present time may, possibly, be one of rest between two periods of increasing crime—a pause, such as came to the former country in the late 18th and early 19th centuries.

CHAPTER XV

AN ETHICAL THEORY OF CRIME.

OUT of the teachings of natural law, which, whether we like it or not, whether we aid or oppose it, is driving the world forward to higher and higher planes of life, of intelligence and mutual helpfulness, comes the idea of crime, and the necessity for the appearance of the criminal in every human community. Crime is an inevitable social evil, the dark side of the shield of human progress. The sifting processes of natural selection continue within the domain of social life, rejecting, through social pressure, both weaklings and workers of iniquity. Anti-social individuals, or malefactors, result from the persistent tendency to variation, manifest in all life. They become criminals through processes of social selection, during which individuals refusing to live up to the social standard of right action are punished by the community, and their actions become known as crimes. Anti-social acts occurred probably long before the punishment of such conduct by the social group;[1] certainly ages before there was any recognition of acts as wrongs against society. Originally the forms of anti-social conduct were very few in number; they have become many with the progress of civilization. The great majority of acts now punished, and rightly punished, as crimes by modern nations, either are unknown among low savages, or are not considered as wrong and immoral. Very often such acts are not really evils in a low stage of social development. Certainly they are not punished by the social group as wrongs against itself;

[1] See page 31.

they have not yet become crimes. To this extent, therefore, crime is a social product;—not that anti-social conduct is a product of social forces, but that society has been compelled to enlarge continually its categories of anti-social acts, to broaden out persistently the field within which certain acts are prohibited as injurious to the social welfare, and to punish as criminals the increasing number of the disobedient, who refuse to submit themselves to this ever-extending social pressure. The increase of crime, which is due to wise changes in the criminal law or its administration (induced by a rising social standard of right action), without any increase of anti-social conduct, promotes civilization and tends to social betterment; but, statutes and administration remaining the same, an increase of crime must mean an increase of anti-social conduct, which assuredly does not promote civilization.

Society's conflict with the criminal is one of the chief factors in social evolution, and since the field of this conflict has broadened down the ages, it is but natural that crime has tended to increase, and in fact has increased with the growth of knowledge, intelligence and social morality. This increase of crime largely takes the direction of acts in opposition to new social prohibitions, which are neither accidental nor whimsical, but inevitable consequences of the increasing complexity of life. In general, new crime follows lines of greatest resistance to the new life of society.

The preservation of life upon the earth and its gradual upward development have resulted, even in the lowest animal forms, from the operation of two great, unchanging, ethical principles, or laws of growth.

The first is the fundamental law of adult life. It is the law of self-support, of self-interest, of earned benefits. "Whatsoever a man soweth, that shall he also reap."[1] The

[1] St. Paul, *Galatians*, vi, 7.

adult must in general take the consequences of his own character and conduct—the survival of the fittest resulting.[1]

The second of these great principles may be called the law of the family. It is the primary law of self-sacrifice, the law of unearned benefits to offspring immature and helpless, without which the species must inevitably perish.

Every kind of living creature must yield obedience to these laws, or degenerate and disappear from the earth. This is true equally of the social and the unsocial forms of life. Disobedience, however ignorant and unintentional, means death.[2]

The elevation of the individual, largely at the expense of his power of reproduction, seems to have been the greatest work of nature; this elevation being measured in terms of size, strength and activity of body and of brain.[3] Nature has always insisted upon this continuance of individuation, upon the necessity for each living creature to strengthen and develop itself as the price of life and prosperity. This has been accomplished mainly through the operation of the law of self-interest, of earned benefits. New and useful variations have been provided thus with the opportunity to grow and perpetuate themselves, and the consequences have been most important.

Later than the laws of the family and of adult life appears another great ethical principle, nature's great secondary law of self-sacrifice, the law of society, the law of mutual benefits; which is perhaps best expressed in the words: "Do unto others as ye would they should do unto you."[4] Far more and different qualities are required in an individual to fit him for life in a community than will suffice for welfare in

[1] Spencer, *Justice*, p. 60.

[2] Even among the simplest protoplasmic existences the operations of both these laws may be dimly traced. Adults must always give of their strength to their progeny, but the demands of the second law are as yet very small.

[3] See page 3.

[4] St. Matthew vii, 12, and St. Luke vi, 31.

isolation. The social being must not only care for himself, his own life and that of his mate and offspring, but he must help care for others also, his comrades, and in supplying his own wants must not interfere seriously with the like opportunity of others to supply their wants. Thus the liberty of each to develop and strengthen himself fully is limited by the necessity for a like liberty for all.[1] Without obedience to this law social life is an impossibility. Even the lowest social group has some needs in opposition to the self-regarding desires of its members singly; and thus two inexorable natural laws—the law of adult life providing for individuation, and the law of society providing for the social welfare—are apparently in direct antagonism, the one to the other. From the pressure of these laws upon each social group, and the adjustment of their antagonisms, results the criminal class, the creation of ever more numerous forms of crime, and the persistent increase of criminality upon the earth. The most civilized and progressive states have the most crime, and more crime as civilization increases; and this seeming multiplication of evil is not a sign of degeneration and decay, but of prosperity and upward growth to higher planes of life, of love, and mutual helpfulness.

Progress always means greater strength, actual or potential. This strength takes many forms, from purely physical to intellectual and moral forces. Throughout the ages progress has in the main taken the direction of increasing power to fight well; at any rate it is most easily measured in such terms. For long the gain was chiefly, almost entirely in physical strength, and at first all progress was enormously expensive. The shallow seas swarmed with microscopic life, which has left records of its existence throughout the rocks of our mountains, and in the coral reefs of ocean.

[1] Spencer, *Justice*, pp. 46, 60.

Myriads of undeveloped types perished. Practically helpless before external dangers, these low organisms were swept into destruction in whole groups by the crude natural forces around them. Some few survived for a season, growing strong through fortunate changes, in a more kindly environment. Of these, some learned gradually to modify their environment to meet their needs. A few have continued and prospered until now. Always development has been necessary; always growth into new strength has been demanded as the price of dominance upon the earth.

During the age of Reptiles the mastery went to creatures of great size and enormous physical strength, but with little intelligence. Natural selection seemed working along a low plane of individual self-interest. The first great primary law was shaping life and seemed to rule alone. But in united effort there is greater power than any gigantic brute can possess, and social life, with its mutual helpfulness against enemies and stimulation of mental development, became the prime requisite for success in the struggle for existence, the great means to the attainment of a higher, a more unselfish life. A higher type of strength was coming in, with boundless possibilities for the future along lines intellectual and moral. For with social life comes not only the development and the victory of intelligence and mutual aid over brutishness and self-sufficiency—it is also the beginning of the victory of altruism over selfishness, of the love of others over the love of self.

The most successful forms of life are gregarious; they have become social, and by the sharing of each other's dangers, joys and pains, have grown stronger, more intelligent, more loving. As intelligence develops, the period of youthful immaturity grows longer, the young are more helpless and need a more extended training, the demands of the primary law of self-sacrifice become larger and more exacting; but parental love cares for these things—obedience to this law of the family is so natural and customary that its neglect is rare. But the shield which social life casts around each individual member of the band preserves him in part, and more fully as life attains higher planes, from the immediate action of outer physical forces which have hitherto maintained the operation of the first great law—the law of earned benefits—securing the survival of the fittest. This fundamental rule of adult life is not abrogated, its strength is no wise lessened; but its immediate pressure is in part transferred from the individual to the social group. Thus society becomes, as it were, responsible to nature for the acts of all its members; for the danger immediately arises that the adult may no longer receive, in general, the good and evil consequences of his own character and conduct—that those ill fitted to live, and either negatively or positively harmful to the community, will be preserved, causing the weakening and final destruction of the body social, and the death of the individuals composing it.

Herds of wild horses or wild cattle are stronger than the strongest of the solitary beasts of prey. When united they will not only defend themselves successfully, but will even trample their enemy to death. Only when through fear, or some other cause, the group ranks are broken and mutual aid ceases, can the lion kill his victim.[1] Almost all that is best in life is cultivated directly by this communal living together, with its mutual helpfulness and mutual self-restraint. Society confers unnumbered benefits upon its members, but the individual must do his part; as more is given him, from him more is required. In a word, the social being must live up to a certain standard of right action; and since association has in part removed from him the pressure of crude

[1] Kropotkin, pp. 702–712.

natural forces, and these forces would now be utterly inefficient in producing the type of character requisite, society must itself compel its members to live up to this necessary standard at its peril, on pain of social and individual degeneration and destruction. This compulsion is fundamentally instinctive, and at first largely unreasoning, but it becomes with time a process distinctly willed and shaped by the social group. It is primarily, and for all time, an effort of nature to promote upward growth by a less wasteful process, using the awakened individual intelligence, combined with the inherited social instinct, to induce evolution from within the group, by encouraging useful variation from the average, thus producing the leader, and punishing harmful variation, —thus ultimately converting the mere malefactor into the criminal. Intelligent, educative, social selection is thus substituted more and more fully, by the workings of natural law, for the crude, destructive, physical selection which is at first exclusively dominant. Social pressure from within the group unites with the pressure from without to uplift and socialize the individual. One of the most important forms of this inner pressure is called among men criminal prosecution and punishment.

A social group is fundamentally a kindred group. Its members feel a resemblance among themselves, and a sense of safety and of pleasure develops. There is general likeness with individual variation. A social type is being formed. Divergence from this type is disliked, and antagonistic variation meets with conscious or unconscious persecution. "Relatively unintelligent though they are," writes Herbert Spencer, "inferior gregarious creatures inflict penalties for breaches of the needful restrictions, showing how regard for them has come to be unconsciously established as a condition to persistent social life. No higher warrant can be imagined," and therefore we may accept "the law of equal freedom as an ultimate ethical principle, having an authority transcending every other." [1]

Morality seems in its beginnings to have been social rather than individual,[2] a morality of action rather than a morality of motive. The moral act, the good act, is that which conduces to the social welfare. The good individual is he whose conduct aids his social group. Morals, ethics, Sitten (German) all mean habits, customs, established ways. The moral act was originally the customary act. Among the lower animals, which possess not the moral sense—the knowledge of what is right and wrong, and consciousness of power to choose between them—the customary act is that which has been enforced by nature's inexorable laws. It is a right choice for them, but they do not know that it is right. We find moral actions before a perception of what is moral. Good and bad are insisted upon by stern processes of selection, and destruction of those which do not grow aright, by laws of nature and nature's God. There are no mistakes here. Not until human society is reached, and the moral sense developed with higher intelligence, do acts become regarded and named as good and evil, right and wrong. It is then that mistakes begin to be made by the social group, the good being called bad, and punished, and the bad, good, and rewarded. Ultimately nature judges and

[1] Spencer, *Justice*, p. 61, and see Chapter II of this book. The claims of nature upon society, that the operation of its laws upon the individual must be maintained by human legislation, have often been recognized by the nations of mankind. As Sir Henry Sumner Maine well puts it: "The happiness of mankind is, no doubt, sometimes assigned, both in the popular and in the legal literature of the Romans, as the proper object of remedial legislation; but it is very remarkable how few and faint are the testimonies to this principle, compared with the tributes which are constantly offered to the overshadowing claims of the Law of Nature." *Ancient Law*, p. 79.

[2] "In ancient times," writes Maine, "the moral elevation and moral debasement of the individual appear to be confounded with, or postponed to, the merits and offences of the group to which the individual belongs." *Ancient Law*, p. 127.

chooses between social groups; those which obey her laws prospering, and those which disobey degenerating and disappearing from the earth. Even among savages "who make hatchets of stones and rub sticks for a fire," we can see, writes Tylor, "that morality and happiness belong together—in fact that morality is the method of happiness."[1] This is undoubtedly true of the lasting happiness of the social group, and in this low stage of social development, the happiness of the individual is most closely intertwined with the continued welfare of the horde to which he belongs.

But the morality necessary among such people is something very different, much lower, more crude and simple than that demanded among civilized nations.[2] The moral man among savages—the man possessing the type of character requisite for the performance of acts most useful to the social group—is the ferocious fighter, cruel and bloodthirsty, the man who insists on his right of personal vengeance for every fancied wrong, the despotic and brutal tyrant. Might makes right. The hero of the stone or bronze age would be the criminal of to-day. Early morality, early ideas of good and evil, were suited to the needs of the dark ages, were necessary for the uplifting of a low humanity to the next higher stage of development.

With increasing intelligence, and with growing interdependence of social life, there is a progressive enlargement of ethical view, and a widening and strengthening social demand that the individual shall live up to this higher morality, avoiding more and more actions seen to be socially harmful, and imitating more and more fully the growing ideal of the social type. For as Dr. James Martineau has well said:[3] The authoritative measure of our duty to our fellow men is (in every age) "the mutually understood ideal." "Only in

[1] Tylor, *Anthropology*, p. 408. [2] *Ibid.*, pp. 408–410.
[3] *Types of Ethical Theory*, ii, 121, 123.

proportion as men have come to understood concurrence on matters of right have they claims inter se."[1] The social mind has reached a certain estimate of conduct as good or bad, and the bad actions which the community punishes as wrongs against itself it calls crimes.

This is the explanation of crime and of the necessity for its punishment. Individual variations, actively antagonistic to the prevalent social type, exist in all the higher social groups. Commonly they are social laggards, who have not kept pace with the average development toward the social ideal. The rebellious social laggard is the true criminal; other laggards belong to the pauper class. Even the higher animal societies collectively punish the most dangerous anti-social acts. Much the same conduct, with a few additions, is punished by the lowest human societies now known upon the earth; and, as social life attains to higher planes, more and more actions become socially harmful, are generally recognized as such, and added to the list of crimes—that is, the list of actions which society punishes as wrongs against itself, for the sake of the general welfare, for the preservation of the social life, for the elevation of the individual toward the ideal of the social type.

Thus the production of crime and criminals is one of the saving processes of nature, substituting a lesser for a greater evil, promoting upward progress at a smaller cost. For if nature had not induced this increasingly severe social selection and pressure within the group, toward the elevation of the individual and the improvement of the type, then that primitive and unreasoning form of pressure from physical

[1] This sets bounds to the acts which are rightly criminal in each stage of evolution. Individuals may and do have a much higher estimate of good and bad, but until they convince society that their standard is the true one, crimes remain as before. The measure of a man's duty to society is fixed by the social estimate of good and evil; his duty towards God is co-extensive with his own ideal, and often goes far beyond the just claims of men upon him.

forces without the group, which always persists, must have continued alone in operation, destroying countless individuals and groups, without, if we may so express it, the attempt to educate them into the true lines of their upward development.

But it must not be thought that this social education consists solely, or even chiefly, in a process of persecution and punishment of noxious members of the community. It has a brighter and most important side in the instinctive admiration and imitation of natural leaders, strong individuals, like their fellows, only somewhat better representatives of the developing social type. These two great socializing tendencies—strong natural forces—the one of instinctive abhorrence and persecution, and the other of equally instinctive admiration and imitation, are present in all the higher social groups; they work together in absolute harmony, and along the line of progress they induce, social pressure becomes more and more strongly developed with increasing social evolution. This pressure is partly conscious and partly unconscious, in both directions, of praise or blame, of honor or persecution. The limits of the field of crime are largely coterminous with the extent of conscious persecution and punishment by the social group for wrongs against itself, and they are being extended continually with the progress of civilization.

The criminal is the man who obeys too completely the commands of nature's first primary law—the law of self-interest, of irresponsible self-development. Often he is the man of the uncurbed ages, when brute strength and unscrupulous cunning were more important, and persistent self-seeking more justifiable than now. The strongest always rules, and it is well for the world that it should rule, for the strongest is in general the best—the least bad where all now seem to us to have been very bad. But the nature of strength has changed, or rather, new and higher forms of strength have appeared continually, and this process will continue, higher strength being accompanied by a higher morality.

Throughout the chapters of this book evidence has been given to show how in every stage of human history the needed steps of progress, strengthening the social group, have resulted from the enforcement of new social prohibitions, creating new forms of crime and multiplying criminals. In Chapter III we have seen how the three great primitive crimes—treason, incest, evil-witchcraft—strike at the very life of society; the imperative necessity that such acts be punished; the instinctive abhorrence and passionate desire for vengeance felt by every normal member of the community; the speedy and often ferocious punishment. Later has appeared the necessity for the coming of the king, the great war leader, the expression of the unity of the people, who can do no wrong, and the wide extension of treason laws fostering his authority and securing his power.[1] A strong religious belief, binding the people firmly together in reliance upon the help of superhuman powers, is also a distinct military advantage. A powerful religious organization is in many ways a most important step in social progress. This is built up and maintained by the punishment of sin and heresy as crimes.[2]

The uniting of many little warring peoples, of the same or different races, into a strong nation has frequently resulted from the fusing and centralizing power of a victorious and mighty king, aided by a strong and proselyting Church. Even the best of religions has often been taught by the

[1] See page 61, and Chapter VI. "The first steps towards civilization can neither be taken nor maintained by primitive nations without the intervention of an energetic despotism." Waitz, *Anthropology*, p. 359.

[2] See Chapter VI, p. 134, *et seq.*

sword, and enforced upon unwilling peoples by criminal punishments. Thus the heathen Saxons of the continent were Christianized by Charlemagne, and the petty Anglo-Saxon kingdoms united into the English nation.[1] As Walter Bagehot has well shown, the greatest need of primitive peoples is law, strong law; it being much more important at first that the law should be strong than that it should be just. "Nation making is the occupation of man in these early ages, and it is war that makes nations;"[2] first war and subjugation, followed by strong law—mostly criminal law—and the fusing, unifying pressure of sure punishment for all rebels. Such work is cruel, but necessary, for it makes for the permanent uplift and strengthening of the human race. The stiff-necked individualism of primitive man had to be in large part crushed out of him, and this has always been the manner of its accomplishment, the way of human domestication and socialization. The process made many criminals.[3]

Robbery and theft, murder and homicide, are, as we have seen, not crimes among low savage races. How and why mankind has converted these acts into crimes as civilization developed, it is hoped that the reader already knows. Un-

[1] See also page 354.

[2] Bagehot, *Physics and Politics*, pp. 21, 25, 50, 77.

[3] See Chapter VI. After national unification and consolidation have been accomplished, all the great progressive modern nations have found it necessary to do away with criminal prosecution for conscience sake. Religious crimes have ceased in England, the United States, Germany, France, Italy and even in Spain; for it was found that the enforced weight of almost unchanging religious beliefs was crushing out all individuality, all hope of helpful variation and upward progress. Spain, France and Italy for many centuries continued the criminal prosecutions of the Inquisition, chose their crimes wrongly, and stunted their national growth by their own evil choices; for nature inexorably visited upon these nations the evils they had provided for themselves. But there is undoubtedly a strong argument to be made in favor of criminal punishment for religious offences during the early days of nation-making and the socializing of man.

doubtedly the criminalizing of such conduct greatly strengthened the nations, through increased security, confidence, and economic prosperity.

In modern times the great civilizations of the world have been taking a more and more industrial and democratic character. New life, upward growth, is largely in this direction. New forms of crime are mainly industrial and social. Laws of forgery and fraud and fraudulent bankruptcy, statutes creating new forms of theft, factory and mines acts, and other legislation of social guardianship, prevention of cruelty to children and animals, education laws, prohibitions of multitudinous little annoyances and damaging acts, the criminal prosecution of drunkenness—all such are manifestations of the rising standard of our recognized duty to our brother man, and are most influential in raising that standard still higher, and in stimulating the lagging members of the community to a more healthy, more social, more truly moral life. There is no doubt also that with the rapid spread of knowledge and development of intelligence, with the diffusion of practical Christianity and brotherly helpfulness among all classes, our civilized nations have grown stronger against foes without. Compare the armaments of the great nations of Europe and America with the war power of the uncivilized, laggard, and unprogressive nations of the world, and who can doubt this? No one who understands the facts can believe even in the possibility of a great Mohammedan invasion and conquest of Europe in modern times, and a few thousand European and American soldiers can capture and hold Pekin, the capital of China, and dictate terms to three hundred millions of people. Our strength is not to be expressed merely in guns, warlike equipment, and the wealth to provide more such. The men behind the guns, intelligent, patriotic, disciplined and mutually reliant—these are the major part of our strength, and they are the product of an era when there is more crime than in any past age, because more kinds of conduct are recognized now to be socially bad, and punished for the general uplift to a civilization still better, stronger and more moral.

Although the progressive welfare of the individual may be considered as the great end of life, yet the preservation and prosperity of the social group must take precedence of the preservation of the individual, for membership in a community is the chief means for his upward development and well-being. The occasional destruction of an individual, or even of many individuals, may be necessary for the welfare of the social group. Such losses may be inflicted by foes without through warfare, or they may be inflicted by the community upon itself through punishment. In either case society not only has the right but is in duty bound to sacrifice the individual for the general welfare. The death penalty for heinous crime is as justifiable, if society deem it necessary for its well-being, as is the demand upon the citizen-warrior to meet death upon the battle-field, or upon the doctor to remain steadfast at his duty in the plague-stricken city. The good of society is the prime reason for the punishment of criminals, and their reformation is justifiable only when it conduces to this end.

As an ethical standard, the law of adult life, if unlimited, certainly teaches the duty of the individual to grow strong by securing for his own use all possible good things of life, irrespective of the welfare of others—might making right. Nature's first limitation to this rule of selfishness is found in the imperative necessity for the care of offspring: a limitation enforced among the lower animals by insensate physical forces around them. The second great limitation is found only within social groups, and is enforced through the mediation of social beings, largely through social punishment.

We have, therefore, on the one hand, the great fundamental law of adult life—the law of self-support, self-interest and earned benefits—the necessity for continued individuation, the permanent good in physical strength, in independence and self-reliance, in courage even in isolation. The law of self-development is not negatived, scarcely even subordinated, but the sphere of its operations has been limited gradually by the working of nature's two great altruistic laws. Notice that these laws both conduce to the upward development and strengthening of the individual, and yet, with this higher evolution, especially in the intellectual and moral field, with the longer infancy and greater helplessness of childhood, with the increasing complexity of social life and differentiation of employments, the limitations which these altruistic laws put upon the operation of the rule of self-interest become ever greater, more extended and more imperative.

It is the old, old problem of the rights of the individual versus the welfare of society. Some liberty must be permitted, the individual must have the opportunity to grow, to develop his powers, individuation must continue. On the other hand, even in animal communities there are some restraints upon the noxious waywardness of individuals, and with higher evolution these social demands become ever more numerous, and society more sensitive to inner harms, more able and ready to punish for them. Not only does the criminal law cover an ever widening field of duties of the citizen to the state, and also to his fellowcitizens, because an injury to one becomes, and is recognized as being more and more an injury to all, but the duty of parents to children is defined and largely regulated by criminal statutes. Society is no longer contented with negative commands, it enjoins positive duties also;—not only, thou must not kill or cripple thy child or fellow-man, under penalty of punishment as a criminal; but also, thou must have thy children educated, thou must guard thy operatives in factory and mine from all unnecessary dangers. There must be a progressive equilibrium established between the rights of the individual and the needs of society, between a man's duty to himself and his duty to his fellow citizens. The rights of one must be balanced continually with the rights of all, for only in this way can persistent, yet conservative progress be assured.[1] The nation that does this is the nation that advances continually in civilization, strength, morality and leadership upon the earth.[2]

But this ever nicer adjustment of mutual rights and duties means constant friction, and constant education by new social prohibitions, increasing forms of crime, and inducing multitudinous acts of petty rebellion (*i. e.*, crimes) against society. For penal laws are not enacted and enforced unless the need for repression is recognized, and opposition will probably be more frequent in a community in proportion to its progressiveness, and to the extent of individual liberty enjoyed; that is, in proportion to the opportunity for variation and individuation in obedience to nature's great primary law of self-development. It takes time and hard pressure to convince men fond of freedom that conduct, until recently considered harmless, is bad and must be abandoned.

Nature thus compels nations to make selection of a progressive social education, and to enforce it by group pres-

[1] "Social necessities and social opinion are always more or less in advance of law. We may come indefinitely near to the closing of the gap between them, but it has a perpetual tendency to re-open. Law is stable; the societies we are speaking of are progressive. The greater or less happiness of a people depends on the degree of promptitude with which the gulf is narrowed." *Maine*, p. 24.

[2] Rome, the Teutonic States that succeeded to her heritage (see pp. 62–3), England, Germany and the United States all bear witness that the enduringly successful nations are those in which wise conservatism is infused with a little leaven of progressiveness—nations where individual liberty is so highly prized that a large and fitting sphere is secured for its development, as the price of union for the commonweal.

sure. A wise social education means strength, civilization, happiness, leadership; an unwise, means weakness, decadence, and national death. For nature chooses inexorably among the nations those which on the whole make for the uplift of mankind to better things—that is, nations which in the main serve God well, for God is served wherever man is bettered. The survival of the fittest means "the success of the most civilized, or of those who potentially at least represent humanity's progress."[1] The laws of nature are working out on large lines the good of all. Nations are the instruments, and those that do the work well prosper. Whether or not a nation is to prosper depends mainly upon its own choices—what type of man it holds up to honor and imitation, and what type it dislikes and punishes. Higher civilization implies increasing interdependence between man and man, the social body becomes more and more sensitive to little rights and wrongs, the kinds of conduct injurious to its welfare become more numerous, social prohibitions are multiplied. There are many new forms of crime, many new forms of evil, many new criminal acts recorded in the statistics.

Crime, therefore, results from the limitation of nature's law of self-interest by her altruistic laws. The anti-social individual who will not submit himself to these limitations, but insists upon acting in opposition to social necessity, he is the typical criminal. Increasing crime is a direct consequence of the enlarging spheres of operation of these two great ethical principles or laws, necessitating care for family and mutual helpfulness among fellow members of a community; in other words, it results from the growth of civilization, the development of knowledge, intelligence and social morality. The demands of a nobler fatherhood, of a grandly

[1] Washburn Hopkins, "England and the Higher Morality" *The Forum*, January, 1900.

widened sense of brotherhood, have resulted in a continued multiplication of social prohibitions, and an ever larger host of criminals, punished that society may grow aright, that true liberty may be secured to the great majority of citizens to develop their powers fully under the shield of law. Crime is the reaction against growing pressure toward a higher altruism, a larger mutual helpfulness, a nobler, stronger civilization. It is part of the price we are paying for this growth to better things.

Now at last we can see that that which the poet dreamed and longed for is true in very deed, for the goal of this great mass of evil, enlarging through the many centuries of social life upon the earth, is the goal of social welfare fore-ordained from the foundation of the world, it is the goal of human good.

> "Oh yet we trust that somehow good
> Will be the final goal of ill."

The giant, Humanity, has been at work, ever rolling an increasing weight of crime up the mountain of social progress. Sisyphus-like the task has seemed; for the ponderous mass has fallen back many, many times, wiping out the pathway made, so that portions of the work had all to be done anew.[1] But the steepest gradient will not be found near the top, and it is quite possible that the easier ascent is even now being attained by one or two of the most advanced nations.[2]

[1] In times of anarchy, like Stephen's reign in England, evil deeds cease to be punished, and cease even to be regarded as crimes. (See pp. 151–153.) Where forms of crime are wrongly chosen, as in Spain, Italy and France throughout the centuries of the Inquisition (see pp. 353–355), and national sickness and degeneration results, a return to health means that the conduct wrongly punished must have been made non-criminal, and the forms of crime proper for their stage of civilization substituted.

[2] The peculiar and new crimes of any era take the direction of greatest resistance to the new life of society. Given an understanding of the way in which a nation

is advancing toward its ideal, a statesman can recognize the early social promptings toward the creation of a new form of crime, and may introduce wise legislation looking toward this end, in time to meet half way the increasing demand for social punishment, thus advancing the nation along its true path without the severe suffering and friction, due to clashing interests, which have often been the forerunners of wise enlargements of the criminal code.

> "He who would win the name of truly great
> Must understand his own age and the next,
> And make the present ready to fulfill
> Its prophecy, and with the future merge
> Gently and peacefully, as wave with wave."—*Lowell.*

The wise lawmaker, by the initiation of needed criminal legislation, before social suffering makes the demand imperative, may do much to promote this peaceful blending of present and future along lines of true upward progress.

APPENDIX I

SPECIAL FORMS OF ENGLISH CRIME.

STEALING was punished from earliest historic times with greater severity than almost any other offence. "It is certain," writes Stephen, "that at every period some thefts were punished with death."[1] Yet at first it was not a crime, but a harm to an individual, which he might punish or not, as he chose, if he had the power, or could secure the aid of society in the prosecution of the offender. Even when theft in general had been made felony in England, many classes of things—important things—were regarded by common law as non-stealable, as late as the sixteenth century. Thus, land and things growing out of the earth could not be stolen, but only "movable personal property." Deeds, charters and instruments relating to real property could not be stolen, for such deeds were declared to "savour" of the realty, and were therefore excluded from the possibility of larceny. Only things possessing a definite value could be stolen, and "valuable" in early days "implied serious practical importance, as opposed to mere fancy or amusement."[2] Thus, many animals, such as peacocks, mastiffs, hounds, spaniels and tame goshawks, could not, it was calmly argued (19 Hen, VIII., p. 2, no. 11, 1528),[3] be subject to larceny "car ils sont proprement choses de plaisir plus que de profit." It was even thought "no felony to take a diamond, rubie, or other such stone (not set in gold or otherwise) because they be not

[1] Stephen, iii, 129.
[2] *Ibid.*. 143.
[3] See *Year-Books*.

of price with all men, howsoever some men do hold them both dear and precious."[1]

Upon such subjects the common law was very vague and uncertain. It was believed that a "fraudulent taking" was essential to larceny, and fraudulent breach of trust was not regarded as a crime until a very late date.[2] Thus, a servant, or any one intrusted with the management of property, was probably unable to make himself a criminal by its misappropriation.[3] At most, the offender was guilty of a civil wrong. But the legal decisions are contradictory, and "fraudulent convertion" was sometimes declared felony, and then again no-felony, by common law. Gradually a mass of statutes came into existence to supply omissions and correct defects,[4] which statutes were consolidated by a law of 1827, and again in 1861, by 24 and 25 Vic., c. 96.

Thus, in the development of English civilization, it has slowly become established: that theft is crime, rather than a mere tort; that documents and records relating to land, etc., can be stolen;[5] that a servant misappropriating his master's property, or a fraudulent trustee, is a criminal; that the man who takes timber or minerals from another's land without his consent is a thief, as is also the man who takes a valuable dog, peacock or precious stone. Many men have been, and are being punished as criminals for such offences—acts in opposition to new social prohibitions, created and enforced under the influence of increasing knowledge, intelligence and social morality.

Slave trading and slavery were stamped as crimes of the greatest enormity only after long agitation. We have seen

[1] See J. Hales, quoted by Stephen, iii, 143.

[2] Stephen, iii, 144.

[3] *Year-Books*, 1471 (49 Hen. VI, p. 14, no. 9, and 3 Hen. VII, p. 12, no. 9).

[4] For a list of such statutes see the repealing act (7 and 8 Geo. IV, c. 27), 1827.

[5] See (8 Hen. VI, c. 12, § 3) 1429, the first statute of this class.

how the business was considered thoroughly honorable in Elizabeth's days, and that the virgin queen herself shared in the profits of such expeditions. In 1786, one hundred and thirty ships, carrying 42,000 slaves, were engaged in this perfectly legitimate occupation. In 1787 was formed "The Society for the Suppression of the Slave Trade." In 1791 and 1798 the question of abolition was debated in Parliament, but the majority was opposed. Beginning with 1806, a series of acts rapidly changed slave-trading from a lawful business into a capital crime. These were, 46 Geo. III., sess. 2, c. 52, 1806; 47 Geo. III., sess. 1, c. 36, 1807; 51 Geo. III., c. 23, 1811; and several others, all consolidated in 5 Geo. IV., c. 113, which largely increased the number of acts punishable. A statute of 1837 (1 Vict., c. 81, § 1), removed the death penalty. The law had done its work. Slave trading had ceased.

Smuggling was everywhere prevalent along the English coasts during the latter half of the eighteenth and early nineteenth century, induced by the heavy taxes and great expansion of commerce. It was not a crime, despite severe laws against it, for it remained generally unpunished, and the public conscience approved of the traffic, until duties were largely reduced. Even Adam Smith expressed his sympathy with smugglers, and the nation supported them by buying their goods, and not enforcing the laws against them. The "free-trader was repaid if he saved one cargo out of three," and "he frequently saved all," and grew wealthy by his ventures.[1] Bands of armed smugglers "loaded waggons and pack-horses on the open beach, and met with no opposition from the customs officers." In half a year, "1835 horse loads of tea, and 1689 of wet and dry goods were safely landed on the Suffolk coast," while about "2000 hogsheads of spirit" were run annually "on the coasts of Hants, Dorset and Devon,

[1] See *Reports of Parliamentary Commission.*

where it took nine years for the customs officers to capture a like amount." When duties were reduced, the public no longer favored the traffic, and the marine police succeeded in punishing many of the smugglers and in practically suppressing their trade. This is a good instance of the determination of crime by the prevalent social standard of morality.

The robbery of ships in harbors and of stores in dock yards were common offences in the reign of George III., and were not successfully punished at first. There were "innumerable receivers" for the stolen goods, and "hardly any preventives" to such robbery, but the nation did not approve such deeds, and a more efficient police soon checked the evil.

Duelling was an "affair of honor," and certainly not a crime until the present century.[1] In 1830, the survivor in a duel was declared guilty of murder by two judges, and three years later the seconds were likewise declared to be criminals. The middle classes were becoming strongly opposed to this habit of the gentry, and juries were found willing to convict the principals, but not the seconds. About 1843 a society was formed for the abolition of duelling, and the evil practice received its death blow, when, in 1844, the articles of war imposed cashiering as a penalty for this offence.

Intervention in Foreign Hostilities. Private interference in foreign hostilities was not a crime until the nineteenth century. Public opinion highly favored soldiers of fortune, who sought military service at their pleasure.[2] Such conduct was first declared to be criminal by the American government, in acts of 1794 and 1818. England followed suit in 59 Geo. III., c. 69.

Rogues and Vagabonds. Laws against vagrancy were many

[1] But see *State Trials*, ii, 1034 and 1042, for a decree of the Star Chamber against duels, showing early attempt to repress.

[2] See Froissart's *Chronicles*.

in the eighteenth and early nineteenth centuries, and more and more actions have been included as misdemeanors of this class, until now, "any person of bad character who prowls about, apparently for an unlawful purpose, is likely to be treated as a rogue and a vagabond."[1] Probably such laws were still more inclusive in the middle ages, when they were largely decreed against desertion of work and residence, and attempts to raise wages, but the laws were not generally enforced. Now, we strive to punish only those "who really prefer idleness to parish relief," or honest work. The efforts to suppress such offenders by a vigorous police have greatly increased.[2]

Laws punishing *conspiracy in restraint of trade* have been the occasion of very bitter discussion in modern times. The great question at issue has been: Within what limits are trade unions justifiable? Freedom of trade is a new thing. For many centuries the regulation and limitation of industry was an important part of the duty of Parliament.[3] The "Combination Laws" are so many attempts, long persisted in, to make all combinations of laborers to raise wages criminal.[4] The later statutes practically decreed that a laborer may go where he pleases, and make the best individual bargain he can for his toil, but he must not aid in bringing the pressure of numbers either upon employers or his fellow workingmen. If he does this he becomes a criminal in the eyes of the law. Apparently the only freedom sought was freedom of employers from coercion by the employed; but in those days the franchise was very greatly restricted, and the upper and middle classes made these statutes, which were finally

[1] Stephen, iii, 274; for statutes see 17 Geo. II, c. 5; and 5 Geo. IV, c. 83, 1824.

[2] Stephen, iii, 275.

[3] See *Statutes of Laborers*, regulating wages, etc.

[4] See 2 and 3 Edw. VI, c. 15, 1548; the Consolidation Act (5 Eliz., c. 4), 1562; (7 Geo. I, st. 1, c. 13) 1720; and (40 Geo. III, c. 60) 18co; which last made the penalty imprisonment at hard labor for two months.

repealed in 1824–25. But, as the statute law was narrowed, the common law was expanded to fill its place, and judicial decisions against laborers reduced the liberty they expected from the repeal of the combination laws almost to nothing. Finally, an act of 1875 specially protected all "combinations in contemplation or furtherance of trade disputes,"[1] and the persistent attempts to make trade unions, as such, criminal, have failed.

A similar attempt, now very prominent in the United States, to make trust combinations, as such, criminal, is likewise doomed to failure; for both trade unions and trusts, despite the many evils connected with them, are necessary instruments in the upward growth of civilization. The aim should be wise legal regulation, not criminal suppression, which is indeed almost impossible.

[1] Stephen, iii, 227.

APPENDIX II

STATISTICS OF ENGLAND AND WALES.

THE statistics of indictable offences from 1853 to 1860 present a strange phenomenon. The totals mount from 29,359 in 1854, to an average of more than 53,000 in 1857–61, for the same classes of offenders. Does this great vault in the statistics really mean that the actual amount of these old crimes in England was multiplied suddenly in a like degree? The evidence does not warrant this conclusion. The great recorded increase falls wholly under the head of simple larceny, and was due to the enforcement of the Criminal Justice Act of 1855, which relates only to such offences.[1] Undoubtedly, social repression for acts of petty theft greatly increased at this time, but it seems impossible to believe that such conduct had not been truly criminal for many years previous. When death or transportation were the only legal penalties for a larceny of forty shillings, or even five shillings, such conduct may not have been crime, because society would not often inflict such punishments; but this was at the end of the eighteenth and beginning of the nineteenth century, and since then social pressure has been growing steadily stronger, as the following table reveals. It is most probable, therefore, that the great increase in the statistics for indictable offences in 1857 does not mean a corresponding growth in the actual amount of such crime among the people. The increase of delinquency came earlier, when various kinds of petty larceny and other offences were re-criminalized by society, after the introduction of milder penalties.

[1] See *Judicial Statistics*, 1857. Introduction, p. xiii.

TABLE SHOWING THE RAPID INCREASE OF CONVICTIONS AND PUNISHMENTS FOR CERTAIN OFFENCES AS THE PENALTIES BECAME LESS SEVERE.

Shooting at, Stabbing Wounding, etc.	Total Convicted.	Sentenced to Death.	Executed.	Transportation, Life to 7 yrs.	Penal Servitude.	Long term Imprisonment.	Six Months and under.
In the year 1817	26	26	12				
In the year 1827	35	35	6				
In the year 1837	41	36	0	2		3	
In the year 1847	118	4	0	42		72	
In the year 1857	208	9	0	11	58	130	
House-Breaking.							
In the year 1817	152	152	0				
In the year 1827	240	240	0				
In the year 1837	403	0	0	294		109	
In the year 1847	506	0	0	172		334	
In the year 1857	568	0	0	10	171	387	
Simple Larceny.							
In the year 1817	6,420	0	0	1,300		935	4,047
In the year 1827	8,358	0	0	1,897		1,141	5,152
In the year 1837	10,409	0	0	1,877		916	7,546
In the year 1847	12,778	0	0	1,180		992	10,577
In the year 1857	5,793[1]	0	0	3	783	1,232	3,614
Forgery, etc.							
In the year 1817	62	62	18				
In the year 1827	46	46	4				
In the year 1837	42	0	0	31		11	
In the year 1847	121	0	0	40		81	
In the year 1857	184	0	0	6	80	93	2

The very small totals of commitments for all indictable offences in the early years of the nineteenth century (4,605 in 1805), points to the de-criminalizing of many forms of evil conduct, and a corresponding decrease in the actual amount of the nation's crime. The growth of intelligence and humanity among the English people seems to have been directly responsible for this decrease, contrary to the general

[1] This does not include the many thousands convicted by Courts of Summary Jurisdiction, under the Criminal Justice Act of 1855, but shows the decreased use of the higher courts for the trial of such offenders.

trend of the evidence and argument of this book. The explanation is simple. The nation demanded more righteous penalties, deeming the punishment of death, or even transportation for minor crimes, greater evils than the acts themselves. There was strong evidence—as shown in Chapter XI.—that many offences, "not of atrocious nature," but punishable with death, were "never brought under the review of magistrates at all," so great was the reluctance to prosecute. Among the evil acts very rarely punished, Judge Colquhoun mentioned shoplifting and various other larcenies, forgery, housebreaking in the daytime, highway robbery, horse, cattle and sheep stealing, burglary without entering the house, acts of violence on the person, frame breaking, and various other minor offences. Many of these evil acts had doubtless ceased to be crimes from lack of social punishment. Some of them, we are told, were fast losing in the public mind the idea of evil formerly associated with them. This is interesting and important as showing the rapid lowering of the social standard of morality, when acts rightly criminal are no longer punished as crimes; and if this be true, its counterpart appeals even more strongly and naturally for our belief, namely, that the enforcement of new and wise social prohibitions is very influential in elevating the moral standard of the lower masses of the people. The English nation was not powerless to arrest and punish dangerous malefactors, as the death penalties for murder (see page 260), and the convictions for burglary[1] abundantly prove, but it deliberately chose to leave many of its laws unenforced for a time, rather than that minor evils should be punished too severely under existing criminal statutes. It did not attempt to substitute lynch law, for that is practically never used for minor offences.

[1] Total convictions for burglary in the years—

1817	1827	1837	1847	1857
374	368	232	346	473

Passive opposition to the enforcement of the cruel laws, and urgent recommendations for change were the means employed. The rapid increase of social prosecution and punishment for old offences of wounding, forgery, housebreaking, and various kinds of simple larceny, from 1817 to 1857, as less severe penalties were legalized, is strong evidence that these acts were not really crimes at the beginning of the nineteenth century, when the total of all punishments for indictable offences was very small indeed.

One of the most striking characteristics of the old judicial statistics was the inclusion among serious crimes of a great mass of acts of petty larceny, and other minor offences against property, while many forms of even serious violence against the person remained unnoticed and unpunished. This would indicate that the social conscience condemned one of these two great classes of evil acts much more strongly than the other, and history proves that this was so. Even most desperate attacks upon the person, including worst attempts to commit murder, were not declared serious crimes until 1803, and this law was again greatly extended in 1829 and 1861; while common assaults were regarded as so highly natural, and occurred so frequently unpunished, that the English people were thoroughly hardened to them, and certainly did not think of them as crimes until long after 9 Geo. IV., c. 31, 1829, which for the first time made such conduct legally punishable by fine and imprisonment, on conviction before justices of the peace. In the same year the metropolitan police force was established, and seven years later, in 1836, the borough police; but it was not until 1857, by 19 and 20 Vic., c. 69, that the establishment of a disciplined police force was made compulsory throughout all the counties of England and Wales. The nation thus greatly increased its ability to arrest and prosecute for minor acts of evil, as well as for more heinous offences. Meanwhile the methods of procedure in the criminal courts were being greatly simplified. In the *Judicial Statistics* for 1857–58 (page V.) we read: "From year to year the jurisdiction of justices has been enlarged, important classes of offenders have been added," but "no previous attempt has been made to show in any connected form the nature and amount of the summary proceedings in criminal matters, a large branch of the administration of justice which begins and ends as a police proceeding. All that has heretofore been known of these *now* very important adjudications has been from prison returns, in which the actual numbers committed only have been shown. The summary jurisdiction of justices, that is, the power to adjudicate at once and punish without the intervention of a jury, *has received very great extension within the last few years.*"

The old means of social repression and punishment in England had become more and more painfully unfit to meet the needs of the developing industrial civilization. Society would take great pains, and incur great expense oftentimes, to apprehend and convict a murderer, but on account of the great difficulty of bringing minor malefactors to justice, busy people thought it almost better to let them escape, unless caught in the act, than to spend so much time, energy and money in securing their punishment. The times were ripe for reform, and the statutes which made compulsory an organized police force, and greatly widened the powers of courts of summary jurisdiction, contained also many new social prohibitions. By such means there was made possible a repression of minor acts of evil, such as had been undreamed of hitherto. In the police returns for 1857, the first year of the enlarged judicial statistics, "the offence first in magnitude is assault." There were 60,695 common assaults, and 12,750 assaults on peace officers. The work of the trained police force induced these last offences, and the faithful performance of police duty resulted in the arrest and prosecution of these 60,695 other peace-breakers, who would otherwise have remained for the most part unpunished. In that same year 75,859 persons were prosecuted for drunkenness; under local acts and by-laws, 21,112; under police acts, 25,913; and under wilful damage and trespass, 13,583. Until 1847, juvenile offenders were punishable as severely as hardened criminals, and transported or imprisoned with them; but because of the terrible severity of the laws, bad children were probably permitted to escape, for the most part. In other words, children could hardly make themselves criminals, by their evil actions. In our day the number of such criminals is very large, because reformatory penalties have induced social prosecution.

BIBLIOGRAPHY

(A partial bibliography, mostly of books and magazine articles referred to in the notes.)

FIRST PART

Ancient Law, Animals and Savage Men.

(CHAPTERS I–IV INCLUSIVE)

Alcedo, A. de. *Geographical and Historical Dictionary of America,* etc. From the Spanish, with large additions by G. A. Thompson. London, 1812.

Angas, G. F. *Savage Life and Scenes in Australia and New Zealand.* London, 1847.

Austin, John. *Lectures on Jurisprudence.* London, 1869.

Bagehot, Walter. *Physics and Politics.* London, 1872.

Bailey, J. "Wild Tribes of the Veddahs in Ceylon." *Transactions of the Ethnological Society, N. S.* Vol. ii. London, 1863.

Bancroft, H. H. *Native Races of the Pacific States.* New York and San Francisco, 1874–82.

Barrow, Sir John. *Travels into the Interior of Southern Africa.* London, 1801.

Bastian, Adolf. *Der Mensch in der Geschichte.* Leipzig, 1860.

Beccaria, C. B. (Marquis) of Milan. *An Essay on Crimes and Punishments.* Dublin, 1767.

Beecham, John. *Ashantee and the Gold Coast.* London, 1841.

Bell, John. *Travels from St. Petersburgh to Divers Parts of Asia.* Edinburgh, 1788.

Bonwick, J. *Daily Life and Origin of the Tasmanians.* London, 1870.

Boyle, Frederick. *Adventures among the Dyaks of Borneo.* London, 1865.

Brehm, A. E. *Merveilles de la Nature.* Paris, 1891.

Brett, W. H. *Indian Tribes of Guiana.* London, 1852.

Brooke, Charles. *Ten Years in Sarawak.* 1866.

Bruce, James. *Travels to Discover the Source of the Nile.* Edinburgh, 1805.

Brunner, Heinrich. *Deutsche Rechtsgeschichte.* Leipzig, 1887–92.

Burton, R. F. *Pilgrimage to El-Medineh and Meccah.* London, 1857.

Burton, R. F. *City of the Saints and Across the Rocky Mountains to California.* London, 1862.

Burton, R. F. *Lake Regions of Central Africa.* London, 1860.

Burton, R. F. *Mission to Gelele, King of Dahome.* London, 1864.

Campbell, Sir John. *Wild Tribes of Khondistan.* London, 1864.

Catlin, George. *Letters, etc., on the North American Indian.* Philadelphia, 1857.

Cherry, R. R. *The Growth of Criminal Law in Ancient Communities.* London, 1890.

Codrington, R. H. "Social Regulations in Melanesia." *Journal of the Anthropological Institute.* London, 1889.

Collins, David. *An Account of the English Colony of New South Wales.* London, 1798.

Cook, Capt. James. *First Voyage.* Edited by W. Wharton. London, 1893.

Copway, G. (Indian chief.) *History of the Ojibway Nation.* Boston, 1850.

Crantz, David. *History of Greenland.* London, 1767.

Crawford, John. *History of the Indian Archipelago.* Edinburgh, 1820.

Crawley, A. E. "Sexual Taboo." *Journal Anthropological Institute.* London, 1895.

Curr, E. M. *The Australian Race.* Melbourne, 1886.

Dalton, E. T. *Descriptive Ethnology of Bengal.* Calcutta, 1872.

Dalzel, Archibald. *History of Dahomy.* London, 1793.

Danks, B. "Marriage Customs of the New Britain Group." *Jour. Anth. Inst.* London, 1889.

De Butts, Lieut. *Rambles in Ceylon.* London, 1841.

Dobrizhoffer, Martin. *History of the Abipones.* London, 1822.

Dorsey, J. Owen. "Omaha Sociology." *Smithsonian Institute Reports.* Bureau of Ethnology. Vol. iii. 1884.

Drury, Robert. *Madagascar.* London, 1831.

Du Chaillu, P. B. *A Journey to Ashango Land.* London, 1867.

Earl, G. W. *Native Races of the Indian Archipelago: Papuans.* London, 1853.

Earl, G. W. *Kolff's Voyages of the Dourga.* London, 1840.

Earl, G. W. *The Eastern Seas.* London, 1837.

Ellis, William. *Polynesian Researches.* London, 1859.

Ellis, William. *History of Madagascar.* London, 1838.

Elmira Reformatory, Year-Books of.

Encyclopædia Britannica. Ninth Edition. Edinburgh.

Encyclopædia of Law. American and English. 1898.

Evans, E. P. *Evolutional Ethics and Animal Psychology.* New York, 1898.

Falkner, T. *A Description of Patagonia.* Hereford, 1774.

Ferre, E. "Evoluzione dell' Omicidio." *Archivio di Psichiatria.* Vol. iii. Torino, 1882.

Fitz Roy, Admiral Robert. *Voyages of Adventurer and Beagle.* London, 1839.

Forbes, F. E. *Dahomey and the Dahomans.* London, 1851.

Forsyth, Capt. James. *The Highlands of Central India.* London, 1871.

Franklin, Sir John. *Narrative of a Journey to the Shores of the Polar Sea.* London, 1823.

Gardiner, A. T. *Narrative of a Journey to the Zoolu Country.* London, 1836.
Godden, G. M. "Nágá and Other Frontier Tribes of North-East India." *Jour. Anth. Inst.* London, 1897.
Grey, Sir George. *Journals of Two Expeditions in Australia.* London, 1841.
Grieve, James. *History of Kamtschatka.* Glocester, 1764.
Griffith, William. *Journals of Travels in Assam*, etc. Calcutta, 1847.
Guzman, D. Alonzo Enr. de. *Life and Acts.* (1518 to 1543.) London, 1862.
Haddon, A. C. "Western Tribe of Torres Straits." *Jour. Anth. Inst.* London, 1890.
Hall, Capt. Charles T. *Life with the Esquimaux.* London, 1864.
Harkness, Capt. H. *Description of a Singular Aboriginal Race*, etc. London, 1832.
Hearn, W. E. *The Aryan Household.* London, 1879.
Hodgson, B. H. *On the Aborigines of India; Kocch, Bodo and Dhimal Tribes.* Calcutta, 1847.
Hodgson, B. H. *Journal of Asiatic Society of Bengal.* Vol. xv.
Holmes, O. W., Jr. *The Common Law.* Boston, 1881.
Humboldt, A. von. *Travels to the Equinoctial Regions of America.* London, 1853.
Hunter, W. W. *Annals of Rural Bengal.* London, 1868.
James, William. *Principles of Psychology.* New York, 1890.
Jones, Peter. (Indian chief.) *History of the Ojibway Indians.* London, 1861.
Journal of the Ethnological Society, N. S. London.
Jubbulpore Expedition, Report of the Ethnological Committee of. Nagpore, 1868.
Kane, Paul. *Wanderings of an Artist among Indians of North America.* London, 1859.
Keating, Wm. H. *Expedition to Source of St. Peter's River.* London, 1825.
Kolbe, Pierre. *Déscription du Cap de Bonne-Espérance.* Amsterdam, 1743.
Kropotkin, P. A. "Mutual Aid among Animals." *The Nineteenth Century.* Vol. xxviii. 1890.
Krusenstern, Capt. A. J. von. *Voyage Round the World.* London, 1813.
Lang, G. S. *The Aborigines of Australia.* Melbourne, 1865.
Lichtenstein, Henry. *Travels in Southern Africa.* London, 1812–15.
Lindt, J. W. *Picturesque New Guinea.* London, 1887.
Livingstone, David. *Missionary Travels and Researches in South Africa.* London, 1857.
Lombroso, Cesare. *Archivio di Psichiatria.* Torino.
Lombroso, Cesare. *L'Homme Criminel.* Paris, 1887.
Low, Hugh. *Sarawak.* London, 1848.
Lubbock, Sir John. *Prehistoric Times.* London, 1869.
Lubbock, Sir John. *Origin of Civilization.* New York, 1874.
Lubbock, Sir John. *Ants, Bees and Wasps.* New York, 1882.
Lumholtz, C. S. *Among Cannibals.* London, 1889.
MacDonald, Arthur. *Criminology.* New York, 1892.

Macdonald, J. "Manners, Customs, etc., of South African Tribes." *Jour. Anth. Inst.* London, 1890.
MacGahan, J. A. *Campaigning on the Oxus.* New York, 1874.
Macpherson, Lieut. *Report on the Konds of Ganjam and Cuttock.* Calcutta, 1842.
Maine, Sir H. S. *Ancient Law.* London, 1870.
Malcolm, Sir John. *A Memoir of Central India.* London, 1824.
Malcolm, Sir John. *Transactions of the Royal Asiatic Society.* Vol. i. London.
Marchi, E. "La Delinquenza negli Animali." *Archivio di Psichiatria,* etc. Vol. xix. Torino, 1898.
Marsden, William. *History of Sumatra.* London, 1783.
Marshall, Lieut.-Col. W. E. *A Phrenologist among the Todas.* London, 1873.
Martin, John. *An Account of the Natives of the Tonga Islands.* London, 1817.
Mason, F. "Dwellings, Works of Art and Laws of the Karens." *Journal of the Asiatic Society of Bengal.* Vol. xxxvii, Pt. ii. Calcutta.
Mason, F. "Physical Character of the Karens." *Ibid.* Vol. xxxv, Pt. ii.
Mathew, John. "The Australian Aborigines." *Journal of the Royal Society of New South Wales.* Vol. xxiii. 1889.
May, J. W. *The Law of Crimes.* Boston, 1893.
Michie, Alex. *Siberian Overland Route.* London, 1864.
Mitchell, H. W. *The Evolution of Life.* New York, 1891.
Morgan, C. Lloyd. *Animal Life and Intelligence.* Boston, 1891.
Morgan, L. H. *Ancient Society.* New York, 1878.
Morgan, L. H. *League of the Iroquois.* Rochester, 1851.
Muccioli, Alessandro. "Degenerazione e Criminalitá nei Colombi." *Archivio di Psichiatria,* etc. Vol. xiv. Torino.
Nansen, F. *The First Crossing of Greenland.* London, 1890.
Pallas, P. S. *Travels through the Southern Provinces of the Russian Empire.* London, 1802–3.
Parkman, Francis. *Jesuits in North America.* Boston, 1874.
Parkyns, Mansfield. *Life in Abyssinia.* London, 1853.
Perelaer, M. T. H. *Ethnographische Beschrijving der Dajaks.* 1870.
Petroff, Ivan. "Report on the Population of Alaska." *United States Census* (10th), 1880.
Pinkerton, John. *A General Collection of Voyages and Travels.* London, 1808–14.
Powell, J. W. "Wyandotte Government." *First Annual Report of the Bureau of Ethnology.* Washington, 1881.
Prescott, W. H. *Conquest of Mexico.* New York, 1855.
Prescott, W. H. *Conquest of Peru.* New York, 1855.
Reade, W. W. *Savage Africa.* London, 1864.
Rochefort, C. C. de. *Histoire Naturelle et Morale des Iles Antilles de l'Amérique.* Rotterdam, 1658.
Romanes, G. J. *Mental Evolution in Animals.* London, 1885.

Rousseau, J. J. *Le Contrat Social.* Paris.

Rowlatt, Lieut. E. A. "Report of an Expedition into the Mishmee Hills." *Journal of the Asiatic Society of Bengal.* Vol. xiv. Calcutta.

Schoolcraft, H. R. *Indian Tribes of the United States.* Bureau of Indian Affairs. Philadelphia, 1853–6.

Science of Man. (Journal.) May 22d, 1889. Sidney, Australia.

Scouler, John. "Indian Tribes Inhabiting the Northwest Coast of America." *Journal of the Ethnological Society.* Vol. i. London, 1848.

Shooter, Joseph. *The Kafirs of Natal and the Zulu Country.* London, 1857.

Sibree, James, Jr. *Madagascar and Its People.* London, 1870.

Smith, E. R. *The Araucanians.* London, 1855.

Southey, Robert. *History of Brazil.* London, 1822.

Spencer, B., and Gillan, F. J. *The Native Tribes of Central Australia.* London, 1899.

Spencer, Herbert. *Descriptive Sociology.* New York, 1873–81.

Spencer, Herbert. *Principles of Biology.* New York, 1898.

Spencer, Herbert. *Principles of Ethics.* New York, 1892.

Spencer, Herbert. *Principles of Sociology.* New York, 1883–97.

Spix, J. B. von, and Martius, C. F. P. von. *Travels in Brazil.* London, 1824.

Sproat, G. M. *Scenes and Studies of Savage Life.* London, 1868.

Steinmetz, S. R. *Ethnologische Studien zur ersten Entwicklung der Strafe.* Leiden, 1894.

Stewart, Lieut. R. "Notes on Northern Cachar." *Journal of the Asiatic Society of Bengal.* Vol. xxiv. Calcutta.

Thompson, George. *Travels and Adventures in Southern Africa.* London.

Thomson, A. S. *The Story of New Zealand.* London, 1859.

Tod, Lieut.-Col. James. *Travels in Western India.* London, 1839.

Tod, Lieut.-Col. James. *Annals and Antiquities of Rajasthan.* London, 1829.

Tregear, E. "The Maoris of New Zealand." *Jour. Anth. Inst.* London, 1890.

Tuckey, Capt. J. K. *Narrative of an Expedition to Explore the River Zaire.* London, 1818.

Turner, George. *Samoa.* London, 1884.

Tylor, Edward B. *Anthropology.* New York, 1888.

United States Census. 1890.

Vega, Garcilasso de la. *First Part of the Royal Commentaries of the Yncas.* (1609). London, 1869–71.

Waitz, Theodor. *Anthropologie der Natur-Völker.* Leipzig, 1862.

Waitz, Theodor. *Introduction to Anthropology.* London, 1863.

Wake, C. S. *Evolution of Morality.* London, 1878.

Warren, W. W. "History of the Ojibways." *Collections of the Minnesota Historical Society.* Vol. v. 1885.

Westermarck, Edward. *The History of Human Marriage.* London, 1891.

Williams, T., and Calvert, J. *Fiji and the Fijians.* New York, 1859.

Winterbottom, T. M. *Account of the Native Africans in the Neighborhood of Sierra Leone.* London, 1803.

Wyndham, W. T. "Aborigines of Australia."

Zurita, Al. de. *Rapport sur les différentes Classes de Chefs de la Nouvelle Espagne.* Paris, 1840.

SECOND PART

THE ARYAN RACES OF EUROPE

(CHAPTERS V TO XV INCLUSIVE)

Accounts and Papers. English Public Documents.

Adams, H. (editor). *Essays in Anglo-Saxon Law.* Boston, 1876.

Alonzo, Giuseppe. "Maffi." *Archivio di Psichiatria.* Vol. vi. Torino, 1885.

Amos, Sheldon. *The History and Principles of the Civil Law of Rome.* London, 1883.

Anglo-Saxon Chronicle. Edited by B. Thorpe. London, 1861.

Annual Register. London, 1819–20.

Bacon, Sir Francis. *Works.* 10 vols. London, 1803.

Barrows, S. J. "New Crimes and Penalties." *The Forum.* New York, Jan., 1900.

Baxter, Richard. *An Abridgment of Mr. Baxter's History of his Life and Times.* London, 1713.

Benedict, of Peterborough. *Gesta Regis Henrici Secundi,* etc. (1169–1192). London, 1867.

Besant, Walter. *Fifty Years Ago.* London, 1887.

Block, Maurice. *L'Europe Politique et Sociale.* Paris, 1892.

Bosco, A. *Sulla Statistica della Delinquenza in vari Stati d' Europa.* Roma, 1898.

Bracton, Henricus de. *De Legibus et Consuetudinibus Angliae.* Edited by Sir Travers Twiss. London, 1879.

Brinkerhoff, R. *Prevention of Crime.* Circular No. I. Board of State Charities, Columbus, Ohio.

Britton. *Ancient Pleas of the Crown.* Nichol's Edition. Oxford, 1865.

Burnett, Bishop Gilbert. *History of the Reformation of the Church of England.* Oxford, 1829 and 1865.

Cæsar, C. Julius. *Commentarii de Bello Gallico.*

Cicero, M. Tullii. *De Legibus, De Re Publica, De Oratore, In Verrem.* Lipsiæ, 1855–1863.

Clarenden, Edward, Earl of. *The History of the Rebellion and Civil Wars in England.* Oxford, 1704.

Clarenden, Edward, Earl of. *State Papers.* Collected by the Earl of Clarendon. Oxford, 1767.

Coke, Edward. *Institutes of the Laws of England.* London, 1797.

Corpus Juris Civilis: Institutiones et Digesta. Berolini, 1899.

Craik, G. L., and MacFarlane, Charles. *The Pictorial History of England.* London, 1849.

Cummin, Patrick. *A Manual of Civil Law.* London, 1865.
Doddington, George Bubb. *The Diary of the Late,* etc. London, 1823.
Domesday Book. London, 1783–1816.
Du Boys, Albert. *Histoire de Droit Criminel des Peuples Anciens,* etc. Paris, 1845.
Durkheim, Émile. *Les Règles de la Méthode Sociologique.* Paris, 1895.
Eadmer. (Eadmeri Monachi Cantuariensis.) *Historiæ Novorum in Anglia.* (1066–1122.) Londini, 1623.
Ellis, Havelock. *The Criminal.* London, 1892.
Encyclopædia Britannica. "The Inquisition." Edinburgh.
Ferri, Enrico. *Criminal Sociology.* New York, 1896.
Florence of Worcester. (Florentii Wigorniensis.) *Chronicon ex Chronicis.* Londini, 1848–9.
Freeman, E. A. *The Norman Conquest.* Oxford, 1870.
Fuller, Thomas. *The Church History of Britain.* London, 1842.
Gellius, Aulus. *Noctium Atticarum.* Libri xx. Lipsiæ, 1871.
Giddings, Franklin H. *Principles of Sociology.* New York, 1896.
Giffin, Sir Robert. *Growth of Capital.* London, 1889.
Glanville, Ranulph de. *Tractatus de Legibus,* etc. London, 1673, Translated by John Beames, London, 1812.
Goodwin, Frederick. *The Twelve Tables.* London, 1886.
Green, J. R. *The Making of England.* London, 1885.
Green, J. R. *The History of the English People.* London.
Gummere, F. B. *Germanic Origins.* New York, 1892.
Hale, Sir Mathew. *The History of the Pleas of the Crown.* Philadelphia, 1847.
Hallam, Henry. *Constitutional History of England.* London, 1854.
Hamilton, A. H. A. *History of Quarter Sessions.* London, 1878.
Hawkins, William. *A Treatise of the Pleas of the Crown.* London, 1824.
Henry of Huntingdon. (Henrici Huntendunensis.) *Historia Anglorum.* London, 1848 and 1879.
Hobart, Sir Henry. *The Reports of that Reverend and Learned Judge,* etc. London, 1678.
Hoegel, Hugo. "Vergleichende Ubersicht der Statistik der Strafzumessung (etc.) in Oesterreich." *Statistische Monatschrift.* 25 Neue Folge 4. Wien, 1899.
Howell, T. B. *State Trials.* (1163–1820.) London, 1809–28.
Hudson, William. *A Treatise on the Court of Star Chamber.* In *Collectanea Juridica.* Vol. ii. London, 1792.
Ihering, Rudolf von. *Vorgeschichte der Indoeuropäer.* Leipzig, 1894.
Jonnès, Alex. M. de. *Statistique de L'Espagne.* Paris, 1834.
Johnson's Universal Cyclopædia. "The Inquisition." New York, 1898.
Judicial Statistics of England and Wales.
Judicial Statistics of Ireland.
Judicial Statistics of Scotland.
Kemble, J. M. *The Saxons in England.* London, 1876.

Kovalevsky, M. *Modern Customs and Ancient Laws of Russia.* London, 1891
Lappenburg, J. M. *England Under the Anglo-Saxon Kings.* London, 1845.
Latro, Porcius. *Declamatio contra Catilinam.* In *Gai Salusti Crispi*, etc. Vol. i. Basiliæ, 1852.
Letourneau, Charles. *L'Evolution Juridique.* Paris, 1891.
Lingard, John. *A History of England.* London, 1825.
Lombroso, C., and Ferrero, E. G. *The Female Offender.* New York, 1895.
Luttrell, Narcissus. *A Brief Historical Relation of State Affairs from Sept., 1678, to April, 1714.* Oxford, 1857.
Mackenzie, J. S. *Manual of Ethics.* London, 1894.
Magna Charta. *The Great Charter.* Edited by Wm. Blackstone. Oxford, 1759.
Maitland, F. W. *Domesday Book and Beyond.* Cambridge, 1897.
Maitland, F. W., and Pollock, F. *History of English Law.* Cambridge, 1895.
Martineau, James. *Types of Ethical Theory.* Oxford, 1885.
May, T. E. *The Constitutional History of England.* New York, 1874.
Mayo-Smith, Richmond. *Statistics and Sociology.* New York, 1895.
Mayo-Smith, Richmond. *Statistics and Economics.* New York, 1899.
Mears, T. Lambert. *The Institutes of Gaius and Justinian.* London, 1882.
Mirrour of Justices. Edited by W. J. Whittaker. Seldon Society Publications. London, 1895.
Mulhall, M. G. *Dictionary of Statistics.* London, 1892.
Neal, Daniel. *The History of the Puritans.* London, 1822.
Northumberland. Three Early Assize Rolls for. Surtees Society Publications. Durham, 1891.
Ortolan, J. L. E. *Explication Historique des Instituts.* Paris, 1870.
Pike, L. O. *History of Crime in England.* London, 1873–6.
Plini, C. (Secundi.). *Naturalis Historiae.* Lipsiæ, 1878.
Ranke, Leopold von. *A History of England Principally in the Seventeenth Century.* Oxford, 1875.
Report on Forgery from the Select Committee on the Criminal Law of England. 1824.
Riley, H. T. *Memorials of London and London Life.* (1276–1419.) London, 1868.
Rogers, J. E. Thorold. *Six Centuries of Work and Wages.* New York, 1884.
Rotuli Parliamentorum. London.
Rushworth, John. *Historical Collections.* 8 vols. London, 1659–1700. 5 vols. London, 1680–92.
Schoell, Rudolfus. *Leges Duodecim Tabularum Reliquæ.* Lipsiæ, 1866.
Select Pleas of the Crown. Edited by F. W. Maitland. London, 1888–9.
Seignobos, Charles. *Political History of Europe since 1814.* Edited by S. M. Macvane. New York, 1900.
Statesman's Year Books. London.
Statistico Italiano. Annuario. Roma.
Statistik des Deutschen Reichs. Especially Vols. 1888, 1893, 1896–1898.

Statistique de la France. Annuare. 1892–94. Paris.

Statistique de la Justice Criminelle en France. Especially Vols. 1880–81 *et seq.*

Statutes of the Realm of England. Folio edition. 1819.

Stephen, Sir James F. *History of the Criminal Law of England.* London, 1883.

Strype, John. *Annals of the Reformation in the Church of England,* etc. London, 1728.

Strype, John. *Memorials of Thomas Cranmer.* Oxford, 1812.

Strype, John. *The History of the Life and Acts of Edmund Grindal.* London, 1710.

Strype, John. *The Life and Acts of Mathew Parker.* Oxford, 1821.

Stubbs, William. *Constitutional History of England.* Oxford, 1887–91.

Stubbs, William. *Select Charters.* Oxford, 1884.

Suetonius, C. *De Vita Cæsarum.* Liber vi. *Nero.* Lipsiæ, 1877.

Tacitus, Cornelius. *Annales.* London, 1872.

Tacitus, Cornelius. *Germania.* London, 1889.

Thorpe, Benjamin (Editor). *Ancient Laws and Institutions of England.* London, 1840.

Thurloe, John. *A Collection of the State Papers of John Thurloe, Esq.* London, 1742.

Traill, H. D. (Editor). *Social England.* New York, 1897.

Walpole, Horace. *Memoirs of the Last Ten Years of the Reign of George the Second.* London, 1822.

William of Malmsbury (Willelmi Malmesbiriensis). *Gesta Regum Anglorum.* Londini, 1840.

William of Newburgh (Willelmi de Newburgh). *Historia Rerum Anglicarum.* Londini, 1856.

Williams, Piere. *Reports of Cases in the High Court of Chancery.* London, 1787.

Year Books of the Reigns of Edward I. and Edward III. Edited and Translated by A. J. Horwood and L. O. Pike. London, 1866–1885.

INDEX

[Numbers refer to pages.]

TABLE OF ERRATA.

Page 2, line 11. For a new crime, read a new form of crime.
Page 5, line 1. For become, read became.
Page 31, line 6. For second, read third.
Page 31, note. Omit the words Civilization Through.
Page 107, last line. For 17th century, read 16th century.
Page 120, line 6. For dint, read duit.
Page 121, line 30. For Ephors, read Ephetae.
Page 128, note 3. For Haphaestus, read Hephaestus.
Page 179, line 14. For Dispensers, read Despensers.
Page 182, line 19. For Ordainors, read Ordainers.

STUDIES IN HISTORY, ECONOMICS AND PUBLIC LAW

EDITED BY THE

FACULTY OF POLITICAL SCIENCE OF COLUMBIA UNIVERSITY.

VOLUME I, 1891-2. Second Edition, 1897. 396 pp.

Price, $3.00; bound, $3.50.

1. The Divorce Problem—A Study in Statistics.
By Walter F. Willcox, Ph. D. Price, 75c.

2. The History of Tariff Administration in the United States, from Colonial Times to the McKinley Administrative Bill.
By John Dean Goss, Ph. D. Price, $1.00.

3. History of Municipal Land Ownership on Manhattan Island.
By George Ashton Black, Ph. D. Price, $1.00.

4. Financial History of Massachusetts.
By Pharles H. J. Douglas, Ph. D. (*Not sold separately.*)

VOLUME II, 1892-93. 503 pp.

Price, $3.00; bound, $3.50.

1. The Economics of the Russian Village.
By Isaac A. Hourwich, Ph. D. (*Out of print.*)

2. Bankruptcy. A Study in Comparative Legislation.
By Samuel W. Dunscomb, Jr., Ph. D. Price, $1.00

3. Special Assessments: A Study in Municipal Finance.
By Victor Rosewater, Ph. D. Second Edition, 1898. Price, $1.00.

VOLUME III, 1893. 465 pp.

Price, $3.00; bound, $3.50.

1. History of Elections in the American Colonies.
By Cortlandt F. Bishop, Ph. D. Price, $1.50.

Vol. III, no. 1, may also be obtained bound. Price, $2.00.

2. The Commercial Policy of England toward the American Colonies.
By George L. Beer, A. M. Price, $1.50

VOLUME IV, 1893–94. 438 pp.

Price, $3.00; bound, $3.50.

1. **Financial History of Virginia.** By W. Z. Ripley, Ph. D. Price, $1.00.

2. **The Inheritance Tax.** By Max West, Ph. D. (*Out of print.*)

3. **History of Taxation in Vermont.**
By Frederick A. Wood, Ph. D. Price $1.00

VOLUME V, 1895–96. 498 pp.

Price, $3.00; bound, $3.50.

1. **Double Taxation in the United States.**
By Francis Walker, Ph. D. Price, $1.00

2. **The Separation of Governmental Powers.**
By William Bondy, LL. B., Ph. D. Price, $1.00

3. **Municipal Government in Michigan and Ohio.**
By Delos F. Wilcox, Ph. D. Price $1.00.

VOLUME VI, 1896. 601 pp.

Price, $4.00; bound, $4.50.

History of Proprietary Government in Pennsylvania.
By William Robert Shepherd, Ph. D. Price, $4.00; bound, $4.50.

VOLUME VII, 1897. 512 pp.

Price, $3.00; bound, $3.50.

1. **History of the Transition from Provincial to Commonwealth Government in Massachusetts.** By Harry A. Cushing, Ph. D. Price, $2.00.

2. **Speculation on the Stock and Produce Exchanges of the United States.** By Henry Crosby Emery, Ph. D. Price, $1.50

VOLUME VIII, 1896–98. 551 pp.

Price, $3.50; bound, $4.00.

1. The Struggle between President Johnson and Congress over Reconstruction. By Charles Ernest Chadsey, Ph. D. Price, $1.00.
2. Recent Centralizing Tendencies in State Educational Administration. By William Clarence Webster, Ph. D. Price, 75c.
3. The Abolition of Privateering and the Declaration of Paris. By Francis R. Stark, LL. B., Ph. D. Price, $1.00.
4. Public Administration in Massachusetts. The Relation of Central to Local Activity. By Robert Harvey Whitten, Ph. D. Price, $1.00.

VOLUME IX, 1897–98. 617 pp.

Price, $3.50; bound, $4.00.

1. English Local Government of To-day. A Study of the Relations of Central and Local Government. By Milo Roy Maltbie, Ph. D. Price, $2.00.

   Vol. IX, no. 1, may also be obtained bound. Price, $2.50.
2. German Wage Theories. A History of their Development. By James W. Crook, Ph. D. Price, $1.00.
3. The Centralization of Administration in New York State. By John Archibald Fairlie, Ph.D. Price, $1.00.

VOLUME X, 1898–99. 500 pp.

Price, $3.00; bound, $3.50.

1. Sympathetic Strikes and Sympathetic Lockouts. By Fred S. Hall, Ph.D. Price, $1.00
2. Rhode Island and the Formation of the Union. By Frank Greene Bates, Ph.D. Price, $1.50.

   Vol. X, no. 2, may also be obtained bound. Price, $2.00.
3. Centralized Administration of Liquor Laws in the American Commonwealths By Clement Moore Lacey Sites, Ph.D. Price, $1.00.

VOLUME XI, 1899. 495 pp.

Price, $3.50; bound, $4.00.

The Growth of Cities. By Adna Ferrin Weber, Ph.D

VOLUME XII, 1899-1900 586 pp.

Price, $3.50; bound, $4.00.

1. History and Functions of Central Labor Unions.
   By William Maxwell Burke, Ph. D. Price, $1.00.
2. Colonial Immigration Laws.
   By Edward Emberson Proper, A.M. Price, 75c.
3. History of Military Pension Legislation in the United States.
   By William Henry Glasson, Ph.D. Price, $1.00.
4. History of the Theory of Sovereignty since Rousseau.
   By Charles E. Merriam, Jr., Ph.D. Price, $1.50.

VOLUME XIII, 1901. 570 pp.

Price, $3.50; bound, $4.00.

1. The Legal Property Relations of Married Parties.
   By Isidor Loeb, Ph.D. Price, $1.50
2. Political Nativism in New York State.
   By Louis Dow Scisco, Ph. D. Price, $2.00.
3. The Reconstruction of Georgia.
   By Edwin C. Woolley, Ph.D. Price, $1.00.

VOLUME XIV, 1901.

1. Loyalism in New York during the American Revolution.
   By Alexander Clarence Flick, Ph. D. Price, $2.00.
2. The Economic Theory of Risk and Insurance.
   By Allan H. Willett, Ph. D. Price, $1.50.
3. *To be announced later.*

VOLUME XV, 1901. 427 pp.

Price, $3.00; bound, $3.50.

Civilization and Crime. By Arthur Cleveland Hall, Ph. D

The set of fifteen volumes (except that Vol. II can be supplied only in unbound nos. 2 and 3) is offered bound for $50.

For further information apply to

Prof. EDWIN R. A. SELIGMAN, Columbia University,
or to THE MACMILLAN COMPANY, New York,
London: P. S. KING & SON, Orchard House, Westminster.

Bei Fragen zur Produktsicherheit wenden Sie sich bitte an:
If you have any questions regarding product safety,
please contact:

Walter de Gruyter GmbH
Genthiner Straße 13
10785 Berlin
productsafety@degruyterbrill.com